Finding All Things in God

Finding All Things in God

Pansacramentalism and Doing Theology Interreligiously

*with an emphasis on the mediation
between theology and spirituality*

HANS GUSTAFSON

◆PICKWICK *Publications* · Eugene, Oregon

FINDING ALL THINGS IN GOD
Pansacramentalism and Doing Theology Interreligiously

Copyright © 2016 Hans Gustafson. All rights reserved. Except for brief quotations in critical publications or reviews, no part of this book may be reproduced in any manner without prior written permission from the publisher. Write: Permissions, Wipf and Stock Publishers, 199 W. 8th Ave., Suite 3, Eugene, OR 97401.

Pickwick Publications
An Imprint of Wipf and Stock Publishers
199 W. 8th Ave., Suite 3
Eugene, OR 97401

www.wipfandstock.com

ISBN: 978-1-4982-1798-9

Cataloguing-in-Publication data:

Gustafson, Hans.

Finding all things in God : pansacramentalism and doing theology interreligiously / Hans Gustafson.

xvi + 340 p. ; 23 cm. Includes bibliographical references and index.

ISBN: 978-1-4982-1798-9

1. Religions—Relations. 2. Dialogue—Religious aspects. 3. Theology in literature. 4. Panentheism. I. Title.

BL410 G95 2016

Manufactured in the U.S.A.   12/03/2015

Contents

List of Figures | vi
Preface and Acknowledgments | vii
Introduction | xi

Part 1: "Tell Me Your Story"
1 "There's a Lot of Medicine in that Water" | 3
2 Theology and Spirituality | 23
3 Foundations of Sacramentality | 47
4 The "Protestant Principle" and Sacramental Caution | 69
5 A Rahnerian Pansacramental Proposal | 80
6 Louis-Marie Chauvet: Beyond Aristotle and Aquinas | 112

Part 2: "Believing is Seeing"
7 Sacramental Spirituality | 123
8 Thomas Merton: Sacramental Spirituality and Place | 131
9 Nicholas Black Elk: Sacramental Spirituality and Descandalizing Multiple Religious Identity | 153
10 Dostoevsky and Wendell Berry: Sacramental Spirituality and Literature | 183

Part 3: "Finding All Things in the Divine"
11 A Philosophy of Sacramental Mediation | 207
12 Panentheism | 245
13 Suffering in God and World | 270
14 Towards a Pansacramental Theology of Religious Pluralism and Doing Theology Interreligiously | 288

Bibliography | 313
Name Index | 329
Subject Index | 335

Figures

Fig. 1.1: Looking north from York Island, near Point Detour (photo by Hans Gustafson) | 3

Fig. 3.1: *Matȟó Thípila* (Devil's Tower), Wyoming (Wikimedia Commons photo), https://commons.wikimedia.org/wiki/File:Devils_Tower_Darton_1900.jpg#file/ | 51

Fig. 8.1: Gal Vihara, Sri Lanka (Wikimedia Commons photo), https://commons.wikimedia.org/wiki/File:Polonnaruwa.jpg/ | 141

Fig. 8.2: Sunset from Gull Island, near Juneau, Alaska (photo by John Bianchi) | 143

Fig. 8.3: Bear Harbor, looking south (photo by Hans Gustafson) | 146

Fig. 8.4: Bear Harbor, looking north (photo by Hans Gustafson) | 147

Fig. 8.5: Needle Rock (photo by Hans Gustafson) | 148

Fig. 8.6: California Redwoods (photo by Hans Gustafson) | 149

Fig. 8.7: Coast near Bear Harbor (photo by Hans Gustafson) | 151

Fig. 11.1: Close-up from Rembrandt's *Return of the Prodigal Son* (Wikimedia Commons photo), https://commons.wikimedia.org/wiki/File:Rembrandt_Harmensz_van_Rijn_-_Return_of_the_Prodigal_Son_-_Google_Art_Project.jpg#file/ | 225

Preface and Acknowledgments

THE MOST ENJOYABLE PART of working on this book was the process of learning from the several readers and editors who contributed their invaluable insight and critique along the way. There are probably too many to mention, so please forgive me for overlooking any.

I thank Anselm K. Min for providing extensive and constructive critique throughout, Andrew Dreitcer for introducing me to the contemporary conversation in the study of spirituality, and Nancy van Duesen's direction in exploring the role of sacramentality in medieval thought. I also thank Philip Clayton for the exploration of panentheism. I thank Michael J. Himes, Bruce Morrill, and Bill Lambert for sparking my fascination with the powerful language of sacramentality as a young undergraduate at Boston College. I thank Michael Byron for introducing me to the theology of religions and for pushing me to constantly reexamine the implications of various claims. I thank my colleague John Merkle of the Jay Phillips Center for Interfaith Learning at Saint John's University and the University of St. Thomas in Minnesota for his support in this overall project and helpful assistance with understanding the rich thought of Abraham Heschel.

I thank my wife Audrey for her patience and support along the way. I also thank my parents, Ethel and Jeff, who have supported me since birth. Though they are not alive to see the publication of this book, they are more a part of it than anyone.

I thank all of the reviewers and respondents to the various articles and several presentations I have made over the years that drew from this book. All of you helped me to sharpen my thought and produce a more coherent manuscript. I am grateful to publishers and editors who have granted me permission to use these works in preparation of this book. These include Inter-Disciplinary Press; *The Heythrop Journal* and Wiley-Blackwell; Fons Vitae; *Journal of Ecumenical Studies* and University of Pennsylvania Press; *Literature and Theology* and Oxford University Press Journals; *The Way* and the British Jesuits. Various sections from part I (chapters 1–6) appear in "Sacramental Mediation between Theology and Spirituality," in *Spirituality in the 21st Century: Explorations*, edited by John L. Hochmeier and William S. Schmidt, 63–82 (Oxford: Inter-Disciplinary Press, 2013); "Sacramental Mediation between Theology and Spirituality," in S*pirituality: Theory, Praxis and Pedagogy*, edited by Martin Fowler, John D. Martin III, and John L. Hochmeier, 341–48 (Oxford: Inter-Disciplinary Press, 2012); and "Sacramental Mediation between Theology & the Contemporary Study of Spirituality," paper presented at the First Global Conference on Spirituality in the 21st Century: At the Interface of Theory, Praxis and Pedagogy (Prague, Czech Republic, March 20–22, 2011). Excerpts from chapter 4 were presented as "Luther and Loyola in Context: Spirituality, Saintliness and Divine Communication," paper presented at the Upper Midwest Regional Meeting of the American Academy of Religion, Luther Seminary (St. Paul, Minnesota, April 13–14, 2007); and "Sacramental Caution and Finding God in All things: Sacramentality and Spirituality in Luther and Loyola," paper presented at the 59th annual meeting of the Renaissance Society of America (San Diego, California, April 5, 2013). Part of chapter 5 first appeared as "Collapsing the Sacred and the Profane: Pan-Sacramental and Panentheistic Possibilities in Aquinas and Their Implications for Spirituality," *The Heythrop Journal* 9 (2011). Chapter 8 was first presented as "Place and Selfhood in the Later Years," paper presented at the 12th General Meeting and Conference of the International Thomas Merton Society, Loyola University (Chicago, Illinois, June 9–12, 2011); it was first published as "Place, Spiritual Anthropology, and Sacramentality in Merton's Later Years," in *The Merton Annual: Studies in Culture, Spirituality, and Social Concerns, Volume 25*, edited by David Belcastro and Joseph Raab, 74–90 (Louisville: Fons Vitae, 2013). Chapter 9 was presented as "Multiple Religious Belonging and Interfaith Panentheistic Spirituality in the Liberal Theology of Nicholas Black Elk," paper presented at the annual meeting of the American Academy of Religion (Chicago, Illinois, Nov. 17–20, 2012); "What a Christians might learn about Sacramentality from the Spirituality of Nicholas Black Elk?" paper presented at the annual convention of the Catholic Theological Society of America (St. Louis, June 7–10, 2012); "Revisiting the Multiple Religious Belonging of Nicholas Black Elk in the Context of the Catholic Sacramental Imagination," paper presented at the annual meeting of the American Academy of Religion (Baltimore, Maryland, Nov. 23–26, 2013); and published as "Descandalizing Multiple Religious Identity with Help from Nicholas Black Elk and His Spirituality: An Exercise in Interreligious Learning," *Journal of Ecumenical Studies*, 51.1 (2016). Chapter 10 first appear as "Sacramental Spirituality in *The Brothers Karamazov* and Wendell Berry's Port William Characters," *Literature and*

Theology 27 (2013) 345–63. Chapter 11 includes sections that first appeared in "Substance Beyond Illusion: The Spirituality of Bede Griffiths," *The Way* 47.3 (2008) 31–48; and presented as "Sacramentality as a Philosophical Model of Mediation and Reconciliation: with an Emphasis on Christian Theology and Spirituality," paper presented at annual Moberg Conference on Sociological Perspectives on Reconciliation, Bethel University (St. Paul, Minnesota, Feb. 22–23, 2013). Chapter 13 includes a section on suffering that was first presented as "The Awe-Filledness of Awfulness: Experiencing God in Suffering," plenary paper presented at *Wondrous Fear and Holy Awe*: A Meeting of the Society for the Study of Christian Spirituality, University of Notre Dame (South Bend, Indiana, July 2, 2013). Chapter 14 includes sections that were first presented as "Pansacramentality as a new model for the God-World Relationship in Panentheism," paper presented at the Upper Midwest Regional Meeting of the American Academy of Religion (Luther Seminary, St. Paul, Minnesota, April 6, 2013); "Interreligious Panentheistic Approaches to a Changing Planet in Comparative Theology and Interfaith Studies," paper presented at the annual convention of the College Theology Society, University of Portland (Portland, Oregon, May 28–31, 2015); and published as "Interreligious and Interfaith Studies in Relation to Religious Studies and Theological Studies," *StateofFormation*.com, January 6, 2015.

Introduction

TALKING ABOUT THE DIVINE and experiencing the divine have served as two basic activities of Western religious persons, whether socially constructed, anthropologically innate, or a combination thereof. Many claim to experience God through particular religious experience. This is spirituality, broadly speaking. Many also talk with others about their experience of God in pursuit of universal knowledge about ultimate reality or, at the very least, a shared narrative or set of complementary narratives that correlate with their own particular experience and posits claims about the divine as such. Talking about the divine, in particular, is the doing of theology. Dwelling either solely on God (or the Gods for that matter) as such or spiritual experience as such, apart from one another can run the risk of forgetting religious roots, ignoring the particular experience of others, and lacking a shared significance. Dwelling solely on experience can lead to missing the forest for the trees while dwelling solely on the divine can lead to missing the trees for the forest. A good forester will account equally for both the particular trees and the forest as such, as well as paying attention to both the emergent undergrowth and the old deadwood. In this book, I advocate for becoming like the forester in the exploration of theology and spirituality, without losing sight of one for the other. In so doing, theology and spiritualty via (pansacramentalism) are held in intimate conversation with each other while paying attention to both classical and contemporary claims about God as such and spiritual experience. To maintain sight of both forest and trees, God and experience, this book puts forth a method of mediation: (pan)sacramental and symbolic mediation.

The tension between theology and spirituality, and the need to retain their interdependence, is by no means a new endeavor. In this book, I offer one promising approach for maintaining their interdependence while recognizing that it is certainly need not be the only approach. I term this approach a philosophy of pansacramental and symbolic mediation, in which all things hold the potential to function as sacramental and symbolic mediators between God and the experience of God. Sacraments (not just the "seven" or "two," but all things), as symbols, mediate between particular spiritual experiences of the divine and the universal theological implications that arise from them. They maintain the tension between our metaphorical forest and the trees: God and our experience of God respectively. Sacramentality, sacraments, and symbols, remain a part of all religious traditions, both explicitly and implicitly. They beckon a continual return to them for critique and (re)evaluation, both new and old, in emerging contexts.

In what may seem like a journey through a forest comprised of an eclectic collection of diverse trees (and whole forests), this book represents the inherent interdisciplinary nature of the study of religion, theological reflection, and especially the study of spirituality. For this reason, the voices represented in the following pages are diverse, but all strive to express the divine while respecting the particularity of their contextual experience of the divine. In an interdisciplinary field such as the study of religion, one of the main tasks is to strive for an understanding of the relationship between and amongst the trees in order to see the forest. Further, it is to recognize that there are multiple forests and it is appropriate to attempt to strive to make some sense of the relationship between and amongst whole forests. Lurking among the trees within the forests, while at times attempting to climb them into the canopies in order to catch glimpses of the forests both below and beyond, in this book I set out as the forester seeking understanding. Remaining a part of the forest and trees, I tread with, hopefully, a sense of great humility. With this in mind, I strive for, to some degree, but not wholly, what Raimon Panikkar strove for, in his 1988–89 Gifford Lectures, when he said, "these meditations do not constitute a system of a scientific hypothesis intended to prove something else. I would like to believe that they are truly *philo-sophia*, which is perhaps the only true human *Sophia*."[1] This project does not advocate for a system, but rather seeks *Sophia* from a philosophy of sacramental and symbolic mediation.

Part I (chapters 1–6) sets the stage by introducing the main categories of the book: sacramentality, theology, and spirituality. Chapter 1 reviews the history of the problem of theology and spirituality becoming divorced from one another while also tracing the history and development of the term spirituality. This leads to the proposal of a working definition of the term spirituality drawn from scholars of the contemporary study of Christian spirituality such as Sandra M. Schneiders, Bernard McGinn, and Philip Sheldrake. Finally, chapter 1 previews the approach of constructing

---

1. Panikkar, *The Rhythm of Being*, 14 (italics his).

a philosophy of sacramental mediation, which carries implications for the remained of the book. Chapter 2 opens by establishing the history of the relationship between theology and spirituality before providing a view of the current situation today. Chapter 3 turns to the foundation of sacramentality by offering a brief history of sacramental theology and its philosophical foundations. It begins with an explanation of the Hebrew root -zkr, "to make memorial," in so far as it serves as a foundation for understanding the functionality of sacramentality. New Testament sacramentality is then reviewed in the context of the Latin term *sacramentum* and Greek term *mysterion*. A review of the Last Supper serves as a model for sacramental experience and functionality going forward. *Sacramentum* through the middle ages is then reviewed in more detail in the work of Augustine, Isidore of Seville, Hugh of St. Victor, Peter Lombard, and Thomas Aquinas. Chapter 4 raises the caution of the Protestant Principle in approaching sacramentality represented by Luther and Paul Tillich. It might be argued that no purview of the concept of sacrament in the Christian West is complete without a recognition of the influence of the Reformers The aim of chapters 3–4 is to provide a foundational history of sacramentality prior to exploring the sacramental theology of twentieth-century theologian Karl Rahner. Thus Chapter 5 narrows from the broad scope of sacramental theology in general to the particular sacramental theology and vision of Karl Rahner. According to a 1978 poll of North American theologians, Karl Rahner ranked behind only Aquinas and Tillich, and ahead of Augustine and Luther, as having the greatest influence on their own thinking.[2] Over three decades later, it is hard to imagine that Rahner has fallen too many positions on such a list. In fact, while interest in his theology remains strong, some of the unexplored corners of his work are continually being probed and illuminated. His writings on spirituality, for instance, continue to elicit wider interest and acceptance evidenced by the recent publication of his compiled essays, *The Mystical Way in Everyday Life*.[3] Perhaps this emerging interest in his mystical and spiritual theology prove accurate the insightful comment by Phil Endean who recognizes that, "the problem is not that Rahner's theology and spiritual vision have been tried and found wanting: they have been found difficult and left untried."[4] Rahner has offered one of the major modern sacramental theologies in the West, proffering an organic grace-filled cosmos which sacramentally expresses God in and through all things; I refer to this theological cosmology as pansacramental. In order to examine Rahner

2. Kelly, *Karl Rahner*, 1.
3. Rahner, *The Mystical Way in Everyday Life*.
4. Endean, "Introduction," *Spiritual Writings*, 29.

properly, chapter 5 necessary reviews some of his basic Thomist tendencies followed by an overview of his theological project in general. His "symbolic reality" is then explained, after which I stress his pansacramental cosmology and explore panentheistic possibilities therein. Rahner's theology of symbol and sacrament provide the basis for the philosophy of sacramental mediation and pansacramental vision put forth in this book. Chapter 6 moves the conversation beyond Aristotle and Aquinas by reviewing the postmodern sacramental theology of Louis Marie Chauvet as an alternative, but no less inadequate, to an Aristotelian substance metaphysics-based sacramental theology.

Part II (chapters 7–10) shifts the focus from the universality of sacramental theology to the study of particularity in sacramental spirituality. Chapter 7 examines the spiritual implications of the Ignatian Principle, a principle that in many ways formed Rahner's spiritual identity as a Jesuit. Since the study of spirituality, as lived religious experience of the divine in the world, involves the examination of particular lived experience, part two presents three particular case studies in sacramental spirituality. Chapter 8 examines Thomas Merton and the theme of place in his later years. Merton's contemplative method is correlated with the narrative from his later journals as he sought to find a new semi-permanent place to live. Chapter 9 examines the spirituality of Nicholas Black Elk through the lens of interreligious theology while entertaining the possibility of, and offering an attempt to de-scandalize, multiple religious belonging. In particular, it examines the role of sacramental mediation in the spirituality of his native Lakota tradition and its promise for learning across religious traditions. Chapter 10 turns to the medium of literature and examines the sacramental worldviews that come out in Fyodor Dostoevsky's *The Brothers Karamazov* and Wendell Berry's Port William novels. These three case studies provide data of particular lived religious experience in three different contexts.

Part III (chapters 11–14) provides the most constructively robust and original theological work of the book in laying out a proposal for understanding of finding all things in the divine via pansacramentalism. Chapter 11, drawing on Hegel's method of *sublation*, sets out to reconcile the universality of theology (part I) with the particularity of spirituality (part II). After applying Hegel's method to theology, spirituality, and sacramentality, it discusses the philosophical functionality of sacraments as symbols. Great care is taken to correlate with, and distinguish from, one another both symbols and sign. Inspired by Paul Ricoeur, I propose a criteriology of sacrament as symbols by suggesting that sacraments, as functional religious symbols, concretize by a) particularizing the universal, b) subjectifying the objective, and by c) rendering inner-reflection experiential. Further, sacraments, as symbols, invite transformative participation. Finally, this chapter suggests that emphasis on sacramentality offers a boon to the turn to relationality in contemporary philosophy by exposing, and therefore abolishing, false dichotomies. Chapter 12 explores panentheism, both classical and contemporary approaches. As an emerging concept in philosophical theology, panentheism posits all things in God and God in all things in order to combat pantheism's radical emphasis on God's immanence and classical Christian theism's alleged emphasis on God's transcendence. In this way, it strives to balance God's immanence with God's transcendence. Given panentheism's diversity, chapter 12 reviews seven prominent panentheists in so far as they contribute to the conversation on "panentheistic pansacramentalism" in chapter 14 and the relationship between and among God, world, person and the place of suffering in chapter 13. The seven panentheists (some explicit and others implicit) are Thomas Aquinas, Friedrich Schelling, Karl Rahner, Arthur Peacocke, John Polkinghorne, Gregory Palamas (and *theōsis* in the Eastern Orthodox Christianity), and Matthew Fox. Chapter 13 turns to the reality of suffering in the world and the challenge it presents to a panentheistic and pansacramental worldview. A view of reality that advocates for all things having the potential to serve as representations of God in time and place ought to take seriously the reality of suffering in the world. Further, it ought to wrestle with the implication that suffering too might serve as a sacramental representation of God in the world. In this regard, this chapter turns to the work of Martin Buber's Hasidic pansacramentalism, Abraham Joshua Heschel's theology of divine pathos, Jürgen Moltmann's Christian application of Heschel's thought, and entertains the possibility of a provisional panentheism in the context of a Polkinghornian realized eschatology and soteriological panentheism. Chapter 14 attempts to set the pansacramental view proposed in the book into a context of doing theology interreligiously. It proposes "panentheistic pansacramentalism" as a new model for understanding the God-world relationship. This view relies on the metaphors of the relation of the artist to her art and the mother to her child. This model is then applied to the context of interreligious encounter by sketching a beginning to a pansacramental theology of religious pluralism. A method for doing theology interreligiously follows which offers an example based on the content of this book, and is then placed within the context of the interdisciplinary field of interreligious studies. It concludes with some very brief comments on potential avenues for theological exploration going forward.

PART 1

"Tell Me Your Story"

1

"There's a Lot of Medicine in that Water"

"THERE'S A LOT OF medicine in that water," Danny, the Ojibwa caretaker of Point Detour campground, declared in reserved tone of humility. He reverently stared out over the icy cold waters of *Gichigami* (Lake Superior), from the northernmost point of Wisconsin on Red Cliff Indian Reservation. He paused, slowly exhaled, and then turned to me with a warm smile. Nothing more is said as he tossed some full garbage bags in the back of his rusty 82' Ford pickup and rumbled away down the dirt road.

Fig. 1.1: Looking north from York Island near Point Detour

Prior to Danny sharing his medicinal proverb with me, we had been swapping stories about the lake. I had been leading sea kayaking trips on the lake for a few months for persons of all abilities (and living with disabilities) from cities near and far. Danny had been praising the lake for its ability to heal in ways beyond our knowing. Further, he had been encouraging me to continue to bring people up to the lake and get them out on the water in any and every way possible. As a kayak guide I was intentional about attuning myself to the rhythms of the lake. Throughout the nights, sleeping in the tent, I'd always have one ear open seeking to calculate the size and frequency of the waves. During morning, noon, and night my eyes constantly scanned the horizon for storms, wind puffs, white caps, or anything of concern for small watercraft. I had become good at reading the lake, but this lake is a master of guises and disguises.

I had (and have) met countless of people with a passion for this truly superior lake, be it for its great recreational opportunities, beauty, purity, power, and of course, its vastness, but never had I met (nor have I met since) someone like Danny, who spoke about the lake in a way that transcended all of these categories. He talked about the lake's 'Spirit' as that which affected him and made demands on him (e.g., life in and around Red Cliff revolves around the lake and her moods), but also served him (healed him like medicine and provided him with a purpose) in return. Danny had never lived off the Red Cliff reservation in his forty-five years of life to that point. He told me he couldn't leave the lake. He told me the lake had saved his life more times than he could count. Danny had oriented his life around the lake and in return, he reports, it has given him life. He had developed what I would refer to as a spirituality; perhaps it is a *Gichigami* spirituality.

Mircea Eliade tells a similar story, in his journals, of an American philosopher inquiring of a Shinto priest about his theology, which elicited the priest's now famous reply, "we have no theology, we dance."[1] I recount this story here not to suggest the futility of theology, but rather to point out that any theology without such a deeply girded spirituality (such as dancing or living attuned to the Spirit of *Gichigami*) runs the risk of being irrelevant, or downright nonexistent (e.g., "we have no theology"). On the other hand, if the divine or the sacred is somehow disclosed through the spiritual experience of dancing (or in the icy cold waters of *Gichigami*), then the questions of what, who, and how the divine is (theology), is intimately wrapped up in living in and experiencing the divine (spirituality). Philip Sheldrake accurately points out that if a theology is to be complete, then "it needs to be *lived* just as much as it needs to be studied and explained."[2] So keep dancing and stay attuned to the 'Spirit of the Lake,' by no means should one refrain

---

1. Eliade, *No Souvenirs*, 31.
2. Sheldrake, *Spirituality and History*, 3 (italics his).

from these activities, but do not avoid the attempt to reflect on and ask questions about it. Keep open the dialogical road between spiritualities and their reflective theologies. Further, remain open to finding the divine in and through the everyday realities that we may not first expect (e.g., dancing and lakes). This book is concerned precisely with these tasks: asking if and how all things may be understood as sacred while maintaining the interdependence between theology and spirituality, and the study of spirituality.

A preliminary fundamental concern this book addresses is the potential gulf between academic theology and spirituality and the philosophic functionality of sacramentality.[3] After examining this alleged gulf between theology and spirituality (which is presumed problematic), I will propose a way, a solution, to bridge the gulf and retain the interdependence between the two. *Theology* and *the study of spirituality*, without doubt, require further elaborative definition, which is given below. The solution I propose lies precisely in articulating what I will term a 'philosophy of pansacramental mediation.' In short, through the constructive task of articulating a philosophy of pansacramental mediation, the two fields (theology and the study of spirituality) can be understood as related and interdependent. In this opening chapter I begin first with an overview of the problem as such; that is, I will explain why this ought to be understood as problematic and will provide a history of the problem. Second, I will offer a brief history of the term "spirituality" and articulate they manner in which it is employed in this book. Third, I will sketch my general approach going forward in this book.

The Problem and Its History

A foundational presupposition for the book is that it is problematic for the fields of theology and the study of spirituality to operate in separate quarters unrelated and independent from one another. In order to adequately demonstrate this and propose a solution, the terms *theology* and *spirituality* must be articulated and distinguished.

In recent years significant scholarship has gone into defining the term spirituality and distinguishing it from other like terms such as theology, mysticism, religion, spiritual theology, mystical theology, monastic theology

3. Though this book is written from a Christian perspective and examines Christian spirituality in particular, there remain many implications for the broader study of spirituality as such.

and asceticism. In fact, only a few hours are required to thumb through the pages of the major academic journals[4] devoted to the study of spirituality to realize that most articles, regardless of whether or not they deal specifically with the method or definition of spirituality, will still indeed provide such boundaries. This demonstrates perhaps a lingering insecurity among the scholars of spirituality to defend their field against those who may seek to either delegitimize it or subsume it into one of many other fields, most notably theology and, maybe to a lesser extent, religious studies.

Notable scholars in the emerging field of the contemporary study of spirituality include Sandra Schneiders, Philip Sheldrake, Bernard McGinn, Philip Endean, Keith Egan, Bradley Hanson, and Andrew Louth to name only a few. Though all of these scholars are committed to the contemporary study of spirituality, they do not perfectly agree with one another about the exact parameters of the field. To be sure, there is great overlap and agreement concerning much of the terrain to be covered; however, there is no agreement on where the boundaries lie precisely thus demonstrating the permeability of its borders (perhaps both to the advantage and detriment to the field). A field with porous boundaries, especially one which seemingly overlaps significantly with theology, can understandably cause much confusion. What follows is my attempt to distinguish the two fields (theology and the study of spirituality) from one another by drawing on the previous scholarship of those mentioned above. I begin here with a brief overview of the two fields and how I employ them.

Theology	Study of Spirituality
study of God, the Gods, or the divine	study of lived religious experience
strives for *universal knowledge* of God, the Gods, or the divine	strives for *particular knowledge* of experience
objective	subjective
reflective	experiential

Theology is a term applied to the critical and thematic study of God (of the Gods or the divine as such) in pursuit of universal knowledge and coherence. It is the task of the theologian to further understand faith (or lack thereof). Thus I uphold the classical definition of the term as *fides quaerens intellectum*, or as Anne Clifford puts it, as "the process of bringing faith to

---

4. E.g., *Spiritus* (formerly *Christian Spirituality Bulletin*), *The Way*, *Spirituality Today* (formerly *Cross and Crown*), *Révue d' histoire de la spiritualité* (formerly *Révue d'ascétique et de mystique*), etc.

understanding through disciplined, critical reflection."[5] The absence of faith need not disqualify one from the doing of theology, for the concept of God/s or the divine may provide sufficient ground for reflecting or thinking about them as concepts or realties towards which one might ascent (or negate). Most specifically, the theology I have in mind here is the theology currently taking place mainly in the academy which pursues questions of divinity through critical, and constructive, descriptive and prescriptive ways. It seeks to systematically and consistently correlate its primary content, which consists of theological ideas, concepts, events, themes and experiences. This includes theologies that seek to know the concrete conditions of personal experience and correlate them with revealed, or otherwise known, knowledge of the divine (e.g., various theologies of liberation). Within Christian theology, this can involve synthesizing, in a consistent manner, the Trinity (if applicable and accepted), Christology, pneumatology, ecclesiology, scripture, revelation, soteriology, ethics and quite a few others. Its object is *universal* in that it strives to understand universal claims about God, even if the only universal claims attainable are negative (e.g., *via negativa*). Theology may draw on *particular* data (such as the specific Christology of Julian of Norwich and the conversion experience of Augustine), but it seeks *universal* positions (such as who Christ is for all, the nature of conversion as such, or the knowledge of God as such). In other words, one goal of theological exploration is to acquire universal knowledge to be applied across the spectrum of particularity. Context remains important to theology, to be sure, but it remains secondary in importance regarding knowledge. Christian systematic theology seeks its object through a methodology of integrating horizons (including scripture, doctrine, history, experience, etc.). These horizons include the particular, yet a primary goal of theology is to clarify language and develop concepts that apply universally. This is not to reduce the distinction between theology and the study spirituality to simply a matter of differentiating between universality and particularity, but also involves the difference between objective and subjective, reflective and experiential, and others mentioned later.

Spirituality,[6] being perhaps as nebulous a word as possible in the parlance of our times, can be understood in contradistinction to theology in

---

5. Clifford, "Re-membering the Spiritual Core of Theology," 20 (parenthesis omitted).

6. It is not uncommon for a person to deem herself "spiritual, but not religious" (SBNR). Philip Sheldrake refers to this distinction as "sharp and unhelpful" since it proposes to replace religion with a vague and meaningless understanding of spirituality detached from history, tradition(s), and community. In so doing, he argues, it often isolates persons from one another and reduces communal interdependence. However,

its object of study, which lies precisely in the *particular*. More specifically, the content of the contemporary study of spirituality[7] concerns ones 'lived religious practice or experience.' In short, it is what Philip Sheldrake terms, "the study of 'felt experience' and 'lived practice' in ways that, while not detached from theological tradition, overflow the boundaries that positivist theology tends to set."[8] It is in the twentieth century that the academic study of 'spirituality' has (re)emerged, prior to which it was, in large part, collapsed into mystical theology, monastic theology, ascetical theology or simply within the broader field of theology in general. Prior to going further with the definition I intend here, and before I sketch the rough boundaries and significant contours of the field, I offer a necessary and foundational history of the term.

A History of "Spirituality"[9]

The term "spirituality" (*spiritalitas*) did not surface until the fifth century in a document originally ascribed to Jerome, later Faustus of Riez, but it was most likely anonymous. The context of the document is one in which the writer is encouraging his audience to live a life according to the (Holy) spirit, thus he tells the reader to "act as to advance in spirituality."[10] To grasp what the anonymous author might have had in mind it is necessary to trace the root, noun *spiritus* and adjective *spiritalis* or *spiritualis*, back to its Pauline usage.

---

this colloquial distinction can be quite helpful if employed to distinguish between subjective religious experience and organized, institutionalized religion. Further, those who self-identify as SBNR can derive great meaning in articulating their faith identity in this manner. Regardless, this definition of spirituality employed in the SBNR label is one that I *do not* have in mind when I use it here in this book (Sheldrake, *A Brief History of Spirituality*, 1).

7. Note here that this project deals with the *contemporary* study of spirituality, and not necessarily *spiritual theology, mystical theology,* and *ascetical theology* as such. These terms are mentioned in more detail below.

8. Sheldrake, "Spirituality and Its Critical Methodology," 15.

9. For a more comprehensive overview of the history of the term, refer collectively to the following: Principe, "Toward Defining Spirituality"; Sheldrake, *Spirituality and History*; Schneiders, "Theology and Spirituality;" Schneiders, "Spirituality in the Academy;" Leclercq, "Introduction;" Alexander, "What Do Recent Writers Mean by Spirituality?"; Mursell, "Prologue," *The Story of Christian Spirituality*, 9–10; McGinn, "The Letter and the Spirit."

10. "*Age ut in spiritualitate proficias*" found in Pseudo-Jerome Epistle 7 (pl 30, 114D-115A), quoted from Jean Leclercq, "Introduction," *The Spirituality of Western Christendom*, 280.

In his first letter to the Corinthians, Paul employs the Greek word *pneuma* (n) and *pneumatikos* (adj.), from which we get the Latin translations *spiritus* (n) and *spiritalis* (adj.) or *spiritualis* (adj.) respectively. The context involves Paul referencing the Holy Spirit in his encouragement to the people in the community founded at Corinth. Thus Paul writes to them, "as it is written, 'What no eyes has seen, nor ear heard, nor the human heart conceived, what God has prepared for those who love him'—these things God has revealed to us through the Spirit; for the Spirit searches everything, even the depths of God."[11] A few chapters later, Paul again claims that "anyone united to the Lord becomes one spirit with him."[12] Both Philip Sheldrake[13] and Walter Principe[14] note that Paul here is not placing the spiritual in opposition to the physical, corporeal, or material (Greek *soma*, Latin *corpus*),[15] as if somehow the two aspects are mutually exclusive, but rather he places it in opposition to all that is unspiritual.

For instance, in addition to 1 Corinthians, if other undisputedly authentic Pauline epistles, such as Galatians and Romans,[16] are taken into account, this becomes apparent. In these texts life according to the spirit (Greek *pneuma*, Latin *spiritus*) is always placed in opposition to life according to the flesh (Greek *sarx*, Latin *caro*) or the body, which does not entail physical, corporeal materiality, since 'the flesh' or 'the [human] body' can refer to a person's mind, will, and/or heart equally.[17] For Paul, then, the spirit entails all that lies within the human person (including the physical corporeal aspects) that is, or can be, orientated toward "God's Spirit" (Greek *Pneuma Theou*, Latin *Spiritus Dei*), while the flesh refers to all that lies within the human person which combats this divine orientation. Thus, as Principe points out, "for Paul the opposition is not between the incorporeal or non-material and the corporeal and material, but between two ways of life,"[18] the life according to the spirit and the life according to the flesh. Hence, Sandra Schneiders notes that, "both the spiritual and the unspiritual person are alive, possessed of body and soul. The Spiritual person

---

11. 1 Corinthians 2:9–10.
12. 1 Corinthians 6:17.
13. Sheldrake, *Spirituality and History*, 42.
14. Principe, "Toward Defining Spirituality," 130.
15. Likewise, Paul places *pneumatikos* and *spiritualis* in opposition to *sarkikos* and *carnalis* respectively, not to *somatikos* or *corporalis*.
16. See 1 Corinthians 3:1–3; Romans 7–8; Galatians 3; 5:13, 16–25.
17. Principe, "Toward Defining Spirituality," 130.
18. Ibid.

is one who is indwelt by the Holy Spirit of God,"[19] and thus it should not be assumed that somehow the spiritual person transcends, shuns, or goes beyond corporeality. This original Pauline understanding of spirit is crucial for retaining a place for the corporeal and thus maintaining an adequate understanding of a philosophy of pansacramental mediation as it pertains to the study of spirituality.

It is possible to trace the origins of the root term back further than Paul, in a certain sense. Paul, in his employment of the term *pneuma*, draws on and develops the Hebrew *ruah*, meaning 'breath,' in reference to the breath of Yahweh. Though, as Schneiders notes, the root *spiritus* does not precede Pauline Christian usage in the New Testament.[20]

This first use of the term 'spirituality,' as we know it, which did not come about until the fifth century and was employed in the Pauline manner detailed above, remained rather consistent in its usage through the twelfth century. However, Principe cites a rare occurrence of the term in the ninth century by the Benedictine Candidus of Fulda who uses it in a non-Pauline fashion by contrasting it to *corporalitas* or *materialitas*.[21] Candidus was ahead of his time in this usage, though by the twelfth century this understanding began to take root. Perhaps Candidus took Paul's understanding of 'the flesh' to mean the material physical aspect of the body alone thus instigating the idea that 'spirituality' was inherently opposed to the bodily and materiality.

With the onset of scholasticism in the twelfth century and thereafter, the meaning of the term began to shift more drastically. The Pauline understanding waned while it took a meaning that was more opposed matter; however, neither understanding completely died. In fact, the key theological figure of this period, Aquinas, sought to hold onto both senses of the term as employed in his *Summa*. He mostly uses the Pauline version of the term, though he also places it in opposition to corporeality a number of times.[22]

Drawing on Raymond Klibansky, Nancy van Deusen has suggested that the introduction of Plato's *Phaedo* in the mid-twelfth century supported the idea that the body and soul (of which the spirit is a part as proposed in Plato's theory of the tripartite soul in the *Republic*) functioned in a reciprocal and complementary manner, yet fostered the "attitude of contempt

---

19. Schneiders, "Theology and Spirituality, 258.
20. Ibid.
21. Principe, "Toward Defining Spirituality," 131.
22. According to Principe, in Aquinas' writings, "*spiritualitas* occurs about seventy times (by comparison with the word *spiritualis*, which is found some five thousand times) (Principe, "Toward Defining Spirituality," 131).

towards the visible world ... prevalent in the accepted Christian doctrine."[23] In the *Phaedo*, Socrates suggests to Cebes and Simmias, that although every pleasure and pain

> has a sort of rivet with which it fastens the soul to the body and pins it down and makes it corporeal, ... the soul secures immunity from its desires by following reason and abiding always in her company, and by contemplating the true and divine and unconjecturable, and drawing inspiration from it ... After such training, my dear Simmias and Cebes, the soul can have no grounds for fearing that on its separation from the body it will be blown away and scattered by the winds, and so disappear into thin air, and cease to exist altogether.[24]

Van Deusen recognizes, in particular, the influence of the *Phaedo*'s discussion on the reciprocity between the corporeal (body) and incorporeal (soul) set forth in the analogy of "a musical instrument" (the *lyra*) and "tuning the strings" (attunement) of that instrument.[25] This analogy is raised by Simmias vis-à-vis Socrates proposed body/soul relationship cited above. Whereas Socrates advocates for the existence of the soul beyond the corporeal, Simmias objects that the corporeal is what precisely makes the incorporeal possible and present. Simmias suggests,

> You might say the same thing about tuning the strings of a musical instrument, that the attunement is something invisible and incorporeal and splendid and divine, and located in the tuned instrument, while the instrument itself and its strings are material and corporeal and composite and earthly and closely related to what is mortal. Now suppose that the instrument is broken, or its strings cut or snapped. According to your theory the attunement must still exist—it cannot have been destroyed, because it would be inconceivable that when the strings are broken the instrument and the strings themselves, which have a mortal nature, should still exist, and the attunement, which shares the nature and characteristics of the divine and immortal, should exist no longer, having predeceased its mortal counterpart.[26]

Here the body is obviously analogous to the corporeal musical instrument (the *lyra* or harp) and the soul is analogous to its incorporeal attunement. For Simmias, if the soul is tied to the body and the body perishes, then so

23. Klibansky, *The Continuity of the Platonic Tradition*, 29.
24. Plato, "Phaedo," 66–67; 83d–84b.
25. Van Deusen explores this in "The Harp and the Soul."
26. Plato, "Phaedo," 68; 85e–86b.

too must the soul perish with it. This raises the question about whether the body or the soul is "stronger and more durable,"[27] than the other. Of course, Socrates (Plato) will ultimately maintain that the former is not to be valued as high as the latter, for according to van Deusen, the main thesis of the *Phaedo* is that "the spiritual world of pure ideas exists apart from specific, concrete, material disclosure of these ideas, as the concept of beauty without a specific manifestation which is qualitatively beautiful."[28]

The influence of the *Phaedo*'s suggestion of the soul (as a kind of incorporeal attunement or harmony or right adjustment) set in complementary distinction to the body (the instrument), may have contributed to the attitude of neglecting the corporeal visible world in favor of the invisible spiritual world of pure ideas precisely because the distinction itself was raised. However, van Deusen is clear that the body and soul are not to be understood in a dichotomous fashion, but rather they function interdependently in a reciprocal and complementary way. This analogy fosters corporeal-incorporeal harmony and supports the argument for the preexistence of the soul. Van Deusen writes, "To a degree of simplicity which seems obvious, Plato meshes the incorporeal invisible concept of soul attunement with a clear image—the harp. The attunement is invisible, immaterial, beautiful, divine, and pure, whereas the harp is material composite, earthy, and perishable. Attunement exists before entering the instrument just as the soul exists before its incorporation into the human frame."[29] Likewise, as the *Phaedo* suggests, attunement exists after the "human frame" (the body) perishes and thus we encounter an undeterred Socrates who imbibes the hemlock confidently like a true martyr dying for that which he believes. Van Deusen suggests that with the translation of the *Phaedo*, the new understanding of the soul as attunement emerged. She points out that "the only place [harp, harmony, and soul] occur together and within dialogue in the fourteenth century is in Plato's Phaedo. In its recent translation in Latin, the Phaedo had become available to the Latin-reading educated pubic for the first time."[30] With its accessibility came the distinction between body and soul set in the analogous context of the instrument and attunement, corporeal and incorporeal. The power of symbols (harp, harmony, etc.) and not necessarily the theory set forth in philosophical tracts and treatises, van Deusen argues, is what find themselves into common popular culture. The symbolic power of the *lyra* analogy for the relationship between body and

---

27. Ibid., 69; 87a.
28. Van Deusen, "The Harp and the Soul," 387.
29 Ibid., 390.
30. Ibid., 397.

soul functions as one factor which may have led to the cultivation of a "spiritual life" directed at the denial and disciplining of the "bodily life."[31]

A third usage of the term arose during this time as well. This usage was juridical in that *spiritualitas* (translated here 'lords spiritual') designated the 'material' goods that belonged to the ecclesiastical estate or clergy in contrast to *temporalitas* which referred to the stately property of the king or prince. Though furthest removed from the Pauline sense, this third sense became the most commonly used between the thirteen and sixteenth centuries.[32]

It was not until the seventeenth century, the so-named "golden age of theology"[33] that new developments began to take place in the meaning of the term. Most notably these changes took place in the context of French arts, literature, philosophy and religion.[34] The word was used to denote the spiritual life in its personal and affective aspects regarding one's relationship with God. In addition, the term also became affiliated with enthusiasm and quietism. These two movements, in their association with the word *spiritualité*, contrasted the term with other popular seventeenth century buzzwords such as 'piety' (Pietists), 'devotion' (Francis de Sales and William Law), and 'perfection' (John Wesley and the Methodists).[35] Thus it is in this era that the term became strongly associated with the human drive, via participation and co-operation, for interior perfection, especially in reference to those tasks and duties that go beyond what was considered proper for the ordinary Christian. During this time and into the eighteenth century,

---

31. The diversity of Plato's legacy should not be overlooked, and one should be careful not to conflate Plato with Platonism and Neoplatonism. For instance, although Socrates exhibits detachment from the body, he does not seem to carry any positive bitterness nor hatred toward it. Keith Ward suggests that "Plato's overall view expresses a dialectic between two extremes—one that the world is evil and to be escaped from, and the other that the world is a 'blessed god,' a perfect finite image of divine beauty. There is actually no 'final system' in Plato's works." (Ward, "Why Plato was not a World-Hating Totalitarian," 11). Neoplatonism takes an almost Gnostic view of the body in that the body serves as the source of all that is bad and lowly. Perhaps it is the development of this Neoplatonist view of the body, in conformity with the newly translated *Phaedo*, that contributed most to the medieval tendency to separate the body from the soul in such a drastically dualistic manner.

32. Principe, notes that "in the mediaeval vernacular the Latin word *spiritualitas* gave rise to such forms as *esperitalité*, *espiritualité*, *espirituauté*, and *espérituaulté* in French and *spiritualty* or *spirituality* in English. In both languages these words were first used for the spiritual-religious realm or for ecclesiastical persons or properties" (Principe, "Toward Defining Spirituality," 131–32).

33. Schneiders, "Theology and Spirituality," 259; and "Spirituality in the Academy," 681.

34. cf. Principe, "Toward Defining Spirituality," 132.

35. Sheldrake, *Spirituality and History*, 43.

in the wake of the European Reformations, within Roman Catholicism, the term was mostly dropped in order to provide distance from the quietist and enthusiastic movements.

The eighteenth century gave rise to the lively debate over whether the call to lead a life of Christian perfection (that is, a 'spiritual' life) is universal; that is, is it meant for all ordinary Christians, or only meant for some? Is it only reserved for those extraordinary mystically-inclined Christians? In some aspects, this debate has never been definitively answered. The Second Vatican Council settled it for its constituents by falling on the former side; that is, all Christians are called to the same spiritual life. The debate also centered on how to understand the Christian call in relation to its mysticism and asceticism. Both mysticism (and mystical theology) and asceticism (and ascetical theology) are important enough, at the very least, to touch on in a book such as this. Thus, I will mention how these two terms square with theology and the study of spirituality in the next section. In short, the term 'spirituality' became an umbrella term to "refer to the spiritual life as a whole in all of its stages beyond the most rudimentary observance of the commandments,"[36] and thus included both mysticism and asceticism within its fold.

With the emphasis remaining largely on devotion, the nineteenth century did not provide many significant developments for the term. However, there was more weight placed on the experiential implications. Schneiders points to the nineteenth century as the one in which the academic study of spirituality took root, inaugurated by Pierre Pourrat's four-volume study of its history.[37] Additionally, in the late nineteenth century the term was sometimes applied to aspects of other religions, most notably to the perceived superior aspects of modern Hinduism[38] that supposedly went positively beyond the materialism of the West. In many respects, this definition looms today in the popular usage of the term 'spirituality.'

In the twentieth century (and into the present century), spirituality as a term denoting the inward life of perfection held strong, though it also began to take on more particular meanings. This is to say that today we have come to speak of not only spirituality but of spiritualities. The contemporary meaning of the term, and the one intended when employed in this book,

---

36. Schneiders, "Theology and Spirituality," 259.

37. Pourrat, *Christian Spirituality*.

38. Principe credits this development due to "a special interest by some in modern Hinduism and the resulting exchange between such Hindus as Swami Vivekananda (1862–1902), sister Nivedita (Margaret Elizabeth Noble) (1867–1911), Annie Besant (1873—1933), and others with persons of Western culture" (Principe, "Toward Defining Spirituality," 133).

drawing on the contemporary study of spirituality in the academy, has been reinvigorated and redefined by thinkers such as Sandra Schneiders,[39] who is often considered the grandmother of this emerging field. She has provided useful categories within which spirituality can be reframed and studied. Her contribution will mentioned in the next chapter.

The Approach of This Book

One aim of this book is to demonstrate, through articulating a philosophy of pansacramental mediation, that theology and spirituality (lived religious experience) are interdependent and in need of one another for their adequacy. Another aim is to offer a view of the God-world relationship that shares kinship with panentheistic accounts, but articulated through pansacramentality. Further, as chapter 14 argues, one of the most effective ways to do theology and articulate it clearly in today's pluralistic world, is to do it interreligiously; that is, in conversation with other religions. A pansacramental proposal such as the one offered in this book entails putting forth an understanding of sacramentality supported by reason, coherence, and philosophical categories. To be clear, this is a study on *sacramentality*, not *the* sacraments (whether one adheres to seven or two or another quantity). Chapter 3 goes into this understanding of sacramentality in more detail. A sacrament is a revelatory experience of the divine[40] which is both signifying and symbolic; it signifies by pointing to something real beyond itself (to the divine), and it functions symbolically by making present (re-presents), through materials of worldly experience, that to which it points (the divine). As symbols, sacraments overcome dichotomies such as the so called sacred/profane dichotomy (metaphysical)—the natural and supernatural—and the past/present dichotomy (time), and as such, bridge (or dissolve) these divisions. If the presupposition that a good God created a good world is accepted, and thus the cosmos is potentially saturated with God's grace (God's self), then the possibility of recognizing the cosmos as potentially containing an infinite number of sacraments is reasonable (hence a proposal for pansacramentality). In other words, every finite being as such functions as a potential mediator of the grace (the divine) and therefore is a potential

---

39. Sandra M. Schneiders notes that, "spirituality as an *academic field* is the study of spirituality as an *existential phenomenon* (the material object) under a formality (the formal object) which distinguishes it from theology, on the one hand, and religious studies, on the other (Schneiders, "Approaches to the Study of Christian Spirituality," 15).

40. A Christian might say it is manifestation of God's grace; grace being understood as God's self-extension in the world in some manner.

sacrament. Grace here is understood as God's self-communication, thus a sacramental experience recognizes God as substantially present in time and space. A *potential* sacrament becomes an *actual* sacrament when someone recognizes and appreciates it as such. In chapter 14 offers some brief remarks on judging the authenticity of a sacrament, for some set of criteria are needed to avoid falsely identifying something a sacrament that promotes oppression, marginalization, and injustice (to name a few). A sacrament reveals the divine; it reveals God (or the Gods for that matter). It is a manifestation of the sacred in (and perhaps through) the profane (ordinary), thus shattering this false dichotomy altogether. A sacrament, through particularity, makes visible the invisible universal divine.

Karl Rahner's sacramentality theology (founded on Aquinas) is employed in this book since it adequately serves and supports a commencement point from which I offer my pansacramental proposal. Chapter 5 is devoted to sketching his understanding of sacramentality and concept of symbolic reality. In short, his transcendental worldview envisions the whole creation (the cosmos) as holding infinite sacramental potential, which for him is predicated on the founding (constitutive causation) of Christ, whom he deems the self-expression of God in time and space.

Sacramentality, hinted at above throughout, can serve as a solution to the problem by filling the potential gap between systematic theology and the study of spirituality. Since sacramental language mediates between a *particular* spiritual experience of a human person and the *universal* theological implications (knowledge of God) that stem from it, it provides a means to understand a particular experience of God in relation to the universal significance of God. Sacramentality functions as a mediator between the subjective particular (spiritual experience) and the objective universal (theological knowledge). Sacramentality stands with one foot in each field on the threshold where spiritual human experience meets systematic theological reflection, and mediates between particular phenomenological experiences of the divine (spirituality) and the making of universal claims about the divine as such (theology). Sacramentality invokes a particular experience yet provides a universal understanding of reality concerning how that particular experience is related to the universality of God.

In this way, a sacramental experience can yield universal knowledge about God for all persons and all creation. For instance, if one maintains, with the author of 1st John, that God is *agapē* (perfect self-gift), then one can experience God in concrete particular experience (spirituality); yet such an experience carries a universal message of ultimate significance, which might be that God is *agapē* for all (a theological claim). Michael J. Himes reminds us of the well-known scene in Dostoevsky's *The Brothers Karamazov* in which an elderly woman has come to Fr. Zosima for advice on how to regain her faith.[41] She asks Zosima how one can prove the existence of God and thus regain faith. He responds,

> one cannot prove anything here, but it is possible to be convinced . . . by the experience of active love. Try to love your neighbors actively and tirelessly. The more you succeed in loving, the more you'll be convinced of the existence of God and the immortality of your soul. And if you reach complete selflessness in the love of your neighbor, then undoubtedly you will believe.[42]

God cannot be understood apart from concrete experience in the world, after which theological reflection on the universal nature of God can be made. The move from the concrete particular (active love of neighbor) to the theological universal (claiming that God is *agapē*) can be facilitated by employing sacramental language which preserves and respects the particularity of experience, yet is able to transcend the concrete to the universal. If the elderly woman were to take Fr. Zosima's advice and go out and manifest active love concretely in the world (in time and space), she would be (re) presenting God in the world (in time and space). This is a sacrament to be sure, but to make the move from a concrete particular manifestation of God in the world to a universal claim about God, the language of sacramental mediation plays a clarifying role in the conversation. If the Christian is to maintain her claim that Jesus of Nazareth represented God in time and space, then she ought to have a way to talk about how God can concretely and authentically render God's-self present in time and space. One promising way is through sacramental language.

Only the particular is visible, that is, it is empirical, corporal, material, and/or experientially present (e.g., concrete love, tree, mountain, lake, person, dog, etc.), but sacramentality is precisely the ability of something that is visible and particular to point beyond itself to the universal while simultaneously pointing within itself by rendering present. By showing that sacramental language can adequately describe the universal significance of a spiritual experience without negating its particularity, an argument can be made for sacramental significance. Louis-Marie Chauvet claims, "that Christian identity cannot be separated from the sacraments means that faith cannot be lived in any other way, including what is most spiritual in it . . . What is most spiritual always takes place in the most corporeal."[43] There must remain a way to do constructive theology without losing sight

41. Himes, *Doing the Truth in Love*, chapter 4.
42. Dostoyevsky, *The Brothers Karamazov*, 56.
43. Chauvet, *The Sacrament*, xii.

of the particular corporeal significance of experience. Rahner's sacramental metaphysics can provide a beginning to the articulation of a way (by no means the only way) that allows for the corporeal context to remain important. It does not subjugate the particular context of a given experience, but rather uses the particular as a means of pointing beyond itself toward its ground and being, namely the universal reality of the divine.

As a mediator, sacramentality makes the particular universally relevant. It is not completely unlike, perhaps, the study of ethics or morality, a field which deals with the mediation between concrete actions and potentially universal behavioral maxims. However, morality does not have metaphysics or philosophy of symbolism as its primary focus, whereas here in this book these remain more of primary focus. I will strive to explain what goes on in the particular concrete and its relevance for the universal understanding of reality.

In this book, I attempt to demonstrate how sacramentality retains a tension between particularity and universality.[44] A view that neglects the former runs the risk of becoming overly idealistic, abstract, unrealistic and theoretically detached from common everyday experience. A view that neglects the latter flirts with trivialization, relativism, and indifference; thus Daniel Boyarin is accurate when he writes, "a theology of difference can produce an indifference."[45] This would mean, for my project, an indifference towards particular sacramental experiences without striving to correlate them with each other in a holistic manner, or seeking to draw from them universal implications. It is only in maintaining this sacramental tension that the particular can retain its uniqueness without becoming insignificant, and the universal can remain grounded without drifting into the vast emptiness of complete abstraction, detachment, impracticality and uselessness.

This books is also an attempt to articulate the relationship between God and world using pansacramental language. Since the claim is made that all things can potentially be understood to be in the divine, various panentheistic accounts are considered (chapter 12). Further, if it is the case that all things are in God, the reality of suffering as somehow being in God and God in suffering needs to be dealt with. This is done in chapter 13.

---

44. Anselm Min takes on a project with a similar methodology but with a different goal: constructing a theology of [geopolitical] solidarity. He writes, "My proposal, therefore is for a theology of tension, tension between particularity and universality. A self-complacent theology of universality is an imperialist theology insensitive to the particular. A self-complacent theology of particularly may be a good political tract or a good sociological analysis, but it is not Christian theology." (Min, *The Solidarity of Others in a Divided World*, 138).

45. Boyarin, *A Radical Jew*, 235. Also quoted in Min, *The Solidarity of Others in a Divided World*, 139.

Finally, chapter 14 argues for method of doing theology interreligiously going forward as an appropriate way of doing theology in pluralistic world. To demonstrate, the final chapter gives a brief example which draws on the breadth of this book.

The specific contribution to the catalog of scholarship this book makes is an interdisciplinary proposal that seeks to mediate between the religious fields of theology and spirituality precisely through proffering a philosophy of sacramental mediation while also drawing out the implications for theology of religious pluralism. Existing literature in sacramental mediation is limited. There are relatively no studies (to my knowledge) that attempt to do what this book proposes: a reconciliation of theology and spirituality *via* sacramentality. There are, of course, numerous publications on sacramental theology (Louis-Marie Chauvet, Herbert Vorglimer, etc.), and with the (re-)emergence of the study of spirituality in the West there are now publications dealing with the intersection between theology and spirituality, sacramentality and spirituality, and maybe even philosophy and spirituality. However, there are no major works on the intersection of theology and spirituality (with an examination of their interdependence) precisely through sacramentality, sacramental mediation nor sacramental language.

Perhaps the most exhaustive and relevant work on the intersection between spirituality and theology is Philip Sheldrake's *Spirituality and Theology*, in which he attempts to bridge "the historic division between love and knowledge in the human approach to God."[46] Sheldrake approaches the subject through the central Trinitarian theme, which he believes to be the most adequate unifier of the two fields.[47]

Kenan Osborne, in the final chapter of his *Sacramental Theology*, comments on "sacraments and Christian spirituality."[48] His treatment of the subject explores sacramental spirituality through the lens of post-Vatican II Rahnerian theology and commences from a Christocentric sacramental view. In particular, he treats the ecclesial dimensions of sacramental life and the individual sacraments, which stem from the ecclesial community, as lived experiences and sources of spirituality. In his brief nineteen pages he does not attempt to examine sacramental language as a mediator between

---

46. Sheldrake, *Spirituality and Theology*, vii.

47. Sheldrake notes the sacramental approach briefly when he writes, "It is often assumed that theologies of the human person or sacramental theology provide the best starting points for examining the connection between spirituality and theology." However, he offers no examples nor any such thinker that has sought mediation between the two fields through sacramental theology, so I asked Professor Sheldrake directly and he very kindly and graciously referred me to Kenan Osborne and Ann Loades.

48. Osborne, *Sacramental Theology*, 119–38.

theology and spirituality, nor how it functions as such. Thus, his project diverges from this book. No doubt, Osborne's work represents one of the more substantial contributions to sacramental spirituality, but says little about how sacramental spirituality interacts, and can be reconciled with, theology.

Ann Loades, in "Sacramentality and Christian Spirituality,"[49] examines the intersection of sacramentality and spirituality through nature, *poiesis* (the task of human making), family, politics, society, church, music, worship, stillness, silence, and Christ as sacrament. Her article is spiritually motivated; that is, it seeks to demonstrate the role sacramentality plays in the spiritual life of an individual. It does not primarily concern theology, rather the author presupposes the validity of Christian sacramental theology. This book differs in its emphasis on exploring the theological and philosophical foundations of sacramental functionality and correlating it with spirituality.

Alejandro García-Rivera, in his article "Interfaith Aesthetics: Where Theology and Spirituality Meet,"[50] comes closer to what I propose in his employment of aesthetics as a meeting place for theology and spirituality However, his goal remains different. His goal is constructive interfaith dialogue via the spiritual communion resulting from appreciation of spiritual art, thus high-lighting the aesthetical meeting point between theology and spirituality. His short piece says very little about how or why this works. This book, although offering a significant contribution interreligious and interfaith theology, dwells more on sacramentality *as such* as a means of demonstrating the interdependency of these two fields. Further, this book includes an examination of the philosophical foundations upon which sacramental theology has been built and sustained, whereas García is more interested in spiritual communion with, and appreciation for, other religious traditions through spiritual aesthetics.

Frank Fletcher supports Ghanaian theologian Kwame Bediako in his assertion that "the West is declining in adherence to Christian Faith because its cultural meanings which are constitutive of the human and the cosmos tend to suppress human sacral imagination and the sacramentality of the cosmos."[51] Though a good boon for why sacramentality remains critical for the survival of theology and religion in the West, the article offers no in-depth theo-philosophical basis for sacramentality as such.

David Brown, in *God and Enchantment of Place: Reclaiming Human Experience*, examines an aspect of what this book sets out to do. He "argues

---

49. Loades, "Sacramentality and Christian Spirituality," 254–68.

50. García-Rivera, "Interfaith Aesthetics: Where Theology and Spirituality Meet," 178–95.

51. Fletcher, "Towards a Contemporary Australian Retrieval of Sacral Imagination and Sacramentality," 1.

for the importance of experience of God as mediated through place in all its variety."[52] In other words, he entertains the sacramentality of place as an experiential mediator of God and "argues for their reinstatement at the centre of theological discussions about the existence of God."[53] Brown's text is prime resource for examining how places function sacramentally, but does not specifically treat how sacramentality as such philosophically functions as mediator between experience of place and the experiences' resulting theological reflection.

Many works in this area either dwell solely on sacramental theology, the role of sacramentality in spirituality, or generically treat the intersection of theology and spirituality.[54] Though these resources offer a good start in pointing out the need to retain the tension between theology and spirituality, they yield little on how the two interact through the theo-philosophy of sacramentality. This is the void the books intends to satisfy. By probing the sacramental field of theology, and the philosophical foundations upon which it relies, the two fields of theology and the emerging field of the contemporary study of spirituality can be brought closer together. This is a voice, though hinted at here and there by many, that has been left faint and is one this book intends to raise.

The overall methodology employed strives promote pansacramentality as a mediator, especially when applied to the reconciliation of theology and [the study of] spirituality, which have been separated due to, in large part, an overly intellectual method stemming from the onset of Scholasticism and the Enlightenment onward. A cloud of suspicion of anything seemingly subjective (or 'non-objective') was born which cast shadows of doubt on any fields pertaining to mystical, spiritual, or religious experience. On the other hand, as Sheldrake aptly points out, those not trained in theology or philosophy of religion may be equally suspicious of seemingly 'objective,' tightly knit and coherent theories of theology and philosophy of religion. This book addresses this need and brings the two back into interdependence and mutual conversation. A solution, as proposed above, is precisely one of sacramental mediation. Sacramentality offers *one* promising way but

---

52. Brown, *God and Enchantment of Place*, backcover.

53. Ibid.

54. These articles include: Allen, "The Restoration of Sacramentality in a Post-Modern World"; Berling, "Christian Spirituality: Intrinsically Interdisciplinary"; Boeve and Leijssen, eds.,*Sacramental Presence in a Postmodern Context;* Crowley, "The Crisis of Transcendence and the Task of Theology"; Anne F. Kelly, "To 'reconstitute the World' the Sacramental Imagination and a Spirituality of Embodiment"; O'Connor, "Sensuality, Spirituality, Sacramentality"; Schneiders, "Spirituality in the Academy"; Vogel, "Sacramental Living."

not the *only* way to reconcile these two fields within the Christian tradition, and possibly in other religious traditions as well.

This books' contribution to the conversation is precisely this: retaining the importance of the sacramental in the doing of academic theology and its relation to spiritual experience (and as applied in a pansacramental theology of religious pluralism) in the world and in relation to the divine. Rahner claims that

> such a spirituality of the future will also always be one that finds concrete expression and an ecclesial manifestation historically and sociologically in the sacraments of the Church, even though the concreteness of the relationship between the existentiality and the sacramentality of the self-realization of the Christian as such is in principle very variable even now and consequently can change considerably in the course of history.[55]

If it is as Rahner claims, that the spirituality of the future will always find expression in sacramentality and the Christian of the future will be a mystic ("or he or she will not exist at all"[56]), then sacramentality, I contend, is and will remain vital in the doing of Christian theology (and perhaps any theology whether it be Jewish, Christian, Muslim, Hindu, Sikh, Pagan or otherwise). Through an examination of the underlying philosophical claims, whether metaphysical (Aquinas) or symbolic (Chauvet), Rahner's claim, this book aims to show, can be demonstrated. In other words, sacramentality (its language and mediation) remains crucial in the doing of Christian theology in the academy due to its ability to retain the legitimacy of lived spiritual experience.

---

55. Rahner, *The Practice of Faith*, 18.
56. Ibid., 22.

2

Theology and Spirituality

BEFORE THE PRESUPPOSITION SET forth in the first chapter is addressed (the potential gulf between theology and spirituality), this chapter traces the historical relationship between theology and the study of spirituality. This chapter has two main sections, both significant in their aim and scope. The first section lays out the history of the relationship between theology and spirituality. The second section offers an impression of the current landscape today between the two fields. In so doing, the alleged problematic nature of their divorce or separation will be addressed.

The History of the Relationship

From Paul through the patristic era[1] up till the onset of Scholasticism, the Pauline sense of *spiritualitas* (life in the Spirit) remained, more or less, part of a unified theological whole; that is it was a part of a theology that had few, if any, divisions. Distinctions among moral theology, spiritual theology, dogmatic/systematic theology and biblical theology were absent at this point. Theology in the patristic sense was, by and large, what might be referred to today as Biblical theology or scriptural commentary, which seeks

1. Philip Sheldrake remarks, "There is disagreement about how long this [patristic] period may be considered to have lasted—so, for example, the Protestant tradition has tended to accept the Council of Chalcedon in 451 C.E. as an approximate end. The Eastern Orthodox would include such figures as Gregory Palamas who lived from 1296–1359. Others use the term somewhat broadly, to describe the whole period up to the development of the 'new theology' of scholasticism in the West in the twelfth century" (Sheldrake, *Spirituality and History*, 45).

knowledge of God and faith based on a rigorous hermeneutical method and scriptural exegesis. All theological pursuits were grounded in scripture as their primary starting point. For instance, Origen, who is sometimes deemed the first major systematic theologian, is most well-known for his scriptural hermeneutics and his allegorical method of interpretation which yielded three distinct 'senses' of scripture (literal, moral, spiritual). It was largely upon this method that a customary medieval reading of scripture grew. The method contained no division or sub theological fields, but was one unitary holistic pursuit.

Since all (perhaps most) of the major scriptural commentators and theologians of this era were in pastoral positions, it followed that their theology was largely pastoral, liturgical, and ecclesial. This naturally lent itself to placing a priority on explaining to the faithful basic doctrines and practices. Further, all faithful Christians of this time were considered capable of attaining 'life in the spirit' and thus the call to mysticism was universal. Mysticism (the quest for grasping, understanding and/or living in the 'mystery'), then, for the patristic era, differed from the later medieval and reformation periods, which shifted emphasis to refer to a more esoteric subjective experience and union with God via a rigorous spiritual path involving exercises and disciplined ascetic tasks. Mystical theology in the patristic era involved solidifying the fundamentals of key doctrines (the Incarnation, the Trinity, the so-called official Sacraments) for the church. It is in and through these basic doctrines that life in the spirit was thought to be attained. This is neither abstract nor subjective, but aims at bringing the faithful into the mystery of God, which inherently involves participation in the sacramental life of the church and the revelation of God in the Trinity and the Incarnation.[2] Pseudo-Dionysius, an appropriate representative of the patristic mystical tradition, emphasized the personal surrender to God in the process of understanding the 'mystery' of attaining the life in the spirit. Philip Sheldrake reminds us that in Dionysius, "the later interest [of medieval mysticism] in subjective experience is not present."[3]

In addition to their pastoral context, the majority of the patristic theologians were set in a monastic context (and therefore living in a community that promoted celibacy), from the upper class (and therefore received an elite education), and of course were men. This context, to be sure, shaped their resulting theology. To be clear, this era maintained a unified theology, with no divisions or branches (to its benefit as well as to its detriment), that sought a synthesis of mysticism, doctrinal clarity, reason, and biblical

2. Sheldrake, *Spirituality and History*, 46.
3. Ibid., 47.

exegesis. What might be referred to as spiritual theology (not necessarily the contemporary study of spirituality as such) was found therein, particularly in its Origenian method of scriptural interpretation.

The breach, divorce[4], or break between theology and spirituality is not clearly denoted in history. Various scholars have differing opinions concerning when and what served as the most influential factor contributing to the breach. There are a number of factors which, without doubt, helped to bring it about. These include, but are not limited to, scholasticism, the (re)emergence of Aristotelian philosophy, the contrast of the spiritual with the corporeal, the advent of sub-divisional theological fields, the European Reformations, the Enlightenment, greater (over)specialization in academia, and the scientific-historical-critical method, to name the major ones.

With the onset of Scholasticism, the so-called 'New Theology,' in the middle ages came early signs of fissures between theology and spirituality, which heretofore had, for the most part, been held together in a single unitary theological pursuit for God as discourse about God.[5] Theology had been done primarily under the auspices of monastic males, and Scholasticism shifted that locus for doing theology to the schools where the new theologians developed a more systematic form of theology drawing on new sources such as ancient Greek philosophy (Aristotle). The twelfth century demonstrates a shift to the new attitude of ordering (*ordinatio*) religion in general, thus rendering to each thing its proper relationship and placing emphasis on measure, order, legalism, political frameworks, discipline, ceremonies, ecclesiastical offices, and duties.[6] Bernard McGinn recognizes this when he writes, "medieval society of the eleventh and twelfth centuries was avid for order, in this sense of putting things in order, across the whole range of its creative endeavor."[7] This new obsession with order found its way to the university in theology resulting in scholasticism, particularly taking hold in the schools of urban Northern Europe.

---

4. Both Philip Sheldrake and Keith J. Egan refer to the breach as a 'divorce.' See Sheldrake, "Chapter 2: The Divorce of Spirituality and Theology," in *Spirituality and Theology*, 33–64 and Egan, "The Divorce of Spirituality from Theology."

5. Andrew Louth points out that for "the Fathers *theologia* is strictly discourse about *God*" (Louth, *Discerning the Mystery*, 3).

6. Jean Leclercq points out that it is important to state what one means by 'scholasticism' due to prior disputes over the term. "Today, it is more generally agreed that the scholastic method is characterized not by the use of Aristotle but by the teaching procedures, principally the *quaestio* applied to the *sacra pagina*" (Leclercq, *The Love of Learning and the Desire for God*, 2).

7. Bernard McGinn credits this recognition to R. W. Southern, *The Making of the Middle Ages*, 153.

This new theology, with its precision oriented method, posed a threat to the existing theological method of monastic theology (since prior to scholasticism, theology was primarily done by monks in monastic settings). Scholasticism sought to appropriate the faith in a new way, which seemed more intellectual. It represented a new posture, attitude, or orientation toward theology. At its core, scholasticism did not necessarily seek new answers to theological questions, but rather provided a new method. It went beyond the mere citation of authorities. Matthew Fox reminds us that,

> What the West has forgotten about scholasticism is that it was, in its healthy days, a radical intellectual movement that came to Europe from Islam and that was essentially *a methodology of asking questions*. This is why it appealed to the radical new movements of the renaissance of the twelfth and early thirteenth century: it assisted the overthrow of the established intellectual methodology of simply citing authorities, usually fathers of the church.[8]

In Aquinas's *Summa*, the confluence of the Patristic and Scholastic approaches is evident. Citation of patristic authority is subjected to the scrutiny of reason and the philosophical categories of Aristotle, 'the Philosopher,' which naturally entails a deliberate effort to properly distinguish one thing from another. Jean Leclercq provides a helpful distinction when seeking to understand how these two methods of theology might differ by noting that the monastic emphasizes *credo ut experiar* (I believe in order to experience) while the scholastic emphasizes *credo ut intelligam* (I believe in order to understand).[9] In other words, the monastics were less interested in the knowledge (*scientia* to be placed alongside all other human knowledge) yielded by scripture, and more interested in wisdom (*sapientia*) as it pertains to salvation from God.[10]

Since these schools were often under the direction of local bishops, understandably their theology differed from monastic theology. Further, since the bishops obviously served as major controllers of ecclesiastical affairs, it is reasonable that their theology took on a more pastoral, apologetic, and ecclesiastical tone in contrast to the more mystical and ascetical monastic theology. Scholastic theology sought answers to questions and concerns that did not burden the monastics. Embedded in the urban universities, scholastic theology sought to integrate itself with the liberal arts

---

8. Fox, *Sheer Joy*, 20 (italics his).

9. Bernard McGinn credits this recognition to Jean Leclercq, *The Love of Learning and the Desire for God*, 367.

10. McGinn, *The Growth of Mysticism*, 368.

and incorporate knowledge from sources outside scripture alone. Bernard McGinn quotes Hugh of St. Victor in characterizing this attitude, "Learn everything; you will see later that nothing is superfluous."[11] A good example of this might be Aquinas' synthesis of Aristotle and the Christian tradition.

Not all scholastics were unified in their theological conclusions. Of course there remained a wide range of differing opinions, but they shared a general scholastic attitude, orientation, and method. Some (perhaps many) medieval theologians cannot be easily placed into one camp or another (e.g., Thomas Aquinas). The point here is that this contrast in theological method helped to set the stage for the problematic divorce between theology and spirituality. Scholasticism naturally encouraged a move away from analysis and consideration of the spiritual life and replaced it with a more 'scientific' approach to dogmatic and moral concerns. This is why many scholars point to the advent of scholasticism as a major culprit in the separation of these two fields.

The number of key medieval theologians worth looking at is far too great for the scope and parameters of this chapter. However, there are three that stand out from the rest that deserve a closer look, namely, Peter Abelard, Bernard of Clairvaux and Thomas Aquinas. The conflict between Abelard and Bernard has been recognized by some[12] as 'symbolic' of the conflict between monastic theology and scholasticism. Symbolic or not, its importance remains central to understanding the breach between the two fields, for the two figures, in their conflict with each other, represent the older monastic method and the newer scholasticism. Abelard is heralded as perhaps one of the greatest logicians of the middle ages and certainly a top-tier scholastic. He contributed to the revival of Latin philosophy and defended the use of reason in the doing of theology. Among other things, he is remembered for his conflict with Bernard, who served as the living icon[13] for the contemplative monastic tradition. Bernard was truly *the* twelfth century mystic (who also enjoyed fame as a crusader, politician, poet, and writer). He excelled in both religious and political life in France and eventually all of Western Europe.[14]

Abelard operated in the scholastic system while Bernard's audience was primarily monastic. Taken as representatives of these two camps

---

11. McGinn quotes Hugh of St. Victor and Charles Henry Buttimer, *Hugonis De Sancto Victore Didascalicion De Studio Legendi*, 115.19–20 in *The Growth of Mysticism*, 369.

12. Louth, *Discerning the Mystery*, 5; and Jones, "Spirituality and Theology," 164.

13. Dante, in the *Paradiso* of his *Divine Comedy*, casts Bernard as the "elder clad like the folk in glory" who guides Dante to Mary and the vision of the Trinity.

14. McGinn, *The Growth of Mysticism*, 164.

respectively, they give clear insight about some of the fundamental points of tension. Abelard's greater confidence in the role of reason clashed with Bernard and his fellow anti-dialecticians,[15] who held that truths of religious faith were plain and thus no careful scrutiny via dialectical reason was required in order to discover them. Further, according to the anti-dialecticians, if the plain sense of a religious sentence (scripture) was not clear, then reason would be of no assistance. Abelard, and those who held a greater confidence in reason, were seen as only confusing and distorting the plain sense of a proposition of faith, and thus were railed against. He had little patience for Bernard and his monastic reason-denying ilk. He outright rejected the notion of a plain meaning to begin with, and endorsed his dialectical method of questioning, gathering (often opposing) answers, and finally discerning a meaning, if one was to be had. According to Abelard, it is often the case that when citing authorities (a trait preferred by the monastic method) one is often led to the possibility of citing equally reliable, yet conflicting, authorities. This forces one to use reason in order to discern the appropriate meaning.[16]

These two figures are often cited as representatives of the monastic-scholastic conflict and therefore symbolically foreshadow the theology/spirituality divorce. In fairness to both Abelard and Bernard, we should recognized that neither of them blindly dug their heels in their respective camps. For instance, though Abelard clashed with Bernard and the anti-dialecticians, he held even less respect for those who posed as dialecticians (pseudo-dialecticians) and over-estimated the strength of reason. Abelard believed that, unlike himself, they did not recognize the limits of reason nor did they put stock in any authority. He believed that authorities did hold persuasive force and further, that some truths may simply lie beyond the limits of reason. In this respect, this would put Abelard somewhere in the middle between these pseudo-dialecticians and Bernard (and the anti-dialecticians). We should also be careful not to judge Bernard too narrowly and deem him a mere blind fideist. He did, in fact, hold some confidence in the intellectual faculties, though he always tempered this confidence with caution and intellectual humility. Intellect, he believed, was part of human nature; however, due to his Christian belief in 'the Fall' and the human condition of being tainted by sin, it (the intellect) operates imperfectly and remains vulnerable to corruption and pride. Thus all true knowledge begins

---

15. Anti-dialecticians resisted the use of the scholastic method of dialectic in seeking and grasping religious truth.

16. King, "Peter Abelard."

in "the self-knowledge of humility."[17] Even though these two serve as the symbolic representatives of the monastic-scholastic divide, they both still held to the idea that knowledge and faith each play central roles in the pursuit of knowledge about, and ascension to, God.

Not long after this conflict surfaced, the medieval world produced one figure who held these two sides together, perhaps more than any other theologian in the West up to his era. This was Thomas Aquinas.[18] Aquinas was neither a strict rationalist nor a fideist.[19] Nor can he be categorized as a strict dogmatist or a skeptic. Matthew Fox, the Episcopalian theologian and scholar of Aquinas, believes Aquinas is best labeled a mystic,[20] while Thomist scholar Brian Davies prefers simply to refer to him as a Christian Saint and thinker.[21] Whatever label is applied to him, his influence cannot be doubted. As both a monk and a scholastic it is not surprising that he represents a *via media*, an inner harmony, between scholasticism and monasticism, though this may seem to have been lost on some (perhaps most) of his followers. This is observed by Marie-Dominique Chenu when he points out that sixteenth century Thomists had, "lost the eminent spiritual equilibrium of their master which would have enabled them to understand, assess and

17. McGinn, *The Growth of Mysticism*, 201.

18. Aquinas fulfilled "more than anyone else the essential medieval program of a marriage between faith and reason, revelation and philosophy, the Biblical and the classical inheritances . . . He represents the medieval mind par excellence, and the Middle Ages are the parent and source of all the divergent streams in the modern world, like a mother whose many children went their own various ways. [He represents] a unity of ingredients that were later to separate . . . For one brief, Camelot-like moment it seemed that synthesis was possible" (Kreeft, *A Summa of the Summa*, 13).

19. "Aquinas's balanced appreciation of the respective roles of reason and faith within the unity of the theological horizon also makes it possible to avoid the dichotomy or rationalism and fideism. He rejects arrogant rationalism by insisting on the subordination of reason to the principles of faith as a servant to a master. He rejects fideism by insisting on the essential role of reason in supplying the philosophical presuppositions of faith, defending faith against its opponents, deducing other truths from the *revelata*, and in general rendering the content of faith humanly intelligible and plausible" (Min, *Paths to the Triune God*, 43).

20. Aquinas "was not a rationalist. On the contrary, he was a mystic . . . This is where Aquinas's amazing balance shows itself: he exercised to the full, it seems, both hemispheres of his brain" (Fox, *Sheer Joy*, 27).

21. "One might just as well say that Aquinas was both a theologian and a philosopher. Much of what he says can be read either as philosophy or as theology. It is, perhaps, most accurate of all simply to call him a Christian thinker, though this should not be taken to mean that his thought can be divided into two: a system of philosophy, founded solely on reason, and—based on and completing this—a system of revealed theology . . . He was also, of course, a Christian saint" (Davies, *The Thought of Thomas Aquinas*, 14).

assimilate the rational values of this second Renaissance . . . their theology had lost the spirit of daring as well as its original freshness and had forgotten the need of continual rediscovery."[22] Aquinas himself sought truth wherever he could find it, be it from Aristotle, ancient philosophy, Islamic philosophy, the Fathers, monastic spirituality, revelation, scripture or reason.

Aquinas had sought to keep the spirit of contemplation in union with scholastic theological speculation,[23] though in the process of producing his work, it may be that, by dividing his *Summa* into parts, he unfortunately laid the groundwork for enduring divisions within the theological field as a whole. He subdivides the *Summa* into parts dealing with 1) God (the principle and *telos* of humankind), 2) humankind (including anthropology, purpose and ethics), and 3) Christ (humankind's means back to God), and in so doing establishes theological subdivisions, such as dogmatic and moral theology. Sheldrake makes the point that content pertaining to the life of the Christian fell under the rubric of moral theology, thus distancing it from other theological divisions.[24] This led to, as Sandra Schneiders has recognized, the removal of spirituality from "being a dimension of all theology" to "a subordinate branch of theology."[25] This resulted in further subdivisions of theological branches and gave birth to the trend of specialization in academia which only grew in the centuries to come. For the reasons outlined above, many contemporary scholars[26] of spirituality point to the rise of scholasticism as the main catalyst for this breach between theology and spirituality, since it eventually led to, as Chenu has declared, the "false modern idea that there is opposition between mysticism and scholasticism."[27] However, as seen in Aquinas, this opposition need not exist. It is part of the task of the contemporary study of spirituality (and this book), to recover that unity and lay to rest such 'false modern ideas.'

As scholasticism gained steam in the ensuing centuries, the pursuit of mysticism and monastic spiritual theology were increasingly viewed with suspicion. Francois Vandenbroucke interprets the 14th century as decisive in the fate of these two fields. He recognizes the widening breach due to "a degenerative speculative mysticism on one hand and the character of

---

22. Chenu, *Nature, Man, and Society in the Twelfth Century*, 33.
23. Sheldrake, *Spirituality and History*, 49.
24. Ibid.
25. Schneiders, "Spirituality in the Academy," 685.
26. Philip Sheldrake, Sandra Schneiders, Eugen Megyer, Keith Egan, Bernard McGinn, and Andrew Louth.
27. Chenu, *Toward Understanding Saint Thomas*, 63.

Devotio moderna on the other."[28] Perhaps the most well-known representative from this century is Thomas à Kempis, the spiritual writer of the renowned work *The Imitation of Christ*, a model of the *Devotio moderna* movement.[29] This work, and movement, focused on interior attitudes in working towards perfection. A leading representative of the fourteenth century spiritual renewal was Gerard Groote who sought to systematize interior prayer. *Devotio moderna*, as a precursor to pietism, sought to sync the outward *figura* (which encompasses both the inner seen substance and the outer incisive form; the inner character and outer gesture) with the inner state of grace. The influence of both *Devotio moderna* and pietism on the development of spirituality cannot be understated. It was an interior pursuit of perfection in an era in which mysticism was increasingly seen as too subjective and psychological to be taken seriously. It had deviated too drastically from the synthesis Aquinas had achieved under his usual clear metaphysical and (seemingly) objective language. Further, spirituality was being gradually separated from concrete experience, whether it was moral theology, ecclesiology, and/or liturgy. Amidst such a climate, "an interest developed in specific experiences and activities: prayer, contemplation and mysticism," Sheldrake writes, "and growth was conceived more and more in terms of ascent, whereby the active life was merely a preparation for the contemplative and was thus viewed as a 'lower' way."[30]

Ann Clifford, in her article "Re-membering the Spiritual Core of Theology,"[31] places the initial point of the 'dis-membering' of theology from spirituality in the fourteenth century, but acknowledges that deeper chasms opened up by the time of the sixteenth century reformations, a point at which the tension between the two fields became antagonistic. With Clifford, Regina Bechte points to the sixteenth century as a crucial turning point for these two fields, particularly due to "the specialization which marked the end of the medieval synthesis and the beginnings of the modern era [which] had had its impact on theology."[32] This played out further, of course, in the ensuing Enlightenment. Alan Jones takes a similar approach in his article "Spirituality and Theology,"[33] in which he diagnoses the source of the divorce in an academic obsession with 'over-specialization.' In arriving at this

---

28. Vandenbroucke, "Le Divorce Entre Théologie Et Mystique," 372–89.

29. For a substantive overview of this movement and its writings, see John H. Van Engen, ed., *Devotio Moderna*.

30. Sheldrake, *Spirituality and History*, 52.

31. Clifford, "Re-membering the Spiritual Core of Theology," 19–21.

32. Bechte, "Theological Trends," 305.

33. Jones, "Spirituality and Theology," 161–76.

conclusion, he draws on Dorothy Sayers, who attributes the obsession to the scientific method of definition, segmentation and separation.[34] She writes about "the increasing segregation of specialists in their own specialties, so that the scientist is not expected to study theology nor the theologian to study science, nor either of them to be an artist or a poet."[35] If this is indeed the case, it is understandable why theology (done by the theologian) need not be concerned with mysticism (experienced by the mystic) nor spirituality ("lived religious experience").

The Reformation set Roman Catholicism and Protestantism on their separate trajectories, and with them also went their approaches to spirituality. On the Catholic side are the Spanish mystics (Ignatius of Loyola, Teresa of Avila, St. John of the Cross) and Francis de Sales. Sheldrake recognizes these individuals to be without "the terminology of later 'ascetical' or 'mystical' theology, [which] developed [later] in the eighteenth century and [became] common currency in the late nineteenth century."[36] However, they showed the clearest signs of coming close to practicing what is referred to by the contemporary study of spirituality,[37] which focuses on the particular experience of lived religion, and not just a mere interior climb up the ladder of perfection. On the other hand, the new Protestant offshoots maintained a more pronounced suspicion of theological knowledge being derived from experience or methods of seeming self-perfection as to avoid (or, at the very least, to maintain caution regarding) any dangerous idolatrous self-sanctifying or salvific meritorious processes. Attempts to merit perfection on one's own, be it through mystical or ascetical means, was seen as possible works righteousness. Instead, the cornerstone of spiritual piety for the reformers resided in 'divine monergism,' the faith in God alone to initiate and accomplish everything pertaining to salvation.[38] According to Sheldrake, the "classic Protestant emphasis was on God as the sole source of holiness. The classic Catholic emphasis was on the practical consequences in the life of the individual Christian of justification and redemption."[39]

In keeping with the uniqueness from their continental ancestors, the Anglo-Reformation took its own approach to spirituality. Emerging in the

34. Ibid., 165.
35. Sayers, *Further Papers on Dante*, 88.
36. Sheldrake, *Spirituality and Theology*, 44.
37. Sheldrake, *Spirituality and History*, 53.
38. Sheldrake, *Spirituality and Theology*, 46.

39. Ibid., (parenthesis omitted). Here Sheldrake also argues that classical Protestantism never developed the idea that theology and spirituality were opposed since the two, from the very outset of the reformation movement, were inherently included in the doing of theology.

seventeenth century, and taking their primary cues from *The Book of Common Prayer*, the English produced an emphatically ethical spirituality. Their spiritual method was, in large part, aimed at guiding persons in right living through a spiritual means such as prayers, meditations, art (such as poetry) and devotional readings.

The seventeenth and eighteenth centuries brought on the Enlightenment which has received notable attention as a contributor to the divorce of spirituality and theology. The Enlightenment produced the so-called 'modern' frame of mind which entails, among other things, a new found confidence "that there is a *method*[40] by which we can reach the truth"[41] whether it be through empiricism or Cartesian clarity and distinct perception. The method sought to expose all of the dark corners of knowledge. Commencing in doubt and ignorance, the method cast a climate of suspicion on anything seemingly subjective (more accurately, anything 'non-objective'), thus any fields pertaining to mystical, spiritual or religious experience remained in doubt. The distinction that began in the middles ages between, on the one hand, an affective piety separated from doctrinal theology and, on the other, an overly intellectual and removed speculative and scientific theology, had become solidified during the Enlightenment. In such a climate, we might reasonably understand why theologians would, in order to legitimatize themselves as scientists and hope to be taken seriously, distance themselves from the subjectivity of spiritual theology.

Romanticism, in a sense, sought a return to what T.S. Elliot referred to as 'sensibility' and what Wordsworth understood to be 'feeling intellect.' It called for a return to the unity of the two halves of head and heart, thought and feeling, and so on.[42] However, this only resulted in further specialization (perhaps over-specialization). Andrew Louth notes that art and aesthetic experience, in particular, received the brunt of such marginalization in its being relegated to the sidelines of life, thus settling in the fringe sphere of extraordinary experience cut off from "any real context in life."[43] This mentality, Louth argues, impacted theology. For instance, the Romantic spirit in the field of religion, beginning with Schleiermacher, only set the essence of religion apart as something to be grasped by the 'cultured.' Further, argues Louth, the theological "cracks and divisions go deeper and have been

---

40. E.g., Scientific method, Cartesian epistemology, the historical-critical method, etc.

41. Louth, *Discerning the Mystery*, 7 (italics his).

42. Ibid., 1.

43. Ibid., 2.

there longer"[44] as evidenced by the endless sub-dividing of theology and the continued 'remoteness' of theologians (although this is perhaps changing in the current era as more theologians are embracing interdisciplinary approaches). Louth concludes that "one way in which the division in theology manifests itself is in the division between theology and spirituality."[45]

Mystical theology and ascetical theology were gradually replaced in the twentieth century by the term 'spiritual theology.' The two former terms were not completely dropped from religious and theological terminology, but rather spiritual theology was seen as more comprehensive than the other two. Mystical theology is primarily concerned with an extraordinary experience of the union with the divine, something not necessarily considered accessible to most ordinary believers, whereas ascetical theology is primarily concerned with the pursuit of interior perfection. However, until around the time of the Second Vatican Council, spiritual theology, as a field, remained subordinate to both dogmatic and moral theology. Though perhaps there are advantages for employing 'spiritual theology' over and above the narrower ascetical and mystical theology, one detriment might be that it has contributed to the confusion of the term spirituality today. The concern here is whether the term adequately represents what people mean when they employ the word. Additionally, prior to Vatican II (and for some time after), the term 'spiritual theology,' as employed by the Roman Catholic tradition, had "a tendency to be individualistic, to ignore the social dimensions of Christian spiritual life and to reduce the ecclesial aspects of spirituality to participation in the sacraments."[46]

In the current post-Vatican II twenty-first century context, "'spiritual theology' has given way to a more dynamic and inclusive concept known as 'spirituality.'"[47] It is that which is studied by the contemporary study of spirituality. Prior to moving ahead and defining further the contemporary study of spirituality, I will briefly distinguish it from four other fields, all of which are by no means mutually exclusive from it, but included in it to various degrees. These fields are mystical theology, spiritual theology, monastic theology and ascetical theology.

Mystical theology can be distinguished from the theology *of* mysticism. The theology of mysticism,[48] as used by Rahner, refers to the "systematic

---

44. Ibid.
45. Ibid.
46. Sheldrake, *Spirituality and History*, 54.
47. Sheldrake, *Spirituality and Theology*, 55.
48. Rahner, "The Theology of Mysticism."

theological reflection *on* mystical experience;"⁴⁹ that is, it is a reflection on the experience of the mystical. Mystical theology, on the other hand, used in the pre-medieval era, refers to the nebulous (mysterious?) knowledge of God that comes through the *mystic* experience itself. In short, theology of mysticism is reflection on the mystical experience, which thus produces knowledge, whereas mystical theology is knowledge that comes precisely from the mystical experience, without reflection. Note here that mystical theology, systematic theology, and any other theology may apprehend the same truth, but through different means.

Ascetical theology refers to the reflection on knowledge apprehended through asceticism, which is the polishing or refinement of one's life through spiritual exercise such as prayer, fasting, watching, and the like. Whereas mysticism yields knowledge through extraordinary experiences of the divine, asceticism yields knowledge through a rigorous striving on behalf of the subject. Ascetical theology, involving a striving on behalf of the person for perfection, is not dissimilar from spiritual theology.

Spiritual theology, as noted above, is that branch of theology that blossomed in the seventeenth century and is concerned with striving after interior perfection through mystical and ascetical avenues.⁵⁰ This term, perhaps more than the others mentioned here, is most often confused with the contemporary study of spirituality. It is often placed under the auspices of either dogmatic or moral theology. Jean Leclercq employs this meaning of 'spiritual theology' when he speaks of 'monastic theology' as "a spiritual theology which completes speculative theology."⁵¹

Monastic theology, though a type of spiritual theology, is the most particular of the types mentioned here. Monastic theology refers to theology done by monks in monasteries. It often includes knowledge apprehended through asceticism and mysticism, but also includes the authority of scripture and the Patristic figures. These sources are not unique to monastic theology alone. On the contrary, scripture and Patristic thinkers may be sources for many (perhaps most) theologies (such as scholastic theology), but the difference here may lie in the context and method by which one goes about appropriating those sources. Monastic theology, as opposed to scholastic theology, incorporates experience (be it mystical, ascetical or other) into its reflection, whereas scholasticism, as Leclercq writes, "puts experience aside" and, should it so desire, operate on a plane of impersonal

---

49. Schneiders, "Spirituality in the Academy," 688.
50. Ibid., 689.
51. Leclercq, *The Love of Learning and the Desire for God*, 223.

and universal metaphysics.[52] With these definitions laid out, I now proceed to the situation today and the field being referred to as the contemporary study of spirituality.

The Situation Today

One aim of this book is to make an argument for why theology and the study of spirituality ought to be inherently linked. Both fields examine religion from different angles and ask different questions. Theologians make claims about the divine and provide explanation and elaboration on how these claims cohere with one another. Likewise, mystics, saints, and those who claim to spiritually access the divine (via 'lived experience') claim to know God through particular experience and make claims about the nature of the human spirit and how it accesses the divine. Both claim knowledge of the divine, yet through different epistemic means, or as Schneiders puts it, the two do not differ on *what* is apprehended, but *how* it is apprehended. They have different sets of data, yet claim a shared source and object: the divine. Before commentating on the current relationship between the two fields, I will offer a more in-depth review 'the contemporary study of spirituality.'

To elucidate the definition (if possible) and parameters of the emerging field of the contemporary study of spirituality, I rely on three primary scholars whom I understand to be among the most lucid, definitive, and deliberate in their explanations of the field. Further, these three have not only offered insight into definition of the field, but have made significant contributions to the various studies within the field itself. These three thinkers are Sandra Schneiders, Bernard McGinn, and Philip Sheldrake.

Defining the field, or the term itself, can be a tricky matter indeed. Since it is true that, as Sheldrake says, "Spirituality is one of those subjects whose meaning everyone claims to know until they have to define it,"[53] then defining it will be the burden of what follows in the next few pages. Thus far I have been intentionally referring to the study of spirituality as 'the contemporary study of spirituality,' as that is the preferred nomenclature given to it by the small, but growing, number of scholars devoted to it. The qualifier 'contemporary' has been affixed to denote its uniqueness from the various ways it has been approached throughout history.

Sandra Schneiders broadly defines the discipline as "the field of study which attempts to investigate in an interdisciplinary way spiritual experience

---

52. Ibid.
53. Sheldrake, *Spirituality and History*, 40.

as such."[54] More specifically, she says it studies a contemporary understanding of spirituality which "refers to the experience of consciously striving to integrate one's life in terms not of isolation and self-absorption but of self-transcendence toward the ultimate value one perceives."[55] The object of study, notice, if one were to study 'contemporary spirituality,' is precisely 'experience' as such, whereas for theology, it is God (or the gods) as such.

To begin with, Schneiders offers four helpful negative statements, that is, what the contemporary study of spirituality is not. First, it is not (or nor longer) exclusively Roman Catholic. Secondly, it is "neither dogmatic nor prescriptive."[56] Thirdly, it is "not concerned with 'perfection'" nor fourthly, is it concerned with the "interior life."[57] Positively, she offers at least four major characteristics of the field that distinguish it from theology. First, since it is interested in 'experience as experience,' it is inherently interdisciplinary because it seeks to utilize any and all modes of knowing about experience. Second, it takes a descriptive-critical approach, not a prescriptive-normative one. The goal is to know the nature of experience (descriptive) and critique its authenticity (critical). It is not an application of theological principles to life and practice, as one might do when engaged in moral theology. Third, it need not be sequestered to one particular religion or tradition (and for this reason remains exceptionally open to interreligious and ecumenical dialogue). Since the goal is not always coherence of theological principles, but the understanding of experience as such, spirituality can account for a diverse range of religious experiences. Finally, much like the first, spirituality is a holistic "inquiry into human spiritual experience [and] is not limited to explorations of the explicitly religious, i.e. the so-called 'interior life,'"[58] thus it should not be reduced to mere mystical and/or ascetical theology. All facets of human experience remain important to the discipline such as psychological, exterior-bodily, social, historical, aesthetical, intellectual, and others.[59]

Sheldrake offers four characteristics of contemporary spirituality that help distinguish it from the 'spiritual theology' common to the early twentieth century. First, it is not exclusive to the Christian tradition. Second, it is not just a mere prescriptive application of dogmatic theology to concrete religious life. Third, it is less concerned with delineating the contours of

---

54. Schneiders, "Spirituality in the Academy," 260.
55. Schneiders, "Theology and Spirituality," 684.
56. Ibid., 264–65.
57. Ibid.
58. Schneiders, "Spirituality in the Academy," 693.
59. Ibid.

perfection, but rather seeks to 'survey' the various human responses to the divine mysteries. Fourth, it goes beyond the sole concern for the interior life, but seeks to understand all facets of the human experience as it relates to the divine.[60]

Like theology, spirituality employs a similar methodology of seeking to integrate horizons (including scripture, doctrine, history, experience, etc.) but differs in that its object is not universal knowledge about the divine nature of God (or the gods), but knowledge of human nature (or the human spirit) as mediated through particular religious experience. A question primarily motivated by *theology* might be 'what does the conversion experience of Ignatius of Loyola teach us about the nature of God,' while a question primarily motivated by the study of *spirituality* might be 'what does the conversion experience of Ignatius of Loyola teach us about the way Ignatius, as a human subject, knew, responded to, and experienced God?' Put another way, theology seeks to know the *nature of the divine* exhibited in such an experience while the contemporary study of spirituality seeks to know the *nature of human experience* in relation to the divine exhibited in the experience. Thus, theology strives for knowledge of divine nature while spirituality strives for knowledge of human experience. Christian Spirituality need not be reduced to a mere philosophical anthropology for it differs in that it seeks knowledge of "the conscious human response to God" or of the Pauline "life in the spirit."[61]

In her influential 1989 article, "Spirituality in the Academy," Schneiders distinguishes between two basic approaches in defining spirituality: 1) "from above" (dogmatic position) and 2) "from below" (anthropological position).[62] From above, spirituality is subordinated to dogmatic theology, and is defined as the "life of the Christian communicated by the Holy Spirit and governed by divine revelation."[63] Schneiders argues against the former position and in favor of the latter, "from below," which she understands to be, as Jean Claude Breton explains, "a way of engaging anthropological questions and preoccupations in order to arrive at an ever richer and more authentically human life."[64] In other words, she reduces the approaches to spirituality to either a theological (from above) or anthropological (from below) approach. Thinkers such as C.A. Bernard, James Wiseman, Bradley Hanson, Kenneth Leech, and Louis Boyer (and possibly Rahner, von

---

60. Sheldrake, *Spirituality and History*, 58.
61. Ibid., 45.
62. Schneiders, "Spirituality in the Academy," 682.
63. Ibid.
64. Breton, "Retrouver les Assises Anthropologiques de la Vie Spirituelle," 101.

Balthasar, Jordan Aumann, and Walter Principe as well[65]) might be considered to be representatives of the former while thinkers such as Jean Claude Breton, Sandra Schneiders, Edward Kinerk, Michael Downey, and Rachel Hosmer (to name a few) might be considered representatives of the latter.[66] Bernard McGinn cautions against the reduction of methodologies to only two when defining spirituality and, in so doing, offers a third possible approach, namely the *historical-contextual approach*. This approach "emphasizes spirituality as an experience rooted in a particular community's history rather than as a dimension of human existence as such."[67] Representatives for this third approach might include thinkers such as Rowan Williams, Urban T. Holmes, André Vauchez, and Philip Sheldrake. Though McGinn recognizes a third possible approach, he acknowledges that any one approach on its own ultimately falls short. Instead he advocates "that all three options remain in the conversation."[68]

McGinn recognizes that "at the present time," no universal and fully adequate definition for contemporary spirituality may exist—nor may it ever exist—and this is not to its determinate. Instead, he understands this "open warfare . . . [to] actually be an advantage."[69] It may encourage lively debate amongst its scholars to further hash out the contours of the field, while at the same time remaining open to a broad spectrum of possibilities.

Sheldrake, in his 1994 article, "Some Continuing Questions,"[70] raises some rather basic (and I believe commonly overlooked) questions regarding situating spirituality in relation to theology. To begin with, he recognizes that, in large part, the relationship between the two not only depends on how spirituality is defined, but how theology is defined as well. He points out the danger of scholars of spirituality sometimes reducing the term theology to that which inherently excludes spiritual concerns, matters of spirituality, and/or concrete realization of faith. This conception of theology, writes Sheldrake, "would not correspond to the search for a contemporary

---

65. These last four particular thinkers place significant emphasis on 'transcendence,' and as McGinn argues, build "upon a distinction between a generic notion of spirituality based upon human hunger for transcendence and specifically Christian spirituality which is to be measured by the norm of revelation (which does not necessarily have to mean that Christian spirituality is just a specialization of dogmatics" (McGinn, "The Letter and the Spirit, 31).

66. McGinn, "The Letter and the Spirit," 30–33.

67. Ibid., 33.

68. Ibid., 35.

69. Ibid., 34.

70. Sheldrake, "Some Continuing Questions," 15–17.

theology 'from below'"[71] like we perhaps find in theologies that are inherently spiritual such as the theology of Karl Rahner and many liberation theologies.

Sheldrake also suggests that though much has been made of the contemporary study of spirituality as a "self-implicating"[72] field, theology is just as much so.[73] This is the claim that one must have *fides* in order to *quaerens intellectum* and thus satisfy Anselm's classic definition of theology. This claim can be appropriately challenged. One might argue that a position of confessional faith is not a necessary prerequisite for the doing of theology. Theologian Michael Himes tells the story of his experience as a graduate student at the University of Chicago under the tutelage of Paul Tillich. Tillich would enter the classroom on the first of the semester, stand at the front of the classroom, pause, and then look out at his students while he uttered the single word, "Gott" in a thick, German, accent. Another pause followed by Tillich declaring, "Whatever came into your head when I said the word 'God,' is not God."[74] Tillich's main point is that no matter what we say or think about God is inadequate. A further point might be made here that if theology is simply "talking about the divine," then anyone with the concept of God (even if they never utter the word) is a theologian, regardless of their implication in the field, no matter how inadequate. The contemporary study of spirituality, on the other hand, has been defined, in essence, as self-implicating, meaning one cannot study spirituality without 'lived religious experience.' Thus in order to be considered a legitimate scholar of spirituality, one must be a player on the field, and not just in the stands. In the doing of theology however, if we take the definition suggested above drawing on the Tillich story, one need not be on the field, but may remain in stands.

71. Ibid., 15.

72. This assertion is made routinely by thinkers in the field of contemporary spirituality, beginning with Schneiders. See Lane, "Writing in Spirituality as a Self-Implicating Act," 53–69.

73. Even the academic field of "religious studies," conventionally understood as an interdisciplinary attempt to study the phenomena of religion from an outsider and/or secular perspective without self-implication or confession, has increasingly come under questioning. Oddbjørn Leirvik, drawing on Gavin Flood's chapter "Dialogue and the Situated Observer" from Flood's *Beyond Phenomenology,* critiques "the idea of 'the detached, epistemic subject penetrating the alien world of the other through the phenomenological process.' Instead, Flood writes, 'the subject must be defined in relation to other subjects.' Flood goes as far as to say that religious studies thus become 'a dialogical enterprise in which the inquirer is situated within a particular context or narrative tradition, and whose research into narrative traditions, that become the objects of investigation, must be apprehended in a much richer and multi-faceted way" (Flood, 143; Leirvik, "Interreligious Studies," 15).

74. Himes, *Doing the Truth in Love,* 9.

Regardless of one's approach to theology, the need for critical examination in both fields remains clear.

Further, offering too broad of a definition for the contemporary study of spirituality may result in simply renaming a field that already exists. For instance, if it is simply about human experience, why then can this concern not be addressed in the more established fields of anthropology, sociology, and phenomenology? Further, and perhaps a more obvious concern, is one that both Sheldrake and McGinn hint at: though it is clear that the study of spirituality and theology refer to distinct fields and methods, is it the case that spirituality is adequately distinct from religion as such? McGinn is concerned with reducing our spiritual method to the anthropological approach alone. He writes, "In trying to determine what spirituality is by taking the anthropological route alone, it may well be that all we have come up with is another name for religion." This does not seem to be a new issue, since today the terms spirituality and religion are often used in tandem,[75] but are somehow assumed to be different.

Schneiders tackles this issue in her article "Religion vs. Spirituality: A Contemporary Conundrum," in which she seeks to make sense of the more recent expression, "I'm spiritual, but not religious." She reintroduces a previous opinion that of her three conceived relationships between spirituality and religion (strangers, rivals, or partners), partnership is the most helpful. To do so, she defines spirituality anthropologically; that is, spirituality is a basic and a fundamental characteristic of what it means to be human. This understanding of spirituality allows for a broad understanding thus making it more appropriate to speak about spiritualities in the plural. Schneiders also reiterates her fundamental understanding of the term in that it "denotes experience of conscious involvement in a project of life-integration, which is pursued via self-transcendence toward ultimate value."[76] Thus, it is not an abstract idea or theory (e.g., a pure mental concept), nor is it an accidental experience (e.g., brought on by a drug overdose), but an effort to integrate all life experience towards one's ultimate concern. This understanding of spirituality can then be particularized (e.g., Christian Spirituality, Lakota spirituality, *Gitchigami* spirituality, Norse *Ásatrú* spirituality, etc.) to specific traditions and contexts.

---

75. For instance, Phyllis Tickle, popular writer on religion in America for general lay readers, employs the terms sacred, religious, and spiritual all interchangeably and synonymously. Though she acknowledges that many understand these in distinction, she credits this to the current state of the society in its striving toward the sacred (Tickle, *Re-discovering the Sacred*).

76. Schneiders, "Religion vs. Spirituality, 167.

Religion, on the other hand, reports Schneiders, "at its most basic [level is] . . . the *fundamental life stance* of the person who believes in transcendent reality."[77] It involves total creaturely dependence on the principle of life and is the "root of any spiritual quest."[78] It can denote a spiritual tradition and/or an institutionalized foundation of a particular spiritual tradition. In popular usage, religion is often set apart as distinct from spirituality precisely due to its institutionalized components. Perhaps this is what is often intended by those who identify as 'spiritual, but not religious.' Schneiders reminds us that religions are set apart from spiritualities in that "they are [institutionally] organized in particular patterns of creed, code, and cult."[79] These patterns, often cultural, are not always present in every particular form of spirituality.

Religions give rise to particular spiritualities because "if a spirituality of a religious tradition is to be made available to others there has to be a way of initiating people into the mystery that has been discovered by or revealed to the founding figures and of sustaining them in living it."[80] In short, a spirituality can rise out of an institutionalized religion, and, in turn, the task of theology can be understood, as it is so often, as the reflection upon religion (and its particular spiritualities); that is, it is the 'second step.' Spirituality is lived religious experience of God and theology reflects on that experience and talks about God.

Himes states it thusly, "if we understand theology as a reflection on the deepest roots of all human experience in order to see how all experience relates to our being believers, then theology and experience become very relevant to one another, indeed . . . Theology is the attempt to give the right name, the deepest and truest name to what is going on."[81] Religion, then "is the name of a way of life and action; theology is a name for reflection on the ground, meaning and goal of that way of life and action."[82] According to Schneiders, religions are related to spiritualities in that they are both born(e) out of intense (perhaps mystical) experience. Religion provides a way to make this experience and worldview available to others.[83] On the

---

77. Ibid., 168 (italics hers).
78. Ibid.
79. Ibid., 169.
80. Ibid., 170–71.
81. Himes, *Doing the Truth in Love*, 87.
82. Ibid., 90.
83. There are, of course, critics of this view that religion or spirituality grow out of experience. For instance, George Lindbeck, in his well-known postliberal cultural-linguistic approach to religion and experience, argues that spiritual experience grows out of, and is informed by, religious language and not the other way around as Schneiders

one hand, religions can promote fundamentalism, extremism and dangerous theocracy, yet on the other hand they can provide a way to collectively and communally access this spirituality. As a result, today we are seeing the proverbial throwing out of the baby with the bath water in a total rejection of religion altogether. "Such global rejection of religion," writes Schneiders, "involves a failure to distinguish between the authentic and life-giving religious tradition and the spirituality to which it gives rise on the one hand, and its institutional form on the other. It is a classic case of curing a headache by decapitation."[84]

Schneiders offers several reasons for why this might be the current trend. She, along with others, points to some reasons for why the emerging culture of postmodernity provides a welcoming and incubating environment for the growth and development of spirituality. In other words, postmodern culture may offer insight as to why there might be a seemingly 'global rejection of religion' and an increasing openness to spirituality. Postmodern sentiment fosters the rejection of foundationalism, meta-narratives, and "claims to normatively or non-negotiable ultimacy by any institution or agency."[85] Sheldrake points out that both the spiritual mystic and the postmodern embrace an apophatic knowing; "all religious language is relative" and "reminds us that religious definitions are to be treated as provisional."[86] This provides a safe space for spirituality to operate. Sheldrake adds, "postmodernism seems to enable religious traditions to be themselves. It frees the notion of 'God' from the constraints of rational philosophy and the need to justify belief in rational terms."[87] With spirituality, postmodernism shares a common foe in its rejection of certain lingering aspects introduced by the so-called Enlightenment. It has assisted spirituality in wrestling itself free from the purely rational constraints that once served as the sole arbiter in the quest for truth. The postmodern is suspicious of the human capacity for reaching essential truths and instead places emphasis on the particularity of one's context and culture. In this regard spirituality too places emphasis on one's particular culture and context when analyzing lived religious experience.

With their master narratives and universal worldviews, some major world religions, certainly Christianity, are often interpreted to be at odds with postmodern inclinations. However, this is not necessarily the case

---

here seems to be claiming (Lindbeck, *The Nature of Doctrine*, chap. 2).

84. Schneiders, "Religion vs. Spirituality," 171.
85. Ibid., 173.
86. Sheldrake, *Spirituality and Theology*, 29.
87. Ibid., 10.

for spiritualities. There are several postmodern tenets which bode well for spirituality which may simultaneously explain the recent and growing interest in spirituality and the waning interest in institutionalized religions. As Schneiders observes,

> The Christian religion is intrinsically difficult to reconcile with a postmodern sensibility. By contrast, a non-religious spirituality is often very compatible with that sensibility precisely because it is usually a privatized, idiosyncratic, personally satisfying stance and practice which makes no doctrinal claims, imposes no moral authority outside one's own conscious, creates no necessary personal relationships or social responsibilities, and can be changed or abandoned whenever it seems not to work for the practitioner.[88]

What Schneiders describes is a popular understanding of a privatized spiritual understanding of religion. This popular definition of spirituality makes it unmistakably "more compatible with a postmodernism sensibility" than traditional religion. Schneiders argues that this understanding of spirituality or religion, as a purely private and personal endeavor devoid of any social or historical commitments, though a legitimate form of spirituality, is "not an optimal formula for the spiritual life of individuals." Rather, she argues that the optimal context for spirituality is within religion itself. First, a privatized spirituality that lacks roots and self-criticism is prone to extremism and fanaticism. Second, spirituality must have a theological structure for critical support. Third, a purely private religion or spirituality faces the possible danger of eventually fading away with the passing of the person. In short, she argues that "the quest for God is too complex and too important to be reduced to a private enterprise."[89] For Schneiders, a personal spirituality may still be considered a spirituality, though removed from its optimal social context. Despite her rather rigorous criteria for establishing an optimal set of conditions for spirituality, I am inclined to view spiritualities with a broader lens by accepting those that may satisfy some of her criteria but not all (e.g., doctrinal claims, in certain contexts may in serve as an obstacle to spiritual experience and its absence may in fact promote or facilitate a robust spirituality).

Certainly volumes could be filled on the relationship between religion and postmodernism. This book is not the place to attempt such a feat, but rather the concern here is to understand how religion and spirituality function in relation to one another in the current postmodern context. If

---

88. Schneiders, "Religion vs. Spirituality," 173.
89. Ibid., 176–77.

anything, Schneiders' 2003 article points to some of the main reasons why, in a postmodern context, interest in religion (institutionalized) is waning and interest in spirituality is growing. This might also help to explain why, in part, "spirituality as a research discipline is gradually taking its place in the academy as a legitimate field of study." The danger, of course, is that religion becomes completely phased out while spirituality continues to grow in popularity completely disconnected from religion. The challenge is to seek ways to retain their connection and interdependence. Though this is not the direct concern of this book, it is certainly related. A more direct concern, rather, is to retain the interdependence between theology and spirituality, but closely related is maintaining a link to religion.

To restate, theology is a 'second step' to both religion and spirituality since it serves as a critical, and sometimes (perhaps often) systematic, reflection on either that particular spirituality or religion (sometimes institutionalized). J. Matthew Ashley writes, "most theologians are now comfortable with the recognition that theology is a 'second step.'"[90] If this is the case, then the overall thrust of this book, in offering an argument for a (pan) sacramental mediation between spirituality and theology, might best be understood as putting forth a means to get to this second step.

The current state of affairs might be described as follows: despite their common source and similar goal, the study of spirituality and theology can potentially become completely disengaged from one another and end up having little (perhaps nothing) to do with one another. This is not only evident in the historical outline laid out above, but is made clear in contemporary practice. Theology, especially rigorously philosophical and systematic theology, *can* devolve into an isolated mental task dwelling solely in the world of theory, concept, and abstraction. It *can* become a strict mental gymnastics (though entertaining at times) devoid of practical application and coherence with lived experience. For example, from the early Christology of the New Testament communities, to the Trinitarian theology of the Patristic theologians and early councils, to the philosophical theology of Aquinas, to Calvin's emphasis on God's sovereignty, to the transcendentalism of Rahner, profound ideas about the nature of God are proffered. Justin Martyr explains that Jesus is the eternal *logos*, Aquinas teaches that God is *ipsum esse subsistens*, and Augustine, following the Patristic theologians, teaches God as one and three in perfect Trinitarian relationship. These traditional Christian theological concepts fit nicely and neatly together in a system of thought, but can sometimes be void of direct relation to practical human experience. Doctrinal concepts that grew from the liturgical life and

---

90. Ashley, "The Turn to Spirituality?" 15.

practices of the church can become empty and outdated in new contexts. These concepts are in danger of becoming empty, but this is not to say that they are insignificant and unhelpful. Nor is this to say that they cannot be (and/or have not been) correlated with religious experience. Rather, the idea here is that the optimal context for theology entails spiritual consultation; that is, it needs the contextual element of lived experience to nourish, concretize, and nuance its significance. Without being in conversation with spirituality, theology flirts with practical meaninglessness. On the other hand, spirituality *can* easily become detached from any theological reflection and devolve into a *possibly* meaningless isolated quasi-religious incoherent conglomerate.

In related fashion, F. LeRon Shults recognizes a few of the modern trends which have led to this potential breach between theology and spirituality. Most specifically, he argues that "shifts in the meaning and use of three concepts—matter, person, and force—have played a particularly influential role"[91] in the relationship between the theological doctrine of the Holy Spirit and spirituality. He argues that "many systematic theological treatments of the doctrine of the Holy Spirit have been relatively detached from the practical concerns of spiritual pilgrims and directors. The healing of this dichotomy has been facilitated by a broader and growing interest in integrating spirituality and theology in general."[92] This book represents one major attempt to heal this dichotomy.

Why do the two fields need one another as dialogue partners? For one, both are interested in the manifestation of the sacred. Theology tends to how we ought to talk about these manifestations and how they might universally cohere with one another within a tradition and with other traditions, while the study of spirituality tends to the particularity of each manifestation itself in seeking to express the human response to the divine. Both fields share a common object and source: understanding the divine, yet diverge in their primary concerns. The challenge is to keep the two in dialogue. Certainly there might be many ways to retain the tension between the two. In this book I propose *one* solution to do so: *a philosophy of pansacramental and panentheistic mediation.*

---

91. Shults, "Spirit and Spirituality," abstract.
92. Ibid., 272.

3

Foundations of Sacramentality

BUILDING ON THE OVERVIEW laid out in the opening chapters, this chapter provides a working history of sacramental theology in the West and a necessary background of the concept of sacramentality as such, its usage, and major issues confronting sacramental theology from its Hebrew roots through the modern era. First, I examine the Hebrew root -*zkr* ('to make memorial') in its serving as the Hebraic foundation of Christian sacramental and symbolic theology. Second, I discuss sacramentality in the New Testament as a basis for drawing out the uniqueness of sacramentality in the Christian tradition. Third, I offer a brief history of *sacramentum* from Augustine (354 c.e.) to Aquinas (1274 c.e.). In chapter 4 I discuss the Protestant reluctance to accept any highly organized conception of sacramental theology, and in chapter 5 I provide a thorough examination of one of the most influential proposals of sacramental theology in the modern era, that of Karl Rahner.

Making Memorial as Making Present

An examination of the Hebrew Bible's emphasis on ritual, history, and memory serves as a good commencement point in the examination of sacramentality, since sacramental events and experience draw and build on the Hebraic conception of ritualistic memorial making. Most specifically, the concern here is to draw out the intention behind the Deuteronomist's use of the Hebrew root *zkr*,[1] which means 'to remember' or 'to make memorial,'

---

1. *Zikkaraon* or *azkarah* translates most often (in the Septuagint) to the Greek *mnemosunon* or *anamnesis*. However, according to Xavier Léon-Dufour, these Greek terms

and refers to what occurs in a ritual commemoration of a past event (e.g., *Pesach*).

Hebrew Bible scholar Brevard Childs' approach assists in situating the term within its cultic and historical context. The goal here is to discern what is meant by memorial (*-zkr*) by the Deuteronomist, the supposed post-exilic author(s) and redactor(s) from roughly 580 b.c.e. Childs, like most recent Hebrew Bible critics, argues that what is meant by the Deuteronomist goes significantly beyond any simple and intentional inner reflection on the past, such as a psychological reflection on the past as one does when she reviews a photo album. Rather, 'to make memorial' involves an encounter with past historical events that are dynamic in character and can be reinterpreted by each successive generation in light of their own experience. Since the God of the Hebrew Bible is a dynamic God (i.e., YHWH acts in history through redemptive reality and natural miracles), past events can be actualized and revisited in the present.

Memorial did not always have this connotation. Prior to the Babylonian Exile, to make memorial functioned in its cultic form without a strong element of actualization. Thus there are two meanings, the pre-exilic cultic meaning and the post-exilic meaning. Childs helpfully frames it by distinguishing between the cultic understanding of God's memory (as in 'God remembers') and Israel's memory (as in 'Israel remembers').[2]

The cultic understanding of memorial (*-zkr*) prior to the exile served as a means to continually remind God of Israel's presence in order that God remember the commitment made to them. In this sense, Israel's 'making memorial' through cultic ritual was intended to evoke God's attention. The post-exilic understanding of the verb to make memorial (*-zkr*) functions as a calling to the mind the past in order to evoke action. The theological emphasis is added after the exile in that "to remember was to actualize the past, to bridge the gap of time and to form a solidarity with the [cultic] fathers."[3]

Before examining the theologically strengthened version of the term, the central question is raised: why the change of meaning in the first place? More specifically, how did the term come to entail the element of actualization? Childs argues for the possibility that the tradition entered a period of

---

are not to be equated to the Hebrew root *zkr*, since they do not contain the element of an "act of recalling to memory." He writes, "neither *mneia* ('mention,' 'anniversary'), nor *mnema* or *mnemeion* ('emblem,' 'commemorative monument,' 'tomb'), nor *mneme* ('the faculty of memory,' 'a psychological type of remembrance')" have this element (Léon-Dufour, *Le Partage Du Pain Eucharistique Selon Le Nouveau Testament*, 131).

2. Childs, *Memory and Tradition in Israel*, 74.

3. Ibid.

crisis out of which emerged a new theological meaning for how Israel makes memorial (–zkr) through actualizing the past.

The crisis here, Childs maintains, stems from being redeemed from the exile in Babylon which separated Israel from the Sinai Covenant and Temple worship. The dilemma arose concerning how to remain faithful to the covenant of old as later generations were becoming centuries removed from the redemptive events in their past. The Deuteronomist, writing in the post-exilic period, had the challenge of discerning how to reinstate the old tradition in a new and contemporary way. Second Temple Judaism was threatened by the possibility of severing the tradition from its old cultic forms. How does the Deuteronomist retain a place for the redemptive events of the past and situate them in Second Temple Judaism in a participatory way? Childs suggests the answer lies in strengthening the theological significance of 'making memorial,' and thus providing a way for contemporary Israel to actualize the past and participate in its older cultic forms. The new post-exilic age accommodated the liturgical shift "from concern with ritual minutiae to centre in joyous expression of thankfulness for Yahweh's benefits which are attributed solely to his election of love,"[4] thus secularizing sacred traditions of the past. In order to retain the sacred nature of past traditions, memory takes on a new element of actualization in that the past is actualized (in some sacramental manner) through making memorial. This element of actualizing the past remains crucial for the overall thrust of sacramentality.

The new meaning of *zkr* explains what occurs when Israel actualizes (in 'making memorial') its past redemptive events (e.g., the Exodus, wandering in the wilderness, the Conquest of the Promised Land) through making memorial. For Israel, "to remember was to call to mind a past event or situation, with the purpose of evoking some action."[5] Here the term 'actualization' can be ambiguous thus taking on several meanings. Childs helps to sort out the proper Hebrew understanding from amongst two inadequate definitions. These are the mythical theory and the historical theory, which are at odds with one another. The proper Hebrew conception of actualization splits the difference between these theories in that it contains features common to both yet has its own unique qualities as well. This more appropriate understanding is best explained by prefacing it with a brief description of the other two theories.

---

4. Ibid., 78.
5. Ibid., 74.

The mythical theory[6] suggests that the concept did not originate with Israel, but was borrowed from "the mythopoeic thought of the Ancient Near East."[7] This theory argues that the cult is dependent on the concept of myth in that it dramatically re-enacts the redemptive events, which function as myths, in order to access, or actualize, the mythical reality (that seems to lie in the past). The cult requires myth to remember and recall its past.

Myth here, as employed in the field of cultural anthropology, is timeless in its character, meaning that it is not assigned to a chronologically fixed point in time. Myths are stories that communities recount about themselves and where they came from in order to convey what they consider to be the deepest and most profound truths about their culture. They may be wrapped in stories that are not literally true, but their literal falsity is overshadowed by the deeper metaphysical truths. For example, recall the Lakota myth of *Matȟó Thípila*[8] (Devil's Tower National Monument in Crook County, Wyoming). Though there are various versions of the story (e.g., Lakota, Cheyenne, etc.), they all tell the tale of either a group of boys or girls being chased by a bear (notice, the literal truth of whether it was boys or girls is irrelevant). Showing compassion on the children, *Wakan Tanka* ("Great Spirit") rescued them by raising them up on a pillar of granite to a place of high safety where the bear could not harm them. Attempting to climb the tower, the bear failed and slid down the granite column in cartoonish fashion scraping its claws down the side leaving symmetrical corduroy ridges around the tower. The literal truth here takes a back seat to the more important truth that *Wakan Tanka* is to be understood as a protector and provider. The myth provides a colorful vehicle to transport this message.

---

6. Here represented by Mowinkel, *Psalmenstudien*, II.
7. Childs, *Memory and Tradition in Israel*, 81.
8. "Bear Lodge" (Lakota).

Fig. 3.1: *Mathó Thípila* (**Devil's Tower**), **Wyoming**

The story of *Mathó Thípila* might best be understood as a hybrid of myth and legend, since a myth is a sacred story about origins without reference to historical individuals or geographical places. In other words, myths are set in non-geographical locations (e.g., Garden of Eden), beyond chronological time (e.g., in the very beginning), and may include characters that go beyond anything we know (e.g., talking serpents or giant granite climbing bears). However, a legend is set in history, and in geographical locations (e.g., Wyoming or Egypt). Legends contain characters that are real historical individuals (e.g., Moses) and convey what happened when and where, but more importantly, like myths, they provide deep profound truths and wisdom to the people (e.g., *Wakan Tanka* is a protector, YHWH is a redeemer, etc.). The mythical conception of actualization can function in both myth and legend. However, Childs concludes that this understanding of actualization is ultimately incompatible with that of Israel since it disregards Israel's view of reality, which is fundamentally historical in character. For Israel, a historical event remains forever fixed in time and is unrepeatable.

The historical-analytic understanding of actualization also falls short in its reactive stance to the mythical theory. Through its employment of historical analysis, it theorizes 'actualization' as a transportation of the liturgical participant (he or she 'making memorial') back in time to the original historical redemptive event, thus providing experiential identification with the original historical participants. Where the mythical conception denied the original events of historical legitimacy, this historical-analytical theory insists that original historical events retain their once-and-for-all chronological character and remain fixed in time.

Neither theory can be fully reconciled with *zkr* as *actualization* in the Biblical tradition. On the one hand, the historical-analytic theory is compatible in its insistence that redemptive events are historical, thus retaining their once-and-for-all character and locked in time. However, it fails to recognize the dynamic and transcendent character of the original historical event. While the mythical theory fails to recognize the historical fixedness of the original event, the historical-analytical theory is denies the dynamic character of the original event in historically fixing it *too* much. In other words, the historical-analytical theory denies the possibility of 'reverberation' of the original event; that is, the original redemptive event cannot reverberate beyond its original entry into chronological time. An authentic understanding of *actualization* must accommodate this possibility for reverberation. Childs affirms this when he writes, "biblical events can never become static, lifeless beads which can be strung on a chronological chain."[9] Though a Biblical understanding of actualization may certainly retain elements from each theory, it must also go beyond them.

A proper conception of actualization in the Hebrew Bible must allow the important biblical events in the redemptive history of Israel to have a life of their own. There is no return to the past for the participants, but rather past events reverberate through time into the present. Childs' approach to *actualization* synthesizes the two inadequate theories, the mythical and the historical-analytic. Drawing historicity from one and participation from the other, Childs defines actualization in a way that remains faithful to the fundamental characteristics of Israel and their metaphysical worldview. Childs' conception of actualization squares well with the post-exilic worldview of Israel since, for Israel, events in history are understood to retain their once-and-for-all character and are thus unable to be repeated in the same fashion at a different time. These events remain significant since they are understood as determinative. They determine redemptive history in that they alter history and are thus significant. They operate as only a beginning and are thus not static like the historical-analytic theory maintains, rather they are dynamic in the sense that each generation can experience these

---

9. Childs, *Memory and Tradition in Israel*, 83.

determinative events in a new way. Since redemptive history never ceases and continues into the future, an immediate encounter (participation) takes place for each successive generation.

Successive generations participate by entering into redemptive time (made possible by the timeless reverberation of the redemptive events). For instance, the commemoration of the Hebrew *Pesach* enters into the redemptive reality made possible through the reverberation of the original Passover event in Egypt. To be sure, each initial redemptive event remains fixed in chronological time, but the dynamic quality of the event acts as a vehicle by which redemptive reality continues ('reverberates') throughout the history of Israel. A quality of time, a certain condition of reality (redemptive reality), entered chronological time at the Exodus and the redemptive event itself reverberates in time and transforms all reality beyond it into redemptive reality thus challenging each generation to respond. It is "not a mere subjective reflection, but in the biblical category, a real event occurred as the moment of redemptive time from the past initiated the genuine encounter in the present."[10] The seeds of sacramental thought begin to emerge here.[11]

Childs suggests that the proper definition of actualization, as used by the Deuteronomist, is "the process by which a past event is contemporized for a generation removed in time and space from the original event."[12] When Israel responds to her redemptive reality through memory, she enters into redemptive history which makes the present an Exodus experience. As postmodern sacramental theologian Louis-Marie Chauvet proclaims, "In its Passover memorial, Israel *receives its past as present*, and this gift guarantees a *promise* of a future."[13] Israel enters the same redemptive reality while remaining in the present chronological point in time because that chronological barrier is overcome by the redemptive reality of the original redemptive determinative events. "The past of its origins is snatched out of its 'pastness' to become the living genesis of today."[14]

In short, "to make memorial" (*zkr*), as employed by the Deuteronomist, is an immediate encounter with the original redemptive event itself. Redemptive events in the Biblical tradition (and beyond) are understood to be dynamic and living and are thus unable to be lost to the past. Each generation experiences anew the same determinative events of the past by

---

10. Ibid., 84.

11. For an instance of this in my own personal experience, see Gustafson, "Encountering the Painful Past in the Present."

12. Childs, *Memory and Tradition in Israel*, 85.

13. Chauvet, *Symbol and Sacrament*, 234.

14. Ibid., 233.

reinterpreting them in light of their own experience in responding to the God who meets them in history. Due to the original event's redemptive reality and dynamic character, each new encounter with it is understood to be just as valid as the original.

New Testament Sacramentality

The New Testament, and the Christian tradition, built on the Deuteronomist's understanding of memorial. Prior to exploring its influence on the meaning of sacrament and symbol in the New Testament, I first offer here a brief preliminary explanation of the term sacrament (although the concept of sacramentality as such will be examined at length in chapters five and eleven), stemming from its Greco-Roman etymological origins (*sacramentum* and *mysterion*).

Sacramentum and Mysterion

The Latin term *sacramentum* was first used in the pre-Christian era as a term for a deposit (understood as a monetary pledge) made in a temple under legal contract. Later it gained its more popular usage to connote the swearing of an oath, in a legal court or a military outfit, to the supreme commander or to the gods of Rome. Tertullian was the first to employ the term within a specific Christian context to refer to an oath sworn under divine covenant such as marriage, baptism, and the Eucharist. By using *sacramentum*, Tertullian used an existing term to explain how a Christian ritual, such as baptism, is to be understood as sacred. As Christianity came to dominate the Greco-Roman landscape and as the native polytheism waned, the original pre-Christian understanding of *sacramentum* was replaced by its Christian usage as a referent to any sacred symbol or ceremony.[15]

In the Greek New Testament, the word Paul uses to refer to the Lord's Supper and baptism is *mysterion* which was a sacred ritual in which a hidden meaning is revealed through symbolic presentation.[16] In the colloquial Greek of that period, it referred to something that was hidden, concealed, or secret. *Mysterion* was a common aspect of all the 'mystery cults' of the time, and in their context it referred to a moment in which a person, in a flash of insight, recognizes the truth of something. It is a moment in which reality is revealed in some manner, a flash of ultimate reality. These mys-

---

15. Martos, *Doors to the Sacred*, 4.
16. Ibid., 22.

tery cults sought to find the deepest meaning of reality and life amidst the superficiality they perceived in Greco-Roman religion and its symbolically divine emperor. Their *mysteria* sought to get beyond (or behind), through rites, this superficiality and penetrate to the depths of existence and its meaning.

Sacramentality and sacraments predate the Christian tradition. Joseph Matos reminds us, "There were sacraments in the Greek and Roman religious world of early Christianity. There were the formal sacraments of the official state religion: oaths and offerings, oracles and auguries, public festivals and family devotions. There were also the sacraments of the mystery religions: symbolic rituals that dramatized deeper religious meanings for those who sought them."[17] By highlighting different aspects, both the Greek *mysterion* and Latin *sacramentum* contribute to the meaning of the Christian understanding of sacrament. *Mysterion* highlights the individual aspect of a sacrament (such as a momentary flash of personal insight into ultimate reality) and *sacramentum* highlights the communal aspect (such as an oath made between persons).

The Last Supper

Recall the previous section on the post-Exilic Hebraic understanding of 'memorial' (*zkr*) as a reverberation of a past event into the present. Recall that it connotes a bringing forth of the past into the present as something real and action provoking. It is a making present and not just a looking back on past events with warm recollection.[18] The principal memorial feast from the New Testament is the Last Supper. The earliest written record of its institution comes from Paul's first letter to the community in Corinth[19] around 57 c.e. It describes the original event of Jesus breaking bread, pouring wine, giving thanks, and then providing instruction to do likewise in his *remembrance*. The occasion for the letter, and the narrative of the Last Supper, is to remind the faithful in Corinth of the origin and purpose of the feast, since apparently some had lost sight of this. The point to notice here is that the feast is to be done in memorial of the original redemptive event, which is the original last supper at which Jesus actually did and said these things (according to the synoptic Gospels). There is a combination of both word and ritual present here, through which the memorial is enacted. The redemptive event founded by Jesus (his death as a salvific event) is understood to be

17. Ibid., 23.
18. Vorgrimler, *Sacramental Theology*, 47.
19. 1 Corinthians 11:23–25.

made present through sacramental reverberation. A similar process is present in the New Testament accounts of baptism as well (Rom. 6:3–4).

In both sacramental events, a gift of the past is given to those celebrating it in the present. It is the gift of Jesus' self, death, and redemptive reality. In the act of Jesus' self-giving, he is understood to become a sacramental mediator and reverberate into the future events. Thus when a sacramental feast takes place, Jesus is recognized as being present in time; that is, he is made present as part of the reverberating redemptive reality that he brought about in the original chronological event of absolute self-giving. Christian sacramental theology is to keep in mind the Jewish roots from which it grew, since "Jewish thinking shaped the origins of the Church's sacramental life; it interprets the sacraments as present saving events, through the making-present of Jesus Christ in the Holy Spirit."[20]

How this actual presence of Jesus, or any original redemptive event from the past brought to the present for that matter, is understood to take place and actually manifests is not always clear. On the one hand, most agree that "the meal, the bread, and the cup were undoubtedly understood as sacramental in the sense that by sharing them in memory and imitation of Christ the early Christians experienced a presence of their own risen Lord which was different from their ordinary awareness of him."[21] However, on the other hand, how this presence actually takes place becomes a well debated issue in the centuries to come. Further, it is reasonable to inquire whether the presence is a pervasive corporate (collective) one, meaning Jesus' presence is in the group's making memorial (eating, drinking, praying), or rather the presence is more localized in the bread and wine itself. This ambiguity is further highlighted when the gospel accounts are compared.

The author of the Gospel of Luke, like Paul, is unclear about what Jesus is referring to when he says "This cup is the new covenant in my blood."[22] Is Jesus referring to the cup, to the wine, or to something else? It is not clear. It is not as clear as it is with the other synoptic writers (Matthew and Mark), who offer a more direct and ostensive explanation. Jesus says, "This *is* my body . . . [and] . . . this *is* my blood."[23] The crucial point, of course, becomes the same one President Bill Clinton asked in 1998, "it depends on what the meaning of the word 'is' is."[24] A more preliminary question

---

20. Vorgrimler, *Sacramental Theology*, 48.
21. Martos, *Doors to the Sacred*, 215.
22. Luke 22:20.
23. Mark 14:22.
24. U.S. President Bill Clinton, Grand Jury Testimony on the Monica Lewinsky Case, 1998.

that might be asked, as pointed out by several Protestants, is whether the word 'is' was even employed in the original saying of Jesus. The text is written in Greek but Jesus spoke a dialect of Aramaic, which does not have the Indo-European linguistic device of copulas linking subjects and predicates. This renders the phrase, "This *is* my body . . . [and] . . . this *is* my blood" to "This my body . . . this my blood," effectively removing the 'is.' The Greek language adds this in translation and thus, so goes the argument, one should not make the assumption that Jesus strictly identified the bread and wine with his body and blood.[25]

Joseph Martos offers support for this Protestant inclination for a couple of reasons. First, it would be odd for Jesus to refer to the wine as his blood since to do so was both forbidden by, and repulsive for, the religion and culture. Second, it was common for the Jewish tradition to interpret the ritual of eating ceremonial food and drink in a symbolic manner, such as the Passover meal. He argues that reason dictates that Jesus would have intended this over the more ill-fitting conclusion of Jesus intending identification of bread with body and wine with blood.[26]

The gospel of John differs from the synoptic in its inclination to combat the Gnostic tendency to deny anything material, which most certainly includes the identification of Jesus with anything corporal such as bread and wine. Thus, the emphasis on Jesus' humanity is more pronounced in the fourth gospel (despite it having the highest Christology), and with it the early Christian communities using this text more strongly identified Jesus with the actual bread and wine. This is curious given that the Jesus of the fourth Gospel makes no mention of the bread and wine at the last supper. There is however a significant section on 'the bread of life' (in reference to the manna from heaven provided by YHWH during the period of wandering in the wilderness) in which Jesus claims to be the "bread of life."[27] Many scholars agree that the author of John has intentionally combined the so-called 'signs source' with a discourse source (which includes "I am" sayings), thus sign sayings (e.g., feeding the five thousand with bread and bread from heaven) are often followed by an "I am" saying (e.g., "I am the bread of life"). This combination of word and deed are understood to bring about the sacramental effect of representing God to the people. However, unlike the synoptic Gospels, the gospel of John does not employ the Greek word for miracle, but rather refers to these events as signs (*mysteria*) since their

---

25. Martos, *Doors to the Sacred*, 216.
26. Ibid.
27. John 6:35.

function is to show the people who Jesus is, unlike a miracle which is more demonstrative of one's power.

Catholic and Protestant scholars are often divided on the interpretation here. The former emphasize the anti-Gnostic tendency of the text (thus entailing identifying Jesus more closely with the very bread as such), while the latter urges the reader to interpret the claim 'I am the bread of life' more metaphorically similar to the claim 'I am the light of the world.' The texts probably reflect the sentiment of their authors and the communities using the text, and is not to be taken as a direct transcription of Jesus' own words. Martos points to John 6:55–56, which is perhaps the clearest in the gospel that reflects the authors' (of the gospel of John) take on this: "my flesh is true food, and my blood is true drink. Whoever eats my flesh and drinks my blood remains in me and I in him."[28]

By the end of the first century and into the early second century, early Christian communities were drawing connections between the Last Supper event as a significant mark (a reverberation) in redemptive history. Its significance demanded commemoration (-*zkr*) and to be made present through ritual, regardless of whether the presence of Jesus comes through the elements of the bread and wine or a more pervasive communal mechanism of collective awareness. Even later developments in the interpretation of the Last supper (e.g., emphasize on sacrifice) do not negate the task to do it "in memory."

Sacramentum from Augustine to Aquinas

Moving from memory to *sacramentum*, this section traces the development of the latter as conceived by the most significant post-canonical thinkers in Western sacramental theology through to the time Thomas Aquinas. In particular, these thinkers are Augustine, Isidore of Seville, Hugh of St. Victor, Peter the Lombard, and Thomas Aquinas.

Augustine of Hippo (354–430)

Augustine defined a sacrament, at its most fundamental level, as a sign of a sacred thing or reality. Taken in its broadest sense, anything can be understood as sacramental on the basis that all creation is from God and thus can function as a sign of God.

---

28. John 6:55–56; ibid., 216–17.

In his *De Doctrina Christiana*, Augustine discusses "signs" and their importance. He begins by defining a sign as, "a thing which of itself makes some other thing come to mind, besides the impression that it presents to the senses."[29] Some Signs are natural, such as smoke which signifies fire, while others are signs people use to communicate with one another and concern the senses by making use of the eyes, ears, and other senses (e.g., nodding of the head). Words occupy the dominant role among humans when it comes to using signs, for language is used to communicate ideas (conceived in the mind) to others. Words, as signs, reveal the hidden ideas of our mind and present them to others. A significant portion of Book II in *De Doctrine Christiana* centers on the introduction of signs, especially as they pertain to language and use in scripture.

Metaphorical signs have a figurative significance and therefore contain a hidden meaning to be plumbed. Augustine warns that "ignorance of the things make figurative expressions [in scripture or elsewhere] unclear when we are ignorant of the qualities of animals or stones or plants or other things mentioned in scripture for the sake of some analogy."[30] Imagine here one reading scripture without sufficient knowledge of these figurative expressions. For example, without knowing about such expressions (e.g., snake, olive branch, hyssop, etc.) the analogies, and the meanings behind them, may be lost. The same can be said of biblical numbers such as forty, ten, three, four, five, seven, etc.

Augustine mentions signs that might be used by "pagan superstition," but should not be discounted on this fact alone. For example, pagan traditions utilize music does not render music as such 'superstitious' or 'pagan.' The same is true for most arts such as theater. Similarly it is with the alphabet. Just because it is said that the God Mercury is its patron, does not mean we should avoid using it. According to Augustine, all truth is God's truth and belongs to God alone regardless of where it is found, be it in the Christian tradition or pagan literature. There are signs that are divinely instituted and there are signs instituted by humans. Of those instituted by humans, some are superstitious while others are not. If it is instituted by humans and promotes the worshipping of idols or the created order as such, then it is 'superstitious.' It is superstitious if it involves making a 'contract' with God, or what might be referred to as 'magic' in the sense of being an attempt to manipulate nature through human activity alone (e.g., understanding a 'rain dance' as literally and mechanistically causal regardless of the subjective dispositions of the human agents). Further, Augustine insists that it is

---

29. Augustine, *On Christian Teaching*, Book II, 1.
30. Ibid., Book II, 59.

superstitious of astrologers to presume to predict the character and destiny of a human agent based solely on his or her calendar birth date. He recommends that all of these superstitious human institutions ought to be avoided by the Christian believer. He continues that there are also those signs which are instituted by God and discovered by human investigation. Some of these concern the mind while others concern the physical senses. He writes, "the study of definition, division, and classification, is not in itself false; and it was not instituted by man, but discovered as part of the way things are."[31]

In Book III of *De Doctrine Christiana*, Augustine delves deeper into the uniqueness of the Jewish people and their understanding of divine signs. He contends that the slavery Israel was subjected to placed them in the unique position to recognize (discover) the truth of monotheism.[32] Their slavery, writes Augustine, ingrained in them the belief of a single God for all; a God whom they are unable to see. Since their slavery cut them off from the material-corporeal world more dramatically than others (e.g., their Egyptian masters), then they were in a position to look for hope from outside nature (e.g., pantheistic cosmological theism) and idols (e.g., statues, structures, etc.). In the process, they looked beyond nature to the unseen world for their God, and this God had to be greater than all local corporeal matter. This is a concept of God in which God trumps all natural Gods and is therefore a single God. The signs imposed on them during their time of enslavement, writes Augustine, "drew the thoughts of those who observed them to the worship of the one God who created heaven and earth."[33]

These signs could be interpreted, by Israel, in a spiritual manner as revealing something hidden and beyond the signs themselves. Furthermore, contends Augustine, since these Israelite interpreters were receptive to the Holy Spirit, they sold their possessions (since material things were of no spiritual value in themselves) and formed a new cult. Augustine recognizes that this was unlike the Gentile churches that created statues as Gods to worship, since they did not have the spiritual toolset to interpret signs as pointing beyond themselves to that which is both beyond nature and unseen. For the Gentiles, these signs were interpreted in so far as they pointed to veneration of the created order themselves. For example, the God Neptune represents all aquatic features of the cosmos (oceans, seas, rivers, lakes, tributaries, etc.) and suggests worship of the thing itself. The difference here is that for Augustine (and the Israelites), a sign is not to be identified with the

---

31. Ibid., Book II, 129

32. However this is disputed by many Hebrew Bible and Rabbinical scholars who recognize the development of monotheism as coming much later, perhaps as late as Amos.

33. Augustine, *On Christian Teaching*, Book III, 23–24.

thing (it signifies) itself, whereas for the gentiles the sign points to the thing itself and thus leads to idolatry. In the history of the Christian tradition, especially in the Protestant tradition, this concern for idolatry is continually raised as it pertains to the sacraments. Augustine's main concern here is to warn the reader of the danger of falling into pantheism and mistaking the sign of God for God's very self, which is also a form of idolatry. Instead, the sign (such as the cosmos) should lead one to love and worship the creator of the cosmos, not the cosmos itself. He writes, "If you relate such signs to the actual things signified by them, and commit your soul to worshipping them, you will still not be free from the oppression and the delusion of this servile and carnal condition."[34]

Augustine emphasizes the importance of the agent's understanding of a sign, for one who venerates a meaningful sign without understanding its meaning becomes enslaved to that sign. However, she who venerates a meaningful divinely instituted sign and understands its significance is not enslaved. She does not worship that thing as such, but rather worships the thing (God) to which all other things are related. Such a person is spiritually free.[35] Augustine uses the example of Christ's body and blood in the celebration of the Eucharist, in which the recipient understands these signs. When this is the case, then he "recognizes with an inner knowledge what they are related to, and consequently venerates them not because of any carnal slavery but because of his spiritual freedom."[36] Likewise, he or she who mistakes the signs for the things themselves falls into idolatry and the signs are rendered useless.

Augustine also raises the distinction between the literal and the figurative (metaphorical). He warns about interpreting something literal that was meant figuratively and vice-versa. He provides guidelines for discerning whether something found in scripture is meant figuratively or literally. In short, his rule is as follows: "anything in the divine discourse that cannot be related either to good morals (love of God and neighbor) or to the true faith (the understanding of God and neighbor) should be taken as figurative."[37] His main goal here is to stress the necessity of a prior knowledge when seeking to uncover the hidden meanings of figurative language (signs).

Important to Augustine's contribution to the history of understanding *sacramentum* is his distinction between the sacrament itself and its effects. This results in making the point that the saintliness (and/or sinfulness) of

---

34. Ibid., Book III, 28.
35. Ibid., Book III, 30.
36. Ibid., Book III, 32.
37. Ibid., Book III, 33–34 (parentheses mine).

the priest who administers the sacrament is of no importance since it is God who causes the sacramental effect, not the minister. This also safeguards against any magical understanding of sacramentality in which causality is understood to take place due to the effort on behalf of the (ad)minister (priest) and/or the recipient. Further still, it solidifies within Catholic sacramental theology an assumed distinction between a sacrament and its efficacy, or fruitfulness. Therein, Augustine leaves open the question of efficacy as dependent on the disposition of the recipient (*ex opere operato* vs. *ex opere operantis*). Finally, Augustine held that with sacraments come grace (sanctification). In other words, sacraments are vehicles through which the purpose of the Incarnation is achieved in persons. We begin with Augustine here since he laid the major foundation from which to approach sacramentality in the West. It is upon this foundation that subsequent thinkers approached the subject.

Isidore of Seville (560–636)

Isidore of Seville contributed the next major development in the history of Western sacramental thought. In his most important and well known work *Etymologies* (*Origines*), he put forth a definition of sacrament that became widely employed throughout the early Middle ages. According to Isidore, "A *sacramentum* is a bond given in support of a promise, and it is called a *sacramentum* (lit. 'holy thing') because to violate a promise is a breach of faith."[38] Here Isidore upholds the traditional Latin understanding of the term as a sacred oath. Later in the document he references it specifically as a military oath.[39] However, he also recognizes the sacredness of the term in his discussion on the sacraments in general. He writes, "These things [baptism, unction, Eucharist] are called sacraments for this reason, that under the covering of corporeal things the divine virtue very secretly brings about the saving power of those same sacraments—whence from their secret (*secretus*) or holy (*sacer*) power they are called sacraments."[40] This last reference to sacraments gets at the Greek *mysterion* dimension. It emphasizes the revealing of hidden depths and meaning of reality. Though the substance of Isidore's writing on *sacramentum* is concise, his contribution and influence over the medieval landscape of sacramental theology is great. It was often the case that anything with the stamp of Isidore's authorial name on it gained immediate doctrinal credibility. This was the case with the references

38. Isidore of Seville, *Etymologies*, V.xxiv.29
39. Ibid., IX.iii.52–53.
40. Ibid., VI.xix.40.

to *sacramentum* that were included in his famous *Etymologies*, which came to be *the* textbook of the early Middle Ages for most educational institutions. In fact, it was often used in lieu of the many primary texts to which it referred. Simply by this fact alone, the references of *sacramentum* and the explanations Isidore applied to it helped to solidify and promulgate its definitions into the middle Ages. Thus any overview of medieval sacramental theology remains incomplete without reference to Isidore.

Hugh of St. Victor (1096–1141)

Hugh of St. Victor, theologian, philosopher, and mystic, produced a masterful and influential text on sacramental theology; this is his *De sacramentis christianae fidei* (On the Sacraments of the Christian Faith). Not only is it considered one of the great works of the middle ages, but is a chief work in any short list on sacramental theology. In Book I he puts forth what many consider to be the first formal definition of sacrament in the history of theology. Expanding on Augustine's simple definition ("a sign of a sacred thing"), Hugh writes, "a sacrament is a corporeal or material element set before the sense without, representing by similitude and signifying by institution and containing by sanctification some invisible and spiritual grace."[41] Hugh claims this definition is so fitting and perfect that it is true in all cases for all sacraments. Throughout the document Hugh applies the term *sacramentum* in three particular ways, each of which refers to a specific theological model. These models are a medical model of salvation (*sacramentum* likened to medicine), a military model of defending against the devil (*sacramentum* likened to a weapon), and a signifying model in which visible signs point to invisible realities (*sacramentum* likened to a sign). In all cases *sacramentum* is rendered an instrumental good set in the context of that to which it strives, the intrinsic good of God's self and reality.

One significant contribution Hugh makes to sacramental theology in this document is his distinction between *sacramentum* and *res sacramenti*; that is, the sacrament as such and the reality it contains, or the reality to which it points. This distinguishes clearly between a sacrament's material elements and its hidden reality. For instance, his medical model portrays the condition of the human agent as an unhealthy patient who receives medicine, the *res sacramenti*, from the physician, God, administered by the priest in a vessel, the *sacramentum*. In Hugh's words, "the physician gives, the minister dispenses, the vessel preserves spiritual grace which heals the

---

41. Hugh of St. Victor, *On the Sacraments of the Christian Faith*, Book I, 9, II.

recipient."[42] In other words, the doctor (God) prescribes the medicine (*res sacramenti*, grace) to the patient (human beings) who then receives the medicine in a bottle (*sacramentum*) from the pharmacist (priest). Hugh writes, "the sacraments themselves are the medicine itself, and, when these are applied to us corporeally without through the ministers of sacred dispensation, the wounds of our souls are cured invisibly so that cured and healed we may be able to attain to the promise of perpetual life."[43] Thus, it is the medicine (*res sacramenti*) from God that cures whilst the vessel and priest do not, for they only serve as a means of making present and dispensing the medicine corporeally. Thus it is the sacraments (visible material) that make present the hidden reality of God's grace.

Hugh's work goes a long way in providing clarity to what is often meant by the term sacrament within the context of the Christian tradition. Through the medical model and others, he strengthened the understanding of sacrament as a visible sacred sign that points to an invisible divine reality. Despite these lasting contributions to sacramental theology, his work has its limitations. Hugh emphasizes that a sacrament is a corporeal element used in a sensible manner, which makes present (visible) a spiritual (invisible) grace, instituted by Jesus Christ and is salvific.[44] However, Herbert Vorgrimler calls attention to some of the problems that surface with this understanding of sacrament. For one, even though it ties the sacrament to corporeality and to an institution (by Jesus Christ), it remains unclear about how the grace is contained in the sign. Vorgrimler attributes this primarily to the monastic milieu in which Hugh lived and out of which his work took shape. Hugh was not of the "world at large," thus his definition of sacrament falls short in its address to the world outside the walls of the monastic cloister. Perhaps this was indeed the case, or perhaps Hugh was aware that his theology lacked an explanation of how grace is contained in the sign simply because he did not believe it was important, or perhaps simply because it could not be known or understood.

Within this context of sacraments serving as sacred signifiers, Hugh uses terms *sacramentum* and *mysterium* interchangeably.[45] Further, like Augustine, it is clear that Hugh employed the term sacrament broadly enough to include acts beyond the seven liturgical sacraments such as sacrifices, oblations, tithes, including pre-Christian practices (e.g., Jewish circumcision), and pagan pre-Judaic practices as well, all of which are understood

---

42. Ibid., Book I, 9, IV.
43. Ibid., Book I, 9, V.
44. Vorgrimler, *Sacramental Theology*, 45.
45. Moore, "The Primacy of Faith in Hugh of St. Victor's Sacramental Theology."

as equally complete and efficacious. However, Hugh does recognizes that upon the arrival of Jesus Christ a clear terminus of all the pre-Christian sacraments commences; that is, Christ dons a new sacramental era from his time on.

Peter the Lombard (1095–1160)

Peter [the] Lombard came to Paris in 1136 and studied with Hugh of St. Victor and quickly earned a renowned reputation as a master teacher, scholar, and writer. His magnum opus, *Sententiarum* (*The Sentences*)[46] quickly became the standard text for all introductory theology students, including Thomas Aquinas. In fact, shortly after Lombard's death, regent master at the University of Paris, Alexander of Hales, began to base his lectures on it instead of scripture. The fourth and final book of *The Sentences* deals specifically with sacramental theology. The main breakthrough Lombard made in this area was to introduce the concept of sacramental *causality*. In so doing, some implications followed which involved narrowing the scope of the way sacrament became defined.

Lombard defines sacrament as something which "is a sign of God's grace, and is such an image of invisible grace that it bears its likeness and exists as its cause."[47] This definition deviates little from the previous thinkers; however, there is an added element of causality, which is crucial. This marks the first time in the history of Christian sacramental thought that this concept is put forth. In other words, Lombard is the first to state that the sacrament is a reason for grace; that is, it is the cause (*causa*) of grace.

One implication that stems from the addition of causality is that it narrows the field of what becomes considered sacramental. Second, in order to distinguish sacraments from all other divine signs (that supposedly do not cause grace), Lombard makes the distinction between the sacraments and sacramentals (*sacramentalia*). Sacramentals are signs, but not grace-causing signs. These might include prayers, blessings, ceremonies, holy water, icons, and the like.

The influence of Lombard is significant for a few reasons. One, due to the sheer exposure and popularity of his *Sentences*, his work on sacramental

---

46. *The Sentences* pioneered a new method for doing theology which later served as the blueprint for the famous *Summa Theologica* of Thomas Aquinas. In a certain sense, it opened new frontiers in the doing of theology. Most specifically it amounted to a dialectical method resulting in a collection of sentences (*sententiae*) prompted by questions (*questiones*).

47. Peter Lombard, *Sentences* IV, 1, 2.

theology was immensely authoritative and widespread. Second, he helped to bring focus to the question of what constitutes a sacrament. More to the point, he assisted in getting beyond the vagueness of Augustine's definition which stated that "a sacrament is a sign of a sacred reality."[48] It is Thomas Aquinas, influenced greatly by Lombard, who solidifies sacramental theology in his alleged rigorous philosophical clarity he is known for. Perhaps it was Lombard who planted the seeds that ripened into the theological explosion that is Aquinas' *Summa Theologica*. This is to say that Aquinas owes something, to some degree, to Lombard. Thus, to gloss over Lombard here would be to miss a crucial rung in the historical ladder of sacramental theological development in the West.

Thomas Aquinas (1225–1274)

Thomas Aquinas is, without a doubt, one of the major theological thinkers not only of the middle ages, but of all ages. His impact on theology in general, and certainly sacramental theology, is great. Before sketching his contributions to the history of sacramental theology in the middle ages and its enduring characteristics, it is appropriate grasp an adequate understanding of the Aristotelian onto-metaphysical terms and categories that Aquinas relies on. Failure to adequately understand these can result in a failure to understand his theology.

The Aristotelian categories most important here are substance, accident, matter, and form. According to Aquinas, everything in the world that exists is made up of matter and form; that is, everything that exists contains both of these dimensions. Take a wooden four legged table for example; it is sensible and experiential (empirical) in certain ways: it is seeable, touchable, testable, fragrant, and so on. These sensible experiential ways of knowing the table refer to its matter. It is made up of oak, not maple; it is brown, not black; it has four legs, not three; it is small, not large; it has one book on it, not two; and so on. These sensible aspects refer to the table's material aspects, and thus its matter. The form of the table, on the other hand, refers to the shape. The form is the intelligible concept of a thing. It is a table because it has all the things a table ought to have: legs, a flat top, and functions as a surface upon which items can be placed. The form does not refer to its material aspect, but its shape. In short, the form of a thing distinguishes one thing from another, while the matter of a thing is that by which one is able to determine a thing's form.

---

48. Augustine, *De civitate Dei* 10.5 (CCL 47:277:25–26).

The terms substance and accident are used in reference to the nature and properties of a thing respectively. Substance (*ousia*) refers to the nature of a thing; that is, it is what makes something to be what it is. For example, the substance of a table is *tableness*. This is opposed to accidents which refer to the sensate properties of a thing. The accidents of the table might be brown, four legged, wood, etc. The accidents refer to those aspects which can be sensibly and physically perceived. The accidents are dependent on the substance to exist, whereas the reverse is not the case. Substance is that which exists in itself and does not require another for its existence. For example, the color brown requires something like a table to exist in order for it to be. These Aristotelian categories are the fundamental building blocks of Aquinas' metaphysics without which his sacramental theology is potentially confused.

The sacramental theology of Aquinas upholds the view of sacraments as causes. Though he affirms that sacraments are primarily signs, he insists further that understanding them alone as mere signs is insufficient. Since sacraments are signs, they effect what they signify. In other words, sacraments *cause* what they signify; put differently, they are *causes* because they are signs. Sacraments are causes in the Aristotelian sense. They are instrumental causes[49] used by God as a means to manifest grace in the world. The sacraments are not the first cause of grace, for that title belongs to God alone. Rather sacraments are instrumental in that they function as channels or vehicles through which God acts.

For Aquinas, sacraments are primarily signs though not merely signs alone. The Incarnation is at the center of the Christian theological tradition and theology; it is the definitive vehicle which draws people to God through creation. However, after the ascension of Christ the meaning of the incarnation lives on and continues to be communicated via the church through ritual and practice. The sacraments provide the conduit through which persons can participate in the incarnation. These sacraments, for Aquinas, are signs in a very real way in that they stand for something (they signify God's substance) that cannot be corporeally sensed or empirically verified. Sacraments, then, signify the reality which engraces (sanctifies) and thus signifies the effect produced. This is why, for Aquinas, a sacrament is "a sign of sacred reality inasmuch as it has the property of sanctifying people."[50]

Aquinas deems Christ the first (principle/ source) sacrament from which all other sacraments flow. Jesus Christ, as the man-God, is divine

---

49. A hammer is an instrumental cause in driving a nail into a stud, but the first cause comes from the person swinging the hammer. The job of the hammer is to provide a means for the first cause to achieve its appropriate end.

50. Thomas Aquinas, *Summa Theologica*, III, 60.2.

and human. His earthly life and death were real presentations of God working in and through creation, through which people actually participated in God's life. Thus, after Jesus Christ's ascension in the gospel accounts, the sacraments continue to work by providing a means for persons to actually participate in God's life in a substantial way. As a significant redemptive event in time, the Christ event reverberates throughout time allowing for subsequent generations to participate through 'making memorial' (-zkr). Sacramental memorials cause grace in allowing genuine participation in redemptive events. As Brian Davies puts it, for Aquinas, "Just like the life, death, and resurrection of Christ, the sacraments of the Church are physical signs of genuine causes of grace. They are symbols which make real what they symbolize. Through them we are united to God even in this life. Through them we are made partakers of the divine nature."[51] In short, the sacraments make God present (or re-present) in time and space through corporeal means. To be clear, God is made present substantially in these corporeal things, not accidentally, for the accidents remain.[52]

A book that includes a chapter such as this on the foundations and history of sacramentality in the Western Christian tradition would be incomplete without some commentary on the Protestant response to what was perceived as an overly rigorous and philosophically reliant attempt to understand sacramental functionality. Needless to say, the understanding of sacraments served as one of the central issues in the European Reformations. The next chapter will comment on this prior to the final chapters in part I on the sacramental worldviews of Karl Rahner and Louis-Marie Chauvet.

---

51. Davies, *The Thought of Thomas Aquinas*, 352.

52. This is important to keep in mind, especially in a non-Aristotelian context in which these onto-metaphysical categories remain foreign. Though these terms and categories might remain distant to the 21st century thinker, they were not for the minds of Aquinas and his contemporaries. It was the popular metaphysical language of their time. With this in mind one should not discount the merit of Aquinas' thought based solely on an outdated philosophical vocabulary, but at the very least attempt to recast the thrust of his ideas into current language. Often his entire collection of thought is thrown out solely on the basis of an outdated metaphysical language. Instead, one might reasonably reject these metaphysical categories and demand a reworking of Thomist sacramental language.

4

The "Protestant Principle" and Sacramental Caution

AN OVERVIEW OF THE history of sacramentality in the West would remain incomplete without a brief commentary on the bifurcation between Catholicism and Protestantism concerning the sacraments during the European Reformations of the sixteenth century. In many ways, the Protestant resistance was grounded in a suspicion of a seemingly mechanistic (magical) and superstitious understanding of sacramentality in Catholic theology. Though specific sacraments were brought to the fore in the reformation debates, the underlying metaphysical understanding and language played key roles. This chapter addresses this cautionary Protestant inclination regarding the sacraments through the lens of the two major protestant thinkers, Martin Luther and Paul Tillich. In particular, I address Luther's basic concern about scholastic sacramentality followed by a reflection on Tillich's theology of "the Demonic" as it relates to the Protestant concern for idolatry.

Luther on Sacramentality[1]

The roots of the Protestant inclination towards a sacramental caution can be traced to Luther who, like most thinkers, was deeply influenced by his

---

1. This section draws various content from two papers I presented: Gustafson, "Luther and Loyola in Context"; and Gustafson, "Sacramental Caution and Finding God in All Things."

context. Luther and his theology must be situated in his sixteenth-century Germanic context, which is characterized by a highly intellectual and revolutionary fervor, yet still falling under the auspices of the Holy Roman Empire; that is, many in the land remained loyal to the Pope and the Emperor. It was a society "constantly searching beyond the finite [yielding] an insatiable urge to arrive at the ultimate in all things,"[2] writes Friedrich Richter. The piety of Luther's late medieval Germanic era entailed a growing concern about salvation. Amidst famine, floods, fires, plagues, and harsh winters, the reality of death was an imminent concern for the average citizen. It is from within this context that the concern for salvation arose. To the common query, "How do I know that I am saved?" the nominalist scholastic answer remained *facere quod in se est*: "do what lies within you; do your best." Failing to provide security, this response only led to the next question, "how do I know I've done my best?"

Luther entered the 'Black Cloister of the Observant Augustinians,' a monastic cloister known for their rigorous pursuit of spiritual discipline. Determined to 'do his best,' Luther threw himself into a life of strict discipline in an effort to achieve salvation. He was a pious monk who strictly adhered to his monastic practices. He struggled, and found little success in his attempt, to free himself from the bondage of sin. His pursuit for soulful peace through monastic rigor and penance only resulted in further frustration (scruples). Thus what was supposed to provide security only led to more agony, anxiety and insecurity. With each attempt to destroy his concupiscence, new temptations and struggles arose. Richter, in his work on Luther and Loyola, concludes, "Ignatius possesses one quality which can never be found in Luther, and that is saintliness. Luther never wants to be a saint."[3] Luther sought salvation, not saintliness. His pursuit was singly focused and since it left him insecure regarding salvation, he eventually discarded the method and sought a new way.

Instead of patiently persevering in the monastic life, Luther, due to his continual state of anxiety over his righteousness in the eyes of God (justification), plunged "into feverish activity," which only led to formulating "a partial solution to his spiritual problems in his doctrine on justification."[4] Of course, Luther believed that he did arrive at a solution in his doctrine on justification. This came out of, in part, his abandonment of monastic life on the basis of it being unbiblical. Years later in reflecting on his monastic trial, Luther wrote, "Sometimes my confessor said to me when I repeatedly

---

2. Richter, *Martin Luther and Ignatius Loyola*, 5.
3. Ibid., 51–52.
4. Ibid., 52.

discussed silly sins with him, 'You are a fool . . . God is not angry with you, but you are angry with God.'"[5] Luther's anger with God (and anger with the monastic formula) eventually led him to leave the monastic life disillusioned by its purpose and lack of security regarding salvation. In a stroke of irony, Luther had entered the monastery to overcome his anxiety about salvation, yet the monastic art of reflection only intensified his anxiety.

These younger and formative years spent in monasticism and its failure to alleviate salvific anxiety profoundly informed his theology. Feeling liberated from the monastic life, and therefore the anxiety of sin that went along with it, Luther wrote a letter to his father, "What difference does it make whether I retain or lay aside the cowl . . . do they make a monk? Shall I belong to the cowl, or shall not the cowl rather belong to me? My conscience has been freed, and that is the most complete liberation. Therefore I am still a monk and yet not a monk."[6] Concerning the psyche of the young Luther, Bengt Hoffman points out his, "primary concern was not intellectual, dogmatic rampart building around God's self-disclosure. Rather, Luther was about the business of translating into meaningful theological language a radical spiritual experience of God's justifying and loving presence."[7]

The examination of Luther's theology here highlights one of the central presuppositions of this book, which is the idea that his lived religious experience (spirituality) influenced, to some degree, the construction of his theology. "Practically all well-known accounts of Luther's Reformation theology . . . play down [his] references to spiritual experience,"[8] however I am suggesting here that Luther's theology, in part, grew out of his spiritual experience and his strive for salvific security via monastic rigor. This was confirmed by what he read in scripture (*sola scriptura*), for his scriptural examination "led him to the conviction that the crisis of human life is not overcome by striving to achieve security by what we do, but by the certainty of God's acceptance of us in spite of what we do."[9] In a letter to Duke George of Saxony, Luther writes,

> I was a good monk, and kept my order so strictly that I could say that if ever a monk could get to heaven through monastic discipline, I should have entered in . . . For if it had gone on much longer, I would have martyred myself to death, with vigils, prayers, readings and other works . . . [My] conscience would

5. Luther, *Luther's Works*, 54:15.
6. Luther, "Letter to Hans Luther, Wartburg, Nov. 21, 1521," 5.
7. Hoffman, "Lutheran Spirituality," 127.
8. Ibid., 125.
9. Lindberg, *The European Reformations*, 67.

never give me certainty. But I always doubted and said, "You did not perform that correctly. You were not contrite enough. You left that out of your confession."[10]

In other words, Luther sought salvific certainty by doing what lied within him and doing his best. But when is enough enough? He wanted certainty, for no matter how much he prayed, he could always pray more. Likewise, he could always do more penance, do more fasting, read more scripture, etc. Recall that these 'scruples' over monastic practice surfaced prior to his dispute with Fr. Tetzel over indulgences. He learned from his monastic experience (his lived spiritual experience) that God does not grant grace in exchange for human works. For Luther, grace did not depend on what a person did, but rather on what God does. This idea was informed both by his experience as a monk and his reading of scripture. He knew that absolutely nothing lay within his power that granted him the ability to achieve grace. Thus, when Fr. Tetzel came along and offered indulgences, Luther was all too ready to reject them as theologically inadequate. The issue centered on the degree to which 'grace' depends on human 'cooperation.' For Luther, it did not count in the least, while for Tetzel and Catholicism it counted to some degree in a specific manner.

In his rejection of the value of monasticism and indulgences as a means to procuring grace, Luther began to doubt everything: his vocation, salvation in the Catholic Church, the hope for liberation from sin, and the possibility of attaining Christian perfection, etc.[11] He fell into a despair which ultimately became a 'consoling' dependence on God—a foundation upon which he sought to (re)construct his theological project. Reflecting on the comfort of failure and imperfection, Luther wrote that the Holy Spirit strives after the "Godly, who know their weakness and for this reason are disheartened, to take comfort in the offense that comes from the account of the lapses among the holiest and most perfect patriarchs."[12] In other words, Luther believed one should take heart in and be consoled by the fact that the most noble of seekers (the saints) could not, on their own accord, achieve favor (justification) in the eyes of God. He took this to mean that if the saints could not do it, then surely no one can. Thus, the ordinary believer should not trouble himself over these scruples—for salvation remains out of their hands and in the hands of God.

In *The Babylonian Captivity of the Church*, Luther rails against what he understands to be a corrupted view of the sacraments. He preaches that the

10. Steinmetz, "Luther and Loyola," 9.
11. Richter, *Martin Luther and Ignatius Loyola*, 54.
12. Luther, "Lectures on Genesis 6–14," 166–67; WA 42:278–79.

THE "PROTESTANT PRINCIPLE" AND SACRAMENTAL CAUTION   73

masses have been held captive by the Pope and the Catholic Church, who have withheld access to scripture and duped them into thinking that rituals and sacraments provide a certain path to salvation. A major concern of the document is the sacrament of the Lord's Supper. Luther did not dispute the presence of Christ in the sacrament, but rather rejected the metaphysical foundations upon which the description of that presence relied. He rejected transubstantiation on the grounds that it relied too heavily on Aristotelian philosophical categories, which he deemed unbiblical. Luther cautions the faithful when he writes, "let us not dabble too much in philosophy . . . What does it matter if philosophy cannot fathom this? The Holy Spirit is greater than Aristotle. Does philosophy fathom their transubstantiation?"[13]

In other words, Luther raises the futility of seeking to know exactly how God works and is present. To him, the rigor of the philosophical language only muddied the theological waters instead of fulfilling its original intent of clarity. His reading of the New Testament yielded a narrative of Jesus who did not use Aristotelian metaphysical language, so why should the Church, he perhaps thought. He saw no practical nor theological need to understand how Christ is present, but rather the important thing is that Christ is indeed present. It should be sufficient evidence for the believer simply becasue Jesus says so, no more. So scripture is enough for the theologian here, hence there is no need to resort to Aristotle. Luther quips in his usual biting tone, "What shall we say when Aristotle and the doctrines of men are made to be the arbiters of such lofty and divine matters? Why do we not put aside such curiosity and cling simply to the words of Christ, willing to remain in ignorance of what takes place here and content that the real body of Christ is present by virtue of the words? Or is it necessary to comprehend the manner of the divine working in every detail?"[14] To be clear then, Luther is not rejecting the belief that Christ is present in the sacrament, but rather he rejects the language and philosophical mechanisms by which we presume to talk about and understand this presence. His rejection is based on foreign, "non-biblical," philosophical foundations, such as substance, accident, matter, and form. Luther had a particular aversion to the concept of transubstantiation, which he makes clear when he writes, "The church kept the true faith for more than twelve hundred years, during which time the holy fathers never, at any time or place, mentioned this transubstantiation (this monstrous word and a monstrous idea), until the

13. Luther, "The Babylonian Captivity of the Church," 224.
14. Ibid.

pseudo philosophy of Aristotle began to make its inroads into the church in these last three hundred years."[15]

Luther later concluded that the two qualities of a sacrament are 1) its institution by Christ (if there is sufficient biblical evidence for it) and 2) its valid promise of forgiveness of sin. If it does not satisfy these two criteria, then it is not a valid sacrament. Thus he accepted two sacraments, baptism and the Eucharist, and possibly a third in penance or reconciliation (but he is not as clear regarding the third).

Since this book does not focus on 'the sacraments,' but on 'sacramentality' as such, I shall focus on Luther's protest against the latter; that is, how, for Luther, God sacramentally encounters persons in experience. His answer to this query is hinted above in one of his writings when writes, "Christ is present by virtue of the words;" that is, his spoken words in the Gospel narrative ("this is my body, this is my blood"). Hence, for Luther, one of the primary means through which God communicates is the spoken word, and in particular through the preaching of scripture. He writes, "the gospel should really not be something written, but a spoken word . . . This is why Christ himself did not write anything but only spoke. He called his teaching not Scripture but gospel, meaning good news or a proclamation that is spread not by pen but by word of mouth."[16] Luther's emphasis on removing merit from the individual and instead relying solely on God is evident here, for the Word remains primary to all of God's action in the world. It is through the Word that the world was created, which is founded and grounded upon the Word and serves as a symbolic pointer back to itself as its primordial principle.

Luther preaches that the Word "must be present in every single creature in its innermost and outermost being, on all sides, through and through, below and above, before and behind, so that nothing can be more truly present and within all creatures than God himself with his power."[17] Since the Word is primary, God is most fundamentally encountered in and through preaching and scripture. Thus scripture is necessary, for it prevents heretical distortion of the apostolic message through erroneous preaching. Similar to his monastic experiences, Luther's interpretation of scripture serves as a reminder to the reader that she can do nothing, (she can perform no works) to merit acceptance in the eyes of God. The Protestant inclination to caution against understanding the sacramental as a magical meritorious

---

15. Ibid., 223.

16. Luther, "A Brief Instruction on What to Look for and Expect in the Gospels (1521)," 97.

17. *Luther's Works* 37, 57.

mechanism towards grace, and thus ultimately a fall into idolatry surfaces here. Paul Tillich has, perhaps more than most, articulated this Protestant concern for idolatry in his theology of the 'demonic.'

Tillich's Theology of the "Demonic"

Paul Tillich is one of the few great twentieth-century Protestant thinkers who spent a great deal of time on, and took seriously, sacramentality. Langdon Gilkey, a student of Tillich's and renowned theologian in his own right, writes, "in theological studies, while many of the once-important systems of the first half of this century [twentieth century] are now of more historical than contemporary interest, Tillich's, almost alone, represents *the* theological system with which almost everyone (at least in American theology) must wrestle."[18] Though one might add a few contemporary theological systems to Gilkey's narrow list here,[19] Tillich's remains arguably one of *the* major systems. He holds fast to the importance and need for an intelligible and adequate theology of symbol, though tempered with the usual Protestant caution, which I argue here surfaces most clearly in his theology of, what he terms, 'the demonic.' When a sacrament (which in Tillich's language he refers to as a 'preliminary concern') is elevated to the status of the Godhead (which he refers to as famously as one's proper 'ultimate concern') it becomes 'demonic.' Thus sacramentality should be approached with caution so as to not to confuse a demon (false ultimate concern or idol) for a God (genuine ultimate concern).

Tillich's theology of the demonic (idols) makes intelligible the potential danger of rendering a sacrament or sacramental experience objectively efficacious and thus 'magical' (a human manipulation of nature and grace apart from divine assistance). Tillich emphasizes, perhaps more clearly than all other contemporary thinkers, the essence of the 'Protestant Principle.' This concern for idolatry helps temper the close identification of God with the sacrament found in the theological streams of the Catholic and Eastern Orthodox traditions. Herbert Vorgrimler appropriately reminds us, "We must take quite seriously the Protestant and Lutheran concern [represented here by Tillich] that the fundamental difference between God and the Church not be obliterated, and that God's absolute sovereignty not be obscured by

---

18. Gilkey, *Gilkey on Tillich*, 56 (parenthesis his).

19. I suggest that Rahner's system (taken from his *Theological Investigations* as a whole) serves as the Roman Catholic counterpart to Tillich's system, which represents liberal protestant theology. Thus both Rahner and Tillich serve as two of the major cotemporary foundations from which this book proceeds.

a new kind of ecclesial-sacramental triumphalism. In Rahner's work, God and Church are sometimes brought dangerously close to one another."[20] Tillich's definition of faith as ultimate concern (whether it be *eudaimonia*, happiness, marriage, money, power, or God) renders an incredibly broad and liberal understanding of religion in that religion becomes simply that which one is ultimately concerned with. This entails religiosity inescapable apart from perfect nihilism. However, for Tillich a 'true' ultimate concern (thus the only 'true' religion) lies in God. More specifically, for Tillich, it is the Christian Trinitarian Godhead. 'True' faith is grounded in that ultimate concern for God. The insistence on keeping God primary among all other theological aspects pervades Tillich's system, thus retaining God as the ultimate concern, not a preliminary concern (sacramental status).

When God is rightfully situated as ultimate and primary, everything else then becomes appropriately and potentially sacramental; that is, everything that is not-God remains free to become preliminary concerns, not ultimate. The Protestant concern here advocates for a rightly ordered set of priorities in which, as Thomas More allegedly quipped at the gallows, "God is first." However, when one pursues a preliminary concern as if it were an ultimate concern (God), it then becomes demonic (an idol). Tillich writes, "Religious symbols point symbolically to that which transcends all of them. But since, as symbols, they participate in that to which they point, they always have the tendency (in the human mind, of course) to replace that to which they are supposed to point, and to become ultimate in themselves. And in the moment in which they do this, they become idols."[21] When a symbol takes the place of that which it symbolizes, idolatry results. This is due to the subjectivity of the perceiver, not because the symbol is itself inherently demonic. A symbol can function both creatively (in a genuine sacramental way) and destructively (demonically). For example, when a religious believer elevates scripture (a potential sacrament) to a level that supersedes the Godhead (that to which the potential sacrament points), she is in danger of rendering the sacramental potential of scripture a demonic idolatrous symbol. Of course this does not entail that scripture is evil and demonic in itself, but only that it has the potential to function demonically if not perceived in proper relation to the Godhead (that to which it points). For Tillich, "All idolatry is nothing else than the absolutizing of symbols of the Holy, and making them identical with the Holy itself."[22] The Protestant concern here is that persons may confuse the actual sacrament for God's

---

20. Vorgrimler, *Sacramental Theology*, 39.
21. Tillich, "Religious Symbols and Our Knowledge of God," 44–56, 50.
22. Ibid.

very self, thus Tillich's point here is to remind the faithful that symbols are religious (sacramental) only when subjectively perceived in proper context to God. In doing so, the 'Protestant Principle,' which commenced with Luther, is at work here in Tillich's thought. This principle is eloquently articulated by Paul F. Knitter when he writes,

> The ever-moving searchlight that the Reformation trains on all religion as it warns that religion may be as dangerous as it is necessary. There is a worm within all religion—Tillich called it "the demonic element"—by which it tries to domesticate and capture deity in the security of human knowledge. All religion is in daily need of reformation because all religion, in both blatant and subtle ways, seeks to make itself and its creeds, codes, and cults more important than the revelation and experience it is meant to serve and pass on.[23]

In other words, the demonic element seeks to undermine the value of the sacrament by destructively replacing the symbol for that which it symbolizes. Sacraments (preliminary concerns) point toward, participate in, and (re)present God (the ultimate concern). However, the demonic concern surfaces when a preliminary concern becomes the ultimate concern. "At times . . . these preliminary concerns can be elevated to a position of pseudo-ultimacy, and when this happens, for instance, in liturgical worship or in Bible worship, the preliminary becomes demonic, and the result is a warped legalistic or magical sacramentalism, or a warped biblical fundamentalism."[24] This articulates precisely the Protestant reluctance to commit to an unabated adherence to sacramentalism.

The sacramental caution here stems from what Tillich recognizes as a potential ambiguity that exists in symbols and sacraments. Symbols can function both creatively and destructively (demonically) simultaneously when, for example, a symbol is mistaken for God. Tillich's premise for this assertion is that symbols participate in that which they symbolize. His argument proceeds as follows: Since Jesus Christ, the God-Man, took on fully the human condition, and the human condition is one of fundamental estrangement and alienation from God, then in Christ, God was subjected to everything that it means to be a human: experiencing joy, sorrow, happiness, hunger, cold, loneliness, death, etc. In this way, Christ *participated* in what it means to be a human. If Christ had not taken on death, there would not have been a full and complete existential *participation* in the human

23. Knitter, *Introducing Theologies of Religions*, 55.

24. Osborne, "Tillich's Understanding of Symbols and Roman Catholic Sacramental Theology," 101.

condition by God. "Only by taking suffering and death upon himself," writes Tillich, "could Jesus be the Christ, because only in this way could he participate completely in existence and conquer every force of estrangement which tried to dissolve his unity with God."[25] In other words, Tillich's vision is that God had to become completely immersed in the human condition in order to redeem it. On the cross, God meets sin, life meets death, good meets evil, everything meets nothing, and reconciliation meets estrangement—God's divine "yes" meets estrangement's sinful "no"—and God triumphs via the resurrection in regaining humanity's essential condition, and this is all made possible through the divine participation on behalf of the Godhead. For Tillich, "The human condition is one of separation and alienation from God;[26] but he [God] has brought that separation and alienation to an end by entering into it, by taking it upon himself, by making it his own."[27]

Due to the inherent ambiguity of sacramental symbols, there must be way, a criterion or set of criteria, for which to determine whether or not a sacrament is genuine or demonic. For Tillich, this is Christ on the cross which "is at the same time the criterion of all other symbols, and it is the criterion to which every Christian church should subject itself."[28] It is the criterion against which all other symbols are judged since it is from which all other symbols proceed and participate in reality by making Christ present (or *re*-present via memorial). Tillich's sacramental understanding here is not unlike that of Rahner. "One could say that Jesus is the primordial sacrament, in Tillich's view, only when Jesus, in his humanity, is the primordial sacrament of the ultimate, that which confronts us human beings as being or nonbeing."[29] Jesus on the cross (the symbol for ultimate sacrifice) is the criterion by which all other symbols are to be judged as sacramental or demonic.

To be clear, Tillich is not rejecting sacramentality as such, but rather remains an outspoken Protestant advocate for the importance of an adequate sacramental theology. "Protestantism" he writes, "has devaluated and

25. Tillich, *Systematic Theology*, vol. 2, 23.

26. Lutheran anthropologies generally place a lower and more cautionary view on the human condition. To some extent, the general theological anthropological positions of the Protestant tradition have no doubt contributed to a healthy cautionary view of sacramentality. This is precisely why the Protestant Principle is so important, in that it serves as a tempering agent for a sacramental imagination that may sometimes run the risk of the demonic.

27. Dwyer, "The Implications of Tillich's Theology of the Cross for Catholic Theology," 77.

28. Tillich, "Religious Symbols and Our Knowledge of God," 56.

29. Osborne, "Tillich's Understanding of Symbols and Roman Catholic Sacramental Theology," 106.

discarded the larger number of the symbols on which Catholicism lives . . . Protestantism must rediscover their [symbols'] realistic meaning, must denounce the interpretation of symbols as mere signs, must attempt to discover the germs of a new symbolism in our present life."[30] Further, he maintains, perhaps more than any other twentieth-century theologian, the retention of both the Protestant Principle and the identity of 'Catholic Substance' (what Tillich defines as "the embodiment of the Spiritual Presence"[31] referring to the tendency of Catholic theology to seek God sensually and tangibly in all things via sacramentality). The Protestant Principle, Tillich writes, "needs the 'Catholic Substance,' . . . [and] is the criterion of the demonization (and profanization) of such embodiment. It is the expression of the victory of the Spirit over religion."[32] In a way analogous to Luther, who took the Church to task on its scandalous view of penance and indulgences, Tillich continually calls for faith in that which concerns one ultimately, not preliminarily. As Luther rebelled against indulgences that seemed to manipulate God and disregard any subjective disposition on behalf of the agent, Tillich cautions against the danger of falling into the demonic objectification of sacramental symbols.

Both Tillich and Luther provide an important reminder in their insistence on keeping God first in the Christian approach to sacramentality. Tillich's theology of the demonic remains important in its providing an important critique of sacramental theologies. This is a foundational point for this book and will become increasingly important throughout. In the next chapter, the concern will be to draw out the particulars of Karl Rahner's sacramental theology and metaphysical cosmology. Luther and Tillich's sacramental caution provides an ever present alertness when seeking to appropriate such a sacramental worldview to spiritual experience.

---

30. Tillich, "The Permanent Significance of the Catholic Church for Protestants," 24.

31. Tillich, *Systematic Theology*, vol. 3, 245.

32. Ibid.

5

A Rahnerian Pansacramental Proposal

WHILE THE PREVIOUS CHAPTERS set forth a foundational and historical understanding of sacramental theology, this chapter draws on Karl Rahner and begins to sketch an understanding of the cosmos as pansacramental within a Christian theological worldview. In so doing, the possibility of conceiving the cosmos as sacramentally panentheistic, without negating classical Thomist ontology, is explored. However, it should be noted that I am not scandalized in the least about violating classical Thomist tenets but many do, thus it is my hope that this chapter might serve as an attempt to ease any fears out there among the Thomists about embracing the possibility of a pansacramental and panentheistic view. This involves the exploration of the claim that through pansacramentality, the entirety of the cosmos might be understood as being held within God without reducing God to the cosmos as such. This, of course, is not a claim on the spatiality of God, but rather is a proposal that speaks to the transcendence of God while affirming God's immanence in all things.

The specific understanding of sacramentality held by Karl Rahner (founded in large part on Aquinas) provides the backdrop against which this chapter proceeds. His sacramental theology begins with the salvific and constitutive character of *das Wort*, Christ, as the primordial sacrament from which his metaphysics of sacramental reality flows. He understands the whole of creation (the cosmos) to hold infinite sacramental potential, but predicates it on the founding (causation) of Christ, the self-expression of God in time and space. He writes "the word of God in the strictest and truest sense, therefore, can exist at all only as an event of grace,"[1] and thus as the primordial sacrament. Christ is not only constitutive of salvation, but constitutive of sacramental reality as well; that is, Christ constituted the conditions necessary for sacramental efficacy in history (time and space). Rahner's sacramental theology hinges on his Christological claim that Jesus is the primordial sacrament. The life of Jesus is a symbol of the concrete historical presence of God. On Rahner's theology, Herbert Vorgrimler writes that Jesus "could be called the icon, the image of God pure and simple, the visible epiphany of the invisible essence of God."[2] Jesus, as primordial sacrament, constitutes a definitive shattering of the aforementioned dichotomies. He signifies the real presence of God's eschatological victory and mercy in the world,[3] and as such, establishes sacramental reality. Thus Rahner's theology entails a symbolic metaphysics in which all things hold the sacramental potential to render present God's self via grace.

In an attempt to articulate and clarify this symbolic metaphysics both in this chapter and throughout this book, I draw here on the theology of Aquinas and more specifically, Rahner's sacramental theology. First, I briefly present the key tenets of Thomist ontology paying specific attention to Aquinas' sacramental theology and its Christological significance. Second, I present an overview of Rahner's theology project (anthropology, Christology, ecclesiology) only insofar as it pertains to his understanding of 'symbolic reality,' which I explore thirdly and is foundational for a pansacramental cosmic understanding. Fourth, and finally, drawing on both Aquinas and Rahner, I suggest how the cosmos may be understood as pansacramental and possibly panentheistic (however, chapter six explores panentheism in more detail). A cosmos understood thusly helps to clarify one of the overall thrusts of the book, which proposes a philosophy of pansacramental mediation (chapter 11).

Aquinas and Thomist Ontology

To a certain degree, Aquinas' ontology foundationally serves Rahner's sacramental cosmology. Central to the task of inquiring about the possibility of perceiving the cosmos as pansacramental is an examination of the Incarnation and the so-called sacred-profane dichotomy (or lack thereof). Sacramental theologian Herbert Vorgrimler captures this Christian inclination,

---

1. Rahner, "What Is a Sacrament?" 141.
2. Vorgrimler, *Sacramental Theology*, 30–31 (parenthetical citations excluded).
3. Rahner, *Kirche Und Sakramente*, 66.

a separation of reality into sacred and profane realms is impossible within Christian faith. A sacred realm (i.e., related to the "sacrum," the "holy") would absorb people and things that are removed from the "profane" and are ordered exclusively to God, reserved to God, and close to God alone. In contrast, the incarnation of God in Jesus of Nazareth affirms that the realm in which God comes to human beings, communicating God's own self and remaining with them, is not removed from the world, no matter how depraved that world may seem to us to be.[4]

In question eight of the *Summa Theologica*, Aquinas affirms the presence of God in all things.[5] His Aristotelian metaphysics allow him to make such a claim without lapsing into pantheism. In so doing, he collapses the sacred-profane dichotomy.[6] Anselm Min, in *Paths to the Triune God: An Encounter Between Aquinas & Recent Theologies*, writes, "one of the theological breakthroughs in recent decades has been the overcoming of the dualism of sacred and profane . . . [but] the real breakthrough had already occurred with Aquinas when his Trinitarian, Christological theology of creation saw all nature graced for the sake of glory and made it possible to include *all things sub ratione Dei* in theology."[7] A key implication of overcoming this dualism is precisely the possibility of subjecting all things to the scrutiny of theology and finding God in them (doctrine of divine ubiquity). As a traditional and classical Christian thinker, Aquinas refrains from deviating from this doctrine and finds a way to elevate it to a new level of importance. In his theological metaphysics, the presence of God in all things in and through their existence (*esse*) becomes paramount to understanding the whole of his theological system.

To get at this Thomist structure of cosmological reality, the Aristotelian distinction between substance and accident is important. Further, it remains important for an adequate understanding of his sacramental theology, which I allows for the closing of the sacred-profane dichotomy without compromising the core tenets of a traditional Christian theism. The substance of a thing is expressed and made present through its accidents. That is, things exist by way of their substance made visible by way of their

---

4. Vorgrimler, *Sacramental Theology*, 17–18.

5. "God is in all things; not, indeed, as part of their essence, nor as an accident, but as an agent is present to that upon which it works" (Thomas Aquinas, *Summa Theologica*, I.8.1).

6 The proposed dissolution of the dichotomy between the sacred and profane does not entail that the dichotomy is illusory, but rather the possibility of all things (no matter how seemingly profane/ordinary) contains the potential to become sacred.

7. Min, *Paths to the Triune God*, 41 (italics his).

accidents. God, on the other hand, cannot be thought of quantitatively nor accidentally. Question three in the first part of the *Summa Theologica* is devoted to God's simplicity, referring to the non-complexity ("non-composedness" to coin an awkward word) of God; that is, God is not made up of quantitative parts capable of being divided. In God there is no composition. God is not composed of matter and form, for to be composed of matter entails potentiality of being. In God there is no potentiality, but pure actuality; thus God is not composed of matter and is nothing but pure form.[8] Further, Aquinas affirms God's simplicity in identifying God's essence with God's existence. Unlike creatures, which are suppositions of an essence "(e.g. Socrates has humanness); . . . God does not have Godhead, or divinity, but He is divinity."[9] God is beyond the distinction and is both God's own essence and existence.[10] This being the case, argues Aquinas, God "cannot be a species of any genus,"[11] nor are there any accidents in God.[12] Aquinas concludes that God is indeed altogether (wholly) simple. Practically speaking, it follows that in thinking about God, thinkers ought to refrain from 'picture-thinking' when it comes to mentally constructing God, for God is not a body since bodies are made up of measureable parts.

Naming God, talking about God, and predicating names of God, through analogical predication is possible since God gives being to all things. God is the principal principle (primordial source) and cause of everything, and as such contains within God's self all the perfections of that which God causes. Through analogical predication, one can predicate God without having perfect knowledge of that predicate. One's knowledge of God is limited to analogy based on her experience as a sensible creature. It follows, that all things predicated to God must be done so analogically and not univocally or equivocally. In naming God, according to Anselm Min, Aquinas proceeds in three steps: (1) the way of causality, (2) the way of negation, and (3) the way of eminence.[13]

(1) God is the cause of material things. Due to the likeness between cause and effect, it follows that there is a likeness (similarity) between God and that which God causes. In this case, God, the cause, creates the cosmos, the effect. There is a likeness between God and cosmos, analogically. Through the effects, we can know that God is without knowing what God is.

---

8. Thomas Aquinas, *Summa Theologica*, I, 3, 2.
9. Kreeft, *A Summa of the Summa*, 78n.
10. Thomas Aquinas, *Summa Theologica*, I, 3, 4.
11. Thomas Aquinas, *Summa Theologica*, I, 3, 5.
12. Thomas Aquinas, *Summa Theologica*, I, 3, 6.
13. Min, *Paths to the Triune God*, 172.

Since God is the first cause of all things and all things are good (because they come from God who *is* goodness), then God contains a goodness which exceeds all goodness on earth. The same can be said, perhaps to an even greater extent, about existence. Since God is the principle of all things, and all things exist because they are given existence from God who *is* existence as such (*Ipsum Esse Subsistens*), then God contains a perfected mode of existence which exceeds all existence in the cosmos. For Aquinas, *esse* is the fundamental perfection which is the most adequate and comprehensive way to describe God. (2) The way of negation informs the analogical predication by denying equal identification and absolute similarity between God as such (cause) and God's creation (effects). There remains an infinite inequality between the two. In this way, creatures are denied any finite perfections predicated upon them. Instead, the perfections are properly applied to God in God's infinity. (3) The way of eminence applies the pure perfections to God. "These pure perfections—such as being, goodness, beauty, wisdom, life—belong to God more properly and are predicated of God with greater with greater priority [*per prius*] than of creatures."[14]

In the employment of analogical predication as the proper mode for naming God, the distinction between analogy and metaphor ought to be maintained. Analogy refers to literal application (albeit it analogical) and metaphor refers to the "transfer of a meaning properly found only in a material being to a non-material being."[15] For instance, God can identified as a mountain, metaphorically, but not literally. The prominence of a mountain, properly found only in a mountain, is applied to God in a spiritual sense, but not in a material (literal) sense. God is prominent and a mountain is prominent, but God is not prominent in the same literal/material way as a mountain is prominent. Analogy, on the other hand, refers to literal application. Thus God is literally good, but analogically speaking. For instance, I am good, you are good, and God is good, but we are not good in the same way that God is good. God's goodness is infinite while our goodness is finite. Our goodness contains negated perfection, but God's does not. God's goodness is analogous to ours, but infinitely greater and unequal. "The difference between an analogy and a metaphor, then, is that intelligible content of meaning remains identical in an analogy but changes in a metaphor."[16]

The cosmos for Aquinas is caused by God and is therefore from God. He writes, "every being in any way existing is from God."[17] All that exists

---

14. Ibid, 172 (bracketing his).
15. Ibid., 173.
16. Ibid.
17. Thomas Aquinas, *Summa Theologica*, I, 44, 1.

within the cosmos can be distinguished through the use of essence-existence language. This is to say that in all finite created things, the essence remains distinct from its existence. God, as the principal cause and creator of the cosmos, is beyond such distinction and comprehensibility. The reason for this is that for Aquinas, to create is to create anew; it is to make something from nothing (*ex nihilo*), and only God can do this. Only God can give being since God is being as such. Aquinas writes, "We must consider not only the emanation of a particular being from a particular agent, but also the emanation of all being from the universal cause which is God; and this emanation we designate by the name of creation."[18] One of the effects of creation is existence itself, "which accordingly should be the proper effect of the first and most universal cause, which is God."[19] This is supported by what Etienne Gilson refers to as the "Great Syllogism,"

1. "God is very being (*esse*) by His own essence"

2. "being (*esse*) is innermost in each thing and most fundamentally inherent in all things since it is formal in respect of everything found in a thing"

3. "Hence, it must be that God is in all things, and innermostly."[20]

God sacramentally expresses God's self (*esse*) in the world via creaturely representation or imaging. Analogically, all agents produce something similar to themselves; that is, there exists similarities between the agent and its effects. For Aquinas, there are four ways that God is represented in the world. There are four ways the effects bear the likeness of its cause, God. These four, from lowest to highest, are 1) by vestige, 2) by image, 3) by grace, and 4) the beatific vision. God is represented by vestige (or trace) in non-intellectual creatures, which is to say they hold divine likeness as effects of God, the universal cause. But they do not represent the form of God. The mode of image, on the other hand, does represent God in its own form. Intellectual creatures do this. Their intellectual activities of knowing and loving analogically image that of their creator. In the third mode, God is manifested through the grace and faith of intellectual creatures. The highest mode, then, is "the mode of eternal life or the beatific vision of God's own essence through glory."[21] These are four degrees of representing God and

---

18. Thomas Aquinas, *Summa Theologica*, I, 45, 1.
19. Thomas Aquinas, *Summa Theologica*, I, 45, 5.
20. Thomas Aquinas, *Summa Theologica*, I, 8, 1.
21. Min, *Paths to the Triune God*, 28.

need not always be sharply distinguished from one another, but rather can be understood to exist on a continuum.[22]

The result of a sacramental occasion is such that the realm of the so-called profane (that which is not God) and the realm of the sacred (that which represents God) is collapsed and dissolved in that God is made present in temporal space. This process is made possible in and through sacramentality, which remains vital for any theological project that claims a cosmology in which all things come from God and are in God, as Aquinas has done.

Drawing on Augustine, Aquinas deems a sacrament a "sign of a sacred thing insofar as it sanctifies a human being."[23] Though Aquinas affirms that sacraments are primarily signs, he insists further that understanding them alone as mere signs is insufficient. Since sacraments are signs, they effect what they signify. In other words, sacraments *cause* what they signify, or put differently, they are causes *because* they are signs. They are instrumental causes used by God as a means to manifest grace in the world. The sacraments are not the first cause of grace, for that title belongs to God alone, but rather sacraments are instrumental in that they are channels or vehicles through which God acts. The Incarnation is one of the fundamental pillars upon which Christians might conceivably claim a pansacramental cosmology. It provides an explanation for the claim that all creation ought to be understood as sacramental. It is the definitive vehicle which draws people to God through creation. The sacraments provide the conduit through which persons can participate in the Incarnation. These sacraments, for Aquinas, are signs in a very real way in that they make God present, which cannot be corporeally sensed or empirically verified. They signify the reality which engraces (sanctifies) and thus signify the effect produced. This is why, for Aquinas, a sacrament is "a sign of sacred reality inasmuch as it has the property of sanctifying people."[24]

---

22. Moreover, each degree can be dissected further. For instance, Min recognizes three stages in humans imaging God. "In discussing the human being as imaging God by imitating God's understanding and loving herself, Aquinas refers to the first stage of intellectual existence as 'the natural aptitude for understanding and loving God,' which is founded on the very nature of the mind [*ipsa natura mentis*]. He refers to the second stage of grace as 'knowing and loving God actually or habitually [*act vel habitu*], although imperfectly,' and to the third stage of glory as 'actually [*actu*] knowing and loving God perfectly.' The first type of imaging is found in all human beings, the second in the just, the third in the blessed (*Summa* I, 93, 4)" (Min, *Paths to the Triune God*, 29, bracketed his).

23. Thomas Aquinas, *Summa Theologica*, III, 60, 2.

24. Thomas Aquinas, *Summa Theologica*, III, 60.2.

Along these lines Aquinas deems Christ the first (principle) sacrament from which all other sacraments flow. His earthly life and death were real presentations of God working in and through creation, through which people actually participated in God's life. Thus, after Jesus' time, the sacraments continue to work in this way providing a means for persons to actually participate in God's life. As a significant redemptive event in time, the Christ event reverberates throughout time allowing for subsequent generations to participate through 'making memorial' (-zkr). Sacramental memorials cause and reveal grace in allowing genuine participation in redemptive events. As Brian Davies puts it, "Just like the life, death, and resurrection of Christ, the sacraments of the Church are physical signs of genuine causes of grace. They are symbols which make real what they symbolize. Through them we are united to God even in this life. Through them we are made partakers of the divine nature."[25]

Jesus of Nazareth, as the God-man, is understood as God's self (God's substance) embodied in time and space. Drawing on the hypostatic union, Karl Rahner refers to Jesus Christ as the primordial sacrament, which in Thomist language might refer to the principle (source) sacrament; that is, the divine *Logos* as Jesus Christ is 'the sacrament of sacraments.' According to Herbert Vorgrimler, "the designation 'primordial sacrament' was applied to the Church by Otto Semmelroth and Karl Rahner after the war. [However], to avoid the terminological confusion occasioned by simultaneously calling Jesus Christ the 'primordial sacrament,' and in order to highlight the enduring, qualitative difference between Jesus Christ and the Church, Semmelroth later referred to the Church as the 'root sacrament,' while Rahner called it the 'fundamental sacrament.'"[26] In Rahner's sacramental theology, there is a basic three-tiered hierarchy of sacraments: 1) Christ as the primordial sacrament, 2) Church as the fundamental sacrament, which is "the continuance of Christ's presence in the world,"[27] and 3) the individual sacraments, which flow from the Church. As fundamental sacrament, the Church is "the well-spring of the sacraments in the strict sense," and "from Christ the Church has an intrinsically sacramental structure."[28] The individual sacraments are, "the essential, fundamental realizations of the Church itself"[29] which (re)present redemptive reality in history.

---

25. Davies, *The Thought of Thomas Aquinas*, 352.
26. Vorglimer, *Sacramental Theology*, 36.
27. Rahner, *The Church and the Sacraments*, 21.
28. Ibid., 18.
29. Rahner, *Kirche und Sakramente*, 21.

For Rahner (and Aquinas) the whole cosmos (and all things contained therein) is created by God and thus holds the ability to symbolize God and make God present in time and space. The cosmos is saturated with grace and this grace is made present through sacramental occasions. Christ, as the primordial sacrament, functions as the means through which God expresses and communicates God's self the most perfectly (or least wrongly).

The Christ event, by uniting the natures of the divine (supernatural) and the human (natural), allow for the collapse of the sacred-profane (natural-supernatural) dichotomy. God's taking on matter and form, substance and accident, in time and space creates the conditions necessary for which all things might potentially become sacramental. This is because the Incarnation functions constitutively. Through the Incarnation, God shares in the materiality of the world and thereby embraces the human condition itself. As such, the human condition and materiality become potential sacramental symbols of God. This is to say that the Christ, as the Divine Logos (God's *ratio*), serves as the primordial exemplar (*primodiale exemplar*) for all creation, of which creatures are a part.[30] Just as Rahner makes the claim that the Christ event is 'constitutive' (causal) of salvation, a Christian thinker might also claim Christ as constituting the proper conditions for which all creation can potentially fulfill (self-actualize) its sacramental potential; that is, all things have the potential to express God sacramentally (although, a pansacramental theology may need not rely on Christ for such conditions). Aquinas writes, "all creatures are nothing but a kind of real expression and representation of those things which are comprehended in the conception of the divine Word; wherefore all things are said (John 1: 3) to be made by the Word. Therefore, suitably was the Word united to the creature, namely, to human nature."[31] Hence, the hypostatic union of Christ serves as the primary example (*primodiale exemplar*) for all creatures to seek to fulfill.

The concept of pansacramentality, for the purposes of this book, refers to the concept that all things contain the potential to render the sacred forth (expresses or (re)present the divine). In question eight of the *Summa Theologica*, Aquinas writes, "God is in all things; not, indeed, as part of their essence, nor as an accident; but as an agent is present to that upon which it works."[32] In positing God's presence in all things, not as a part of their being, Aquinas rejects pantheism. Likewise, Aquinas distinguishes Christianity from deism when he writes, "now since God is very being by His own essence, created being must be his proper effect . . . God causes this effect in

---

30. Min, *Paths to the Triune God*, 31.
31. Thomas Aquinas, *Summa Contra Gentiles*, 4.42
32. Thomas Aquinas, *Summa Theologica*, I, 8, 1.

things not only when they first begin to be, but as long as they are preserved in being."[33] This is a rejection of deism since he affirms God's continual action in all things through causality. God continually causes the existence of all things because God's very self is *esse*. God does not stop working like the 'watch-maker' deity of deism, but rather God is continually and intimately involved with creation.[34] Moreover, God is at work (is present) in all things in an 'innermost' way. God's being (*esse* as such) is existence and thus nothing is more present and intimate to all things than God, hence Aquinas writes, "God is in all things, and innermostly."[35]

Rejecting pantheism and deism, he professes a Christian metaphysics in which all things can potentially (re)present God sacramentally (vestige, image, grace, glory).[36] All sacramental potentialities (all things within the cosmos) hold the potential to express God in cosmic time and space. For example, a stone, a tree, a mountain or a lake may (re)present the divine via sacramentality in that they, as effects, body forth the likeness of the divine. Metaphysically, one could argue over how this works, whether transubstantiatially, consubstantially, or neither. Substance metaphysics aside, this is not to say that the water in a lake, understood to be sacred by an individual or community, ceases to be water (with chemical composition of two parts hydrogen and one part oxygen) and materially becomes (or even tran/consubstantiates into) something other than water. The idea here is that when recognized and actualized as sacramental, the water (re)presents the likeness of God in the world.

A parallel can be drawn to the way orthodox Christianity articulates and affirms the hypostatic union in Jesus Christ, in whom both natures (divine and human) remain. The hypostatic union provides the deepest possible presence of God in the world, and as such, God is present as a cause. In the creation, and the taking on, of materiality in the Incarnation, God endows materiality with the potential function of sacramentally. Similar to the hypostatic union in Jesus Christ, both "natures" of the lake remain at the same time, unchanged and unconfused: the mundane (profane?) material nature of ordinary lake water-ness and the sacramentally present divine

---

33. Thomas Aquinas, *Summa Theologia* I, 8, 1.

34. Peter Kreeft provides an example that distinguishes clearly between deism and Aquinas when he writes, "A carpenter does not cause the very being of the house he builds, only its form; therefore when he stops working, the house continues to exist. But if God stopped 'working' (cf. Jn 5:17), the very existence of all things would perish, for this is His work" (Kreeft, *A Summa of the Summa*, 101).

35. Thomas Aquinas, *Summa Theologica* I, 8, 1.

36. For a more in-depth discussion and explanation of Aquinas' ontology and various modes of God's presence, see Min, *Paths to the Triune God*, 26–39.

nature of God, albeit only a trace or vestige. God as expressed in the world (such as in the lake) can be distinguished from God in God's own nature or eternal essence, which remains ultimately mysterious. An orthodox Christian position claims that "God is transcendent in *nature*, not in *place* . . . God is transcendent in His *nature* and immanent in His *presence*."[37] In this way, the lake might be understood to function both mundanely (profanely) and sacramentally (sacredly) thus collapsing the so-called sacred-profane dichotomy.

Rahner's Theological Project

Roman Catholic systematic theologian and ecclesiologist Michael Himes provides one of the fundamental premises for any Rahnerian sacramental theology,[38]

> Things tell you what they are. You don't have to torture the truth out of things. Everything that exists is open and ready to tell you about itself. It's eager to reveal its inner most depths. That's true of everything that exists. But there is a necessary first step, [which is] to ask the right question: 'tell me your story.' That is the key in coming to know anyone or anything. Give an attentive hearing to that story, [because] reality is there to be seen. It's not disguised. It's not hidden from you. It's not hidden behind some veil that you have to tear off. All you have to do is ask the right question, and the right question is always 'tell me your story.'[39]

If this is the first proposition to a Rahnerian sacramental theology, that everything is waiting to tell you what it is, to tell its story, and spirituality is the lived experience of the reality of the divine (ultimate reality), then sacramentality is central since it provides a means for understanding all things as giving themselves away. If reality is ready and willing to give itself to the persons, then persons had better be ready to give ourselves to it by listening attentively; that is, they need to be ready, willing, and open to it in order to understand it. This comes through spiritual experience and is founded on Himes' principle presupposition that "things tell you what they are."

Any understanding of Rahner's theology without an adequate grasp of his spiritual foundation and motivation remains incomplete. The goal here is to flesh out his systematic understanding of sacramental theology in order

---

37. Kreeft, *A Summa of the Summa*, 102n (italics his).

38. This premise is given by Michael Himes as the first proposition in his uncompleted, unpublished, systematic sacramental theology.

39. Himes, "The Last Lecture," min. 7:00.

to situate it within the context of his spirituality To do so, this section offers a tour (albeit brief) through the systematic contours of Rahner's theological project in so far as it illuminates his sacramental worldview. I begin with an examination of his transcendental anthropology followed by a sketch of the systematic inter-weavings of his Christology, ecclesiology and Trinitarian theology. Finally, I illuminate his sacramental theology and vision of 'symbolic reality.'

Central to the contemporary study of spirituality, as a self-implicating field, is the necessity to give sufficient attention to theological anthropology. This is concerned with what it means to be a human in relation to God. In other words, does, and how does, the human person engage the divine through lived religious experience (spirituality)? Is there something unique about the human person which enables her to engage the divine through spirituality? This suggestion should be taken just as seriously when approaching a thinker such as Rahner, whose theology and spirituality build on one another. To situate the two fields in his book, I begin here with an examination of his view of the person: his theological anthropology.

He offers a transcendental anthropology in which the human person must be situated within the context of the reality of *Vorgriff* (preapprehension of being), which is a chief characteristic that endows all human persons. It "expresses the fundamental being and God-orientedness"[40] of humans. This is the pre-thematic trait of the *supernatural existential*, which is the ability of all humans to look ahead, to anticipate, and to be aware of the divine. Drawing on Heidegger, Rahner here coins the phrase "supernatural existential" to refer to the reality of the being of humans as such as preordained and orientated toward seeking and communing with God. God's "self-communication" is present in all persons "in the mode of an offer."[41] Even though this is an ontological reality of all persons, it remains supernatural. It is supernatural in that it is a capacity given to humans by God, without which there would be no possibility of communing with God. Furthermore, even though not all will accept this divine offer, it is still God's self-communication. Rahner writes,

> The free subject can possess himself in the mode of "yes" or in the mode of "no," in the mode of deliberate and obedient acceptance or in the mode of protest against this essential being of his which has been entrusted to freedom, so too the existential of man's absolute immediacy to God in and through this divine self-communication as permanently offer to freedom can exists

---

40. Hoppál, "Karl Rahner's Notion of *Vorgriff*," 451.
41. Rahner, *Foundations of Christian Faith*, 127.

merely in the mode of an antecedent offer, in the mode of acceptance and in the mode of rejection. The mode in which God's self-communication is present with respect to human freedom does not nullify the real presence of this self-communication as something offered.[42]

The human person is necessarily free in this anthropology. The free will of the person manifests itself in the human ability to either accept (recognize and cooperate with) or reject (ignore and thwart) the universal offer of God's grace. In her freedom, the human agent actualizes her 'self' and transcends her limitations and finitude in seeking the Holy Mystery.

With the gift of God's self-communication comes "the necessary condition which makes possible an acceptance of the gift."[43] All persons, regardless of his or her particular religious commitment (or lack thereof), have as a part of their nature, the existential awareness of the "Holy Mystery" (be it explicit or implicit). This is a foundational character of human nature and is not to be considered as simply one among many, but rather is a part of all human experiences. "Such an element in man's transcendental constitution is not the object of an individual, a posteriori and categorical experience of man *alongside of* other objects of his experience,"[44] but rather forms the condition for the possibility of all other objects of experience.

For Rahner, all humans inherently have an awareness of the Holy Mystery (God) as the horizon against which they experience life. This movement toward God is not a move toward an eternally distant God, "but rather in the God of absolute closeness and immediacy."[45] For Rahner, grace enters into the equation as the God given capacity to progress toward the *telos* of the beatific vision, "towards the immediacy of God."[46] Grace is both the goal itself and ability to move towards that goal via transcendence. Rahner writes that "we can say without hesitation: a person who opens himself up to this transcendental experience of the holy mystery at all has the experience that this mystery is not only an infinitely distant horizon, . . . it is not only something mysterious which frightens him away and back into the narrow confines of his everyday world. He experiences rather that this holy mystery is also a hidden closeness, a forgiving intimacy, his real home."[47] The supernatural existential, the experience of God's self-communication,

42. Ibid., 128.
43. Ibid.
44. Ibid., 129 (italics his).
45. Ibid.
46. Ibid., 130.
47. Ibid., 131.

is so enmeshed with the fabric of what it means to be a human, and a part of the everyday world, that "in principle . . . the original experience of God even in his self-communication can be so universal, so unthematic and so 'unreligious' that it takes place, unnamed but really, wherever we are living out our existence."[48]

Fundamental to what it means to be human is the ability to confront ones limitations and finitude, overcome them, and transcend them towards God thus giving rise to indirect knowledge of God. The human ability of transcendence, as the chief character of what it means to be human, entails a cosmology saturated with God's grace offering human persons (*all* human persons) the opportunity to know and beware of God. This is the case since all humans are endowed with this ability to intuit, or indirectly know (be it explicit or implicit), the Holy Mystery in their experience of daily life. Humans, like nature, have a single common goal in seeking to transcend the material world toward the spirit, which lies in the fullness of God as holy mystery.

The goal of transcendence is, in Rahner's terminology, to experience the "Holy Mystery." Rahner rejects the concept of mystery that became commonplace after Vatican I, since it fails to account for the supernatural character of the mysteries of the church and revelation. Further, it treats mystery as provisional, something that will ultimately be revealed. "It is a matter, or so it would seem, of truths obscure and impenetrable for the moment but which will be clarified later on and so finally be adequate to the demands made by human reason for insight and perspicuousness."[49] This is to treat supposedly supernatural mystery no different than natural mysteries. For instance, the truth value of the statement "Lake Superior is the largest freshwater lake in the world by surface area" is a mystery to those who have not done the research, or do not have access to the research. Natural mystery is mystery in the same sense of, for instance, a murder mystery or Sherlock Holmes solving a mystery, which are quandaries that can be solved with sufficient evidence.

Rahner rejects this "murder mystery" understanding of mystery in talking about God. "For the so-called natural mysteries, when regarded clearly, are either not real mysteries at all, or they raise again the question of what makes them mysterious."[50] In positing God as holy mystery, mystery must retain God's incomprehensibility. Unlike a natural mystery, which we may or may not unveil, the holy mystery that is God is infinitely incom-

---

48. Ibid., 132.
49. Rahner, "The Concept of Mystery in Catholic Theology," 111.
50. Ibid., 116.

prehensible both here and now and in the beatific vision. This entails that God as such, as holy mystery, cannot be grasped nor understood by the human mind. God remains holy mystery to both those in this life and beyond. Grace does not unveil the holy mystery, but rather presents God as holy mystery as such. Rahner writes,

> Man, elevated by grace, is the spiritual being which is ontologically directed to the beatific vision. Grace, being strictly supernatural, is ultimately the beatific vision or its ontological presupposition . . . Pilgrim man, still a stranger to the vision of God, can be deceived about the character of absolute mystery in God, because he knows the holy mystery only as the distant and aloof. When he sees God, God's incomprehensibility is the content of his vision and so the bliss of his love.[51]

God as holy mystery remains mysterious in the absolute sense. This does not mean God is unknowable, but rather it means that God is knowable as mystery—as infinitely knowable. Rahner's theological anthropology has a few clear implications for the rest of his system, most specifically for his Christology, theology of grace, soteriology, and metaphysical cosmology.

Transcendence remains foundational for Rahner's systematic theology. His anthropology and Christology are inexorably linked, thus earning the respective titles of 'transcendental anthropology' and 'transcendental Christology.' His Christology is one which understands Jesus of Nazareth as a historical human person who was united with God in such a complete fashion that Jesus' transcendence was irrevocably affirmed. The presupposition for this is that all human beings are oriented towards this encounter and are thus able to achieve it and experience it in their concrete lives. All humans are oriented toward, and naturally yearn for, an absolute savior.

One implication of this view is that humans, like Jesus Christ, are capable of transcendence. They are able to recognize, have knowledge of, and confront their finitude, limitations and dependence. They are able to neglect these, overcome them and transcend them towards their Spirit, their *telos*, or God. This is not just another part of human experience to be placed alongside others, but rather is a part of all human experiences. God (the supernatural) is the horizon against which all existence is experienced as experience (existential). The reality of God, then, is at the very heart of one's anthropological condition. It is through transcendence that one can fully realize his or her divine potential.

---

51. Ibid., 118.

Rahner's Christology commences out of his transcendental anthropology and evolutionary view[52] of the world. His is an "ascending Christology" since it begins with the historical man of Jesus of Nazareth and works towards the eternal Logos of God. The eternal Logos reconciles human persons with the Holy Mystery. The person of Jesus as the Christ offers an anthropological model in that he exemplifies the transcendental potential of human nature in its ability to encounter the finite and strive beyond it (transcendence) towards the infinite (God). Jesus as the Christ (Christology) offers the radicalization, the perfect model, of what it means to be human (anthropology), which is the ability to self-actualize. Transcendence carried to its single highest pitch (as in the case of Jesus) implies that the person can represent God, which is perhaps reminiscent of *theōsis* or divinization in the Eastern Orthodox traditions. Thus Christ's divinity does not contradict his humanity, but rather fulfills it.

It is the human person, along with the world, which "evolves" in this evolutionary worldview. Persons are called to this evolution via transcendence. In responding to the innate call of God in persons (*Vorgriff*), persons transcend themselves and follow their "God-orientedness." This active-transcendence "must be understood as real *self-transcendence*, as surpassing oneself, as emptiness actively achieving its own fullness."[53] In other words, in knowing matter as that which is teleologically ordained to communicate spirit, persons transcend matter. As matter themselves, persons move towards this *telos* as well and, in so doing, assists with the "active transformation of the material world itself."[54] Christ remains God's guaranteed offer of self-communication. "God's self-communication must have a permanent beginning and in this beginning a guarantee that it has taken place, a guarantee by which it can rightly demand a free decision to accept this divine self-communication."[55] Of course, the person remains free to either accept or reject this offer. Accepting the offer entails entering into "the movement of the world and of the spirit."[56] In so doing, a person "really

---

52. Rahner's view of the cosmos as evolutionary is not to be understood in the Darwinian biological sense. For Rahner, the cosmos (created nature) is ever seeking to evolve and self-realize its *telos* by striving (evolving) towards Spirit (super-nature). He understands the cosmos as an ever-evolving organically upward spiral from nature towards super-nature (Spirit, "Holy Mystery," the Divine, or God).

53. Rahner, *Foundations of Christian Faith*, 184.

54. Ibid., 187.

55. Ibid., 193.

56. Ibid., 192.

comes to himself for the first time, and comes to God and to his goal, the goal in which the absolute beginning itself in its immediacy is [the] goal."[57]

Sacramentally, Christ is where it all begins in that the Christ, as God's self-expressing Logos, serves as the primordial sacrament. As primordial sacrament, Christ "is the historically real and actual presence of the eschatologically victorious mercy of God."[58] As such, the Incarnation reconciles God with the material world. This is "the fundamental assertion of Christology . . . precisely that God became flesh, became matter."[59] The life of Jesus is a continuous stream of real symbols through which God self-expresses in a concrete fashion. A real symbol here refers to that which genuinely expresses and presents its being (its inherent symbolic reality) in the world, which is distinct from a mere arbitrary sign, signal or code. In this way, sacraments are real symbols of God. Furthermore, the life of Jesus is a continuous presentation of sacramental symbols in the world. "The sacraments are expressly described in theology as 'sacred signs' of God's grace that is as, 'symbols,' an expression which occurs expressly in this context."[60] Jesus' life, death, and resurrection (re)present God's self in the world. In other words, the person of Jesus Christ happens when God "self-exteriorizes." The Incarnation, Rahner insists, is, "what God wished to be, in free grace, to the world."[61] When God expresses God's self outside of God (outside the Trinity), the divine God-man of Jesus Christ happens. The incarnated Christ stands as the primordial sacrament and functions as a constitutive catalyst for sacramentality as such. Put differently, Christ for Rahner, in and through the Incarnation, constitutes the conditions necessary for created nature to actualize its sacramental potential. Herein lays the emphasis on 'Catholic substance.' The claim that Christ *causes* sacramentality entails important theological implications for Rahner's Christian soteriology and Christian theology of religions, which will come up again below in the section below, in which Ranher's sacramental cosmology is discussed.

Understanding Christ as the primordial sacrament means that He is to be understood as "the real presence in history of the victorious eschatological mercy of God in the world."[62] As a sacramental symbol, Christ makes God present in a real and intentional way. Christ does not function as a mere sign pointing away from himself to God. Rather through symbolic actualization,

---

57. Ibid.
58. Rahner, *The Church and the Sacraments*, 14.
59. Rahner, *Foundations of Christian Faith*, 196 (italics his).
60. Rahner, "The Theology of the Symbol," 241.
61. Ibid., 237.
62. Rahner, *Kirche und Sakramente*, 99.

Christ points inward to Himself and thus to God's very self in the concrete historical world. When God expresses God's self in the world, Jesus Christ, the fully human and fully divine being, happens or appears. This is what is meant by God going out from God's self via self-exteriorization.[63] Hence, since the Incarnation communicates God to the world in and through the very process of communication, the communicative method itself is made divine; that is, in God expressing God's self through the human person of Jesus Christ, the expressive mode of humanity is instilled with divine teleological potential. In and through the reception of God's self, the historical Jesus of Nazareth is at-oned with God (God's self-communication). In the process, Jesus exercised his anthropological trait of transcendence and expressed God in the world as the "absolute savior."

As the "absolute savior," Jesus Christ, according to Rahner, demonstrates the reception and acceptance of God's self-communication. Jesus as savior is a historical person whose life functions sacramentally. Rahner insists that it would be wrong to deem the event of Jesus Christ as the inaugural commencement event in God's agenda of moving the cosmos towards its *telos*, but rather is a definitive, or absolute, point in the process which has already begin. Jesus Christ as the absolute savior marks the irrevocability of "God's absolute self-communication to the spiritual world as a whole."[64] It would also be misleading to deem the Christ event the conclusion of God's self-communication, but rather marks the "climax" and beginning of the fullness of time. "The whole movement of this history of God's self-communication lives by virtue of its moving towards its goal or its climax in the event by which it becomes irrevocable, and hence precisely by virtue of what we are calling the absolute savior."[65]

With reference to soteriology, Christianity for Rahner is the absolute religion and Christ is the absolute norm by which all others ought to be measured. Hence his soteriology is Christocentric. However, this cannot be separated from his anthropology. Since his anthropology maintains the prethematic trait of the supernatural existential, Rahner insists on the universal salvific will of God. Since all humans naturally experience God as the horizon of experience, be it implicitly or explicitly, then God must somehow will the salvation for all, regardless of whether or not one explicitly confesses membership within the Christian Church. Therefore, all persons are potentially 'saved' regardless of their explicit faith commitment or explicit knowledge of Christ. This leads to Rahner's well-known "anonymous Christian"

---

63. Rahner, "The Theology of the Symbol," 239.
64. Rahner, *Foundations of the Christian Faith*, 194.
65. Ibid., 195.

soteriology which accommodates the salvation of all while retaining the absoluteness and uniqueness of Christ as the sole savior and mediator. Thus Rahner's soteriology remains Christocentric, not theocentric. Christ remains at the center moving salvation along *constitutively*; that is, Christ creates the necessary conditions for salvation to take place.[66]

Rahner's anthropology informs, and is intimately connected to, his Christology. Jesus, as a fully divine human, transcended his own human nature and achieved oneness with God. This transcendence is not a onetime event, but rather is a part of a transcendence which takes place in all human creatures. All people have the potential to actualize their mutual intercommunication between self and God, and thus all share the same teleological goal. This transcendence, though potentially taking place in all humans, was actualized definitively only in one person, Jesus of Nazareth, who communicates (via the Incarnation) the potential of human transcendence and self-actualization. Interestingly, for Rahner, the hypostatic union of Jesus and the divine Logos was not a unique instance, but rather served as a communicative symbol of revelation. The God-Man did not enter human existence once and for all, bring it to fulfillment, and leave it behind, but rather communicated the *telos* of self-transcendence to which all human creatures are called. This implies that the Incarnation serves as the climax towards which the whole world is directed. However, it is only a beginning, not an end. The hypostatic union is a union towards which all humanity strives.

In approaching Rahner's understanding of the hypostatic union, the utter humanity of Jesus must be kept in mind. Jesus "cannot simply be God himself as acting in the world, but must be a part of the cosmos, a moment within its history, and indeed at its climax . . . Jesus is truly man, truly a part of the earth."[67] In his humanity, and like all humans are invited to, Jesus "lived out the acceptance of the grace bestowed on him by God and of the immediacy to God which he possess as man."[68] In the hypostatic union, "God lays hold of matter when the Logos becomes flesh, and does so precisely at that point of unity at which matter becomes conscious of itself and spirit possesses its own essential being in the objectifications of matter, that

---

66. In other words, Christ is *causal* of salvation in that Christ *causes* salvation. For example, this view, which is often quite representative of an inclusivist model of Christian theology of religions, claims that a Buddhist or an atheist, regardless of his or her explicit knowledge or practice of the Christian faith can still be saved, through Christ without explicit knowledge of Christ. In this way, they are anonymous Christians if they are faithful to their transcendence.

67. Rahner, *Foundations of the Christian Faith*, 195.

68. Ibid.

is, he does so in the unity of a spiritually human nature."[69] In the process, matter and spirit are joined and at-oned. This self-transcendence demonstrated in the hypostatic union in Jesus Christ serves as a model, for "such an ultimate and absolute self-transcendence of the spirit into God is to be understood as taking place in *all* spiritual subjects."[70]

All persons are invited to participate in this transcendental act by virtue of their humanity. In responding to God's offer of grace (which is offered to all since God universally wills salvation), one can freely accept, participate, and cooperate with it, and transcend via self-actualization toward God. This is divinization and what many Christian traditions might refer to as sanctifying grace. According to this scheme, Rahner does not conceive of a God that saves all, but rather a God that universally wills that all be saved in offering grace to all. Persons, in their freedom, must still respond to (or reject) the offer of grace in an effort to transcend towards God.

Jesus, as the divine logos, serves the communicative function of expressing God's self to the world in the most concrete and definitive way possible. After the ascension, this fully definitive concrete expression is no longer manifest; hence Rahner's insistence on the sacramental function of the *ekklesia*. It is the Church that continues to make Christ present in the world. As Jesus personally (hypostatically) and sacramentally makes God present in history, the Church makes Jesus sacramentally present in history. For Rahner, Jesus and the Church are not just any sacraments, among many, to be placed alongside others, but rather they serve as the primordial and fundamental sacraments respectively. Jesus is the primordial sacrament from which the church flows and the church is the fundamental sacrament from which other sacraments flow.

In the Rahnerian scheme, Christ's presence in time and space (via the church) functions as the commencement point for sacramental theology. He writes, "In the Church God's grace is given expression and embodiment and symbolized, and by being so embodied, is present."[71] Understanding Christ as God's Word expressed in Jesus in time and space implies that the Church, in and through Christ, makes God sacramentally present in time and space. The result of such sacramental occasions yield grace, which Rahner deems as that which happens when God expresses God's self outside of God; that is, grace is God's self-expression outside the Trinity. Since the whole of reality is understood as 'symbolic' according to Rahner, and is

---

69. Ibid., 196
70. Ibid., 198 (italics his).
71. Rahner, *The Church and the Sacraments*, 34.

engraced (grace-given), it holds the potential for sacramentality, though not always actualized. He writes,

> The Church in her visible historical form is herself an intrinsic symbol of the eschatologically triumphant grace of God; in that spatiotemporal visible form, this grace is made present. And because the sacraments are the actual fulfillment, the actualization of the Church's very nature, in regard to individual men, precisely in as much as the Church's whole reality is to be the real presence of God's grace, as the new covenant, these sacramental signs are efficacious . . . this presence (by signifying) of grace in the sacraments is simply the actuality of the Church herself as the visible manifestation of grace.[72]

This hints at the core of Rahner's sacramental theology and begins to make clear the Christological and ecclesiological commencement point in making Christ, and thus God, present. Michael Himes comments, "There are occasions in which the church communicates itself most effectively, when it says as deeply, intentionally and intently as it can, 'This is who we are.' Those occasions are called sacraments . . . Rahner maintained that 'word' is the operative element in the sacraments. The Word of God in the flesh of Jesus of Nazareth; Jesus' great word is the church, and the church's great words of self-expression are the sacraments."[73]

Grace here is understood as God's communication of God's self outside the Trinity. The most basic theological question of all might simply be 'what is God?" If the author of 1 John is taken seriously in his claim that "God is love"[74] (*agapē*), then by applying this predicate to a Rahnerian worldview, one might argue, with Himes, that "God's communication of God's self, God's Word, addressed to us in our world is what we mean by grace . . . God is an eternal explosion of love."[75] This entails that Jesus, the personification of God, is the personification of *agapē* who wholly gave himself over to others. The classic Christian doctrine of the Trinity understands the Godhead as one god in three "persons." For Rahner, all beings are constantly striving to express themselves. The Trinity in the Rahnerian sense might be understood as God constantly expressing God's self and, in so doing, constantly outpouring God's self unto God's self within the Godhead. In the outpouring of God's self outside the Trinity, God demonstrates

---

72. Ibid., 39.
73. Himes, *Doing the Truth in Love*, 106.
74. 1 John 4:8.
75. Himes, *Doing the Truth in Love*, 103.

creativity; that is, creation is the result of God loving (expressing God's self) outside the Trinity.

In this way, God's outpouring of God's self sustains and grounds all that exists. This is not to be understood as a pantheistic cosmology entailing identity and co-dependence between creator (lover) and creation (the beloved), as perhaps Hegel surmised. God would still be God without creating outside the Godhead. It follows that for Rahner all of creation is saturated with grace. The whole universe is engraced since God has loved it into existence through self-expression. Further, this entails that God is to be found in all things since God is communicating God's self through all things. Rahner's insistence on the Ignatian principle of 'finding God in all things' was foundational to both his spiritual and theological development. Central to making such a claim necessitates an adequate theology of grace. In Rahner's approach, diffusive grace is not only present, but experiential. Philip Endean points out that "If grace, the divine self-gift, is necessarily an experiential reality, then *all* grace is mystical. Moreover, if it is God's will that all human beings should be saved and come to knowledge of God's truth, God's grace must be present throughout the creation."[76] This is a central concern of Rahner's; that the Christian God is a God that can be experienced, since God is incessantly self-communicating God's self to all of creation. It serves as one of the foundational presuppositions for this chapter in sketching his vision of the cosmos as sacramental. Further, for the larger scope of this book, the spiritual implications of such a view are striking, in that lived religious experience in concrete reality becomes a real experiential possibility.

Rahnerian "Symbolic Reality"

The main concern of this chapter is to provide an adequate view of Rahner's ontology of symbolic reality and the resulting sacramental and symbolic theology. Since it can be difficult to make sense of his ontology without a preliminary understanding of his Christology, I first offered a brief reflection on the fundamentals of his Christology and ecclesiology above. Geoffrey Kelly properly recognizes this when he observes that for Rahner, "sacraments are fundamentally an outgrowth of his Christology [and] sacrament and symbol are intertwined."[77] For Rahner, a symbol makes present that which it symbolizes. In this way, Christ is understood as a symbol of salvation since Christ makes present the possibility of salvation.

76. Endean, "Introduction," 15.
77. Kelly, *Karl Rahner*, 281.

Sacraments (re)present God via grace, thus they function symbolically as mediators of grace which is God's gift of God's self outside the Trinity. In short, sacraments are symbols of grace. In this way, both Christ and the *ekklesia* serve as symbolic expressions of God and Christ respectively. A central ontological claim of Rahner is that "all beings are by their nature symbolic, because they necessarily 'express' themselves in order to attain their own nature."[78] As symbols, all beings constantly strive to 'tell you what they are.' Further, "all beings (each of them, in fact) are multiple, and are or can be essentially the expression of another in this unity of the multiple and one in this plurality, by reason of its plural unity."[79] In other words, a human being might be multiple in that she has multiple relations to other beings (e.g., mother, daughter, teacher, student, aunt, niece, friend, employee, citizen, and supervisor). However, in her plural unity, she remains one person; that is, she remains the same single solitary unified being.

Rahner writes, "It is therefore true: a being is, of itself, independently of any comparison with anything else, plural in its unity."[80] A being, created in the image of God, contains this plurality in its unity, since the Godhead itself contains the Trinitarian plurality in its unity. For Rahner, each being "possesses a plurality as intrinsic" and this plurality "constitutes itself . . . in such a way that that which is originated and different is in agreement with its origin and hence has the character of expression or 'symbol' with regard to its origin."[81] It follows that persons, as beings, are intrinsically plural in their unity "in agreement with their origin" (God) and are necessarily symbols, for "being is of itself symbolic, because it necessarily 'expresses' itself."[82] Human creatures express their being in this Rahnerian symbolic way of giving themselves away to the other. He writes that each being "expresses itself and possesses itself by doing so. It gives itself away from itself into the 'other,' [and] there finds itself in knowledge and love."[83]

In chapter 11, I provide a more in-depth analysis of the philosophical function of sacraments and religious symbols. In that chapter I distinguish between sign and symbol. Here it is necessary to only offer an overview of the distinction set within a Rahnerican context. Whereas a sign points *out* from itself *towards* reality, a symbol points *in* to itself *as* reality. For instance, a traffic light functions as a sign by pointing to the reality stopping or not

---

78. Rahner, "The Theology of the Symbol," 224.
79. Ibid., 225–26.
80. Ibid., 227.
81. Ibid., 229.
82. Ibid.
83. Ibid., 230.

stopping. It does not function as a symbol and create the reality of stopping or not stopping as such. There is nothing intrinsic to the colors red or green that mean stop or not stop. It could be orange and blue all the same.[84] Symbols, on the other hand, point inward due to their intrinsic meaning. They point to something intrinsic which could not be expressed in any other way.[85] Weeping and laughter function symbolically this way. They are outward signs of an inward experience. They make present that which they symbolize. A sign does not do this. A sign points out to something else (e.g., the reality of stopping or not) while a symbol points inward to its intrinsic meaning by expressing itself externally (e.g., a hug does not point to the reality of affection, a hug *is* affectionate).[86]

For Rahner, symbols are unlike arbitrary signs, signals and codes. Real symbols make real that which they symbolize, whereas a sign merely points to something else beyond it without rendering it present. There is an ontological thrust at work with the symbol, and it is fitting that a pansacramental proposal such as the one I advocate for later in this book begins with the basic principle of a Rahnerian ontology of symbol: "all beings are by their nature symbolic, because they necessarily 'express' themselves in order to attain their own nature."[87] Real symbols make real that which they symbolize by expressing their very being. As such, symbols attain their own nature. A real symbol is a "supreme and primal representation, in which one reality renders another present (primarily 'for itself' and only secondarily for others)."[88]

Rahner's ontology in this sense deviates little from the Thomist position that maintains that a symbol (sacrament) causes what it symbolizes. Rahner writes, "The 'effect' [of a symbol] is the 'cause' itself, in so far as the cause itself is the reality, the 'act' of the material cause, which is becoming its own 'potency.'"[89] By expressing itself, a symbol makes real what it symbolizes. Unlike signs, sacraments act as symbols by making present the reality they symbolize. Unlike signs, which serve as pointers pushing one away from itself, sacraments draw one in to the depth of reality. The process whereby a symbol makes real that which it symbolizes is called 'self-realization.' "The symbol" writes Rahner, "strictly speaking (symbolic reality) is the self-realization of a being in the other, which is constitutive

---

84. Himes offers the example of the traffic light in *Doing the Truth in Love*, 106.
85. Ibid., 106–7.
86. Ibid.
87. Rahner, "The Theology of the Symbol," 224.
88. Ibid., 225 (parenthetical his).
89. Ibid., 232.

of its essence."⁹⁰ Human creatures also have the potential to serve as living sacraments when they self-express, through self-realization, symbolize, and (re)present God (e.g., in community⁹¹). On a cosmological level, since the cosmos is that which happens when God expresses God's self outside the Trinity and imparts grace to all things, then all things constantly strive to self-realize by (re)presenting God in and through itself in time and space. The implications of such a cosmology may lend itself to understanding the cosmos, and all things therein, as maintaining potential sacramentality; thus all reality holds the potential to function symbolically, hence Rahner's preferred term 'symbolic reality.'⁹²

The Trinity remains central to a Thomistic ontological scheme in its insistence that a sacrament effects what it signifies. In a similar way, Christology remains at the center of a theology of symbolic realities. Rahner writes, "The attentive reader . . . will not have failed to remark that the thought of the mystery of the *Trinity* was the constant background of the ontological considerations . . . If a theology of symbolic realties is to be written, Christology, the doctrine of the incarnation of the Word, will obviously form the central chapter."⁹³ Foundational to Rahner's project here is the role of Christ as the absolute and primary symbol of God in the world. Christ is not only constitutive of salvation, but of all created reality as symbolic as well. He insists that Christ remains necessary for both salvation and symbolic reality, which is to say that there must be a means by which the person and function of Christ substantially contribute to, or necessitate, the conditions upon which the world and salvation exist. "Theology of symbolic reality," writes Rahner," is based on the truth that the Logos, as Word of the Father, expresses the Father in the 'abbreviation' of this human nature and constitutes the symbol which communicates him to the world."⁹⁴ The cosmological worldview that views all creation as a potential communicative vehicle to express God's self symbolically is founded and established on the incarnate Christ, who is the expression of God's self in the world. Rahner understands that this "natural depth of the symbolic reality of all things . . . has now in ontological reality received an infinite extension by the fact that this reality has become also determination of the Logos himself or his milieu."⁹⁵ At the center of all reality lies God by virtue of being created by the creator. Thus,

90. Ibid., 234.
91. Matthew 18:20.
92. Rahner, "Theology of the Symbol," 234.
93. Ibid., 235, 237.
94. Ibid., 240.
95. Ibid., 239.

all reality is able to symbolize God, and this is possible *because* of Christ as the primary sacrament. Rahner writes,

> Every God-given reality . . . states much more than itself: each in its own way is an echo and indication of all reality. If the individual reality, by making the all present, also speaks God . . . this transcendence is made radical . . . by the fact that in Christ this reality no longer refers to God merely as its cause: it points to God as to him to whom this reality belongs as his substantial determination or as his own proper environment. *All things are held together by the incarnate Word in whom they exist (Col 1.17), and hence all things possess, even in their quality of symbol, an unfathomable depth, which faith alone can sound.*"[96]

Clearly the Incarnation remains central to Rahner's project, for it not only constitutes salvific conditions, but imports meaning to all creation and history.[97] It makes possible the reality of God speaking definitively to persons in a language that they can understand clearly and concretely. Himes eloquently states, "Jesus of Nazareth is the human translation of the Word, God's perfect self-expression in human terms. Jesus is the Word said in our language, in a way we can grasp as human beings."[98] In this way, the Christ functions primordially and constitutively of symbolic, and thus sacramental, reality.

In the eighth century, St. John of Damascus, representing the Byzantine Church, successfully combated iconoclasm through apologetics grounded firmly and centrally in the Incarnation. St. John writes, "It is obvious when you contemplate God becoming man, then you may depict Him clothed in human form. When the invisible One becomes visible to flesh, you may then draw His likeness."[99] In other words, the Incarnation radically changed history by leaving an indelible mark on the theology of the symbol. Through the Incarnation, he sought to retain the validity of the symbolic icon in Christian life, liturgy and veneration. He argued that since God had become a created human and hypostatically joined the divine and human, then created persons have the potential to image God. Therefore, media (icons, paint, wood, stone, etc.) are able to depict this image. Rahner's transcendental Christology and anthropology are clearly based on a similar argument grounded in the constitutivness of Christ. The media, through which God is depicted, is not God's self nor an idol or a demon, but rather

---

96. Ibid., (italics mine).
97. Vorgrimler, *Sacramental Theology*, 38.
98. Himes, *Doing the Truth in Love*, 104.
99. John Damascus, *On the Divine Images*, 1, 8, 18.

as a symbols, they function sacramentally in depicting God. Painted icons and the incarnation of the Christ in Jesus are not understood as equivalent expressions of God, but rather the point here is that the Incarnation makes possible the potentiality of the icon to serve as a medium for the symbolic expression of God.

Prefiguring Pansacramental and Panentheistic Possibilities[100]

Drawing on both Aquinas and Rahner, in the remaining pages of this chapter I suggest a beginning to how the cosmos may be understood as pansacramental and possibly panentheistic, for a cosmos understood thusly remains clarifying for the overall trajectory of the book. According to Rahner, the universe is what happens when God expresses God's self outside the Trinity, thus all things contain the potency to symbolize grace. Further, it follows that all things are constantly striving to body forth their essence through self-realization. In so doing, God is expressed. This is what is meant by Rahner's 'symbolic reality;' that is, a cosmos in which all things are potentially sacramental, thus a pansacramental cosmos.

A central premise for understanding sacramental language as an adequate mediator is the claim that the cosmos is pansacramental; that is, if the cosmos can be presumed to be filled with God, then it might be understood as containing an infinite reservoir of sacramental potential (e.g., Lake Superior or dancing). This might entail understanding the cosmos pan*en*theistically or pantheistically, which is to say that God is in all things regardless of how one construes it, whether all things are *in* God (panentheism) or all things *are* God (pantheism).[101] The idea here is to examine how a pansacramental understanding of the cosmos is important for grounding the argument about the necessity of sacramental language.

If Aquinas is correct that 'God is in all things, and innermostly,' then to claim that the cosmos is pansacramental and base it on a Thomist theology, is not unrealistic. That much seems clear, but a further question might be asked here: that is, whether some form of Christian panentheism is possible while still retaining many of the classical Christian Thomist tenants. The burden here is to briefly spell out a possible Thomist pansacramentality and

---

100. A version of this section was published as Gustafson, "Collapsing the Sacred and the Profane."

101. At this point, I am not attempting to make an argument here for one of these over the other, since both might accommodate my proposal. However, I prefer panentheism to pantheism for a number of reasons laid out in the final chapters of this book.

inquire about a classical Christian Thomist panentheism. Although I personally have no particular preference for the retention of Thomist language, categories, and philosophy, I realize that many Christian thinkers do.

It would of course be anachronistic to claim that Aquinas was an explicit panentheist. The word itself was not coined until the eighteenth century by Karl Krause.[102] Since there are a variety of panentheisms, it is necessary here to be clear about what is meant by the term. Chapter twelve explains the contours of panentheism in much greater detail, but here it is necessary to introduce the topic. Charles Hartshorne offers some clarity on the matter when he writes, "'Panentheism' is an appropriate term for the view that deity is in some real aspect distinguishable from and independent of any and all relative items, and yet, taken as an actual whole, includes all relative items."[103] God and world are related in that the world is in God and God is in the world, however it might be construed. I suggest that this is one of the fundamental tenets of any panentheism: *the world (all things) is in God and God is in the world (all things)*.[104] A commonly accepted generic definition of the term comes from *The Oxford Dictionary of the Christian Church*, "The Being of God includes and penetrates the whole universe, so that every part exists in Him, but His Being is more than, and not exhausted by, the universe."[105] God need not be reduced to the world in such a view, though some panentheists may hold that. The world might be in God and God might be in the world, yet God's being might go vastly beyond the world. There are many versions of panentheism, thus it is more appropriate to speak of panentheisms.

Within contemporary scholarship on panentheism, one of the main debates takes place over the ontological status of the term "in" in the claim that "all is in God." Panentheists do not all agree on the ontological function of the term "in." In chapters twelve and thirteen I take up some of these various panentheisms and propose a panentheistic pansacramentalism, however for the sake of fleshing out a Thomist panentheism here, which remains the concern of this section, it is sufficient to explicate the term "in" for Aquinas. Recall the "great syllogism" of Aquinas, as expressed by Gilson: "God is very being (*esse*) by His own essence . . . being (*esse*) is innermost in each thing and most fundamentally inherent in all things since it is formal in respect of everything found in a thing . . . Hence, it must be that God is

---

102. Gregersen, "Three Varieties of Panentheism," 28.

103. Hartshorne, *The Divine Relativity*, 89.

104. A popular panentheistic refrain likens God to the sea and all things to fish, thus as all fish are in the sea and the sea is in all fish, so too all things are in God and God is in all things.

105. "Panentheism," in *The Oxford Dictionary of the Christian Church*.

in all things, and innermostly."¹⁰⁶ Thus God, according to Aquinas is in all things by way of being. But how are all things to be understood as "in" God according to a Thomist panentheism?

Prior to addressing the question directly, notice that a key challenge to any Christian panentheistic proposal concerns how to retain the distinction between God and world. In other words, a common question levied against any panentheism, in its failure to completely distinguish between God and world, is: 'if the world no longer existed, then would God also cease to exist?' I suggest here that it is not necessary for a panentheist to maintain God's dependence on the world.¹⁰⁷ God can be understood to be in the world, and the world in God, without reducing God to the world or making God's existence dependent on the world's existence. Working on this presupposition, we can propose an answer to the question of whether or not a Thomist might embrace panentheism, and in the process address the ontological question of how all things are in God.

Aquinas does not employ the language of (or even the word) 'panentheism.' What he does say, however, leaves no reason to think that he would have rejected some construal of a Christian panentheism, though certainly his theology is incompatible with many variations. In question eight of the *Summa Theologica* he writes, "God is in things as containing them . . . it is said that all things are in God; inasmuch as they are contained by Him."¹⁰⁸ With the fundamental tenet of panentheism in mind, on the face of Aquinas' writing here, it would seem that he certainly satisfies, at the very least, one of the components: *God is in the world (all things)*. For Aquinas, God fills all places, not as a body occupies a space (this is accidental), but rather God's very ontological being as *esse* constitutes the necessary conditions by which all things exist in the first place. Thus, God's occupation of a space does not exclude other entities from occupying that very same space simultaneously. The example Aquinas uses is that of the soul occupying all parts of the body without excluding or negating the existence of the other parts. In other words, God provides the very ground of being for all things, and by virtue of that fact alone, *the world is in God (all things)* in that all

---

106. Thomas Aquinas, *Summa Theologica*, I, 8, 1.

107. This might be the argument of Hegel (i.e., logic dictates that the infinite is dependent on the finite; that is, the finite is within the infinite, which entails the presence of God in the world). However, this clearly clashes with Aquinas' theology of creation. Anselm Min articulates this when he points out that for Aquinas, "creation is not a necessary emanation from God's own essence; it is product of God's self-knowledge in the Word and self-love in the Spirit, freely created to share in God's own goodness by participating in the exemplarity of the Son" (Min, *Paths to the Triune God*, 41).

108. Thomas Aquinas, Summa *Theologica*, [I, 8, 1] & [I, 18, 4].

things exist (and subsist) in God, thus possibly satisfying the other half of the panentheistic definition.

I recognize a plurality of panentheisms.[109] Though traditional panentheism might entail the understanding of God as mutable, temporal, and thus influenced by the world, not all forms of panentheism make these claims. For instance, self-described panentheist Arthur Peacocke, along with other notable Eastern Orthodox panentheists,[110] insist on a panentheistic model in which God is not affected by the world.[111] In so doing, they are able to maintain God's omnipotence and immutability. This might be distinguished from fellow panentheists who insist that the world does affect God and thus posit a more dynamic understanding of God.[112] The main point here is that panentheists do not share an understanding of the Godhead. Panentheism is subject to both internal critique (panentheist vs. panentheist) and external critique (non-panentheist vs. panentheist).

For Aquinas, how might all things exist in God? As the uncaused cause and primordial principle of existence, God is more intimate to a thing than a thing is to itself. For God is that which gives being (that which gives God's self, *esse*) to all things and is therefore present to all things. "God is in all things by essence—not by essence of the things themselves, as if God were of their essence,[113] but by God's own essence, because the divine substance is present to all things as the cause of their being."[114] This rejection of pantheism serves as a key distinction to be kept in mind for any attempt seeking to plead the case for a Thomist panentheism (as Matthew Fox has done).[115]

The case for a Thomist panentheism can resonate with, what I term, sacramental panentheism or a pansacramental cosmology. Founded on Aquinas' theology of creation, which commences with God as the first principle, all creation is to be understood as that which is bodied forth by God's self-expression in the world. He writes, "the emanation of all being from the universal cause, which is God; and this emanation we designate by the name of creation."[116] The use of the term 'emanation' here preserves the distinction between creator and creation. In other words, all of creation receives its be-

---

109. For a good overview of the varieties of panentheism, see Culp, "Panentheism"; and Gregersen, "Three Varieties of Panentheism."

110. Andrew Louth, Alexei V. Nesteruk, and Kallistos Ware.

111. Culp, "Panentheism."

112. Many Process theologians claim this.

113. Thus Aquinas rejects pantheism.

114. Thomas Aquinas, *Summa Theologica*, I, 8, 3.

115. Fox, *Sheer Joy*, 67–73.

116. Thomas Aquinas, *Summa Theologica*, I, 45, 1.

ing from God, who is being itself. In this way, all things are to be understood as effects of God and thus allow for the possibility of all rational creatures to know God. According to Aquinas, it is from God's effects that it can be demonstrated whether God exists. This method is held together on the logic that if one knows the effect, then the cause can be deduced. If it is the case that there are effects from God (creation), then it is the case that God exists. This does not entail that we can deduce *what* God is in God's own eternal essence, but it does entail that we can deduce *that* God is. Furthermore, we can know what God is as reflected in the created world; although, this remains incomplete.

Among the *quinque viae*, Aquinas demonstrates God's existence through the Aristotelian concept of motion. Since motion (change) is self-evident in the cosmos, and understood as actualized effects, one is able to reason back to the cause. All things move from potency to act by way of time. With this in mind, an examination of cosmic motion yields the deist formula: for every move there is a mover, for every change there is a changer, and for every mover there is another mover and so on regressively back through time to the first mover (God) that sets the world in motion. Of course, for Aquinas, God is the original mover; the unmoved mover of movers. However, Aquinas is no deist, for God maintains an intimate and continual involvement with the cosmos always and in all ways, which is compatible with most variations of panentheism.

All things are to be understood as effects of God with the potentiality for being recognized as sacramental occasions. Aquinas maintains that all things (effects) are perfected when they return to their source. Effects of God can function sacramentally since they are created by God and, as such, carry the likeness of God.[117] Aquinas writes,

> An effect is most perfect when it returns to its source; thus, the circle is the most perfect of all figures, and circular motion the most perfect of all motions, because in their case a return is made to the starting point. It is therefore necessary that creatures return to their principle in order that the universe of creatures may attain its ultimate perfection. Now, each and every creature returns to its source so far as it bears a likeness to its source, according to its being and its nature, wherein it enjoys a certain perfection.[118]

Anthropologically, this may be understood as the teleological journey of the human person as coming from God and returning to God. This is the

---

117. Thomas Aquinas, *Summa Contra Gentiles*, I, 29, 2.
118. Thomas Aquinas, *Summa Contra Gentiles*, II, 46, 2.

teleological desire for all things; that is, all things aim for a return to their source and *telos* in order to achieve perfection. A further implication entails that all things, including persons and other living creatures, are images of God with the potency and desire to be perfected by returning to their principle: God. In short, a Thomist theology of creation sets the tone and lays the groundwork for positing a pansacramental cosmology and a sacramental panentheism.

∽

This chapter aimed to offer a foundational and influential backdrop for sacramental theology in the Western Christian traditions (e.g., Rahner and Aquinas). It will serve as the basis going forward. However as the next short chapter attempts to show, a Thomist-Rahnerian platform (that employs Aristotelian metaphysics) need not be the only foundational sacramental theology for a pansacramental proposal such as the one offered in this book. The next chapter will turn to the postmodern sacramental theology of Louis-Marie Chauvet in an effort to show an approach to sacramentality that is not dependent on Greek substance metaphysics.

6

Louis-Marie Chauvet
Beyond Aristotle and Aquinas

MANY POSTMODERN AND CONTEMPORARY theologians claim that the ontotheological categories of Thomist philosophical metaphysics no longer provide an adequate framework to address contemporary theological concerns and issues. Louis-Marie Chauvet, the contemporary French sacramental theologian, is one such thinker who found Scholastic theology insufficiently equipped to respond to questions of the time. Here I set out to make the point that though one might rightly find Aristotelian substance metaphysics wanting, this does not entail negating neither the promise of sacramentality to mediate nor the approach to the cosmos as pansacramental. In fact, one may determine that by liberating it from such substance metaphysics, the case for pansacramental functionality it strengthened. This chapter offers one postmodern approach, that of Chauvet, and the boon such an approach might bring to the conversation about sacramentality.

Heavily influenced by European linguists, deconstructionists, and philosophers (e.g., Heidegger), Chauvet's central aim is to make the move from understanding sacraments as causal instruments dependent on 'being' as such and separated from language, to understanding sacraments as symbolic mediators dependent precisely on language. One of his central complaints concerns the addition of instrumental causality (efficacy) to Augustine's claim that a sacrament is "the sign of a sacred thing."[1] In this way, sacraments not only present grace as a sign, but also cause grace as an instrumental cause. Thus what for Aquinas (and his twelfth century cohorts)

---

1. Chauvet, *Symbol and* Sacrament, 13.

was an instrumental cause, for Chauvet becomes a symbolic mediator. The claim I intend to make here is that regardless of which assertion one hitches his wagon to, the fundamental assertion remains: sacramentality and sacramental language remain a crucial "paradigm in which to conceive of divine-human communication."[2]

Central to Chauvet's project is the typical postmodern move in rejecting metaphysics. Following Heidegger, Chauvet states that "metaphysics believes itself to have produced an explanation of being, when in fact it has ontically reduced being to metaphysics' *representations*, utterly forgetting that nothing that exists 'is.'"[3] The complaint is that scholastic theology presumes what many postmodern thinkers find questionable, which is essentially that 'the mind conforms to reality'[4] and is capable of grasping objective reality as such. What is more, they question the claim that language can adequately express the ontological realities it describes. This is further problematized when applied to so-called spiritual realities such as grace. In the way Kant sought to de-ontologize ethics,[5] Chauvet sought to de-ontologize sacramental theology, which is to say both sought to articulate their respective fields without dependence on ontology. Chauvet's postmodern claim here is that reality is a linguistic and symbolic construct imbued with meaning provided by one's cultural context, thus 'reality conforms to the mind'[6] via language.

Religious traditions and cultures all have their own set of rituals, movements, expressions, and thus, in a strong sense, their own unique languages. The world that non-believers live in is different from the world in which believers live in. Likewise, the Protestant world, with their own set of rituals and language, differs from the Catholic world. The presence of the divine is perceived in different ways depending on one's religious context and orientation, and therefore the symbols through which God's presence is manifest varies.[7] However, according to Chauvet, the presence of God is

---

2. Boeve, "Theology in a Postmodern Context and the Hermeneutical Project of Louis-Marie Chauvet," 12.

3. Chauvet, *Symbol and Sacrament*, 26–27 (italics his).

4. Kant's 'Copernican Revolution' in philosophy sought to negate the assumption that 'the mind conforms to reality' and proffer instead the reverse: 'reality conforms to the mind.' In this way Kant might rightly be understood as a precursor to postmodern criticism in his calling into question the modern assumptions of rationalism and empiricism.

5. Of course, Kant's deontology also pertained to the examination of *deon* (duty or obligation) in philosophical ethical theory.

6. See footnote 4.

7. Martos, *Doors to the Sacred*, 122.

unlike the presence of all other things. The presence of God is in the world, "not like a 'thing,' but in the gift of his life and his coming-into-presence."[8] The coming-into-presence is the illumination of the absence; hence God's presence is also paradoxically an absence. What is absent for non-believers is made present (or brought-into-presence) via religious symbols, which are called sacraments. Here Chauvet toes the Heideggerian phenomenological line in his insistence that "genuine presence always entails absence."[9]

Sacramental language (via ritual, expressions, gestures, words, images, vestments[10]) creates reality in that it provides meaning for believers within their respective traditions. Chauvet claims that this meaning and reality are provided not by ontological substantiations and transubstantiations, but rather by linguistic structures which thus, in turn, alter the world and the way one views and speaks about it. For instance, it is through linguistic structures that "aliens become citizens, civilians become soldiers, couples become married, pagans become Christians, laymen become priests, and bread and wine becomes the Eucharist."[11] The Eucharist is "*the symbol par excellence* of the *adesse*[12] of Christ giving his life"[13] since it expresses communion with Christ's self through the emptiness of the broken bread. The broken bread leaves a 'hollow' (an absence) which reveals the spiritual body of the glorified Christ (a genuine presence).[14] The emptiness in the 'hollow' is what makes the sacrament a sacrament, for "it shows that *Christ's presence comes forward through the mode of being open.*"[15] This is not an ontological presence to be understood "under the category of metaphysical Being, but under that of the *symbolic Other.*"[16] Chauvet here is making the assertion that it is not the [tran/con]substantiation of the bread, understood ontologi-

---

8. Chauvet, *Symbol and Sacrament*, 404.
9. Morrill, "Building on Chauvet's Work," *xviii*.
10. Martos, *Doors to the Sacred*, 122.
11. Ibid.
12. a*d-esse*; "presence for."
13. Chauvet, *Symbol and Sacrament*, 406 (italics his).
14. 1 Corinthians 15:44; Romans 8:11. To demonstrate this move from closed to open, Chauvet also highlights the story of the Disciples on the Road to Emmaus. He writes, "this topographically round trip [Jerusalem-Emmaus-Jerusalem] is for us the symbolic support of the turn-around in the disciples' hearts during the telling of the story; a passage from non-recognition to recognition, from closed eyes to opened eyes, from giving up the mission to taking up the mission [from 'absence to presence'], and at the level of the group as such, a transition from a state of breakdown ('Peter went to the tomb by himself' as verse 12 shows) and thus of death to a resurrection of the group as the Church" (Chauvet, *Symbol and Sacrament*, 167).
15. Chauvet, *Symbol and Sacrament*, 407 (italics his).
16. Ibid. (italics his).

cally, that renders the *res* ('reality'[17]) of Christ to be present, but rather it lies precisely in the whole Christ, "the *Christus totus*, the Head *and* members."[18]

The *effectus res* of the sacrament is to be understood through symbolic and ritualistic language, since it is the language itself that brings about the symbolic efficacy.[19] Thus a metaphysical understanding is not required. The shared language employed by the subjects of a given religious tradition is what brings about (effects) their particular experience of the divine (spirituality) and worldview. Chauvet writes,

> In order for the subject to reach and retain its status of subject, it must build reality into a "world," that is to say, a signifying whole in which every element, whether material (tree, wind, house) or social (relatives, clothing, cooking, work, leisure) is integrated into a system of *knowledge* (of the world and of society), *gratitude* (code of good manners, mythical and ritual code ruling relationships with deities and ancestors), and *ethical behavior* (values serving as norms of conduct) . . . By these means, the universe and events form a coherent whole which is called "the symbolic order.[20]

Language functions as the creative instrument that gives rise to the world (comprised of, for Chauvet, mainly *knowledge*, *gratitude*, and *ethics*). Symbols are already present in culture, but persons actively and continually engage and re-engage these symbols and thus continually reconstruct them. In this way, Chauvet understands "the practice of Christian identity, the ongoing formation of Christian identity, as a particular engagement in this essential anthropological structure of knowledge, gratitude, and ethics."[21] The ecclesial context provides the environment within which Christians procure and reorient this symbolic order given to them by "the Spirit of the risen Christ," which includes the sacramental symbol *par excellence* of the Eucharist, for it provides "the sacramental experience of Christ's absence as an indwelling presence compelling believers to action."[22]

The ecclesiastical context provides the "symbolic network"[23] within which believers operate. For Chauvet, the Christian faith is, at its most fundamental level, sacramental in structure. This entails the making present of

17. Chauvet here translates *res* to "ultimate reality" (*Symbol and Sacrament*, 407).
18. Ibid.
19. Martos, *Doors to the Sacred*, 122.
20. Chauvet, *The Sacraments*, 13.
21. Morrill, "Building on Chauvet's Work," xix.
22. Ibid., xx.
23. Chauvet, *Symbol and Sacrament*, 157.

the absent; it is the sacramental (re)presentation of that which is not present via symbolic expression. In and through the linguistic (e.g., scripture, worship, creed, code, cult) and symbolic (sacramental) structures of the faith, truth and meaning are brought forth. In this way, Chauvet believes that "traditional and contemporary claims about the sacraments and sacramentality" can be made and "understood without having to have recourse to an outdated and implausible metaphysics,"[24] such as scholastic Thomism. Further, one might claim that within Chauvet's proposal there is a built-in safeguard against idolatry.[25] If the Christian faith is understood as sacramentally mediated and distinguished from the immediate, then one avoids mistaking the immediate for God's very unmediated self.[26] This is achieved by denying the onto-theological presumptions of 1) forgetting "the ontological difference in the attempt to ground the being of beings in a first being" and 2) separating being from language. Embracing these two tenets leads to idolatry since they mistake God as such for what God is not by attempting to "take hold of God and God's grace" apart from situating them within a contextual framework (symbolic, linguistic, cultural, ritualistic, etc.).[27] Thus, Chauvet proposes a scheme which seeks to replace the understanding of language as instrumentally causal with one in which language functions as a mediator of symbolic exchange independent of onto-theological grounding.

Herein lies the essential foundation of Chauvet's theology of sarcamentality, and his central claim of sacramental symbols as mediators. One of the key distinctions to be recognized in Chauvet's approach as opposed to a substance metaphysics approach, with respect to how a symbol effects reality, is the function of its (the symbol's) efficacy. Make no mistake, for Chauvet the symbol still effects reality; it is "an efficacy which touches reality itself." However, reality as such is understood differently by Chauvet than it is for most substance metaphysicians. For Chauvet, reality is not "a 'substrate' or an ontological 'substance,'" but rather it is that which has "already [been] culturally processed," which is to say it is a reality that has

---

24. Martos, *Doors to the Sacred*, 123.

25. Lieven Boeve makes this claim (Boeve, "Theology in a Postmodern Context and the Hermeneutical Project of Louis-Marie Chauvet," 7, 13). However, Vincent J. Miller argues that in Chauvet's project, "Religious symbols are misused not only by those who assume direct, unmediated presence but also by those who coopt them to ideological ends. Chauvet's theology provides no principle of discernment concerning the possibility of the corruption of the Christian symbol tradition" (Miller, "An Abyss at the Heart of Mediation," 230–47).

26. Boeve, "Theology in a Postmodern Context and the Hermeneutical Project of Louis-Marie Chauvet," 13.

27. Ibid., 7.

been already constructed by language. This reality is the truest (the most real) reality there is. As such, to effect reality, persons engage in the "act of symbolization" which "carries out the essential vocation of language: to bring about an alliance where subjects may come into being and recognize themselves as such within their world."[28]

In order to demonstrate that "symbolic efficacy always takes place within the *socio-cultural order*,"[29] Chauvet offers three examples of indigenous religious rites as reported by Lévi-Strauss, Victor Turner, and Eric De Rosny. All three examples demonstrate rites which strive to alleviate some affliction, whether it is a pregnant Kuna Indian woman unable to give birth (Lévi-Strauss), a Ndembu suffering from physical Illness (Turner), or the paralysis of a Douala in Cameroon. The healing rites of these people, according to Chauvet, are all the "same thing: the ritual "acts on the real by acting on the representations of the real."[30] The rite employed by the healer functions as a language which mediates between the sufferer and her pain (experience), and thereby "permits the person to assimilate an actual experience of pain, otherwise anarchic and inexpressible, into an ordered and intelligible form."[31]

For instance, Lévi-Strauss describes the "shamanistic ritual of giving birth among the [Kuna] Indians."[32] A shaman assists a pregnant woman in pain who is unable to give birth. He does so by singing a long mythical story "of a violent combat, woven together from a thousand incidents, between"[33] essentially good and bad representatives. The good are represented by "sacred images (*nuchu*),"[34] which are protective spirits, while the bad is referred to as Muu, which "has taken possession of the 'soul' of the future mother."[35] The Kuna believe that Muu literally resides in the pregnant woman's uterus and vagina, where the so-called battle is waged. According to Lévi-Strauss, the shaman's song provides "a psychological manipulation of the sick organ."[36] The pain experienced by the pregnant human in the birthing process is "incongruent" with the Kuna worldview and the mythical incantation provides meaning (it provides a language). It thus effects what

---

28. Chauvet, *Symbol and Sacrament*, 130.
29. Ibid., 135 (italics his).
30. Ibid., 138.
31. Ibid., 136.
32. Ibid., 135.
33. Ibid.
34. Ibid.
35. Ibid.
36. Lévi-Strauss, *Anthropologie structural*, 211.

it symbolizes: the victory of good over bad—healing over pain and sickness. Important to this scheme is the necessity of belief and proper disposition in relation the Kuna worldview. Lévi-Strauss points out, and Chauvet agrees, that this rite succeeds only because "the sick person believes in it and is a member of a society that believes in it."[37] It fits within their worldview and thus provides linguistic meaning to reality. The shaman provides meaning for a seemingly meaningless experience; that is, "the shaman relocates [it] within a coherent whole."[38] The woman's acceptance of the rite as that which brings meaning to the 'incongruent element' restores and reestablished it within their cultural and symbolical order, and thus functions efficaciously.

The symbol then, for Chauvet, does not function magically nor instrumentally. The Kuna woman is healed "not only because she knows and understands the connection between the myth and her bodily condition."[39] It is not enough to know the causal relationship between germ and disease, for that knowledge does not cure on its own since it "is exterior to the patient's mind."[40] Rather, it is "the relation between the powers evoked in the myth and the sickness,"[41] which are "interior to this same mind, conscious or unconscious,"[42] that effect the cure—that is, "that releases the physiological processes."[43] Herein lays the symbolic efficacy of myth, which relies on the creation of meaning for foreign elements within a given cultural and linguistic system. The symbol effects the reality it symbolizes, not on the causal functionality of ontological 'substance,' but rather, according to Chauvet who quotes F.A. Isambert's *Rité et efficacite symbolique*, on "the consensus created around the representations, on the one hand, and of the symbolic connection between the representations and what is at issue, on the other."[44]

Set with the context of the Christian tradition, sacraments as symbols, strive for effects that are not purely corporeal, but "spiritual." They seek to effect "grace." Grace is communicated not via the "'metaphysical' scheme of cause and effect, but according to the symbolic scheme of communication through language."[45] For Chauvet, this mode entails "supremely effective"

37. Ibid., 218.
38. Ibid.
39. Chauvet, *Symbol and Sacrament*, 136.
40. Lévi-Strauss, *Anthropologie structural*, 218.
41. Chauvet, *Symbol and Sacrament*, 136.
42. Lévi-Strauss, *Anthropologie structural*, 218.
43. Ibid.
44. Chauvet, *Symbol and Sacrament*, 139.
45. Ibid.

communication since language provides the context in which the subjects relate to one another "within a common 'world' of meaning. It is precisely a *new relation of places between subjects*, a relationship of filial and brotherly and sisterly alliance, that the sacramental 'expression' aims at instituting or restoring in faith."[46] In this way, Chauvet believes he has retained sacramental-symbolic efficacy within a postmodern Heideggerian context and without reliance upon substance metaphysics.[47] In his detailed work, Chauvet applies this model of sacramental efficacy of grace to the Christian tradition and its sacraments, beginning with the body. To address that here would be to venture beyond the scope of this book, for the foundation of Chauvet's theology of sacramentality remains sufficient going forward.

Regardless of whether one adheres to a Thomist ontological, a Rahnerian transcendental, or a Chauvetian linguistic approach to sacramentality, the central thrust of the first part of this book remains consistent. Though some might assert that Chauvet's work negates a Thomist ontological understanding of sacramentality, it does not negate the central thrust of this chapter and the previous chapter. With or without a firm metaphysical understanding of sacramental functionality, the cosmos might still be reasonably understood as pansacramental. Both Aquinas and Chauvet provide historically conditioned approaches to sacramentality. Both draw on the dominant categories of understanding the world in their historical context, namely scholasticism and postmodern linguistic deconstructionism respectively. All three approaches (Aquinas, Rahner, and Chauvet) have both promises and problems. For instance, Aristotelian categories demonstrate the importance of the 'inner' or 'unseen' realities (e.g., grace). Likewise, Chauvet raises the importance of language and its role in bringing meaning to those realities. He provides another way to understand the language of sacramentality and shows why it is crucial in its function of mediating between theology and spirituality.

---

46. Ibid., 140 (italics his).

47. Chauvet does not intend to be simply revisiting the Feuerbachian project of reducing all theology to mere anthropology, or more specifically in this case, to the "socio-linguistic process." To do so, Chauvet believes, "would be to transform theology into nothing more than a peculiar form of anthropology and to diminish the absolute otherness of God. We must say, then, that 'sacramental grace' is an *extra-linguistic* reality, but with this distinction, in its Christian form it is comprehensible only on the (intra-linguistic) model of the filial and brotherly and sisterly alliance established, *outside of us* (*extra nos*), in Christ. Despite grammar, which should never be taken at face value, 'grace' designates not an object we receive, but rather a symbolic work of *receiving oneself*: a work of 'perlaboration' in the Spirit by which subjects receive themselves from God in Christ as sons and daughters, brothers and sisters" (Chauvet, *Symbol and Sacrament*, 140, italics his).

The role of mediation in sacramentality will be further explored in chapter eleven of this project where the emphasis is on how sacramental language (Chauvet) plays a mediatory role between theology and spirituality, and how sacramentality expresses (via Rahnerian 'symbolic reality') the divine in spiritual experience and, what is more, remains crucial in the conversation between the fields of theology and the contemporary study of spirituality. With the theological groundwork of Rahnerian sacramental theology laid out in the previous chapter and the proposed postmodern alternative approach of Chauvet in this chapter, and an understanding of the *universality* of the potential sacramentality of all things set forth therein, the next part of this book (chapters seven through ten) shifts to the *particularity* of spiritual experience and provides an investigation of sacramentality through three case studies of particular spiritual experience.

PART 2

"Believing is Seeing"

7

Sacramental Spirituality

SPIRITUALITIES, UNDERSTOOD AS MODES of lived religious experience, manifest themselves in vastly diverse ways. While part I focused largely on this history of and the theo-philosophical foundations of sacramentality, part II focuses on particular pansacramental spiritualities; that is, part I presented the theory (theology) while the present chapter offers the experience (spirituality), and then part III will explore the interdependence between the two and the resulting implications. In this brief introductory opening chapter of part II, I begin with a commentary on one of the foundational examples of pansacramental spirituality in Western Christianity: Ignatian spirituality and the Ignatian principle. I then offer three substantive case studies, each of which approach sacramental spirituality with various emphases.

The first case study examines Thomas Merton's sacramental spirituality and its concrete influence on his understanding of geographical 'place.' In his late years, 'place' became a dominant theme in his journals as he entertained the possibility of relocating. I draw on his contemplative method and theological anthropology in order to situate his sacramental worldview and its influence on his self-perceived 'place' in the world. His journey for a new place, understood in light of his sacramental spirituality, offers insight into his self-understanding and contemplative method. The role of sacramental language as a mediator offered a constructive medium for Merton as he pursued these questions.

The second case study embarks on a project of comparative theology and interfaith learning, from a Christian perspective, by exploring the spirituality of Nicholas Black Elk, the Lakota Catholic of Pine Ridge, South

Dakota. In particular, I examine four aspects of Black Elk's spirituality: the sacred hoop, the sacred pipe, the making of relatives, and the sacredness of all things. By examining the spirituality of one outside the Christian tradition, the Christian is able to better understand his own sacramental spirituality and become less scandalized by the possibility of multiple religious belonging.

The third case study turns to the literature of Dostoevsky's *The Brothers Karamazov* and Wendell Berry's Port William stories as a source for sacramental spirituality. In particular, I examine anti-dualism in Dostoevsky's *The Brothers Karamazov*, kenotic *theōsis* in Father Zosima, and the pansacramental vision of Wendell Berry's Port William Characters, all of which exhibit a spirituality connected to the sensual as mediated through sacramental categories. In the process a sacramental spirituality surfaces in a way 'of apprehending the whole of reality'—a new 'way of seeing.' The strength of employing sacramental language, which can successfully mediate between God and world, allows for the retention of an immanent God that dwells in the world, yet is not reduced to the world as such (thus a taste panentheism). The gifted prose of Dostoevsky and Berry assists in articulating this spirituality in a manner that strict philosophy and theology might not otherwise be able to do.

The Ignatian Principle

"Finding God in all things" serves as the Jesuit motto of spirituality drawing on St. Ignatius of Loyola of sixteenth century Basque nobility. This Ignatian Principle has grounded the flourishing of the largest Roman Catholic order of priests that relentlessly stresses the importance of education and remaining committed to the mission of representing the way of Jesus in all corners of the globe. His spiritual method has played an important role in affirming God both in and beyond the world. Foundational to this spirituality is a deep and reverent sacramental appreciation of finding God in all things, in which Ignatius provides an approach to understanding the pansacramentality of the cosmos. In this chapter, I draw out his spirituality, situate it within his particular context, and point to some of its theological implications.

In order to understand one's spirituality, it ought to be situated within his or her particular context. Hence, Ignatian spirituality cannot be separated from sixteenth century Spain and Basque nobility. Since the story of Ignatius is quite well-known, it is only necessary to point out a few key contextual details here. Though a contemporary of Luther, it would be misleading to place their spiritualities and respective theologies alongside one another. This would be to oversimplify the matter, for the complexity of their contexts must be recognized in order to interpret their particular spiritualities.

Friedrich Richter, in *Martin Luther and Ignatius of Loyola*,[1] provides an engaging study on the respective contexts of Luther and Loyola. Whereas Luther's context might be characterized as one of progressive, Germanic, intellectual, and revolutionary fervor, Ignatius' context might be characterized as one of conservative, Spanish, mystical and Catholic traditionalism. At the time, Luther's Germanic context was rooted in the mind emphasizing logic, reason, and nature whereas Ignatius' context was rooted in the supernatural and supersensory, which both stressed and went beyond the sensual. Remarkably, the two great figures share much in common. Ignatius was born eight years after Luther and had his profound near-death conversion experience eight years after Luther had his near-death conversion experience. Both struggled with scruples in their ascetic life. Whereas Luther, due to his scruples, left the monastic life and rejected it as unbiblical, Ignatius delved deeper into asceticism with a renewed attitude. Armed with this new religious orientation, Ignatius understood these practices not as a means to merit God's grace, but rather as a means to give thanks to God. Shortly after his temptation to kill a 'Moor' at Montserrat, he writes that he, "decided to do great penances, no longer with an eye to satisfying for his sins so much as to please and gratify God."[2]

Ignatius was raised in the Loyola castle dreaming of knighthood and chivalry, and his first vocational path was that of a soldier, which was cut short when he was struck by a cannon-ball in a local skirmish. Hence, he was not one to neither back down in a fight nor succumb to setbacks, but rather pushed through times of struggle with the stubborn discipline of a soldier. This is evident in his perseverance through ascetic scruples. It is not surprising to find military imagery in his *Spiritual Exercises* and the *Constitutions of the Society of Jesus*. He envisioned the Jesuits as an army of God, made up of soldiers for Christ, subordinate to the Superior General and the commander-in-chief (the vicar of Christ, the Pope), who were sent out on missions throughout the world. With his dream of military fame cut short, Ignatius became determined to "lay aside his [armed battle] garments and to don the armor of Christ."[3]

Ignatius' spiritual method clearly portrays this particular context and military background. A priority of the month-long *Spiritual Exercises* is

1. Richter, *Martin Luther and Ignatius Loyola*.
2. Ignatius of Loyola, "The Autobiography," chap. 2, sec. 14.
3. Ibid., chap. 2, sec. 17.

to lead the retreatant through a discernment process in discovering what God's will is for him or her in the world. It is to discern and accept the mission of God's will. The *Exercises* stress the 'application of the senses' and imagination. For example, in the "Mediation on Hell" in the first week, the retreatant is asked to

> *imagine* the length, breadth, and depth of hell ...
>
> ask for an interior *sense* of the pain suffered by the damned ...
>
> *see* with the eyes of the *imagination* the huge fires ...
>
> *hear* the wailing, the shrieking, the cries ...
>
> by [the] *sense* of *smell* ... *perceive* the smoke, the sulphur, the filth, and the rotting things
>
> by [the] *sense* of *touch* ... *feel* how the flames touch the souls and burn them.[4]

The concrete sensory imagery functions to make impressions on the retreatant progressing through the exercises. Each exercise and mediation follows a similar pattern in order to bring the retreatant to discern the will of God. The heart of this sensual spirituality climaxes for the retreatant in the final contemplation of finding God in all things.

> Consider how God dwells in creatures; in the elements, giving them existence; in the plants, giving them life; in the animals, giving them sensation; in human beings, giving them intelligence ... consider God labors and works for [you] in all the creatures on the face of the earth; ... he is working in the heavens, elements, plants, fruits, cattle, and all the rest—giving them their existence, conserving them, concurring with their vegetative and sensitive activities, and so forth ... Consider how all good things and gifts descend from above.[5]

This passage, and many similar to it throughout the *Exercises*, provides the foundation for the Ignatian principle of 'finding God in all things.' Ignatius' worldview resonates with Aquinas in the sense that all things, people included, strive to realize their *telos* of serving and moving towards God. Thus God is to be found in all things in so far as they reveal, and assist with the movement towards, this *telos*. Rahner, a Jesuit himself, suggests that one must first understand the love of all things before one can find God in all things (the Ignatian Principle). Central to the pursuit of attaining the

---

4. Ignatius of Loyola, "The Spiritual Exercises," *Ignatius of Loyola*, Week 1, 5th Exercise, 65–70 (italics mine).

5. Ibid., Week 4, "Contemplation to Attain Love," 235–37.

love of all things, is the movement towards *indiferencia* and, paradoxically, understanding God as beyond all things. In the context of spirituality, this is the experience of *indiferencia* in one's life, and theologically this entails understanding God as both in all things and beyond all things. This entails the possibility of a panentheistic cosmology. *Indiferencia* here does not refer to a negative apathy to all things of the world, but rather it calls for an indifference to things of the world in order to return back to God and the love of all things. "By *indiferencia* is meant the willing readiness for any command of God, an equanimity resulting from the awareness that God is always greater than all we know of him."[6] In this sense, *indiferencia* is a very positive attitude indeed. Indifference here pertains to remaining indifferent to the pull of worldly desires and one's own selfishness rooted in sin. Think here of a solider following his commanding officer's orders regardless of the soldier's aversion to those orders. The soldier is detached in a certain sense. This Ignatian detachment is the approach of indifference toward the obstacles of the created world in order to free oneself from them and humbly accept the will of God will no matter what that might entail. For instance, remaining indifferent to worldly desires includes rejecting the desire of wealth over poverty, health over illness, and so on. Whatever one's worldly lot may be, the Ignatian call to remain indifferent to it opens one to happily and humbly accepting God's will. Rahner remarks, "From such an attitude of *indiferencia* naturally results in the ongoing readiness to hear a new call from God to tasks other than the present ones; to continually be willing to leave those areas in which one wanted to find and serve God."[7]

Ignatian spiritual piety calls for, then, both an indifference to the world, since God is beyond the world, yet also an openness to finding God in the world through the attainment of the love of God in all things. "In short, such an *indiferencia* is a looking for God in all things."[8] This *indiferencia* begins in the Ignatian call of *fuga saeculi*,[9] thus flight from the world leads back to immersion in the world through indifference. Paradoxically, flight from the world is the way of deeper immersion in the world. This Christian flight from the world is not the negation of the world, which is perhaps more similar to what the Buddhist, Gnostic, or neo-Platonist[10] might hold for differing reasons. *Fuga saeculi* does not entail anti-materialism, nor

6. Rahner, "The Mysticism of Loving All Things in the World according to Ignatius," 154.

7. Ibid., 152.

8. Ibid., 155.

9. "flight from the world"

10. For a challenge to the presumed Platonist rejection of materialism, see Ward, *God and the Philosophers*, 4–13.

does it entail the rejection of the world as some form of cosmic trash, but rather, according to Rahner, the Christian flight from the world "is only the response and necessary gesture toward the God who freely reveals and discloses himself and who gives himself to us in freely given love."[11] In one's acceptance of the God who comes through faith, and not the negation of the world as such, he or she is then "able to accept by grace their service in the world, which is his world and creation after all, as a path to him who is beyond the world," continues Rahner, "so that people will not only encounter the absolute God as in radical contradiction to the world but also as in the world."[12] To immerse oneself in the world with an open will to the will of God, it is first necessary to "flee the world" in indifference and remain open to the discernment process.

One paradoxically detaches in order to attach. One flees the selfish obstacles of the self and world in order to remain open to the God who is beyond the world. She then immerses herself back into God's world open to God's will in all circumstances. Thus, "Ignatius moves from God to the world, not the other way around."[13] After one surrenders to the will of God and becomes indifferent to his or her own will and accepts the will of God, who is beyond the world, he or she is thrust back into the world in order to carry out God's will. This *indiferencia* is manifested in the will of the person. It is similar to how a military solider might negate his own will and submit to the will of his superior and the mission given to him. *Indiferencia*, then, is a necessary prerequisite for the Ignatian principle of finding God in all things.[14] First, one 'lets go' to his or her own will and remains open, or indifferent, to the will of God. Second, one gains the courage to reject all former paths to God as the only paths to God and remains open to looking for God in all things. In short, Ignatius turns empiricism on its head thus rejecting the adage that "seeing is believing" and affirms "believing is seeing." One must come to *believe* in the God, who is beyond all things, in order to *see* God in all things (recall Chauvet's mention of Levi-Strauss in chapter six on necessity of belief in order for a symbol to effect what it signifies). Rahner puts it thusly, "since God is bigger than everything else, he can allow himself to be found in our flight from the world and he can also come to meet us in the streets of the world."[15]

---

11. Rahner, "The Mysticism of Loving All Things in the World according to Ignatius," 152.

12. Ibid., 153.

13. Ibid., 154.

14. Ibid.

15. Ibid., 155.

Within his *Exercises*, Ignatius gives his society the *examen* [of the consciousness], a method of seeking God in all things and receiving the freedom to allow God's will to be carried out in the world. It proceeds in five steps. The first step emphasizes the Ignatian principle of finding God in all things. Before the final four steps (reviewing one's day, contemplating one's emotions, praying, and looking ahead to tomorrow), the first step calls for the recognition of the all-pervasive presence of God, no matter where one happens to be. Since God is the creator of all creation, including persons, and God is in all things by way of their being, God is always present—so goes the thinking here.

In a way reminiscent of Hegelian reconciliation (which is examined more in-depth in chapter eleven), Ignatius has synthesized what Rahner believes the study of religion has mistakenly separated from one another, namely the "flight from the world" on one hand and "mission within the world" on the other hand.[16] Herein is a cosmic worldview which preserves the "infinitely knowable-ity" of God, while allowing for the finding of God in all things. God is deemed "infinitely knowable" in a Thomist-Rahnerian sense, which does not refer to the ease of which one can know God, but rather refers to the idea that there is so much content in God that should be known but cannot be. A distinction must be recognized between the knowability of the content of God and the human ability to know God. It is not as if there is nothing about God to be known, rather a person can know God and since God's content is infinite, there is always more to be known. This entails the unknowable-ity of God in a certain sense. In short, due to God's infinite content to be known, God remains infinitely knowable, thus also unknowable to humans—since humans cannot know God completely and perfectly.

Though Ignatius may not have had a contemporary panentheistic cosmology in mind, his spirituality affirmed a pansacramental cosmology that allows for the manifestation of God in all things. Unlike many panentheistic constructions of the cosmos, Ignatian panentheism (be it ontological or not[17]) places stress on God as beyond the world. It is precisely through this affirmation of God beyond the world that paradoxically allows for God to be found in the world (through all things). For, "God is more than [our images and concepts of God, whether natural or supernatural]. And as the one who is more than the world, God has broken into human existence

---

16. Ibid.

17. Philip Sheldrake notes that, "in Ignatius' sense of the 'liberality' of God, God dwells in all things and all creatures exist in God . . . All that exists, exists only in God . . . He is not reflecting about the ontology of created things but about how humans may perceive and relate to them" (Sheldrake, *Spirituality and Theology,* 141).

and has burst apart this world and what theology calls, 'nature.'"[18] God is simultaneously in nature and beyond nature, thus in Ignatius we find a clear rejection of pantheism and a tendency towards pansacramentality.[19] What allows for this tendency begins in the flight from the world in order to come back to the world in order to find God in all things in a sensual manner, as portrayed in the *Exercises*. Sacramentality and sacramental language assists in bridging this spirituality of Ignatius with an Ignatian theological understanding of God as both in and beyond the world. To borrow a phrase from Rahner (who draws on Aquinas), God remains the 'mystery' that is 'infinitely knowable;' that is, God is knowable only to a certain extent, thus one might find God sacramentally in all things, yet God simultaneously remains infinitely beyond all things.

For the purposes of this book, and especially part II here, The Ignatian principle of "finding God in all things" serves as a backdrop against which the following three case studies can demonstrate the particularity of lived religious experience spirituality). Further, it begins to make clear the pansacramental and panentheistic construction of the cosmos in which the Ignatian motto can be nuanced to "finding all things God" pansacramentally.

---

18. Rahner, "The Mysticism of Loving All Things in the World according to Ignatius," 148.

19. It would be anachronistic to suggest that Ignatius was an explicit panentheist since he did not use this term nor did he delve into its metaphysics. At best, one might make the argument that he has an implicit (and metaphorical) panentheist in similar way that Aquinas was, but I do not find that tenable or necessary at this point.

8

Thomas Merton
Sacramental Spirituality and Place[1]

THOMAS MERTON, PERHAPS MOST known for his contemplative and monastic writings, had the remarkable ability of finding beauty, order and religious significance in even the most ordinary and seemingly insignificant events in life. For instance, he reflects on,

> watching pro football on TV—at midnight!! The Packers beat the Dallas Cowboys—and it was, I must say, damn good football . . . Football is one of the really valid and deep American rituals. It has a religious seriousness which American religion can never achieve. A comic, contemplative dynamism, a gratuity, a movement from play to play, a definitiveness that responds to some deep need, a religious need, a sense of meaning that is at once final and provisional; a substratum, of dependable regularity, continuity, and an ever renewed variety, openness to new possibilities, new chances. It happens. It is done. It is possible again. It happens . . . Final score 31–27 is now football history. This will last forever. It is *secure* in its having happened. And we saw it happen. We existed.[2]

Though a reflection on a seemingly ordinary ('non-spiritual') event, this journal entry illustrates a side of Merton, a true and authentic side, which

---

1. A version of this chapter first appeared as Gustafson, "Place, Spiritual Anthropology, and Sacramentality in Merton's Later Years," and also presented as Gustafson, "Place and Selfhood in the Later Years."

2. Merton, *The Other Side of the Mountain*, 160–61 (italics his).

surfaces often in his journals. The burden of this chapter will be to offer a case study examining how Merton's sacramental spirituality concretely influenced his sense of 'place' and orientation in the world. To assist in conceptualizing 'place,' (geographical place) I draw on Mircea Eliade's *The Sacred and the Profane*, and in particular his elucidation of one's *axis mundi*, for it provides a constructive framework within which to approach the concept of 'home' as such in the context of Merton's later years.

Merton espoused an anthropological vision in which persons are called to seek knowledge of the self via knowledge of God; that is, in knowing the true self more intimately, one knows God more intimately. In so doing, they might see the world sacramentally. This connatural[3] knowing of God and self hinges on contemplation. Merton's spiritual anthropology as laid out in *The New Man* and his explanation of contemplation in *New Seeds of Contemplation* are examined and applied to the personal narratives from his journals. *The New Man* presents the theological anthropology, *New Seeds* provides the contemplative theory, and his journals provide the practice or the data from his own life. Thus, the aim here is to relate his theology and theory with his practice. Merton's consideration of 'place' and where he should 'be' consumes much of the content of the later journals as he frequently considers the possibility of moving to another 'place' on earth, most notably northern California, Alaska, Latin America or even Asia. The journals offer insight into times and 'places' this occurred for Merton. They report when and where Merton understood the world sacramentally. In order to properly situate his journals, I shall first offer a brief review of his spiritual anthropology in *The New Man* and contemplation in *New Seeds of Contemplation*.

Merton's quest for self and place offers a window into the human condition of restlessness, thus many will resonate with the anthropological traits he exhibits such as dissatisfaction, restlessness, the sense of and longing for home, and the search for rootedness. Merton's quest for a new home, set within the context of his spirituality and sacramental vision, provides a striking glimpse into his quest for the 'self,' which remains a central concern for much of his contemplative theory.

---

3. By the concept connatural knowledge, I have in mind the coming to knowledge of something by way of imitation, experience, and practice. Connatural knowledge of God refers to coming to God by imitating and practicing Godly attributes. For instance, by loving *agapeically*, one comes to know the *agapic* love of God and thus knows God more intimately. It street parlance, "it takes one to know one" (see footnote 7).

Spiritual Anthropology

In the *New Man*,[4] Merton lays out his most complete theo-philosophical treatment of spiritual anthropology. He begins with the basic question, 'What does it mean to be human within a theological context?' In so doing, he casts an anthropological vision that draws heavily on the tradition of 'Catholic Substance'[5] in positing the potential sacramentality of all persons via the Pauline notion of 'putting on Christ'. It is perhaps too hasty to say at this point that the 'putting on of Christ' is similar (certainly not the same) to the Eastern understanding of *theōsis*, or divinization, which broadly refers to a person living in and through Christ, or rather having Christ living in and through that person. However, the concept of 'putting on Christ' is often interpreted metaphorically to refer to the immersion into, and the becoming similar to, Christ, not by nature, but by adoption and participation. Christ functions as mediator in the hypostatic union and incarnation, thus persons can understand themselves as potential sacramental mediators in the world; however, this by itself is not identical to the Eastern understanding of *theōsis*. Merton understands the human person as existing in a state of conflict caught up in a tension between life and death, or rather existence and non-existence. In this sense, Merton does not deviate from the classical Augustinian and Thomist emphasis on *esse* and the understanding of evil as non-being (privation). In other words, to live is to be, and to not-be is to not exist.

Anthropologically, this idea might be rephrased in the following way: 'we do not know ourselves because we do not know God, and we do not know God because we do not know ourselves, thus knowing God and knowing oneself are inherently wrapped up with one another.' In other words, discovering God entails discovering one's self as well. Merton writes, "In order to find God, Whom we can only find in and through the depths of our own soul, we must therefore first find ourselves."[6] This is the classical notion of connatural knowledge, the idea that one knows God through knowing one's self and vice-versa, or in common street parlance, "it takes

---

4. Lawrence Cunningham points out that, "the 'new man' of the title is an implicit rebuke to the Marxist claim to building a 'new man'—the theoretical capstone of a classless society. Merton's 'new man' is, in short, an alternative vision to the oft discussed 'new Soviet man' of the Cold War era" (Cunningham, *Thomas Merton and the Monastic Vision*, 82).

5. Used by Paul Tillich in contrast to 'the Protestant Principle.' Sometimes it is also referred to as 'the sacramental principle.'

6. Merton, *The New Man*, 63.

one to know one."[7] Merton embraces connatural knowing in his advocating that the solution to knowing the self entails an attainment of connatural knowledge via 'putting on Christ.' This participatory path remains sacramental in its retention of the possibility that persons might become divinized via Christ through sacramental participation in Christ. In putting on Christ, one participates in a Godly reality in which all things, steeped in God's sacramental self via grace, are seen fully and completely. A Christian believer, such as Merton, might proclaim this way of seeing as the way God intended the world to be seen; that is, this way of seeing entails seeing the world in the manner that Jesus spoke of when he espoused the imminent 'Kingdom of God' in the New Testament. This vision includes one's own vision of the true self.

Mystically, in one's union with Christ (via the putting on of Christ) she becomes a living sacrament and (re)presents Christ in concrete space and time. The result is a new way of seeing[8]—a sacramental illumination in which all things are understood as potential avenues through which the divine is present and communicates. Did Merton ever truly find his true self? Though not the central question of this article, it should not pass without notice; that is, did Merton arrive at connatural knowledge of himself and God? If so, then how might it relate to his spirituality and search for place? Perhaps his later journals can offer some insight to these questions.

Contemplation

In *New Seeds of Contemplation*, Merton examines the practice and goal of contemplation in an accessible manner for both monastics and non-monastics alike. It progresses from negative (*via negativa*) statements about contemplation (what contemplation is not) towards affirmative statements about what contemplation is. For Merton, contemplation "cannot be taught," but "only hinted at." It does not simply lie in pure passivity nor is it a mere psychological passivity. "The contemplative is not merely a man who

---

7. Kreeft, "Aquinas and the Angels."

8. Robert Barron, claims that, "Christianity is, above all, a way of seeing . . . What unites figures as diverse as James Joyce, Caravaggio, John Milton, the architect of Chartres, Dorothy Day, Dietrich Bonhoeffer and the later Bob Dylan is a peculiar and distinctive take on things, a style, a way, which flows finally from Jesus of Nazareth. Origen remarked that holiness is seeing with the eyes of Christ, Teilhard de Chardin said, with great passion, that his mission as a Christian thinker was to help people see, and Thomas Aquinas said that the ultimate goal of the Christian life is a 'beatific vision,' an act of seeing" (Barron, *And Now I See*, 1).

likes to sit and think, still less one who sits around with a vacant stare."⁹ Contemplation is not a pure prayerfulness nor the contentedness found in the liturgical rites. It is not arrived at through "practical reason" alone, nor is it found in trance, ecstasy, emotion nor enthusiasm. It is not the gift of prophecy. It is not a mere acceptance of the way things are in order put one at ease, and it is certainly "no pain-killer."¹⁰ Contemplation is not Cartesian epistemology,¹¹ but rather is more similar to the existential experience of subjective being. In making clear what contemplation is not (partially), Merton offers an understanding of contemplation that involves transcendence and knowledge of the true self in a subjective manner. Contemplation assists in knowing that one's false self is not the true self, but proceeds in an experiential way. "Contemplation," he writes, "is precisely the awareness that this 'I' is really 'not I' and the awakening of the unknown 'I' that is beyond observation and reflection and is incapable of commenting upon itself."¹²

In addition to this *via negativa*, he highlights three additional important themes for grasping what contemplation is. They are 1) the relationship between faith and theology, 2) union with Christ and 3) the vision of a pansacramental cosmology.¹³ Each remains important in so far is it relates to Merton's journal narratives on 'place' and spirituality.

First, the relationship between faith and theology is crucial for understanding contemplation. Faith is the first step towards contemplation since

9. Merton, *New Seeds of Contemplation*, 9.

10. Ibid.

11. Merton places the Cartesian formula for the proof of one's own existence (*dubito ergo cogito ergo sum*) the furthest outside the reality of one experiencing her own existence because it clearly and distinctly reduces oneself to an objective concept only to be grasped via cognitive insight. Furthermore, it reduces God to a mere concept, to a *what*. However, for Merton, "God is not a *what*," not a "thing." . . . There is "no such thing" as God because God is neither a "what" nor a "thing" but a pure "*Who*" (Merton, *New Seeds*, 13). Thus contemplation, as a means towards knowing the true self and God's true self, must retain an emphasis on "the experiential grasp of reality as *subjective*." To do this adequately, God's self must be understood as a subject (as a 'Who'). Merton maintains that pure rationalism, such as one might find in Cartesian epistemology, undermines the project to know the self, since "For the contemplative there is no *cogito* ('I think') and no *ergo* ('therefore') but only *SUM*, I AM" (Merton, *New Seeds*, 9).

12. Merton, *New Seeds*, 7.

13. Merton does not refer to this term, but offers a cosmic vision compatible with a pansacramental cosmology. In his essay 'Symbolic and Sacramental Existence' Martin Buber coins the term 'pansacramentalism' to clarify the distinct features of Hasidic sacramentality (Buber, "Symbolic and Sacramental Existence," 178). More recently, I have made the case for the compatibility of a pansacramental panentheistic theological cosmology with a classical Thomist Christian theology in Gustafson, "Collapsing the Sacred and the Profane."

it marks the transition between theology and faith. In a certain sense, faith steps beyond the limits of theology. Faith, on its own, begins in 'intellectual assent' and picks up where theology leaves off. In other words, faith commences in theology but eventually moves beyond it. Although faith begins in an 'intellectual assent,' it is not wholly intellectual. Theology can only proceed to a limit in the religious quest. Ultimately, it is to be left behind at a certain point at which it is radically purified or altered. 'Radically purified' here is what Merton intends when he writes, "Here theology ceases to be a body of abstractions and becomes a Living Reality Who is God Himself."[14] The higher stages of faith, bordering on contemplation, put to rest analogies and technical theological language about God and seek to rest in the living presence and reality of God's self. Theology is purified when all of the crutches of theological language and analogy are stripped away to reveal a deeper, truer reality of God. "Faith goes beyond words and formulas and brings the light of God Himself."[15] Faith becomes a step towards contemplation, which is ultimately a lived theology—an existential participation in God's own self.

Second, union with Christ remains the heart and goal of the contemplative experience, which is attained by shedding the false self and 'putting on Christ' and sharing in his divinity. Putting on Christ is to model oneself after the inner life of the Trinity in having one nature, yet multiple persons (modes of relationality). In so doing, the contemplative (re)presents Christ. The contemplative becomes her true self, while her false self fades into its own illusion. Thus, contemplation provides a means through which one comes to be and to know the true self. In this way, kenosis entails *theōsis*. Merton writes, "In order to become myself I must cease to be what I always thought I wanted to be, and in order to find myself I must go out of myself, and in order to live I have to die."[16] However, contemplation goes beyond this, for it is an awareness (a *way of seeing*) of the world that renders to each thing its proper relation to God's self.

Third, this new *way of seeing* is a vision of the cosmos[17] as pansacramental. "As we go about the world," writes Merton, "everything we meet

---

14. Merton, *New Seeds*, 148.
15. Ibid., 129.
16. Ibid., 47.
17. I am using the term "cosmos" here in the manner that Raimon Panikkar uses the term kosmos. I employ cosmology, and Panikkar employs Kosmology, "in the sense of the subjective genitive: the *logos*, the word of the kosmos that Man should try to hear and to understand by attuning himself to the music of this world, to the mysteries of the kosmos" (Panikkar, *The Rhythm of Being*, 369). I do not intend the currently popular definition of the term which refers to knowledge resulting from scientific reasoning

and everything we see and hear and touch, far from defiling, purifies us and plants in us something more of contemplation and of heaven."[18] All cosmic things contain the potential to express God in temporal time and space. "God is everywhere," according to Merton, "His truth and His love pervade all things as the light and the heat of the sun pervade our atmosphere."[19] Contemplation is an awareness—a new *way of seeing*—of what is 'really there' in the world. It allows one to grasp reality in an authentic manner. Through the eyes of the contemplative, the world is seen as in God. Further, for the contemplative, the world simply *is*; that is, God just IS, simply being (*esse*), and the recognition of this, albeit at some level profoundly simplistic and incomplete, holds the essence of contemplation.

The Later Journals

In Merton's final journals a constant inner debate (struggle) surfaces over where and how to be in the world. This may surprise those who expect an experienced monk, such as Merton, to be among those who are the most rooted and the least restless.[20] For instance, Merton journals, "I struggle with myself with my own future—and with the fear I will be discovered before I can get away (irrational)—or even that I may die or be shot."[21] Eerily, he wrote these words four months prior to his death in Bangkok. Further, this passage reflects his restlessness and, to a certain degree, his non-rootedness. By looking at the concept of a) home, b) contemplative awareness, and c) the quest for place through the lens of Merton (in particular his journal narratives on the places and times he experienced the world in it is pansacramentality), we can rediscover Mircea Eliade's religious categories of the *axis mundi* and the sacred and profane.

"Home"

Eliade remains a giant in the field of religious studies for his phenomenological study of religion. His classic text on the study of sacred place, *The Sacred and Profane*, has been foundational in the development of categories

---

applied to the physical data of cosmos.

18. Merton, *New Seeds*, 25.

19. Ibid., 151.

20. Like Augustine, Merton typifies one of Augustine's most fundamental claims regarding the human condition of restlessness.

21. Merton, *The Other Side of the Mountain*, 163.

and terms used for analyzing religion. One major concept is the *axis mundi*, "the image of a universal pillar . . . which at once connects and supports heaven and earth and whose base is fixed in the world below."[22] For many traditions, this axis is recognized as located in specific geographical places such as a certain mountain top,[23] town, or river. However, Eliade makes clear that although this remains a fundamental feature of religious oriented persons, it also manifests itself in those who adopt a nonreligious view of the world. In this way, 'profane spaces' (secular, non-religious) can take on religious meaning to the extent that they become an *axis mundi* for certain individuals or groups. This might be, for instance, "a man's birthplace, or the scenes of his first love, or certain places in the first foreign city he visited in youth."[24] These places may be understood as *axes mundi* of a person's individual universe or cosmic orientation.

Though he endlessly pondered the possibility of making a permanent move beyond Kentucky, Gethsemani[25] remained his *axis mundi*. It had become the place around which he oriented his life and world; it was at the center of his universe. He writes, "I will remain a monk of Gethsemani. Whether or not I will end my days there, I don't know—and perhaps it is not so important."[26] Later, when in India reflecting on his future, he writes,

> so far the best indications seem to point to Alaska or to the area around the redwoods . . . I do not think I ought to separate myself completely from Gethsemani, even while maintaining an official residence there, legally only. I suppose I ought eventually to end my days there. I do in many ways miss it. There is no problem of my wanting to simply "leave Gethsemani." It is my monastery and being away has helped me see it in perspective and love it more.[27]

These passages portray a Merton oriented around a place that carries some sense of 'home' despite his lack in desire to permanently reside there in his final years. Perhaps he understood Gethsemani as his 'home' in the way many nostalgically orient themselves to their place of childhood. For instance, I currently orient myself to the geographical place of Minnesota

---

22. Eliade, *The Sacred and the Profane*, 36.
23. E.g., Bighorn Medicine Wheel of the Lakota & Sioux in Wyoming (USA); the sacred mountain Machhaphuchhare outside Pokhara (Nepal), a local sacred place to the deity Shiva.
24. Eliade, *The Sacred and the Profane*, 24.
25. Merton's monastery is the Abbey of Gethsemani near Trappist, Kentucky.
26. Merton, *The Other Side of the Mountain*, 166.
27. ibid., 282.

since it was the place of my childhood, most of my family and friends reside there, and I have spent most of my adult life there. Even when I lived on both coasts of the U.S., I still understood Minnesota as 'home.' I orient myself, both psychologically, consciously and unconsciously, around its geographical location; that is, I understand all other places on earth in relation to its orientation to Minnesota. Thus, Minnesota is at the center of my psychological map; to a certain degree it is my geographical *axis mundi*. Merton does this as well. He writes, "For real solitude, Alaska really seems the very best place . . . the idea of being in Alaska and then going out to Japan or the U.S. strikes me as a rather good solution."[28] Here Merton points out the utilitarian advantage of settling in Alaska in that it provides easy access[29] to both his 'home' in Kentucky and Asia, a place Merton was becoming increasingly interested in.[30] Thus, the pull of Kentucky, as a fixed point of orientation (*axis mundi*), remained an influence on his future considerations of place.

Contemplative Awareness

Prior to his travels in Asia, Merton traveled extensively within the western United States, spending significant time in New Mexico, Alaska and on the coast of northern California. He titled his journal during this period, *Woods, Shore, Desert*, which included poems, impressions, memoirs, travelogues and photographs he had taken. It provides a unique glimpse into Merton's experience of exciting new places in the context of a pivotal point in his life as one searching for a new 'place' in the world. Further, it demonstrates his attentiveness to seemingly mundane ordinary passages of time. For instance, while on the coast in northern California, he writes "A huge shark lolls in the swells making his way southward, close in shore, showing his dorsal fin. Faint cry of a lamb on the mountain side muffled by sea wind."[31] What might be understood as descriptions of insignificant events were intentionally recognized by Merton and logged in the journal. In these episodes, Merton pauses and sees the world in a new way via contemplation.

There are many instances prior to *Woods, Shore, Desert*, which demonstrate this contemplative awareness. Perhaps the most well-known account,

28. ibid., 252.

29. At the time of writing this, Anchorage, Alaska, often served as a mid-way point between the U.S. and much of the Eastern world as passenger airplanes often had to refuel there.

30. Though Merton probably ruled out Alaska for a number of reasons, perhaps one was that it would have been a disadvantageous compromise to settle in a particular place due to its proximity to two more desirable places.

31. Merton, *The Other Side of the Mountain*, 98.

and turning point in the life of Merton, is the experience that has come to be known as the "Vision in Louisville," or the realization "at the corner of Fourth and Walnut." It is a reflection which came to Merton in March of 1958 when downtown Louisville. He writes,

> In Louisville, at the corner of Fourth and Walnut, in the center of the shopping district, I was Suddenly overwhelmed with the realization that I loved all these people, that they were mine and I theirs, that we could not be alien to one another even though we were total strangers. It was like waking from a dream of separateness, of spurious self-isolation in the special world, the world of renunciation and supposed holiness. Not that I question the reality of my vocation, or of my monastic life: but the conception of "separation" from the world that we have in the monastery too easily presents itself as a complete illusion: the illusion that by making vows we become a different species of being, pseudo-angels, "spiritual men," men of the interior life, what have you.[32]

Here, perhaps for the first time, Merton recognizes not only a collapse of the sacred and non-sacred, but the collapsing of the monastic/non-monastic dualism of the world. He realizes that his monastic vocation does not negate his connection to, and responsibility for, persons living outside the monastery. Ten years later, in April of 1968, after visiting a Louisville burger joint, Merton reflects,

> When I was in Lum's I was dutifully thinking, "Here is the world." Red gloves, beer, freight trains. The man and the child. The girls at the next table, defensive, vague, aloof. One felt the place was full of more or less miserable people. Yet think of it: all the best beers in the world were at their disposal and the place was a *good idea*. And the freight train was going by, going by, silhouetted against an ambiguous sunset.[33]

Merton takes note of the world around him and sees things in themselves. "Here is the world," he writes of its brute hard reality. He sees the world in its *is-ness*, its being. In the passage above, it is almost as if the world is staring back at Merton echoing the monotonic refrain, 'Here I am. This is the World. What are you going to do about it?' He recognizes the persons around him as living in the world. Similar to his 'Fourth and Walnut'

---

32. Merton, *Conjectures of a Guilty Bystander*, 140.
33. Merton, *The Other Side of the Mountain*, 78.

experience, he affirms the reality of the world beyond Gethsemani, no matter how 'ordinary.'

On December 4th, 1968, six days prior to his death in Bangkok, while in Colombo (Sri Lanka) observing the rock formations, sculptures and carvings near the temple of Gal Vihara, Merton describes an onslaught of contemplative awareness,

> Looking at these figures I was suddenly, almost forcibly, jerked clean out of the habitual, half-tied vision of things, and an inner clearness, clarity, as if exploding from the rocks themselves, became evident and obvious . . . The thing about all this is that there is no puzzle, no problem, and really no "mystery." All problems are resolved and everything is clear, simply because what matters is clear. The rock, all matter, all life, is charged *dharmakaya*[34]—everything is emptiness and everything is compassion I don't know when in my life I have ever had such a sense of beauty and spiritual validity running together in one aesthetic illumination.[35]

Fig. 8.1: Gal Vihara, Sri Lanka.

Here Merton experiences this 'new way of seeing' as described in *New Seeds*; that is, he welcomes the vision of seeing all things in what he perceives to be their true reality as coming together in God. He describes this experience as one of the most beautiful and spiritually valid he has ever seen, and it comes six days prior to his departure from mortal life. These experiences

---

34. Ultimate Truth (literally "body of truth" or "truth body").
35. Merton, *The Other Side of the Mountain*, 323.

demonstrate clear instances in which Merton recognized the world through a contemplative lens.

The Quest for a 'Place' in the World

"Tell me where you are to be found and I will tell you who you are,"[36] writes Emmanuel Mounier, the twentieth-century French Personalist. This line is a favorite among philosophers, anthropologists, and sociologists of place when seeking to understand a person in the context of their physical and geographical location. However, the context of Merton is more difficult to discern than that of most. He was born in France and spent his youth moving around New York, France, Bermuda and England. He spent his last 27 years at Gethsemani prior to his death in Bangkok at the young age of 53. Thus, the task of articulating who Merton was based on his context is rather complex due to the lack of any fixed place of youth and childhood. If a 'home' is to be affixed to Merton, in any sense of the term, then it would arguably be Gethsemani, the place he spent the majority of his life. Merton recognizes some sense of this in 1962 when we writes,

> Returning to the monastery from the hospital: cool evening, gray sky, the dark hills. Once again I get the strange sense that one was when he comes back to a place that has been chosen for him by Providence. I belong to this parcel of land with rocky rills around it, with pine trees on it. These are the woods and fields that I have worked in, and walked in, and in which I have encountered the deepest mystery of my own life. And in a sense I never chose this place for myself, it was chosen for me (through of course one must ratify the choice by personal decision).[37]

Since Merton lacked a place to be 'from,' the nuanced adage, 'tell me where you are *from* and I will tell you who you are,' might be reasonably negated. However, this would not rule out Mounier's claim. In other words, Merton's 'home,' to the best of one's knowledge, was Gethsemani.

If Merton was rooted in Gethsemani, then why might he have been inclined to find a new place? He cites several reasons in his journals, the most frequent of which pertain to a lack of privacy and dissatisfaction with the leadership and administration of the monastery. Thus, he sets out for the Western United States with several destinations for the purposes of giving

---

36. Mounier, *The Character of Man*, 70–71.
37. Merton, *Conjectures of a Guilty*, 234.

talks, correspondence and leading retreats.[38] Apart from these talks and retreats, another theme emerges in his journals. It becomes evident that Merton also uses the trip as an opportunity to explore the possibility of finding another 'place.' What was he searching for? What type of place? Among the various places he visited, New Mexico, Alaska, northern California and even Asia received the most attention in his journals, and perhaps exerted the strongest pull on him. For instance, the vast empty spaces of the New Mexican desert impelled Merton to write, "New Mexico is one of the places where I might eventually settle."[39] However, despite a couple of visits to New Mexico, the impression made becomes largely overshadowed by both Alaska and northern California.

Fig. 8.2: Sunset from Gull Island, near Juneau, Alaska.

The desire for solitude persisted throughout his travels as he reflected on future locations to settle. He notes, "More than anything I want to find a really quiet, isolated place."[40] Alaska, he concluded, due to its isolation and lack of population, provided the greatest opportunity for seemingly unlimited solitude. He writes, "It is clear that I like Alaska much better than

38. For a well written and synthesized exposition on this West Coast tour and Merton's thematic teachings, see Thurston, "'I Spoke Most of Prayer.'"

39. Merton, *The Other Side of the Mountain*, 163.

40. Ibid., 142.

Kentucky and it seems to me that if I am to be a hermit in the U.S., Alaska is probably the place for it. The SE[41] is good—rain and all."[42] Yet, he remained guarded against the possibility of being too isolated, for earlier he had wrote, "I have no special urge to be a hermit in Alaska, but it is an obvious place for solitude,"[43] and "I tend to find myself thinking a lot about how to live in Alaska . . . The thing is that I can't make sense out of a purely private endeavor to be completely alone, un-bothered, etc. This is nonsense."[44] Merton visited several places throughout Alaska including the Southeast, the tundra and near Anchorage. He found several places that would provide his sought-after solitude and escape from Kentucky, however I suspect none of them struck him as quite right. There is an analytical pickiness that seeps from his journal in his notation over their advantages, though always finding something inadequate about them. For example, when in Yakatat he wrote, "Frank Ryman has a quarter acre of land he offered me—and it is enough to put a trailer on. But it is at the edge of the village. If I lived there I would become very involved in the life of the village and would probably become a sort of pastor."[45] This option was, I suspect, too public for him. He wanted more solitude, but not too much.

Merton spent the last weeks of his life in Southeast Asia, mostly in India. Prior to departure, in Kentucky, he writes, "In eight weeks I am to leave here. And who knows—I may not come back. Not that I expect anything to go wrong—though it might—but I might conceivably settle in California to start the hermit thing . . . Really I don't care one way or another if I never come back."[46] He had been preparing and looking forward to this trip for a long time. His journals give the impression that he had a true sense of destiny or fate about his trip to Asia; it was as if he expected to find something there that he had been searching for his whole life. Reflecting on his flight from the San Francisco airport, he writes, "We left the ground—I with Christian mantras and a great sense of destiny, of being at last on my true way after years of waiting and wondering and fooling around . . . I am going home, to the home where I have never been in this body."[47] Perhaps this is best explained by the understandable excitement and romanticization of

41. "SE" here is in reference to "Southeast Alaska" (i.e. the panhandle) known for its lush evergreen rain forests and abundant wildlife.

42. Merton, *The Other Side of the Mountain*, 193.

43. Ibid., 153.

44. Ibid., 154.

45. Ibid., 192.

46. Ibid., 148.

47. Ibid., 205.

one's first trip to the East, or perhaps we should take serious his reported sense of destiny. Regardless, we might easily imagine Merton in the airplane sitting at the edge of his seat for hours over the Pacific staring out the window while making the occasional recording in his journal, such as "When the stewardess began the routine announcement in Chinese I thought I was hearing the language of Heaven."[48]

Could he have subconsciously known that he was not to return? Could he have subconsciously known that he was indeed headed 'home' in a very definite and ultimate sense?[49] While in Asia, Merton provided few insights about becoming a hermit there. If anything, I suspect Merton overcame his 'honeymoon phase' and romanticized view of Asia and decided that there was no long term place for him there. He did spend a few days in a secluded hut in the Himalayan foothills of northern India outside Darjeeling; however, while there he came to the following conclusion, "With my reaction to this climate at its best and with the noise of the Indian radio in a cottage across the road from the hermitage, I guess it's still Alaska or California or Kentucky for me."[50]

Despite an overly-idealistic vision of Asia, the perfection of solitude in Alaska, and the vast empty nothingness of the New Mexican desert, northern California seemed to resonate with the deepest chord in Merton. In particular, the coastal area due south of Mendocino point caught the eye of Merton. It is the rugged coastal wilderness area known as 'the lost coast,' which Merton points out is the closest point of the lower 48 states to Asia. While visiting a women's monastery (Our Lady of the Redwoods), Merton was introduced to Bear Harbor, which looked out over Needle Rock.[51] The following journal prose captures both the place within the imagination of Merton and his contemplative awareness of that place.

48. Ibid., 208.

49. Merton's last public words demonstrate this eerie destiny towards his ultimate home, which are now famous, "So I will disappear *from view and we can all have a coke or something.*" The first four words of this quote are from Merton, *The Asian Journal of Thomas Merton*, 343; however, the more complete quote, which includes the italicized words, is from *Merton: A Film Biography*, minute 51:28.

50. Merton, *The Other Side of the Mountain*, 293.

51. Today this location is both federally and locally protected within the King Range National Conservation Area and Sinkyone Wilderness State Park.

Fig. 8.3: Bear Harbor, looking south.

About a mile from Bear Harbor, there is a hollow in which I am now sitting, where one could comfortably put a small trailer. A small loud stream, many quail. The calm ocean . . . very blue through the trees. Calla lilies growing wild. A very active flycatcher. The sun shines through his wings as through a Japanese fan. It is the feast of St. Pachomius. Many ferns. A large unfamiliar hawktype bird flew over a little while ago, perhaps a young eagle.[52]

---

52. Merton, *The Other Side of the Mountain*, 99.

Fig. 8.4: Bear Harbor, looking north.

The comfortable setting is illuminated well by Merton and, if he had moved there, one might easily imagine his seamless transition into the rhythms of coastal life. Later, back in Kentucky, he continues to describe the location in more detail.

> Northern California was unforgettable. I want very much to go back. Especially to Bear Harbor, the isolated cove on the Pacific shore where the Jones house is and which, I think, can be rented: the barrier, the reef, the eucalyptus trees, the steep slopes crowned by fir, the voce full of drift-redwood logs—black sand, black stones, and restless sea—the whole show, those deserted pyramids, the hollow full of wild iris, the steep road overhanging the sea, Needle Rock.[53]

The trip to Bear harbor left such a great impression on him that, when back in Kentucky, he devotes the majority of his journal entries to dreaming, analyzing and recapturing those memories. He reflects, after developing his Needle Rock photographs from the first trip, "The Agfa film brought out the great *Yang-Yin* of sea rock mist, diffused light and half hidden

---

53. Ibid., 117.

mountain—an interior landscape, yet there. In other words, what is written within me is there, 'Thou art that.' I dream every night of the west."⁵⁴

Fig. 8.5: Needle Rock

His old home in Kentucky seemed to pale in comparison to what he imagined may be possible on the coast of northern California. He plots and justifies a move to the Pacific under several different arguments, some serious and others not. For example, he appeals to practicality when he asks, "Would I do better creative work alone out by the Pacific? I have a feeling I probably would."⁵⁵ Similarly, he points out a symbolic and spatial justification in its geographical orientation; he writes, "Needle Rock is, I guess, within sight of Cape Mendocino and hence is one of the points south of

54. Ibid., 110.
55. Ibid., 129.

Canada that are nearest to Asia."⁵⁶ Less seriously, he notes the seemingly inferiority of his Kentucky surroundings when he writes, "Then I arrived back here in Kentucky in all this rain. The small hard-woods are full of green leaves, but are they real trees? The worshipful cold spring light on the sand-banks of Eel River, the immense silent redwoods. Who can see such trees and bear to be away from them? I must go back. It is not right that I should die here under lesser trees."⁵⁷ Throughout, he peppers his journal with direct affirmations of his preference for Bear Harbor with statements such as, "I can think of nothing I'd like better than to fly back to California,"⁵⁸ and "But what I want most of all is to spend a couple of months entirely alone somewhere on the shore of the Pacific."⁵⁹

Fig. 8.6: California Redwoods

56. Ibid., 130.
57. Ibid., 112.
58. Ibid., 127.
59. Ibid., 132.

Merton's longing to return to the coast for an extended period of time takes on a language of one longing for a home and place of belonging. In addition to the reasons given at the outset of this section (e.g., solitude), perhaps this is explained by Merton's spiritual yearning. Perhaps he perceived himself as having spiritually plateau-ed in his ongoing quest for the self. Philip Sheldrake, in his article *Human Identity and the Particularity of Place*, recognizes that one element that 'home' represents is "our need for a location where we can pass through the stages of life and develop our fullest 'self.'"[60] Sheldrake's explanation supports, and perhaps clarifies, Merton's restlessness of place and longing to find a new 'home.' Merton's spirituality of self calls for putting to death the old self and finding the newer, supposedly more real, self in Christ. Thus, the real self is acquired through a negation of self. Fittingly and correspondingly, concerning the concept of place and home, Merton writes "The country which is nowhere is the real home; only it seems that the Pacific Shore at Needle Rock is more nowhere than this, and Bear Harbor is more nowhere still."[61] Bear Harbor must have provided something that none of the other locales could—a sense of nowhere, yet at the same time, a very definite sense of somewhere. Whatever it was, there is some indication that Merton thought he had found a place where he could feel at home. He recognized this back in Kentucky, "Lonely for the Pacific and the Redwoods. A sense that somehow when I was there I was unutterably happy—and maybe I was. Certainly, every minute I was there, especially by the sea, I felt I was at home—as if I had come a very long way to where I really belonged."[62]

---

60. Sheldrake, "Human Identity and the Particularity of Place," 49.

61. Merton, *The Other Side of the Mountain*, 110. Some have suggested the possibility that Merton is playing around with words here in his use of "nowhere." "Nowhere" can be broken up to "now here" and when used in this journal quote it functions well in describing a place where Merton felt content in the moment. Present contentment is a popular lesson drawn from Buddhism.

62. Ibid., 122.

Fig. 8.7: Coast near Bear Harbor

I suspect that if Merton did return from Asia, he would not have ended up in Alaska, New Mexico or even somewhere in Central or South America as he sometimes toyed with, but would have worked out a temporary to semi-permanent arrangement in northern California. He certainly gave it the most attention in his journals and sought to justify it in a variety of ways, for it seemed to retain a stronger call than the other candidates on Merton's short list. In no other place did Merton record such vivid contemplative accounts as he did in northern coastal California. One such account that demonstrates his contemplative awareness combined with his longing for a new home and place is as follows, "It was a bright day and the sea was calm, and I looked out over the glittering blue water, realizing more and more that this was where I really belonged. I shall never forget it. I need the sound of those waves, that desolation, that emptiness."[63] Regardless of his musings over Alaska and California, Gethsemani remained his home, around which he oriented his life.

Conclusion

For one who wrote and spoke extensively on 'the self' and being at home in the world, Merton was, to a certain extent, rather restless and not perfectly comfortable with being 'at home' in the world. Perhaps Merton did not

---

63. Ibid., 120.

know himself as well as he let on, or at the very least, as well as others would have liked him to have known himself. Perhaps this restlessness is demonstrated by his quest for a new place in the later years of his life. His journals contain the constant questioning of who he was and where he was going. On August 5th, 1968 he writes, "Maybe I am no true solitary, and God knows I have certainly missed opportunities—made mistakes—and big ones too!"[64] This restlessness, though perhaps disturbing to some (especially those who romantically envision monks as the human strive for perfection), provides a very human side to Merton the monastic, in a similar way to Augustine who, in his *Confessions*, demonstrates his proneness to sexual gallivanting and the human delight found in stealing pears as a boy. Thus, it may not be surprising that it was Augustine who made one of the most profound statements about the human condition when he prays to God, "For Thou hast made us for Thyself and our hearts are restless till they rest in Thee."[65] Like Augustine, Merton will remain an enduring figure in the history of anthropological study and it may not be for his spiritual theology, but rather for his open candor about self, world, and place. Like Augustine, Merton offers a window into the psyche and inner struggle of the human condition placed in the context of existential being in the world while striving to transcend it.

Recall Merton's opening reflection on the religious validity and significance of the football game. He was fascinated with its finality, fixity, and quality of lasting security in the logs of football history—and for this reason, he recognized its religious significance. In a similar fashion, perhaps Merton was searching for security and finality in a new place and new home to lay down new, though impermanent, roots. Places, due to their rootedness in the cosmos, contain the tremendous power to provide one with an *axis mundi* around which orientation of life and self is possible. Merton's quest, with his open candor and transparent journals, provides not only inspiration, but the opportunity for all to catch a little glimpse of their own self and place in the world.

---

64. Ibid., 150–51.
65. Augustine, *Confessions*, book 1.

9

Nicholas Black Elk

Sacramental Spirituality and Descandalizing Multiple Religious Identity[1]

NICHOLAS BLACK ELK'S SPIRITUALITY may be understood, from a non-Native Christian perspective, as pansacramental and panentheistic (though he did not describe it in these explicit terms). It also yields a spirituality and theology characterized by openness. In this examination, which is an exercise in interreligious learning, first I begin with a necessary explanation of my approach, definition of terms, and an introduction to the contemporary conversation regarding Black Elk in light of his religious narrative. Second, I correlate elements of Black Elk's spirituality with Christian theology as mediated through sacramental categories. Third, I entertain the possibility that Black Elk had an authentic multiple religious identity (belonger and/ or participant) and argue that non-Native Christians should welcome the possibility; that is, if Christianity is understood as an open and dynamic religion in the way that many Native traditions are, then Christians should confidently seek new expressions of the divine in the manner Black Elk allegedly did. Finally, I offer a few brief comments concerning this exercise in

1. A version of this chapter first appeared as Gustafson, "Descandalizing Multiple Religious Identity with Help from Nicholas Black Elk and His Spirituality: An Exercise in Interreligious Learning," and was also presented as "Revisiting the Multiple Religious Belonging of Nicholas Black Elk in the Context of the Catholic Sacramental Imagination," "Multiple Religious Belonging and Interfaith Panentheistic Spirituality in the Liberal Theology of Nicholas Black Elk," and "What a Christians Might Learn about Sacramentality from the Spirituality of Nicholas Black Elk?"

interreligious learning as it relates to the content of Black Elk's quest for the divine. Drawing on the most recent and primary Black Elk scholarship in order to reflect on his spirituality from a non-Native Christian perspective, this paper suggests that understanding Black Elk as maintaining a sincere multiple religious identity (both his native Lakota tradition and Roman Catholicism) should not scandalize nor threaten the non-Native Christian believer. In order to examine this, I reflect on the sacramental bridge between Christian theology and Black Elk's spirituality. I will suggest that his Lakota spirituality can coexist and be practiced simultaneously alongside Catholic spirituality without causing scandal (for non-Native Christians).

The relevance of this question (whether non-Native Christians should welcome the possibility of multiple religious belonging or participation in this context) becomes clear in light of Achiel Peelman's assessment of the contemporary situation in which many Native Americans, and indigenous peoples worldwide, "who have become Christian without abandoning their traditional beliefs"[2] and thus live out multiple religious belonging in some manner. He teaches that "What we need to remember here is that, throughout North America, many Native persons and communities continue to struggle with the question 'Can I be both Christian and Indian, or must I choose?' This question stands at the center of our contemporary efforts to move from confrontation to dialogue between Christianity and Native American spiritual traditions."[3] Although this question is ultimately one that requires navigation by those Natives who identify with one or both traditions, the primary concern here is whether non-Native Christians ought to be open to the simultaneous embrace of both. George Tinker frames it thusly, "the problem for mainline european and amer-european Christians is that indigenous Christianity among Indians begins to look less and less like mainline European and amer-european Christianity as Indians determine for themselves how they will interpret the gospel."[4] The claim this chapter sets out to make is that this should not be a problem at all for non-Native Christians, but rather a welcome opportunity for listening, learning, and growing. In other words, the project in this chapter is distinctly one of Christian theology done from a non-Native Christian perspective, which may carry little to no appeal for Native people and/or Native Christians, in an effort to promote Native Christianities like Tinker's.

---

2. Peelman, "Native American Spirituality and Christianity," 346.
3. Ibid., 349.
4. Tinker, *American Indian Liberation*, 15 (sic).

A Necessary Preliminary

Nicholas Black Elk (1866–1950), the Oglala Lakota visionary and son of Crazy Horse's cousin, has been the subject of both debate and inspiration. Inspiration comes from his alleged appropriation of his Lakota tradition via Catholicism, his commitment to religious dialogue, and courageous pursuit for religious truth. Debate has sprung up since John Neihardt published his nationally recognized account of Black Elk, *Black Elk Speaks*, in 1932. It has received criticism for its literal inaccuracy and colonial assumptions which sought to emphasize the mythical aspects of Black Elk's life. The normative view that has emerged among Black Elk scholars is that it is best understood not as an ethnographic or anthropological work, but rather as an artistically crafted literary work. For instance, Damian Costello contests one of the most quoted passages, the "death of a dream," and concludes that it remains a poetic literary invention of Niehardt and was never originally uttered by the "historical Black Elk."[5] Further, the Black Elk of Niehardt comes across as a defeated old man oppressed by the white colonizers only to spend his final days a bitter, tired, and angry victim with his Lakota culture lost to the hands of the white man.[6] This view of Black Elk suggests that his Catholic identity and practice were insincere, or surface level at best, and served only the utility of appeasing the colonizers; that is, in order to survive, Black Elk half-heartedly (or empty-heartedly) acted "as if" he were a faithful Catholic and Catholic catechist. The sincerity of Black Elk's faith commitment(s) remains the subject of considerable debate and is considered in the latter half of this paper. By examining the possibility of Black Elk's "multiple religious identity" (MRI henceforth)[7] I hope to suggest that the frontiers of one's

---

5. Costello, *Black Elk*, 7. See the appendix for a more in-depth commentary on the terms "historical Black Elk" and "literary Black Elk," as well as an overview of current postcolonial Black Elk scholarship.

6. Niehardt's *Black Elk Speaks* covers Black Elk's story to the young age of only 24 (or 27, see footnote 15 and 23) and ends with the massacre at Wounded Knee in 1890. This limited view leaves out his remaining sixty years. The last lines, and most quoted words of the text, read, "And I, to whom so great a vision was given in my youth, — you see me now a pitiful old man who has done nothing, for the nation's hoop is broken and scattered. There is no center any longer, and the sacred tree is dead" (chapter 25). However, Niehardt himself admits to employing his artistic license in portraying his literary Black Elk. He admits, "At times I changed a word, a sentence, sometimes created a paragraph. And the translation—or rather the *transformation*—of what was given to me was expressed so that it could be understood by the white world" (McCluskley, "Black Elk Speaks: And So Does John Neihardt," 239). For this reason, among others, many contest the literal authenticity of *Black Elk Speaks*.

7. A distinction can be made between "multiple religious *belonging*" and "multiple religious *participation*," both employed here under the rubric of "multiple religious

Christian theology might be expanded to welcome the simultaneous embracing of two religious traditions in some manner.

A goal here is to explore the Christian category of sacramentality implicitly or explicitly employed in the spirituality of another. Concerning the terms 'sacramentality' and 'spirituality,' the former refers to that element of the Christian tradition which accounts for the real presence of the divine, God's self, in the world in some way. Sacraments mediate between the divine and the world.[8] This broad view of sacraments allows for an infinite number of potential sacraments, thus sacraments are not to be reduced to a fixed number (e.g., whether one believes in seven sacraments or two). In this way all things hold the potential to mediate the divine in the world. This is the 'pansacramental principle,' which implies a pansacramental view of the cosmos. The term spirituality refers to the lived religious experience of a particular individual in the world. The content of the contemporary study of

---

identity" (MRI). "Multiple Religious Belonging" refers to the simultaneous embracing of, and commitment to, two or more religions. It is a phrase that has surfaced most significantly and recently in *the* text on the subject, *Many Mansions? Multiple Religious Belonging and Christian Identity* edited by Catherine Cornille in 2002. Peter C. Phan writes, "Among recent literature on multiple religious belonging, one work deserves particular mention: *Many Mansions? Multiple Religious Belonging and Christian Identity*" (Phan, "Multiple Religious Belonging," 64, 496n). John Thatamanil has suggested the use of "multiple religions participation" since it is broader and can be used with less scandal. He argues that often in cases of multiple religious *belonging*, there is a dominant tradition which trumps the other(s) in case of conflict. Hence, with multiple religious *participation* one can identify with a single tradition yet participate in other traditions without worrying about wholly adhering to both without conflict and scandal. Perhaps more importantly, Thatamanil argues that "belonging" is not universal and it does not apply to all traditions, especially non-Western traditions. So the question of whether one belongs to the Lakota tradition in the same manner he belongs to Christianity is relevant here, and Thatamanil's suggestion is that perhaps *participation* is more constructive. Further, when a Lakota becomes Catholic, or when a Jew becomes Buddhist, do they cease being Lakota and Jewish? Probably not. This nuance illuminates aspects in these traditions that allow for this, and they might not be equivalent aspects found in Christianity. For all of these reasons, the suggestion here is that perhaps the less exclusive "participation" ought to be given preference over "belonging" when engaging multiple religious identity (Thatamanil, "We Are All Multiple").

8. Note here the likely distinction between Christian and Lakota understandings of the relation between the divine and the world. Care must be taken when seeking to draw lines of similarity between the two traditions' conceptions of the spirit world (or the spirit in the world). The category of sacramentality is likely to fall short in grasping the fullness of the Lakota religious understanding of *Wakan Tanka*. Further, the phrase "God's self" can suggest a concept of a personal God whereas it is unclear and unlikely that Lakota notions of the spirit realm and *Wakan Tanka* proclaim a personal God with a "self." These differences further suggest the fruitfulness of not clinging to a narrow view of sacrament, but rather suggest the benefit of a broad view of sacrament as a mediator of the divine or God (whether personal or impersonal).

spirituality concerns one's 'lived religious practice or experience.' It is what Philip Sheldrake terms, "the study of 'felt experience' and 'lived practice' in ways that, while not detached from theological tradition, overflow the boundaries that positivist theology tends to set."[9] Hence, sacramental spirituality concerns one's particular experience of the divine in the world.

Non-Native Christians have something to learn about their own sacramental tradition from the wisdom of Black Elk's spirituality. It is not unusual to be attracted to a particular idea or practice in another tradition. Often it is the case we are drawn to particular ideas or concepts in other traditions with the hope that we might then be able to retrieve something similar from the roots of our own tradition. Can non-Native Christians recover the sacramental roots of Christianity by learning from Black Elk's Lakota spirituality? Employing this approach entails a word of caution about the possibility of dominating and domesticating Black Elk's practices in a manner unintended. This paper is not an attempt to interpret or reinterpret a non-Christian tradition (that task is for the Lakota). This is not a project to reinterpret Lakota spirituality for the non-Native Christian in a manner that erases differences between traditions. For example, the claim is not that the ritual use of the sacred pipe and the Eucharist are the same without recognizing differences (i.e., the Lakota do not understand the sharing of the pipe as sacramental in the exact same way Christians understand their sacraments). Rather, this paper represents a non-Native Christian perspective on the spirituality of Black Elk with the goal of understanding further the robust theological language of sacramentality already employed in the Christian tradition. This approach to Black Elk's spirituality follows the method Phillip P. Arnold has suggested in his essay, "Black Elk and Book Culture." Arnold writes, "Like John Neihardt's efforts at interpreting the significance of Black Elk's life, all efforts that follow, including the present one, are creative enterprises. Readers of *Black Elk Speaks*, like Neihardt, are *entangled* in the world of Black Elk, and this entanglement assumes that scholarly responses to the book, as well as others, will rise out of a creative integrity."[10]

Pansacramental theology, in large part, assists the Christian with accepting the conclusion sough here: the descandalization of MRI. It allows for a generous amount (an infinite amount) of sacraments. Placing this assertion in the context of Keith Ward's claim that the Christian faith is,

---

9. Sheldrake, "Spirituality and Its Critical Methodology," 15. For the purpose of constructive interreligious learning, I have sought to entangle myself with not only *Black Elk Speaks*, which has been sufficiently critiqued regarding its literal authenticity, but also the main texts of the Black Elk corpus.

10. Arnold, "Black Elk and Book Culture," 93.

at its roots, essentially liberal,[11] and that liberal theology emphasizes "conscientious freedom of interpretation, in a carefully qualified sense, without denying the importance of tradition and authority, in an equally qualified sense, within Christian faith."[12] This paper's position is grounded in the religious sacramental inclination of the Christian tradition while opening up the possibility of pansacramental and panentheistic interpretations of, and within, the entirety of the cosmos. The rich sacramentalism of Catholicism and the Ignatian principle of "finding God in all things" practiced by Black Elk's Jesuit contemporaries may have influenced his way of relating to the cosmos and divine. The late Franciscan Sister Marie Therese Archambault, a *Hunkpapa* Lakota professor, writer, and spiritual director, remarks on the spiritual core of Black Elk, "By placing himself at this center which was simultaneously physical, spiritual and metaphorical, he encountered the Great Mysterious One."[13]

In recounting the elements germane to Black Elk's MRI, this paper relies on the traditional canon of Black Elk scholarship.[14] Born in 1863[15] on the present-day border of South Dakota and Wyoming, he came into

---

11. Ward argues that the three main reasons that the Christian faith is essentially liberal are 1) Paul's teaching in the New Testament that Christians are free from 'the Law,' thus demonstrating Christianity's freedom from written rules and positive affirmation of freedom. 2) "The fundamental Christian experience is encounter with God in Christ. It is not primarily acceptance of a set of beliefs." Therefore, encounter with God "can never be wholly captured in any formula, and it will always have diverse manifestations, as people respond to Christ in different ways." 3) Christianity was born out of an inherent revisionist interpretation of the Jewish tradition in its interpretation of the Messiah as spiritual savior and not a political liberator. Christianity is a tradition that continually reinvents itself given its cultural and philosophical context (Ward, "Liberal Theology and the God of Love," 200–01). Oddly enough, by the term "liberal" here I intend something similar to the way the movement known as Conservative (Masorti) Judaism employs the term "conservative." Obviously not meant in the American political sense, both terms seek to express the yearning to conserve the roots of tradition while remaining open to new and contemporary questions, issues, and historical contexts. Similarly, this is what I also refer to as the doing of radical theology, radical in the etymological sense of going to the root (*radix*), thus recovering, conserving, and preserving the theological roots of a tradition while remaining liberal (open) to transcending it in growth towards new expressions.

12. Ward, "The Importance of Liberal Theology," 40.

13. Archambault, *A Retreat with Black Elk*, 44.

14. For a more exhaustive telling of the Black Elk story, see Neihardt, *Black Elk Speaks*; Michael F. Steltenkamp, *Nicholas Black Elk: Medicine Man, Missionary, Mystic*; Black Elk, "Gift of the Sacred Pipe"; DeMallie, *The Sixth Grandfather*.

15. Michael Steltenkamp, with the support of Black Elk's daughter, Lucy Looks Twice, claims the correct birth-date falls in 1866, not 1863 as Neihardt contends (Steltenkamp, *Nicholas Black Elk: Medicine Man, Missionary, Mystic*, 14).

the world as a member of the Oglala Lakota. At age nine he experienced a divine vision and spent the rest of his life attempting to interpret it.[16]

As a result of the vision, Black Elk became a *wicasa wakan*,[17] spending the rest of his life discerning the vision while striving to fulfill the dual tasks of providing his people with holy guidance and healing while seeking to destroy their enemies. He understood the vision as a call to reveal to his people the sacred road leading to the sacred hoop, at the center of which he is to make the sacred tree blossom. While he continually sought ways to reinterpret and understand his vision in light of historical circumstances, his life was rife with suffering and political tensions as the territory of his people was eventually controlled and converted to reservation land by the U.S. government. At age thirteen he witnessed the battle of Little Bighorn and killed a U.S. soldier. He fled to Canada with the remainder of Sitting Bull's people, only to surrender in 1881 and move onto South Dakota's Pine Ridge Indian Reservation, which currently contains two of the most impoverished counties in the U.S.[18] He spent two years working as an "American Indian" actor with Buffalo Bill's traveling "Wild West Show" and in Europe with a similar outfit led by "Mexican Joe."

In 1889, a Paiute named Wovoka from Nevada brought the message of what journalists referred to as "the messiah craze,"[19] which consisted of a messianic message cast in Native spirituality. The primary vehicle for communicating and telling this message was the controversial 'Ghost Dance.' It stirred controversy and contributed to the events that led to the Wounded Knee Massacre.[20] The main thrust of the Wovoka doctrine was that the Son

16. The vision is recounted in astonishing detail in DeMallie, *The Sixth Grandfather*. Black Elk reports hearing a voice calling him, after which he collapsed with sickness in the tipi. He then saw a vision of two men coming to him from the clouds. He ascended to the clouds with them and met the council of the six grandfathers. They showed him the various regions of the spirit world. These included: "the four directions, the cloud tipi of the six grandfathers, the black sacred road from west to east, the red sacred road from south to north, and the center of the earth." This center served as the axis of the sacred hoop, the home of the sacred tree. In the vision, the first grandfather (the grandfather of the west) gave Black Elk a wooden cup of [medicine] water which symbolized the power to heal humankind. He also received a bow and arrow symbolizing the power to destroy the enemy (DeMallie, *The Sixth Grandfather*, 119).

17. [wee-*cha*-sha wa-*kan*]: holy man, shaman, conduit of spirits (Archambault, *A Retreat with Black Elk*, 10).

18. According to US Census Bureau Data in 2000, five of the seven poorest counties (by per capita income) comprise reservation lands in South Dakota. Six of the seven poorest counties are located in both North and South Dakota.

19. See "The Messiah Craze Spreading," *New York Times*, November 26, 1890, and Sandoz, *Old Jules*, 128.

20. This is a controversial event in US-Native History resulting in an estimated 50

of God, the *wanikiye*,[21] was to return exclusively for the Native people, rid them of the whites, bring back those who had passed away, and thus bring about a return to prior, better, times. The gospel of Wovoka proclaimed the return of the Son for the Natives exclusively, since the whites were understood to have put the messiah to death. Black Elk eventually accepted the Ghost Dance as being related to his vision and thus endorsed its practice.[22]

At age thirty-eight in 1904,[23] Black Elk was baptized and took the name Nicholas.[24] The 'conversion'[25] story has been a topic of controversy.[26] Perhaps the most telling account of the "conversion" story comes from Black Elk's daughter, Lucy Looks Twice, narrated to Steltenkamp.[27] The story recounts Black Elk's attempt to provide *yuwipi*[28] to a sick boy only to encounter Father Joseph Lindebner, a Jesuit priest, who wanted to give the boy his last rites. Lindebner rebuked the *yuwipi* as "satanic" and immediately invited Black Elk to come to the Holy Rosary Mission. Two

---

US soldier fatalities and 200 to 330 Lakota fatalities (Steltenkamp, *Nicholas Black Elk: Medicine Man, Missionary, Mystic*, 71).

21. *Wanikiye* refers to 'savior' or messiah figure. "Sometimes Wovoka himself was identified as the *wanikiye*." (Steltenkamp, *Nicholas Black Elk: Medicine Man, Missionary, Mystic*, 60).

22. Niehardt portrays Black Elk as having regretted following the Ghost Dance visions he received on Wounded Knee Creek. He deems them "lesser visions" to those in his "great vision," which he regrets not depending on (Niehardt, chapter 23). Niehardt frames the regret as a rejection of the Ghost dance visions, but as Clyde Holler has pointed out, Niehardt left out the real Black Elk's report, "I have seen the son of the Great Spirit himself," thus concluding that "the real Black Elk regrets not using a more powerful vision" (Holler, 'Lakota Religion And Tragedy," 35). In other words, Black Elk did not reject the Ghost Dance visions, but rather regretted not following another vision in their place during that particular time leading up to that particular war at Wounded Knee.

23. This assumes Steltenkamp's proposed date of birth of 1866 is correct.

24. He "entered the Church" on Dec., 6th, 1904, the feast of Saint Nicholas; hence Black Elk adopted his name.

25. "Conversion" is a lousy and confused term to use in this context since it often entails exclusivity and leaving one tradition for another. "In Black Elk's case, conversion was not capitulation, nor did it imply substitution of one religion (a failed one) for another (a better one)" (Holler, "Black Elk's Relationship to Christianity," 39). Rather it referred to a sort of multiple religious identity.

26. "Whether coercion, a moving emotional experience, the culmination of inquiry, or a combination of all three was at the root of Black Elk's conversion, he dedicated himself to the communal life of Lakota Catholicism" (Costello, *Black Elk*, 11).

27. Steltenkamp, *Black Elk: Holy Man of the Oglala*, 33.

28. *yuwipi* [you *wee* pi]; "aspect of Lakota religion which uses spirits to perform for the shaman" (Archambault, *A Retreat with Black Elk*, 11). Black Elk made a part of his living as a *yuwipi* healer (Costello, *Black Elk*, 9n).

weeks later Black Elk was preparing for baptism. The power imbalance that existed between the Christian colonizers and Native people (e.g., in politics, social standing, military might), coupled with the reality of forcing Natives to choose Christianity, cannot be ignored.[29] Without question, coercion played a major role in the colonizing strategy of the missionaries. Further, obvious benefits were afforded to those Natives that did "convert" such as employment and educational opportunities. All of this is to suggest that the so-called conversion experience of Black Elk is a complicated and murky matter. It is unclear whether force was employed in pushing Black Elk toward Catholicism. It if was, and it may be likely, it does not necessarily negate the authenticity of his faith commitments. However, this power differential between Native and Christian encounter is highlighted here given the history of oppression and the ripple effect it has had throughout the history of this encounter up to the present day. George Tinker reminds us that "the constant pressure of amer-european settlers and their colonialist federal government worked to slowly erode much of the basic cultural structures and values of Indian nations as part of their strategy to erode the political and economic viability of Indian Tribes."[30] This is relevant because this chapter examines the lived religious experience (spirituality) of Black Elk's Lakota tradition, and this historical ripple effect is a part of it.

The post-conversion years of Black Elk's life, like his early years, remain the subject of much debate, especially as to who the authentic historical and religious Black Elk was. Damian Costello's monograph provides a thorough critique of the current scholarly landscape of the historical Black Elk. He suggests two dominant views exist: 1) the "essentialist" Black Elk, which assumes the Neihardt account is the most authentic and literally accurate, and 2) the "Lakota Catholic Black Elk," which assumes Black Elk to be a sincere and committed Roman Catholic and not the defeated old man in *Black Elk Speaks*, who is simply 'going through the motions' of Catholicism to appease the Jesuits.[31] Costello makes the case for the latter built on an argument that accuses Neihardt of unintentionally falling prey to many colonial assumptions which influenced his presentation of Black Elk.

Costello endorses the view of Michael Steltenkamp, S.J. and Paul Steinmetz, S.J., which paint a contrasting picture of Black Elk as one who sincerely

---

29. "Forcing this choice was so successful as a part of the colonialist strategy in dividing communities and coercing compliance that missionization was further developed explicitly as a political strategy throughout the colonializing process to serve that purpose" (Tinker, *American Indian Liberation*, 7).

30. Ibid., 13 (sic).

31. The Jesuits maintained the most consistent Roman Catholic presence and practice at Pine Ridge during Black Elk's life.

practiced Catholicism for his remaining forty-six years. Steltenkamp and Steinmetz are trained anthropologists with doctoral degrees. They lived and served as priests on the Pine Ridge Reservation with Black Elk. Their view is further corroborated by Black Elk's daughter, Lucy Looks Twice. Costello's rationale for endorsing Steltenkamp is that the more accurate account of Black Elk would most likely come from his Lakota and Jesuit contemporaries who lived alongside him for decades, instead of Niehardt who spent three weeks interviewing Black Elk via a translator.[32] However, reasonable skepticism of Steltenkamp's and Steinmetz's view can be maintained on the grounds that it seems rather probable that two Jesuit priests would be eager to endorse the sincerity of Black Elk's Catholic devotion. For this reason, they are sometimes rejected as Catholic apologists.[33]

Sacramentality and Black Elk's Spirituality

Approaching Black Elk's spirituality from a Christian perspective within a sacramental framework can demonstrate the possibility of accepting sincere MRI as an authentic expression of the tradition. Apart from literature on pan-Native popular spirituality there is little substantive work on the particular spirituality of Nicholas Black Elk, and even less on the influence of sacramentality on his religious beliefs.[34] Costello deems Black Elk a "Lakota Catholic," which probably refers to a devoted Catholic who also happens to be of Lakota heritage. It is unclear precisely what Costello means by this. Was Black Elk a devout Catholic immersed in a Lakota cultural tradition? Was his faith that of a Catholic and culture that of a Lakota, or is this a confused distinction between faith and culture? Or, does "Lakota Catholic" refer to simultaneous dual participation in two religious traditions, or the collapsing of two traditions into one? This lack of clarity is recognized by David Martinez in his critique of Costello's text. Martinez remarks, "it is

---

32. For a more in-depth overview of the various approaches to the historical Black Elk, see Costello's *Black Elk,* in which he treats the views of relevant Black Elk scholars such as Raymond DeMallie, Julian Rice, Clyde Holler, John Neihardt, Michael Steltenkamp, and Paul Steinmetz. Other quality resources include Clyde Hollers' "Black Elk's Relationship to Christianity" and "Lakota Religion and Tragedy: The Theology of *Black Elk Speaks*." For a postmodern critique of Holler's work, see Dale Stover's "Eurocentrism and Native Americans."

33. Costello, *Black Elk,* 14

34. William Stoltzman explores the intersection of Lakota tradition and Christian rituals in his *The Pipe and Christ,* however does not treat sacramentality as such as it pertains to the Lakota beliefs of Nicholas Black Elk.

difficult to tell what is left over other than a heavily syncretized thesis about Black Elk."[35]

This paper suggests the possibility that Black Elk was both Lakota and Catholic in a sincere multireligious capacity which may suggest that he found the traditions not at odds, but rather mutually inclusive and complementary within a Lakota context. The two traditions neither corrupted nor negated each other for Black Elk, but rather converged. In particular, this section examines the role of sacramentality and how it might assist Christians with accepting as sincere and legitimate members of the Christian faith those who claim MRI. Central to this remains the Christian theological openness to sacramentality. There are clear instances of acculturation (perhaps even inculturation), appropriation, and possibly syncretism in various aspects of Black Elk's spirituality (as viewed through the lens of Christian sacramentality). Four of these aspects are treated below in so far as they assist with descandalizing MRI.

1) The Sacred Center

The ritualistic establishment of "the center"[36] in the seven major rites of the Lakota is foundational to Black Elk's spirituality. Ritual (in all traditions

---

35. Martinez, "review of Damien Costello, *Black Elk: Colonialism and Lakota Catholicism*," 1014.

36. Here it may be misguided to declare this making of the center of the sacred hoop an Eliadian *axis mundi*, which is "the image of a universal pillar . . . which at once connects and supports heaven and earth and whose base is fixed in the world below" (Eliade, *The Sacred and the Profane*, 36). For many traditions, this center is found at particular geographic locations which might include a specific river, mountain, or town. The sacred hoop rather, symbolizes the centeredness of the various rites. However, it is interesting to notice that for Black Elk, the sacred tree functioned as the primary symbol of his vision which, Costello argues, 'is in fact a Christian symbol" representing the Christian life of the people (Costello, *Black Elk*, 92). This sacred tree might be understood as reminiscent of an Eliadean *axis mundi*, however it would be a dynamic axis (capable of being located at various geographical places) rather than a fixed central pillar such as a specific mountain or temple. This dynamism and ability to be recognized in multiple places lends itself to an inherent pansacramental vision of the cosmos, in which no place is off limits to the erection of an *axis mundi*. If an *axis mundi* is to be identified in Black Elk's spirituality, the postscript to Niehardt's *Black Elk Speaks* might provide some evidence, but it is probably a stretch. "Pointing to Harney Peak that loomed black above the far sky-rim, Black Elk said, 'There, when I was young, the spirits took me in my vision to the center of the earth and showed me all the good things in the sacred hoop of the world" (Niehardt, *Black Elk Speaks,* postscript). Harney Peak, the highest natural point in South Dakota, stands at 7,244 feet above sea level and is located in the Black Elk Wilderness, a federally protected area within the Black Hills National Forest.

both explicit and implicit) establishes an order and way to approach and understand the world.[37] The center marks the center of the sacred hoop, the center of the dance circle, the center of the community, and the center of the earth, at which the sacred cottonwood tree of life grows. Black Elk tells of the holy man instituting the rite of establishing the center:

> He struck the ground twice at the center for the Earth and then again twice at the center for the Great Spirit. He scraped the ground level, and with a stick which had been purified, and which was first offered to the six directions, he drew a line from the west to the center, and then from the east to the center, from the north to the center, from the south to the center, and then, offering the stick to the heavens, he touched the center, and offering the stick to the earth, he again touched the center. In this manner the altar was made, and . . . it is very sacred, for we have established the center of the Earth, and this center, which in reality is everywhere, is the home, the dwelling place of *Wakan-Tanka*.[38]

Christians here might be reminded of the importance of ritual in their own tradition, especially the promotion of a sacramental worldview. Here Black Elk might encourage the Christian to expand and enrich the boundaries of sacramentality. The center of this sacred hoop establishes a sacred structure to the world which necessitates a ritualistic approach. It is an opening up of the person and the world in order to see the sacred.[39] The sacred hoop itself represents the created world universally and is not to be understood

---

37. For instance, "Coffee in Sweden is far more than an energizing beverage; it is a ritual." That is, this implicit ritual of *fika* (drinking/sharing coffee) in the Swedish culture (and of all Scandinavian cultures) means that, according to Samantha Albert, "Coffee shops in the Nordic countries are a place for community. People sit and talk to their friends." The ritual of sharing coffee orients its participants around a common worldview and set of values that may include sharing community through food and drink for example (Albert, "I'll Have That to Stay Please—Swedish Coffee Culture").

38. Black Elk, "Gift of the Sacred Pipe," 108.

39. A Christian might make the loose parallel to seeing the world through the eyes of Christ and to 'put on Christ' as Paul prescribes. In this way, one seeks to establish a vision of the New Creation on earth. Costello draws this theme out even further correlating the author's vision of the "great multitude" in the book of Revelation with Black Elk's vision, as described by DeMallie, of the "millions of faces behind the grandfathers" (Costello, *Black Elk*, 122). Christian theology might refer to this realized eschatology as 'now and not yet' in that the *eschaton* comes about in the here and now via sacramental glimpses of the sacred on earth, yet remains incomplete. There is no evidence that suggests Black Elk explicitly understood it this way, but rather the point to be recognized here is that the sacramental tradition (with its philosophical categories and language) allows the Christian to remain open to such religious compatibility.

as representing only that geographical real estate within its physical parameters. Rather the hoop represents all peoples and lands and it is within the hoop that *Wakan Tanka*[40] dwells, thus bringing about the divine into real corporeal space and temporality. Archambault explains,

> Black Elk learned that whoever found a center also became the center of the universe and that is where God dwells . . . By placing himself at this center which was simultaneously physical, spiritual and metaphorical, he encountered the Great Mysterious One . . . *the center of oneself becomes the center of the universe. The center of the earth and the center of the person are one and the same.*[41]

Herein the correlation with a pansacramental theology becomes more evident. If the cosmos is understood as a constant self-expression of the divine via God in all things, the sacred hoop illustrates a ritualistic framework within which one becomes simultaneously centered in self and world. In the Lakota tradition Black Elk was understood to be a "conduit between the spirit world and his people, but in a very special way."[42] A pansacramental Christian can understand Black Elk, as Archambault suggests here, as a living sacrament to his people in that he reveals the way and reality of the sacred. However, this would be a claim imposed upon Black Elk from the outside, for there is no evidence that he employed the term 'sacrament' in referring to his function as a visionary.

---

40. *Wakan-Tanka* [wah-*kan* than-ka]: the Lakota-Sioux referent for Great Mystery, Great Spirit, Sacred, Divine and/or God (Archambault, *A Retreat with Black Elk*, 10). Prehistorically, *wakan* (sacred) was separate from *tanka* (great), and thus did not suggest a monotheistic deity. Ethno-historians argue that initially the term was used in a non-monotheistic manner to refer to the "totality of the spirit world, its incomprehensibility, and its mysterious, wondrous power. Over time, however, Lakota prayers that were in English simply came to invoke the Great Spirit, which connoted monotheism. Black Elk's spirituality reflects this shift" (Steltenkamp, *Nicholas Black Elk: Medicine Man, Missionary, Mystic*, 11).

41. Archambault, *A Retreat with Black Elk*, 43–44 (italics hers). Thus, if one places his or herself at the center, a place at which God dwells, then God dwells in that person, perhaps loosely reminding those in the Christian tradition of the Eastern Orthodox understanding of *theōsis* or divinization which refers to the human sharing in the divine life of God in some manner.

42. Archambault, *A Retreat with Black Elk*, 20.

2) The Sacred Pipe

An important ritual in the Lakota tradition is the sharing of the sacred pipe. As reported by DeMallie's record, it surfaces in a prominent place in Black Elk's vision. He receives the pipe from the third grandfather. From a Christian perspective the pipe functions sacramentally and, if there is evidence to suggest that Black Elk understood it in a similar way, it may have contributed to his understanding of the two traditions as compatible. Though "there is no [perfect] parallel to the pipe in the Christian tradition,"[43] it was most often likened to scripture and the Eucharist.

"The peace pipe was the Bible to our tribe,"[44] reports Black Elk.[45] Pine Ridge elder Ben Marrowbone confirms this in his telling of the woman gifting the pipe to the people. She told them, "That pipe—it's a road to take—a road of honesty—a road to heaven. It teaches how to lead a good life, like the Ten Commandments."[46] From a Christian perspective, it sacramentally reveals God's self in a similar manner that scripture might be read sacramentally by devotional readers. It yields a spiritual and moral hermeneutic.

In a similar fashion, the pipe can be compared even more strikingly to the Eucharist. For Black Elk in particular, reports his daughter Lucy Looks Twice, "receiving communion was what he really held sacred."[47] Marrowbone interprets the Eucharist as a gift from God brought through the "white people." In describing Black Elk, he reports:

> Before he converted [to Catholicism], Nick Black Elk talked to Almighty God with that pipe. He learned that some god talked to white people. That's why those catechists believed in the Catholic Church. Nobody said, "Oh, you fool you!" No. That's the great Almighty you are respecting and honoring—in a new way. And just as we were brought the sacred pipe, we now had the sacred bread from heaven.[48]

The Christian might affirm complementarity here, for the Sacred Pipe does not replace nor negate the Eucharist. They are different but not incompatible. Rather the pipe complements the Eucharist and can stand alongside it

---

43. Costello, *Black Elk*, 113.

44. DeMallie, ed., *The Sixth Grandfather*, 334.

45. Costello draws this theme out and points more specifically to the pipe as playing the role of the Torah and Hebrew Bible within the Christian tradition, that is, as preparing the way for the gospel (Costello, *Black Elk*, 112–13).

46. Steltenkamp, *Black Elk*, 105.

47. Paul Steinmetz, *Pipe, Bible and Peyote among the Oglala Lakota*, 158.

48. Steltenkamp, *Black Elk*, 104.

as a valid sacramental ritual. True complementarity here entails a two-way street; both the Catholic Eucharist and the Lakota sacred pipe ceremony remain open to the other bringing something new. If each religion remains open to an internal dynamism and dialogue with itself, then it will prove more successful in surviving and adapting in light of its encounter with the other.[49] Clyde Holler refers to these religions as "living religions" since they are able to "change in response to new circumstances and challenges. This has been especially true of Native American religions, which have changed rapidly and drastically in response to forced cultural change and contact with Christianity."[50] Christians can learn something here from the Native American traditions and their ability to adapt and change (even if due to unwelcomed coercion). As a child, Black Elk "was taught to look for the Sacred wherever, and however, it might appear."[51] Not only is this attitude almost necessary for the survival of any tradition in a rapidly growing globalized and pluralistic world, but also teaches the Christian to remain humbly open to finding the divine in the world in many ways.

The story of the pipe being given to the Lakota by the 'Buffalo Cow Woman'[52] has been likened, by some "pre-reservation Lakota," to Mary providing the gift of Jesus.[53] By participating in the pipe ritual or Eucharist, one participates in the divine in an important, sacred, and sacramental way. From the Christian perspective, the pipe as sacrament often functioned in communal ceremonies and offered a path for the participants to commemorate ('to make memorial') past events and enter into sacred space and time. The Christian need not restrict this sacramental element of commemoration to the biblical traditions alone, but rather can observe its function in other contexts, cultures, and religious traditions. Though it was never "officially incorporated into the Catholic liturgy, the use of the Sacred Pipe was accepted and even participated in by Jesuits."[54] The Sacred Pipe and

---

49. Martin Buber might refer to this as "genuine dialogue," and further still as "sacramental dialogue" in that via genuine dialogue, one "tastes God" through engaging, and being engaged by, the other in a self-implicating way (Buber, *Between Man and Man*).

50. Holler, "Black Elk's Relationship to Christianity," 37.

51. Steltenkamp, *Nicholas Black Elk: Medicine Man, Missionary, Mystic*, 228–29.

52. In Lakota narrative, Buffalo Cow Woman "carried the pipe as if carrying a child." Her "pipe-child helped the people down life's road," thus "it was not difficult for many people to equate her" with the sacred Mary (Steltenkamp, *Nicholas Black Elk: Medicine Man, Missionary, Mystic*, 227–33). Black Elk recounts the Lakota story of the origins of the sacred pipe in the Black Elk, "Gift of the Sacred Pipe," 3–9.

53. Steltenkamp, *Nicholas Black Elk: Medicine Man, Missionary, Mystic*, 227.

54. Costello, *Black Elk*, 35.

other Lakota customs[55] were accepted by the Jesuits and inculturated into the Catholic mass.

Black Elk's openness to new ways of finding the sacred in other traditions teaches a lesson in humility,[56] hospitality,[57] and openness. Non-Native Christians may remain open to the Lakota ways as legitimate and authentic paths to the sacred without reducing them to mislabeled forms of Christian ritual. In other words, as Black Elk accepted communion as an authentic path to the sacred, so too might the non-Native Christian accept the pipe as an authentic sacramental path to the sacred in its own right apart from or within the Christian tradition. This acceptance is reminiscent of the general attitude cultivated by Black Elk in his openness to the sacredness of all things (see pansacrality below).

3) The Making of Relatives

The Lakota rite 'the making of relatives'[58] sought to establish relations among the people by fostering kinship amongst all. Its origins lie in the vision imparted by *Wakan-Tanka* to Matohoshila, a Lakota visionary. By cooperating with the agriculturally based Ree tribe, an enemy of the Lakota, peace was established through this new rite involving corn.[59] This rite was then extended to all the members within the tribe entailing the treatment of others as if they were brothers, sisters, mothers, fathers, cousins, and so on, despite lacking direct ancestral relations. Horizontal and vertical implications[60] stem from this rite; or as Black Elk explains it, there is "a three-fold peace."[61]

---

55. E.g., naming ceremony, lighting the pipe from the alter candles during mass, the making of relatives, wailing and placing the body on a raised platform at funerals (Costello, *Black Elk*, 35).

56. The "recognition of the very possibility of change or growth within one's own tradition" (Cornille, "Conditions for Inter-Religious Dialogue," 21).

57. The "attitude of generous openness to the (possible) presence of truth in the other religion may be called hospitality" (Cornille, *The Im-Possibility of Interreligious Dialogue*, 177).

58. *hunkapi* [hoonh *gah* pee] (Archambault, *A Retreat with Black Elk*, 11).

59. Costello, *Black Elk*, 79.

60. I employ the terms 'horizontal' and 'vertical' simply as symbolic shorthand to distinguish between the human-human relationship and the human-sacred relationship respectfully. I am not affirming nor negating God's absolute transcendence or God's absolute immanence. Black Elk does not use these terms either.

61. Black Elk, "Gift of the Sacred Pipe," 115.

Horizontally, it binds the people together in an external and internal manner; that is, both inter-tribally (between two nations) and intra-tribally (between two persons within the tribe). Vertically, the bond between person(s) and *Wakan-Tanka* is established and reaffirmed. This vertical dimension is described by Black Elk as the first peace,

> which comes within the souls of men when they realize their relationship, their oneness, with the universe and all its Powers, and when they realize that at the center of the universe dwells *Wakan-Tanka*, and that this center is really everywhere, it is within each [person] . . . This is the real Peace, and the others are but reflections of this.[62]

This peace and its reflections shine horizontally between persons and nations.

Black Elk understands that the bond between persons, relatives, and nations receives its power from the perfect peace of *Wakan-Tanka*. The horizontal manifestations of peace between persons and nations, though existing in imperfect ways, make present the sacred center at which God dwells. Hence, Black Elk deems this a rite in which the participant establishes his or her relationship with the cosmos, which reflects the reality of love between persons and *Wakan-Tanka*. Further, the love of *Wakan-Tanka* extends to others within one's nation and without.[63] Spiritually, when one places his or her self in the center of the sacred hoop in this manner, he or she achieves their spiritual pinnacle "in balance with all the sacred directions. [Since] then the powers of the earth and symbols of all these directions coalesce dynamically within the soul of the person who stands at the Center with a pure heart."[64] The standing at the Center with a pure heart might remind non-Native Christians of the call to seek right relationship, or attunement, to God and the cosmos. It resonates with the importance of striving for the sacramental revelation of both God and self in relationship.

4) Pansacrality

After several decades of living, learning, and growing in two traditions open to finding God in all things, Black Elk eventually developed the following vision evident in this narrative from his late years:

---

62. Ibid.
63. Ibid., 101.
64. Archambault, *A Retreat with Black Elk*, 82.

We should understand well that all things are the works of the Great Spirit.[65] We should know that He is within all things: the trees, the grasses, the rivers, the mountains, and all the four-legged animals, and the winged peoples; and even more important, we should understand that He is also above all these things and peoples. When we do understand all this deeply in our hearts, then we will fear, and love, and know the Great Spirit, and then we will be and act and live as He intends.[66]

Similar to Christian pansacramentality, Black Elk finds the dualism of nature and supernature problematic. This is not an amendment of the Lakota tradition by Black Elk in order to conform to the Christian tradition and cosmic worldview. Rather, as Steltenkamp recognizes, even prior to Black Elk, the "use of the term 'supernatural' to explain this mystery [of *Wakan-Tanka*] was tenuous because *wakan* (sacred) realties were so evident in the natural order. No neat separation existed between religion and the rest of Lakota daily life."[67] The development and continual affirmation of these neatly separated categories perhaps owe their existence to medieval and so-called 'enlightened' modern thinking. Pre-modern Christianity and Lakota religion blur the line between the sacred and ordinary to a degree in which one might reasonably claim that all things hold the potential for the *wakan*. For the Christian that believes this nature/supernature dichotomy to be false or problematic, all things within the cosmos, including the cosmos as such, can be understood as holding sacramental potential.[68]

Several scholars report that one of the most positive teachings Black Elk took from his time on the road in Europe and with William F. 'Buffalo Bill' Cody's Wild West Show, was his exposure to Christianity. Despite being unimpressed with most European customs, he returned having been impressed with their faith. He explains, "I know the white man's customs

---

65. *Wakan Tanka*

66. Black Elk, "Forward," xx.

67. Steltenkamp, *Nicholas Black Elk: Medicine Man, Missionary, Mystic*, 11 (parentheses and italics mine).

68. Most Lakota do not employ the term sacramental, but rather might refer to this actualized potentiality as *wakan*, while many Christians refer to it as God's self or grace (God's potential self-extension in the cosmos via sacramental representation). Although I have encountered non-Christian Natives and anti-Christian Natives use the term sacrament to refer to vehicles in their own tradition. A cursory review of the term's origin will reveal its pre-Christian heritage and will show it is by no means a term created and owned by Christianity. From within both Black Elk's spirituality and Christianity, the cosmos can be understood in a panentheistic manner; that is, the divine is in all things and all things are in the divine, yet the divine can be understood as transcendent of the cosmos by potentially existing as other than the cosmos as such.

well. One custom is very good. Whoever believes in God will find good ways . . . Of the white man's many customs, only his faith . . . I wanted to understand."[69] After his conversion in 1904, and upon his return to Pine Ridge, Black Elk sought to understand the faith of the *wasicu*.[70] Archambault speculates that "perhaps his gift of immense spiritual sensitivity opened a way for him to recognize *wakan* when it was manifested within another, very different socio-religious context."[71] Black Elk is portrayed by the many who write about him as a natural interfaith learner open to new paths and new ways present in other traditions. Even Niehardt's Black Elk, in *Black Elk Speaks*, reflects this. Upon joining the Wild West Show, Black Elk reflects, "They told us this show would go across the big water to strange lands, and I thought I ought to go, because I might learn some secret of the *Wasichu* that would help my people somehow."[72]

Phillip Arnold has suggested that Native Christians, such as Rigoberta Menchú of Guatemala and Black Elk, "consistently express a sense of religion that is indigenous in spite of its being Catholic. Their sense of the sacred was/is actively opposed to an understanding of religion as abstract, transcendent, or Utopian."[73] By "Utopian," he is referring to the Christianity of the white European American immigrants who were "placeless,"[74] distinguished from the "indigenous Christianity" of the inculturated natives who were connected to the materiality of the land and place.[75] Arnold attributes to Natives, such as Menchú and Black Elk, the contributions of "creative religious innovations"[76] to Christianity. Although they certainly contributed creative and constructive innovations to Christianity, the inclinations to relate religion to land, place, and materiality were not absent to Christianity. Rather, this sacramental aspect was repressed in some of the Christian traditions pushed on the Natives people (e.g., puritanical and pietistic Protestantism). Arnold is astute in his recommendation that these innovations "can help non-Natives to critically re-evaluate the material dimensions of American religious life."[77] This is certainly the case when combined with

---

69. DeMallie, 8.

70. *wasicu* [wah *shi* chu], stranger, white person (Archambault, *A Retreat with Black Elk*, 10).

71. Archambault, *A Retreat with Black Elk*, 26.

72. Niehardt, *Black Elk Speaks*, chap. 19.

73. Arnold, 107.

74. Ibid., 88.

75. Ibid., 87.

76. Ibid., 108.

77. Ibid.

the retrieval of the sacramental tradition in Christianity. These Native innovations can assist the non-Native Christian in retrieving this aspect of the tradition while broadening the understanding of sacramentality at work in other traditions.

Though Black Elk himself seemed to be extraordinarily perceptive to spiritual experience, the openness of the two traditions for finding the sacred in all things might also contribute to his spirituality. Without such an accommodating tenet, the difficulty of compatibility and complementarity increases. The openness of Black Elk and his Lakota heritage combined with the pansacramentality of the Ignatian principle of 'finding God in all things' as stressed by his Jesuits peers, helped to facilitate the fertile conditions for his MRI. Moreover, he provides non-Native Christians the opportunity to affirm the pansacramentalism of Black Elk's spirituality and accept his MRI without scandal.

Multiple Religious Identity

Black Elk's multiple religious identity (MRI) is made possible, in part, through the sacramental openness of Christianity and Black Elk.[78] If Keith Ward is accurate in his claim that Christianity is essentially liberal at its roots, then the Christian should have little to be scandalized about in Black Elk's MRI. The category of sacrament allows the Christian to permit and invite MRI.[79] Steltenkamp observes Black Elk's inherent openness to the sacramentality of the Jesuit priests, "who appear to have been kindly men who brought a repertoire of ritual that was also a medium that spoke to the heart of the holy-man's religious upbringing. Their 'sacraments' reminded him that *Wakan Tanka* still resided within the nation's hoop,"[80] despite being governed as a reservation under the auspices of the United States.

---

78. This claim draws on the symbolic and sacramental openness of Christian theology and its incarnational view of the cosmos. It does not rely on discerning the precise ontological or historical status of the incarnation since both realist and metaphorical interpretations of the incarnation lend themselves to an incarnational view of cosmos (e.g., for two opposing, yet accommodating, views, see Borg and Wright, *The Meaning of Jesus*).

79. Most often the phenomenon of MRI originates in those coming from the Christian tradition seeking to participate in a non-Christian tradition (e.g., Henri Le Saux, Bede Griffiths, and Raimundo Panikkar). Black Elk, however, presents a different dynamic, that of a 'convert' from a non-Christian tradition to Christianity while retaining his former religious identity (e.g., Manual C. Parekh and Brhmabandhav Upadhyaya). The challenge remains, with both dynamics, in retaining symmetry in relative commitments and avoiding one 'trumping' the other, if at all possible.

80. Steltenkamp, *Nicholas Black Elk: Medicine Man, Missionary, Mystic,* 221 (italics

In his self-described postcolonial and post-Western Christian approach, Costello concludes that Black Elk was indeed a sincere practicing Catholic for his last forty-six years. His critique yields a Black Elk that "is at once a sincere Catholic, a Lakota Holy man, and an active agent fighting for survival in a colonial world."[81] It is unclear, based on his text alone, whether Costello would deem this authentic MRI or an instance of a practicing Catholic who re-appropriated his Lakota worldview to conform to Catholicism, thus negating or amending all incompatible Lakota elements. In a manner similar to Jacques Dupuis' explanation of various Hindu-Christian identities, the interpretation of Black Elk as a Lakota Catholic or Catholic Lakota can be distinguished from the identity of MRI.[82] For instance, to refer to Black Elk as a Lakota Catholic might be to say that he embraced the Lakota culture and the Catholic religion; while referring to him as a Catholic Lakota might mean to say he has joined the Catholic cultural framework with Lakota spiritual beliefs. Neither constitute genuine MRI. Rather, the former identifies Black Elk as one who married the Lakota culture to the practice of Catholic faith, which would ultimately deem Black Elk's religion Catholicism and his culture Lakota (which is rather problematic since there is no clear distinction between religion and culture in the Lakota tradition and for some Catholic contexts as well).

To claim that Black Elk exhibited authentic MRI is to suggest that he simultaneously embraced, to some degree, both the Catholic and Lakota traditions in a religious manner. Authentic MRI entails that, "one no longer only understands the other from the perspective of Christianity, but also comes to understand the Christian tradition from the perspective of the other."[83] In other words, Black Elk's Lakota tradition makes a deliberate and growth-filled impact on his Catholicism as well.[84] The soil for this impact becomes fertile "when and where a religion has accepted the complementarity of religions,"[85] which Black Elk appears to demonstrate to some degree.

---

mine).

81. Costello, *Black Elk*, 21.

82. Jacques Dupuis writes, "To be a Hindu-Christian, for example, might mean joining in oneself the Hindu culture and the Christian faith. Hinduism would then not be considered as a religious faith, strictly speaking, but as a philosophy and a culture, which, with the necessary adaptations, could serve as a vehicle for Christian faith." In this case, the religious belonging would be singular; that of Christianity cast in a Hindu framework (Dupuis, "Christianity and Religions," 64).

83. Cornille, "Introduction," in *Many Mansions?*, 4.

84. This is what various thinkers have referred to as "passing over," which is to encounter "both the other and the religious experience that the other bears within, together with his or her *Weltanshauung*." (Dupuis, "Christianity and Religions,"63).

85. Cornille, "Introduction," in *Many Mansions?*, 2.

This serves as a constructive tenet for non-Native Christians to adopt as well. This openness comes from both the sacramental tradition of Christianity and, as Steltenkamp proposes, the openness of Black Elk and the Lakota *Weltanshauung*.

> In Childhood, Black Elk learned about creation and his place within it. What he learned reveals to some extent how he understood the ways of the *Wakan*. Like his peers, he was taught to look for the Sacred wherever, and however, it might appear. He believed that if one looked, it could be found, and if one listened, it could be heard. The Sacred was not restricted to one vision, one cultural traditional, one conversion experience, or one insight, but was cumulative.[86]

The non-Native Christian can learn from this wisdom of Black Elk and appropriate it through the robust theological language of sacramentality. It is not a coincidence that Black Elk's MRI can be traced through the conduits of spirituality and sacramentality ('symbolic framework'), for these are, as Catherine Cornille has recognized, the two most common ways of "understanding and legitimating the phenomenon"[87] of multiple religious belonging. The first way, through spiritual experience, often presumes, as Steltenkamp has described above, that "all religious traditions are regarded as different expressions of the same ultimate reality and experience."[88] In this manner spiritual experience, as a means for accessing that ultimate reality, functions as a bridge in appropriating the sacred via cultural practices and phenomena.[89]

The second way, appropriation through the symbolic frameworks of the traditions, allows for the possibility of becoming open to MRI. More specifically, this path might entail appropriating the Christian faith to accommodate the symbolic framework of another. For instance, this is evident in Black Elk's hermeneutical exploration of his childhood vision in light of the Christian tradition and message. This can be understood as a complex form of inculturation, a process in which "the Christian faith has been reformulated in philosophical categories belonging to non-Western traditions."[90]

86. Steltenkamp, *Nicholas Black Elk*, 228–29 (italics mine).

87. Cornille, "Introduction," in *Many Mansions?*, 5.

88. Ibid.

89. For this reason Cornille recognizes that it is probably "no coincidence that the individuals who appear most often as examples of MRB belong to the spiritual branches of traditions and that the intermonastic dialogue has offered much of the food for thought on this question" (Cornille, "Introduction," in *Many Mansions?*, 5).

90. Cornille, "Introduction," in *Many Mansions?*, 5.

Some speculate that Black Elk understood the Sun Dance and Sacred Pipe to be Lakota expressions of the Christian gospel message,[91] which would not necessarily entail MRI, but is rather the inculturation of the Christian message into the Lakota culture. Ultimately this would still be the Christian religion cast in Lakota culture. It is not clear that Black Elk understood it this way, but rather he may have understood the two traditions as authentically different yet compatible.[92]

A necessary presupposition for the possibility of MRI, especially in the case of Black Elk, is the understanding of religions as dynamic and open to new expressions of the divine. This view exhibits a liberal theology, which simply refers to an open and dynamic view of God's presence in the world. Keith Ward challenges Christians to become more liberal, in this sense, and to "see that once an understanding of faith as acceptance of exclusively correct propositions is given up, one can no longer simply say that the Christian faith has the only truth, and that all others are wrong. If faith is response to a disclosure of the divine in this community, then why should there not be different disclosures of the divine in other communities?"[93] In other words, it is quite reasonable to accept Black Elk's dual religious identity as an authentic response to his faith rooted in the Lakota tradition and community. Thus it follows that a dynamic (liberal) Christian approach to faith yields an attitude which views "the many religions . . . as parts of the whole religious history of humanity, and Christianity is one community of discernment among others, not the only source of religious truth."[94]

In order for authentic MRI to occur, the traditions involved ought to remain open to adapting to new situations and addressing questions through encounter and 'genuine dialogue' with each other. Thus, genuine *inter*-religious dialogue entails genuine *intra*-religious dialogue. It will be

---

91. Steltenkamp documents an excerpt from a letter written by Joseph Epes Brown to Father Gall which attempts to articulate a "Metaphysics of the Pipe." Brown writes, "to smoke the Pipe is the same as taking the Holy Christian communion. The form of the pipe is the same as the Xian Cathedral, & it too represents the Universe, with God at the Center"(sic) (Joseph Epes Brown, "Letter to Father Gall"). Steltenkamp concludes that "given Brown's understanding, and given Black Elk's innate tendency to see sacred connectedness everywhere, the two men no doubt helped one another find parallels where others might not" (Steltenkamp, *Nicholas Black Elk: Medicine Man, Missionary, Mystic*, 225).

92. Clyde Holler suggests, "it is important to note that Black Elk's commitment to Christ-ianity does not necessarily imply any lessening of his commitment to traditional Lakota religion. This is clearly the understanding of conversion assumed by the missionaries, but it was not necessarily that of the Indians themselves" (sic) (Holler, "Black Elk's Relationship to Christianity," 39).

93. Ward, "The Importance of Liberal Theology," 51.

94. Ibid., 52.

more difficult, though not impossible, for an immovable religion (culturally and spiritually) to converge with and complement other traditions. Both the Christian tradition and Black Elk's spirituality showcase their convergent dynamism. Cornille claims, "Christian identity is not a static and fixed reality but a fluid and dynamic process that defines itself in reaction to concrete challenges that present themselves in changing circumstances."[95] This can be applied to Black Elk and his spirituality. Further, it correlates with Cornille's "rough-and-ready axiom: the more encompassing a religion's claim to efficacy and truth, the more problematic the possibility of multiple religious belonging. Conversely, it thus seems that the idea of belonging to more than one religion can be tolerated only when and where a religion has accepted the complementarity of religions."[96] If the Christian is willing to heed Cornille's axiom and affirm an openness to learn from, and be complemented and taught by, other religious traditions, the more inviting, and less scandalous, will she find the phenomenon of MRI.

Liberalism is not at all opposed to tradition, as Ward makes clear.[97] He embraces a liberalism "which emphasizes such a positive notion of freedom as the condition of the pursuit of personal excellence and creativity. In this sense, liberalism is not seen at all opposed to tradition. It would indeed value it in so far as tradition preserves the fruits of the creative acts of past generations."[98] Black Elk's liberalism respected the tradition of both his native Lakota heritage and his newly found Catholic faith. He was able to root the rich tradition of the Jesuits' sacramentality within his Lakota spirituality. He represented what Ward envisions as one of the great constructive tasks of interreligious learning and dialogue. Ward writes,

> The great religious traditions are histories of developing reflection on the primal disclosures that constitute a tradition. In their meeting, the opportunity exists for conversations in which each tradition is modified by its greater empathy for the insights embodied in other traditions. It is in this way that diversity, and the freedom it requires, can be helpful to the discovery of the partiality in one's own views, and thus of a more expansive truth.[99]

---

95. Cornille, "Introduction," in *Many Mansions?*, 6; see Jeanrond, "Belonging or Identity."

96. Cornille, "Introduction," in *Many Mansions?*, 2.

97. See footnote 11.

98. Ward, "Liberal Theology and the God of Love," 194.

99. Ibid., 198. Ward goes on to recognize, quite fairly, that this is often where "liberal theologians are sometimes accused of syncretism." He defends against this accusation by pointing out that the famous German liberals of the late nineteenth century

Of course there will remain the question of whether true complementarity without compromise can occur. Bringing a second religious tradition into one's own horizon can create challenges. The classical Christian tradition does not outright ban such a task. For instance, Aquinas's assumption of Aristotle and Christianity's blend with Hellenism has been, in large part, accepted by traditional western Christian orthodoxy. However, today some Christians are continuing Luther's project of calling into question the substance metaphysics employed in the classical tradition on the basis of it being unbiblical. In any case of MRI or multiple philosophical identity or multiple religious-philosophical identity, cases of contradiction must be dealt with. It may be possible to reconcile many of these and it is up to the individual believer to navigate this in his or her own harmonization of the traditions. In the case of Black Elk, he was likely able to embrace the traditions he did because there was little theological competition at play. Rather, he was able to accept and reject non-Lakota rituals based on their merit for leading his community towards the spiritual good and freedom.[100] Sometimes (certainly not always) ethical contradictions can arise in the convergence of two or more traditions. When oppressive and unjust elements rear their head in one tradition, they must be dealt with and denied. It is likely that modifications and compromises are inevitable, but this should not scandalize the believer; rather it ought to be received as an invitation to self-criticism and growth. Christians already do this with their own tradition in various ways. It may be that sometimes conflicts cannot be resolved nor reconciled, and elements may have to be outright denied. This exciting and very challenging journey begins with remaining open to the complementarity of religions.

(e.g., Harnack) were not syncretists, but could be accused of giving up central Christian doctrines such as the Atonement, the Trinity, and the Incarnation. Ward importantly points out that, of course, not all liberals agree and one must be intentional with their language when discussing it. He concludes that, "all that really unites these liberals is that they did not feel themselves bound to ancient Hellenistic formulations of Christian doctrine, and they had seen the acids of criticism dissolve away traditional commitment to the literal inerrancy of Scripture" (ibid., 198).

100. Like many non-Christian traditions and non-Western Christian traditions, indigenous traditions usually emphasize belonging (commitment to community) over belief (confessing doctrines).

Concluding Postscript: An Exercise in Interreligious Learning[101]

This chapter serves as an exercise in interreligious learning from a non-Native Christian perspective. By examining the spirituality of Black Elk and his quest to find the God in two traditions, the Christian is able to broaden his understanding of sacramental functionality. A theological implication of this study is that by employing a panentheistic pansacramentality from within a Christian theology of religious pluralism, the Christian can affirm the validity of other traditions (as well as all things) as potential sacramental representations of the divine. Of course there can (and indeed must) remain some criterion or set of criteria against which oppressive, unjust, and contradictory elements can be rejected. However, the Christian must obviously

---

101. Although Christian theology of religions is not a major focus of this paper, I write out of a working perspective of religious pluralism and not necessarily inclusivism, although a Christian might maintain the same claims from some nuanced version of inclusivism. Unlike the Christian inclusivist, I do not suppose that Black Elk's experiences are simply mislabeled encounters with the Christian God, but rather may be distinct Lakota ways of relating to ultimate reality and truth. However, these categories (inclusivism, pluralism, etc.) may ultimately prove unhelpful. There are several different types of religious pluralism. Anselm Min has proposed six types represented by its corresponding advocates: 1) "phenomenalist" (John Hick and Paul Knitter); 2) "universalist" (Leonard Swidler, Wildfred Cantwell Smith, Niniam Smart, Keith Ward, and David Krieger); 3) "ethical or soteriological pluralism" (Rosemary Ruether, Marjorie Suchocki, Tom Driver, and Paul Knitter); 4) "confessionalist" (Hans Küng, John Cobb, Jürgen Moltmann, John Milbank, and S. Mark Heim); 5) "dialectical" (Anselm Min); and 6) "ontological" (Panikkar). The pluralism I advocate for here need not fall neatly into one of these types, but rather might shares kinship with several. For instance, like Hick and Knitter I remain open to the possibility of one ultimate noumenal reality mediated through different phenomenal languages and cultures. Likewise, with Ward and W.C. Smith, I do not find the possibility of a universal theology scandalous; however, the confessionalist pluralism of Cobb and Moltmann (and perhaps S. Mark Heim), and their respect for religious difference, might also accommodate the proposal being made here. Further, Panikkar's proposal of an ontological diversity of the divine as such may also open a door through which monotheists might remain open to polytheists' experience of Gods (even if not perfectly corroborated by polytheists themselves). Though perhaps interesting and relevant to a certain point, Christian theology of religions is not one of the foci of this paper. Rather it is to propose that, from a non-Native Christian perspective, Black Elk's spirituality can be accepted as a legitimate and authentic way of experiencing divine presence. To do so, it may helpful for the Christian to entertain a pluralistic understanding of pansacramental mediation in which all things hold the potential to represent the divine in their own unique and distinctive manner. This religious orientation can increase the promise for constructive interreligious dialogue for the Christian tradition while demonstrating its ability to respond and adapt to the concrete challenges present in the dynamism of the world (Min, "Loving Without Understanding"; Min, *The Solidarity of Others in a Divided World*, 173–97; and Min, *Paths to the Triune God*, 53).

yield to the other tradition the right to reject the category of sacrament and employ its own language. For instance, the non-Native Christian may claim that the spirituality of Black Elk represents authentic sacramental representations of God in a genuine way, and at the same time accept as equally valid the claim of Black Elk that the Christian tradition represents an authentic path to *Wakan Tanka*. However, in such a proposal the content of the Christian God and *Wakan Tanka* may not line up and serve as a focus of conversation, if indeed applicable. The Christian tradition might represent an authentic path to *Wakan Tanka* in its affirmation of pansacramentality; that is, accepting all things as potential mediators of God. For instance, the Lakota

> see *Wakan Tanka* manifest in a variety of ways in the world. Each of these very different manifestations can actually be referred to as *Wakan Tanka*, and yet *Wakan Tanka* is, in another sense, all of them . . . The real complexity of Lakota thought might be hinted at as unity expressed in diversity. To Lakota Peoples each manifestation is *Wakan Tanka*, yet does not exhaust *Wakan Tanka* . . . *Wakan Tanka* is only one.[102]

Black Elk's personal faith commitment, especially his openness to the sacredness of all things discussed above, demonstrated an inherent liberalness in the sense of honoring both his own Lakota tradition while remaining open to the revelation of the *Wakan Tanka* in other traditions. His account of revelation understands all things as the works of *Wakan Tanka*, who "is within all things" and "also above all things."[103] He provides "an account [of revelation] in terms of a unique type of value-commitment and with a tradition of such discernments preserved in a distinctive community."[104] Further, this panentheistic openness assists in engendering a constructive and positive environment within which interreligious learning might flourish.

A non-Native Christianity set within a Lakota context might be understood as another diverse path towards *Wakan Tanka*, the creator.[105] Regardless, the affirmation of the pansacramental principle offers a promising

---

102. Kidwell, Noley, and Tinker, *A Native American Theology*, 59, 60 (italics mine).
103. Black Elk, "Forward," xx.
104. Ward, "The Importance of Liberal Theology," 49.
105. One might even go further, with special care and courage, to equate the content of *Wakan Tanka* with the Christian Godhead; however, doing so will most likely present challenges, and may not be necessary if one were to accept a theology of ontological pluralism such as Raimon Pankikkar has proposed which espouses a Godhead that is ontologically diverse as such, and thus contains both *Wakan Tanka* and the Christian deity (as well as other expressions of God).

entry point into this conversation. The following narrative from Muskogee medicine man Phillip Deere demonstrates this,

> Your missionary ancestors told Indian people that they were worshipping a false god when we pray to the sun. The sun is the most powerful physical presence in our lives. Without it we could not live and our world would perish. Yet our reverence for it, our awe, was considered idolatry.
>
> But your missionary ancestors misunderstood even that much, because we never worshipped the sun. We merely saw in it the reflection of the sacred, the creator, and used its image to focus our prayers of thanksgiving for Creator's life-giving power. It is, for us, a constant reminder of the creative power of God, as we greet the sun in the morning when we first arise and again in the evening. In between, as we go about our day, we constantly will see our shadow on the ground and will be reminded again of God's creative goodness. We can stop, look up, and say a short prayer whenever this happens.[106]

In a manner commencing from the pansacramental principle, two traditions can equally respect one another in their difference, yet complement the other in their mutual theological sharing. Black Elk, as a kind of a natural bridge figure between two traditions, offers an opportunity for interreligious convergence, encounter, and learning. This chapter has sought to argue that Black Elk's spirituality, from a non-Native Christian perspective, aids in understanding and articulating a Christian pansacramental and panentheistic vision while helping to descandalize MRI for Christians.[107] In this non-Native approach to Native spirituality, this paper takes direction from George Tinker who teaches that "the question that is finally important is not 'who are these exotic creature who are so different from ourselves?' but rather, 'how will we together (non-Indian and Indian) build the future differently than we have built the colonial past?'"[108] This paper represents one small step towards building that future by embracing Native and Native Christian spiritual traditions.

---

106. Kidwell, Noley, and Tinker, *A Native American Theology*, 52; and quoted in Tinker, *American Indian Liberation*, 27.

107. I have not sought to impose my view on Black Elk, although I may have unintentionally done so in part. Rather the intent of my examination of his Lakota spirituality is both complementary and complimentary; the former in that his spirituality complements the Christian sacramental tradition, and the latter in praising Black Elk for taking a Christian claim more seriously than many Christians do: the claim that God is in all things.

108. Tinker, *American Indian Liberation*, 4.

Appendix

The phrase "Historical Black Elk" is borrowed from Damian Costello, to refer to the authentic Black Elk. This is placed against the phrase "literary Black Elk" as portrayed by various writers. Costello refers to the "literary Black Elk" as the "essentialist Black Elk" in reference to the Black Elk portrayed by Neihardt and understood as normative by popular culture. Costello contests the "essentialist Black Elk" as normative and instead proposes, what he refers to as, the "Lakota Catholic Black Elk," as the authentic Black Elk.

Further, Costello has sought the historical Black Elk grounded in post-colonial and post-western Christian scholarship in his text *Black Elk: Colonialism and Lakota Catholicism*. He explains, "To understand Black Elk properly, we must place his story within the story of Western colonialism as told by the colonized . . . Black Elk's Catholicism as described by the Lakota community and historical record is normative and more easily understood by relocating it within the framework of postcolonialism and post-Western Christianity."[109]

This postcolonial scholarship, Costello argues, operates within an arena in which colonized peoples have now become scholars and have brought with them their own postcolonial interpretations. This entails a shattering of the old colonial paradigms from which writers such as Neihardt operated. The well-known post-colonial Biblical hermeneut, R.S. Sugirtharajah, emphasizes the complexity involved when attempting to discern the relationship between colonized and colonizer. The older, over-simplified, often binary, categories of colonial thought must be rejected in favor of a broader approach. He writes, "Postcolonialism does not mean that the colonized are innocent, generous and principled, whereas the former colonizers, and now the new colonizers, are all innately culpable, greedy and responsible for all social evils. . . . The current postcolonialism tries to emphasize that this relationship between ruler and the ruled is complex, full of cross-trading and mutual appropriation and confrontation."[110]

The assumption of the 'noble savage' has been challenged and rejected; that is, not all savages are noble nor are all rulers oppressive. Thus, postcolonial thought remains suspicious of the attempt to naively characterize Black Elk as a victim striving for mere survival. This remains too formulaic and oversimplified in its ignorance of a vastly more complex reality. Costello does not fault Neihardt for making these colonial assumptions, but rather

---

109. Costello, *Black Elk*, 60.
110. Sugirtharajah, *The Bible and the Third World*, 279–80.

argues that his work is "understandable in the context of postcolonialism and post-Western Christianity." Neihardt's "biography of Black Elk is essentially accurate but problematic due to its context within Western colonialism and American modernity."[111]

Instead, Costello offers categories which "allow for a unified understanding of Black Elk as a Lakota Catholic agent," entertaining the reality that Black Elk lived as both a sincere Catholic and Lakota simultaneously. He argues that Black Elk was able to reconstruct his Lakota tradition "in light of the Christian narrative" and was thus "at once a sincere Catholic, a Lakota holy man, and an active agent fighting for survival in a colonial world."[112] Costello's post-colonial approach is not immune to criticism itself. For instance, though he justifiably illuminates the failings of Neihardt's colonial assumptions, he fails to account for the possible colonial attitudes and cultural importation on behalf of the reservation Jesuits.[113] Further, it could be argued that Costello's "Lakota Catholic Black Elk" is also simply a partially fictional construct in the same manner that Neihardt constructed his Black Elk, though each author with his own separate agenda.

This chapter is not immune from being accused of colonialism itself. Perhaps the sacramental analysis above is simply a Christian appropriation of the Lakota tradition. Conversely, perhaps Black Elks' vision is simply a Lakota appropriation of the Christian tradition. Moreover, the Ghost Dance and its accompanying message may also fall into this latter category; that is, it is a Native reappropriation of the messiah story. If the Jesuits and the Lakota were to incorporate pipe smoking into the celebration of the Eucharist, we might then reasonably inquire as to which party is guilty of appropriation. Further, is such appropriation scandalous in the first place? These questions are neither uninteresting nor unimportant, however this chapter does not address the normativity regarding one's appropriation of the other. Rather, it engages Black Elk's spirituality from a non-Native Christian perspective with the aim of learning about sacramentality and its possible function in the compatibility of these traditions and the acceptability of multiple religious identity.

---

111. Costello, *Black Elk*, 19.
112. Ibid., 20.
113. Martinez, 1014–17.

10

Dostoevsky and Wendell Berry
Sacramental Spirituality and Literature[1]

DOSTOEVSKY AND WENDELL BERRY depict one of the foundational Christian claims (for both Eastern and Western traditions) with implications for both theology and spirituality. This is the presence of sacramental spirituality in the human experience of the world. The particular lived religious experience (spirituality) of their literary characters reveals a concretization of sacramental mediation between theology and spirituality, as well as between God and world. In this chapter, I employ literature as a case study for sacramental spirituality; that is, literature serves as a lens through which sacramental spirituality might be understood more clearly.[2] Sacramental spirituality is about one's particular experience of God in the world. Pansacramentality is then the idea that all things hold sacramental potential and are thus able to represent God in the world. In particular, this chapter examines anti-

---

1. A version of this chapter first appeared as Gustafson, "Sacramental Spirituality in *The Brothers Karamazov* and Wendell Berry's Port William Characters."

2. In keeping with the spirit of this book, the term "sacramental" is employed to refer to that element of the Christian tradition which accounts for the potential of a person, thing, place, idea, and experience (among others), to represent the real presence of the divine (God) in the world. Sacraments mediate between the divine and the world. This broad view of sacraments allows for an infinite number of potential sacraments, thus it does not intend to reduce sacraments to a fixed number (e.g., whether one believes in seven sacraments or two). In this way all things hold the potential to mediate God in the world, thus maintaining a pansacramental understanding of the cosmos. The term spirituality refers to the lived religious experience of a particular individual in the world.

dualism, kenotic *theōsis*, and the sacramental vision in Dostoevsky's *The Brothers Karamazov* and Wendell Berry's Port William characters.

> To interpret literary texts from a religious perspective is to draw upon a host of theological ideas and to allow these to shape the way one thinks about the worlds that are imagined through literature. Religious thought brings with it certain ways of apprehending the whole of reality, and although the impact of reflecting on the world in the light of God is almost impossible to isolate fully, it influences both what we look for in literary texts and how we think about what we find there.[3]

As Mark Knight suggests above, the goal here is to allow the following texts to help shape the way one thinks about the world. Through the concretization of their characters, they help demonstrate why pansacramentality and panentheism are fruitful resources for thinking theologically and "apprehending the whole of reality."

Proceeding thematically, this chapter focuses on the concepts of antidualism, kenotic *theōsis*, and the sacramental vision. Both Dostoevsky's masterpiece, *The Brothers Karamazov*, and Wendell Berry's novels, serve as a medium through which this sacramental spirituality emerges. Central themes for this spirituality arise from the characters and their experiences. Dostoevsky and Berry remain separated by time, place, culture, and, to some degree, religious orientation. However, both share a basic theological Christian perspective; Dostoevsky writes against the backdrop of Russian Orthodoxy and Berry against an incarnationally and sacramentally-imbued agrarian worldview. I do not intend to suggest that either writer opposes his tradition. In Dostoevsky, there is little that might be deemed scandalous to the Russian Orthodox tradition. On the other hand Berry's commentary against traditional institutionalized religion in America is more explicit; however, I do not interpret Berry as opposing his organized religion in favor of a pansacramental vision. To do so would be setting up a false dichotomy. Rather, Berry is expressing the need to emphasize an aspect of his faith which is often lost within the fold of contemporary Western Christianity: seeing the world pansacramentally. In this manner, I understand Berry's critique in the same vein as Jesus of Nazareth in the New Testament, who did not reject Judaism as such, but the contemporary version employed by its leaders. In any case, the difference and similarities between these two writers' context should not go without notice, for they contribute to the underlying emphasis on their respective sacramental tendencies.

---

3. Mark Knight, *An Introduction to Religion and Literature*, 2.

Dostoevsky and Berry, in their literary characters, effectively concretize sacramental spirituality that clarifies philosophical and theological implications in a manner that can be more accessible than a brute examination of philosophy and theology. In what follows, I draw on these characters as a lens through which sacramental spirituality is concretized. First, I examine the anti-dualism in *The Brothers Karamazov*, second I explore kenotic *theōsis* in Dostoevsky's Zosima, and finally, I turn to the sacramental vision of Berry's Port William characters.

Anti-Dualism in The Brothers Karamazov

The Brothers Karamazov remains a deeply complex text with multiple layers concerning ethics, politics, psychology, philosophy, anthropology, family, religion, responsibility, free will, immortality, God, and others. The burden of this section will be to introduce the anti-dualist tendency of the text as it relates to sacramentality (in particular, the sacramentality of Dostoevsky's Russian Orthodox Christianity[4]). David S. Cunningham, in his chapter, "'The Brothers Karamazov' as Trinitarian Theology," remarks that one of the fundamental motivators behind the formation of Trinitarian theology was the necessity to combat the radical dualism of spirit and matter supposedly prevalent in Platonic and Greek philosophy.[5] Although I may not necessarily share Cunningham's enthusiasm for the claim that the doctrine of the Trinity was developed to primarily combat Gnostic and docetist tendencies and radical monotheism in Christianity, I can affirm that the promotion of incarnationalism and sacramentality does. Regardless of whether or not the Trinitarian doctrine was developed to combat such tendencies, it still allows for a Godhead that is both in the world (immanent) and beyond the world (transcendent). In order to understand the cosmos as one in which persons, events, and things, might (re)present God, yet without reducing God to those persons, events and things (which might entail pantheism), one's theology need oppose both the radical separation of God and the material world (e.g. Gnosticism), and the radical reduction of God to world (i.e. the pantheistic collapse of the God-world distinction altogether). Cunningham recognizes the *via media* functionality of Trinitarian language in its ability

---

4. I am not attempting to interpret the inner psyche of the author nor evoke his definitive theology, but rather draw out some of the reasonable theological implications of the text.

5. David Cunningham, "'The Brothers Karamazov' as Trinitarian Theology," I am indebted to Cunningham's work here as I draw on many of his examples and reinterpret them in light of sacramental spirituality.

to avoid both poles. He demonstrates how this Trinitarian tendency comes out in the *The Brothers Karamazov* in its avoidance of binary oppositions.[6]

Putting the explicit Trinitarian aspects aside, I will focus on the sacramental spirituality that stems from the same concept that allows for the Trinitarian claims of God's immanence and transcendence; that is, the understanding of God's presence sacramentally, and one's experience of it as such, is made intelligible through a sacramental worldview that allows for a God that exists in all things, yet remains beyond all things. The doctrine of the trinity allows for such a move by making available a third option, thus exposing the false dilemma of *either* radical monotheism, in which Jesus' (re)presentation and incarnation of God is denied, *or* gnostic dualism, in which the material fleshiness of Jesus must be denied as divinely significant. Sacramentality allows one to navigate between the suffocating *either/or* polar binaries: *either* God is immanent *or* transcendent, God is *either* one *or* many, one or three, but not both. To simultaneously posit both suggests a scandal to the logical mind, for it offends reason by affirming seemingly contradictory claims at the same time. However, with such a worldview, one misses the point of sacramentality as that which allows for the presence of God, without reducing God. In the text, Ivan Karamazov (governed by logic, reason, intelligence and the categories of the modern enlightenment relative to his brothers) famously struggles with the conceptual existence of God. For Ivan, God is a logical problem to be solved, a proposition to be reasoned out. His mind, which he freely admits is one that operates on the presuppositions of 'Euclidian geometry,' is one that cannot reconcile seemingly opposing binaries such as those previously mentioned. To his younger brother Alyosha, Ivan declares,

> there were and are even now geometers and philosophers, even some of the most outstanding among them, who doubt that the whole universe, or, even more broadly, the whole being, was created purely in accordance with Euclidean geometry; they even dare to dream that two parallel lines, which according to Euclid cannot possibly meet on earth, may perhaps meet somewhere in infinity. I, my dear, have come to the conclusion that if I cannot understand even that, then it is not for me to understand about God. I humbly confess that I do not have any ability to resolve such questions, I have a Euclidean mind, an earthly mind, and therefore it is not for us to resolve things that are not of this world.[7]

---

6. Ibid.

7. Dostoevsky, *The Brothers Karamazov*, 235.

The either/or mentality here is upheld by the mind of Ivan, one that ultimately cannot accept the God of his younger brother, the God of Christianity which strives to account for a God that is *both* in the world *and* beyond the world.

While Ivan is understood as representing the intellectual, his older brother Dmitry stands securely rooted in 'sensuality.' Following an emotionally-charged recitation of Schiller's poem "To Joy," in which joy is found in the world of creation, nature and the sensuality of insects, Dmitry preaches to Alyosha,

> I want to tell you about the 'insects,' about those to whom God gave sensuality: To insects—sensuality! I am that very insect, brother, and those words are precisely about me. And all of us Karamazovs are like that, and in you, an angel, the same insect lives and stirs up storms in your blood. Storms, because sensuality is a storm, more than a storm! Beauty is a fearful and terrible thing! Fearful because it's undeniable, and it cannot be defined, because here God gave us only riddles. Here the shores converge, here all contradictions live together. I'm a very uneducated man, brother, but I've thought about it a lot . . . Too many riddles oppress man on earth.[8]

Alyosha, the youngest, stands between his two brothers, the Euclidean educated Ivan, rooted in reason, and the 'very uneducated' Dmitry, rooted in the immediacy of sensual joy. His religious tradition, which endorses sacramental categories, allows him to mediate between the two brothers. For Ivan, God remains rooted in concepts (e.g. he accepts a God that is pure and simple), while for Dmitry, God is both terrifyingly and beautifully rooted in earthly matter. Language which adequately posits God's presence in matter without reducing God to that matter on the one hand, and without reducing God to the mere affirmation of perfect concepts (e.g., 'God is pure and simple') on the other hand, functions to mediate between God and world while accommodating such an understanding of the Godhead; this language is sacramentality.

---

8. Ibid., 108.

Kenotic Theōsis in Father Zosima[9]

An anonymous contemporary Orthodox monk has declared, "The aim of man's life is union (*henōsis*) with God and deification[10] (*theōsis*)."[11] According to the Christian Orthodox tradition, deification is the human sharing, via grace, in the divine life of God.[12] *Kenosis* refers to the imitation of Jesus' extreme humility, which, according to Paul in his letter to the Philippians, occurred when Jesus "emptied himself, taking the form of a slave."[13] Understood in this Pauline context, the kenotic imitator strives to empty his or her self through humility and baptism, and thus, according to Paul's letter to the Galatians, "put on Christ like a garment." "Putting on Christ" by itself is not *theōsis*, but rather serves as a metaphor to refer to the immersion into and becoming similar to Christ, not by nature, but by sacramental participation. According to Vladimir Lossky, for the Russian Orthodox tradition, "the perfection of the person consists in self-abandonment: the person expresses itself most truly in that it renounces to exist for itself. It is the self-emptying of the Person of the Son, the Divine κέwσις."[14] This path towards perfection manifests itself in the Russian context through "holy foolishness," which,

---

9. On the character of Father Zosima, Dostoevsky wrote, "He could not express himself in other language or in another spirit than that which I gave him . . . I took his person and figure from the Old Russian monks and prelates: together with deep humility [they had] limitless hopes for the future of Russia, about its moral and even political predestination" (Dostoevsky, "Letter to editor Nikolai Lyubimov").

10. Here I employ the terms *theōsis*, deification and divinization synonymously. However, it should be recognized that these terms can take on different meanings.

11. [Anonymous] Monk of the Eastern Church, "The Essentials of Orthodox Spirituality" 108.

12. Vladimir Lossky writes, "The deification or θέωσις of the creature will be realized in its fullness only in the age to come after the resurrection of the dead. This deifing union has, nevertheless, to be fulfilled ever more and more even in this present life, through the transformation of our corruptible and depraved nature and by its adaptation to eternal life" (Lossky, *The Mystical Theology of the Eastern Church*, 196).

13. Margaret Ziolkowski makes an important distinction. She writes, "In speaking of the influence of the act described by Paul on the Russian monastic tradition, it is important to distinguish between the concerns of modern kenosis theology and the kenotic stance embraced by many Russian monks from the eleventh to the nineteenth century. Especially in the nineteenth century a number of European theologians sought to define the extent to which Paul's statement may suggest Christ's renunciation of his divine nature. In contrast to traditional patristic exegesis, which viewed this text as a 'scriptural proof of the divinity of Christ, of his real and complete humanity, and of the unity of His Person' kenotic theories of the incarnation question the simultaneity of Christ's divinity and humanity. Such concerns play no role in the medieval Russian kenotic tradition" (Ziolkowski, "Dostoevsky and the Kenotic Tradition," 33).

14. Lossky, *The Mystical Theology of the Eastern Church*, 144.

as Evgenia Cherkasova reminds us, "can be said to represent the extreme form of kenoticism—standing as it does for radical asceticism, rejection of earthly possessions and ambitions, chastity and purity of intention (represented by insanity), and the tireless challenging of the moral and social *status quo*."[15] This is similar to, though not perfectly the same as, the life of a Hindu *sannyasi* and *sādhu*. I suggest that this tandem action of self-emptying and 'putting on Christ' function as kenotic *theōsis*.[16]

Dostoevsky and his works are marked by the clear influence of both *kenosis* and *theōsis*; that is, Dostoevsky's literary monastic models, Fr. Zosima[17] (in *The Brothers* Karamazov) and Fr. Tikhon (in *The Demons*) represent one striving for such a state. Drawing on the concepts of *kenosis* and *theōsis* in the authentic Pauline texts of Philippians and Galatians respectively, I shall draw out the spirituality of Fr. Zosima. *Theōsis* is inherently sacramental and in striving for *theōsis* kenotically, Zosima's spirituality allows one to see and participate in the world sacramentally. First, I shall offer a brief explanation of deification according Dostoevsky's Orthodox tradition, typified by Gregory Palamas and Vladimir Lossky. Secondly, drawing on Bishop Kallistos Ware, I shall trace four clear implications stemming from kenotic deification evident in the sacramental spirituality of Zosima. These four implications are universality, moral responsibility, practicality, and hope.

Orthodox anthropology, represented by Palamas and Lossky, entails the human capacity for participating in God, in the way of Jesus who participated in God. Thus deification marks the *telos* towards which persons strive. The doctrine of deification can be scripturally based both in the Hebrew and Christian Scriptures, most prominently on the Gospel of John and the Pauline theme of "putting on Christ"[18] and receiving eternal "life in Christ."[19] Additionally, 2 Peter recognizes the innate human potential to become "partakers of the divine nature."[20] Orthodox anthropology em-

---

15. Cherkasova, "The Ambiguity of Suffering: Dostoevsky and the Russian Orthodox Tradition," 7 (italics hers).

16. Cherkasova covers the themes of kenosis and co-suffering (what I refer to as *sobornost*) in Dostoevsky more extensively in her chapter, "The Ambiguity of Suffering: Dostoevsky and the Russian Orthodox Tradition."

17. Zosima is thought to be modeled after Tikhon of Zadonsk and "the three great elders of the monastery of Optina Pustyn,' the last of whom, Amvrosy, was visited by Dostoevsky and had profound impact on the genesis of Zosima's character" (Ziolkowski, "Dostoevsky and the Kenotic Tradition," 34).

18. Galatians 3:27.

19. Romans 6:23.

20. 2 Peter 1:4.

phasizes the Genesis creation story in its recognition of humans as created in the 'image' of God. Lossky explains, "The true greatness of man is not in his incontestable kinship with the universe, but in his participation in the divine plentitude, in the mystery within himself of the 'image' and the 'likeness.'... Man is a personal being like God, and not a blind nature. Such is the character of the divine image in him."[21] Thus, human persons, endowed with the image of God, contain the potential to become complete in God's 'likeness' via participation. This process of becoming complete is understood as union with God and referred to as deification. It is not understood as sentimental union with God in that one might feel some emotional resonance with God and the cosmos, rather for the Orthodox tradition, this is understood as an ontological union via grace.

To avoid reducing God to mere instances of human deification, Palamas distinguishes between God's energies and God's essence. According to Lossky, "this distinction is that between the essence of God, or His nature, properly co-called, which is inaccessible, unknowable and incommunicable; and the energies or divine operations, forces proper to and inseparable from God's essence, in which He goes forth from Himself, manifests, communicates, and gives Himself."[22] This allows for the conceptual construction of human participation in God without becoming wholly God. This saves the doctrine of deification from lapsing into pantheism, in which persons become (and/or participate in) God's very essence. It is in God's energies that one achieves union with God's self, but not God's essence. Since this distinction in God allows for union in, and participation with, God, it also raises the potential issue of dividing God (into energies and essence), which seemingly threatens the retention of God's simplicity. For Palamas, this distinction is real but does not affect the simplicity of God. Joost van Rossum states, "'Palamism' remains unsatisfactory for philosophically minded theologians, especially for those who are trained in western scholasticism."[23] Palamas does not perceive this distinction as a threat to God's divine simplicity since it does not divide God's essence, which remains simple. The Palamite distinction between God's energies and essence might be understood analogously, with caution, as the distinction between the economic and immanent trinities (which might ultimately be accepted as a mystery of faith). Since Palamas was neither a systematic nor a philosophical theologian, dwelling on his theology within the context of Aristotelian categories (such as essence) may eventually fall short. After all,

---

21. Lossky, *Orthodox Theology*, 70.
22. Lossky, *Mystical Theology of the Eastern Church*, 70.
23. Van Rossum, "Deification in Palamas and Aquinas," 368.

"Palamas' God is not the God of Aristotle, but the living God of revelation in the history of salvation . . . In other words, a personal God, and not a philosophical abstraction."[24]

The deified unites with the energies of God, which is to unite with God's self (energies), but not God's essence. In deification, one does not cease being human, but rather retains full personhood in the way Jesus of Nazareth was believed to have remained fully human when hypostatically united with God. However, the difference between Jesus and the deified person is that while Jesus took on God's nature, the deified person takes on God's energies. Deification entails the divinization of the whole person, including material body and immaterial spirit. Kallistos Ware makes this important distinction, "the full deification of the body must wait, however, until the Last Day, for in this present life the glory of the saints is as a rule an inward splendour, a splendour of the soul alone; but when the righteous rise from the dead and are clothed with a spiritual body, then their sanctity will be outwardly manifest."[25] Complete deification of the body remains suspended. However, in this world and life, the soul unites with God. The deified becomes united to God and is 'uncreated by grace;' that is, one becomes a full participant in God. One's human nature remains as it is, but is transfigured by grace. This is the reversion of the human condition from the fallen state, via transfiguration, back towards "its paradisian state,"[26] though the body remains fallen, finite, and sinful.[27]

In Palamas and the Orthodox tradition, the function of grace is emphasized, not only as operative in the world, but more importantly, operative in the union of humanity with God's self. With such a robust view of operative grace in the world, Kallistos Ware recognizes at least four clear implications stemming from kenotic deification, all of which Dostoevsky clearly articulates in Zosima. The four are universality, moral responsibility, practicality, and hope.

First, the call to deification is universal. It is not reserved for a select few, but rather all persons have as their *telos*, deification—and all can achieve it. Though persons "shall only be fully deified at the Last Day," Ware writes, "but for each of us the process of divinization must begin here and

---

24. Ibid., 369.
25. Ware, *The Orthodox Church*, 233.
26. Van Rossum, "Deification in Palamas and Aquinas," 381.
27. Here the Western Roman tradition places more emphasis on the sinful condition of the post-deified individual and the sinful remnants of the human condition.

now in this present life."[28] Lossky concurs.[29] At a young age, Zosima learns this from his older brother, Markel, who died in his late teenage years. Prior to his death, Markel underwent a transformation from a position of skeptical antagonism towards religion to one of all-embracing self-emptying. On his deathbed, Markel teaches, "life is paradise,[30] and we are all in paradise, but we do not want to know it, and if we did want to know it, tomorrow there would be paradise the world over."[31] The implication here might be that all are called to self-empty, like Markel, and 'put on Christ,' thus having paradise. The theme of a realized indwelling paradise continues in Zosima's relationship with 'the mysterious visitor' who offers his own commentary on the idea. The visitor proclaims,

> That life is paradise I have been thinking about for a long time—that is all I think about . . . Paradise is hidden in each one of us, it is concealed within me, too, right now, and if I wish, it will come for me in reality, tomorrow even, and for the rest of my life . . . indeed it is true that when people understand this thought, the Kingdom of Heaven will come to them no longer in a dream but in reality.[32]

Second, deification entails moral responsibility in the present both personally and socially. Sin remains in the deified self, thus there is a constant call to combat the sinful self via moral living. The doctrine of deification is fundamentally grounded in Jesus' great commandment to love both God and neighbor. In Zosima, this comes out most emphatically in the call to self-empty and love one's brother. Rowan Williams' chapter "Exchanging Crosses: Responsibility for All" in his most recent book on Dostoevsky treats this theme in depth. There Williams reminds us that for Dostoevsky and the Russian Orthodox tradition, "taking up the cross with and for another is not a removal of responsibility from the other; rather the contrary."[33] Zosima learns this from his older brother Markel as well, who, on his death bed, had servants attending to him. Markel, proclaims, "If God were to have mercy on me and let me live, I would begin serving you, for we must all serve each other . . . let me also be the servant of servants, the same as they are to me."[34] Later, from the 'mysterious visitor,' Zosima is taught that, "until one

28. Ware, *The Orthodox Church*, 236.
29. See footnote 12.
30. Some translators here employ 'heaven' instead of 'paradise.'
31. Dostoevsky, *The Brothers Karamazov*, 288.
32. Ibid., 302–03.
33. Williams, *Dostoevsky*, 153.
34. Dostoevsky, *The Brothers Karamazov*, 289.

has indeed become the brother of all, there will be no brotherhood."[35] This plays on a number of themes to be sure (*sobornost*,' solidarity, rejection of western isolationism, etc.), but within the context of a kenotic and theotic spirituality, Zosima's concern for self-emptying in order to serve others is evident.

Any examination of Zosima's relation to Markel and the 'mysterious visitor' remains incomplete without recognition of its wider context and the emphasis on personal and social moral duty. Prior to joining the monastery, as a youth, Zosima served in the 'Cadet Corps,' a period which he described himself as "most susceptible to everything,"[36] including "wicked behavior."[37] He became infatuated with an engaged girl, insulted her fiancé and challenged him to a duel. Zosima shamefully drags this innocent man into a duel by playing on his pride to fight for his fiancé. The evening before the duel, Zosima describes an event which changed his life: "Having returned home in the evening, ferocious and ugly, I got angry with my orderly Afanasy and struck him twice in the face with all my might, so that his face was all bloody."[38] Unable to sleep, Zosima awakes early the next morning full of shame, possibly from the impending duel that awaits him with the innocent man; a duel in which Zosima is confident of victory. After a period of psychological introspection, he concludes the shame is neither from his intent to kill an innocent man nor from his fear of possibly being killed in the duel, but rather he concludes, "suddenly I understood at once what it was: it was because I had beaten Afanasy the night before!"[39] This culminates in an epiphany[40] of Zosima's moral shame: "What a crime! It was as if a sharp needle went through my soul."[41] Realizing his abusive actions towards Afanasy, his own servant, he recalls Markel's speech about serving one's servants. He races to Afanasy, kenotically throws himself at his feet and begs for forgiveness. At the duel, he allows his adversary to take the first shot and instead of returning fire, he hurtles his gun into the trees and begs for forgiveness in place of death. He then enters the monastery.

What commences with the least of men, the servant Afanasy, ripples through Zosima on to others. This is most clear in the 'mysterious visitor'

35. Ibid., 303.
36. Ibid., 295.
37. Ibid., 296.
38. Ibid., 297.
39. Ibid., 297–98.
40. Julian W. Connolly examines a few of the most prominent epiphany experiences in the text, sometimes deeming them 'spiritual epiphanies' of 'theophanies' in "Dostoevskij's Guide to Spiritual Epiphany."
41. Dostoevsky, *The Brothers Karamazov*, 298.

who, having learned of Zosima's duel, visits him weekly to learn how Zosima brought himself to act in such a noble fashion. The mysterious visitor is described as holding an official and noble position in town, "universally respected, wealthy, [and] well known for his philanthropy."[42] He confesses to Zosima to have killed a woman fourteen years prior and is free of suspicion. In a manner similar to Zosima at the duel, the mysterious visitor eventually gleans the courage to fulfill his moral duty to publically confess to his crime. The path of kenotically humbling oneself, by freely giving one's own destiny over to the mercy of others (as Zosima did to his adversary), reverberates through Zosima from the least of men (Afanasy) to the most of men (the mysterious visitor). Perhaps more significantly, this kenotic way towards *theōsis* is then impressed upon the young Alyosha who, at the encouragement of Zosima, leaves the monastery, spends the rest of the novel self-emptying, going alongside others, and sharing in the suffering of others. This fulfills what Zosima commands of Alyosha: "you will go forth from these [monastery] walls, but you will sojourn in the world like a monk."[43] Going beyond the monastery, like a commoner, Alyosha embodies the universal call to kenotic *theōsis* and moral duty in the world, though imperfect due to sin. Cherkasova traces this theme in her work remarking, "Ultimately, Dostoevsky's novels demonstrate that by suffering with others we do not increase the ills of the world but partake in a genuinely humane communion, sustained by love and mutual responsibility."[44]

Third, deification is not to be understood as an abstract concept detached from experience, but rather is grounded in everyday practice, which often includes concrete suffering. Cherkasova reminds us that "for Russian Orthodox Christianity, *kenosis* signifies the supreme expression of religious devotion and represents a path that intimately links the sufferer to the image of Christ."[45] The model of *theōsis* provides a blueprint for those aspiring to deification to follow, which includes going to church, reading scripture, prayer, love of neighbor, following commandments, receiving sacraments, and so on. But it goes beyond liturgical action as Ware teaches,

> when we think of deification, we must think of the Hesychasts praying in silence and of St. Seraphim with his face transfigured, but we must think also of St. Basil caring for the sick in the hospital at Caesarea, of St. John the Almsgiver helping the

---

42. Ibid., 301.

43. Ibid., 285.

44. Cherkasova, "The Ambiguity of Suffering: Dostoevsky and the Russian Orthodox Tradition," 15.

45. Ibid., 5 (italics hers).

poor at Alexandria, of St. Sergius in his filthy clothing, working as a peasant in the kitchen garden to provide the guests of the monastery with food.[46]

For the Orthodox, mystical doctrines such as deification call the participant to concrete action in the historical here and now. In so doing, one is transfigured and becomes a living sacrament, resulting in experiencing the world sacramentally. In Zosima's spirituality too, this pansacramental cosmology emerges. Zosima was first assisted in coming to this view as a young traveling monk spending the night on the banks of a large river, where he was befriended by an eighteen year-old ferryman who transported people and goods across the river.[47] Zosima recalls that they "got to talking about the beauty of this world of God's, and about its great mystery. For each blade of grass, each little bug, ant, golden bee, knows its way amazingly; being without reason, they witness to the divine mystery, they ceaselessly enact it."[48] Zosima declares, "All things are good and splendid . . . for the Word is for all, all creation and all creatures, every little leaf is striving towards the Word."[49]

This 'new way of seeing' the world, a pansacramental vision of the cosmos, resonates with Dostoevsky's sacramentalism carried forward by Zosima throughout the rest of the text. Zosima learned it from his brother Markel and it was confirmed by his experience at the river. After his display of humility in the duel, he declares to his fellow comrades,

> Gentleman, look at the divine gifts around us: the clear sky, the fresh air, the tender grass, the birds, nature is beautiful and sinless, and we, we alone, are godless and foolish, and do not understand that life is paradise, for we need only to wish to understand, and it will come at once in all its beauty, and we shall embrace each other and weep.[50]

---

46. Ware, *The Orthodox Church*, 237.

47. It is beyond the scope of this analysis to speculate on Dostoevsky's attempt (if any) to draw on the significance of the river and ferryman in the Hindu and especially the Buddhist tradition, which depicts the river, ferryman, and boat as, among many things, teachers of one's relation to the cosmos. Perhaps it is by the river, with the ferryman, where Zosima first learns about 'the beauty of this world of God's, and about its great mystery.' In his presentation "Comparing the Non-Objectifying Aim of Zen to Christian Apophatic Mysticism," Peter Feldmeier suggested the possible parallel between the Zen Buddhist paradox that 'emptiness is fullness and fullness is emptiness' to the Christian paradox that 'emptiness is divinization and divinization is emptiness;' that is, *kenosis* entails *theōsis* and *theōsis* entails *kenosis*.

48. Dostoevsky, *The Brothers Karamazov*, 294–95.

49. Ibid., 295.

50. Ibid., 299.

Without reducing God to all things in a pantheistic manner, the existence of sin and suffering remains evident in the theology and spirituality of Zosima and the text as a whole. Sin and suffering are to be embraced and loved.[51] Sin as such is not to be loved, but rather sin is to be combated by love. Embracing the sins of others is to strive for deification since it is to live in a manner according to the life of God. In so doing, one recognizes God in all things. This is espoused by Zosima's spirituality and concretized by Alyosha's actions. Zosima teaches,

> Brothers, do not be afraid of men's sin, love man also in his sin, for this likeness of God's love is the height of love on earth. Love all of God's creation, both the whole of it and every grain of sand. Love every leaf, every ray of God's light. Love animals, love plants, love each thing. If you love each thing, you will perceive the mystery of God in things. Once you have perceived it, you will begin tireless to perceive more and more of it every day. And you will come at last to love the whole world with an entire, universal love.[52]

Fourth and final, perhaps the greatest strength of deification is the hope it provides for change in the present. Both the Greek and Russian Orthodox maintain a high standard for the person. Through deification, persons can achieve a high level of participation in God in the world, thus providing a strong call to work towards structural change in order to alleviate systemic social injustices. In fact, Lossky argues that for persons who have achieved some sense of union with God, "the Holy Spirit becomes in them the very principle of a consciousness which opens up ever more and more in the discernment of the divine realities."[53] Further, "In the Holy Spirit all becomes fullness: the world which was created that it might be deified, human persons called to union with God, [and] the Church wherein this union is accomplished."[54]

It might be argued that kenosis possibly parts ways with *theōsis*, especially if deification ought to be concerned with the world (socio-geopolitical affairs). Margaret Ziolkowski argues that in this regard, "Zosima departs most radically from the kenotic tradition narrowly defined in his overtly

---

51. Love here is used in the *agapic* sense; that is, the concretized free self-giving of oneself over to the other. In this way, the sin is something to be combated through love. For instance, as hunger is eradicated by nourishment, sin is to be eradicated by loving.

52. Dostoevsky, *The Brothers Karamazov*, 319.

53. Lossky, *Mystical Theology of the Eastern Church*, 246.

54. Ibid.

nationalistic interests."[55] Zosima is convinced the salvation of Russia rests on the shoulders of the monks, whereas, as Zilolkowski points out that Russian "kenoticism is inherently apolitical, [and] supposedly concerned with its practitioner's spiritual perfectibility and not with participation in world activities."[56] Though Zosima exhibits a departure from traditional Russian kenoticism, it might be reasonably conceived how that tradition could legitimately lend itself to providing hope on a political level. From the life and teachings of Zosima, it is clear that a realized eschatology of paradise is within everyone's grasp and this should provide hope to some degree. As previously stated, Zosima learns from his brother Markel that, "we are all in paradise, but we do not want to know it, and if we did want to know it, tomorrow there would be paradise the world over,"[57] while the 'mysterious visitor' teaches him that, "when people understand [that paradise is hidden in each one of us], the Kingdom of Heaven will come to them no longer in a dream but in reality."[58]

The Pansacramental Vision of Berry's Port William Characters

Wendell Berry's 21st century American fiction is imbued with an inherent sacramentalism which yields a similar anti-dualistic sacramental spirituality.[59] He is a confessing Southern Baptist, which is not uncommon for his time and place in twenty-first century Kentucky. However, the overwhelming sacramental and sometimes Catholic character of his worldview and ethics cannot be denied. Readers of Berry's works know well his distaste for the dualistic, Gnostic, and "other-worldly" tendencies that have crept into modern American Protestantism. This criticism, as well as his emphasis on the sacramental, may be attributed to his context as a Southern Baptist, in which he finds both a lack of, and need for, an emphasis on "this-worldliness."

---

55. Ziolkowski, "Dostoevsky and the Kenotic Tradition," 38.
56. Ibid.
57. Dostoevsky, *The Brothers Karamazov*, 288.
58. Ibid., 303.
59. Norman Wirzba touches on the kenotic element of Berry's writing, especially as it pertains to imitating the divine through mystical experience. In "The Dark Night of the Soil: An Agrarian Approach to Mystical Life," he suggests, I think quite rightly, that Berry's ambitions are mystical. He writes, "If mystics are those who seek to take up the divine pattern of life within their own, then the giving away of one's life will become a defining feature of mystical practice. According to Berry, we have a concrete model to learn from: the soil's fertility" (Wirzba, "The Dark Night of the Soil," 162).

A self-described 'agrarian,' Berry offers a vision of persons living connected to the land in solidarity sharing in life's joys and struggles. His fiction revolves around well-developed characters set in the town of 'Port William, Kentucky,' which Berry refers to as a 'membership' in order to demonstrate the interdependence and necessary belonging of all its citizens. I will draw on these literary works to get at Berry's sacramental vision and spirituality. In so doing, I shall focus on three episodes featuring three different characters within the 'Port William' corpus. They are Jayber Crow, Andy Catlett, and Aunt Fanny.

First, in *Jayber Crow*, the central figure, Jayber Crow, the town's barber who experiences the world in a simple and matter-of-fact way, recognizes the paradox[60] of the popular Christian message. While serving as the janitor for the church, he reflects on the young preachers and their common message to "lay up the treasures in Heaven and not be lured and seduced by this world's pretty and tasty things that do not last but are like the flower that is cut down."[61] These young preachers all had the knack for recognizing and preaching about the perceived fallenness of the world and thus, according to Jayber, did not know where they were. "The preachers were always young students from the seminary," Jayber observes, "they [did not go] to school to learn where they were, let alone the pleasures and pains of being there, or what ought to be said there . . . They learned to have a very high opinion of God and very low opinion of His works—although they could tell you that this world had been made by God Himself."[62] Herein lays the paradox, Jayber notices. The young preachers had created a seemingly sharp distinction between the here and hereafter, world and church, existence now and existence then, earthly life and heaven/hellish life, and so on. Jayber recognizes this Gnostic tendency in the church.

> This religion that scorned the beauty and goodness of this world was a puzzle to me . . . I didn't think *anybody* believed it . . . Those world-condemning sermons were preached to people who, on Sunday mornings, would be wearing their prettiest clothes . . . [They] loved good crops, good gardens, good livestock and work animals and dogs; they loved flowers and the shade of trees, and laughter and music; some of them could make you a fair speech on the pleasures of a good drink of water or a patch of wild raspberries. While the wickedness of the flesh was preached from the pulpit, the young husbands and wives

---

60. Jason Peters examines the contradiction of dualism exposed by Berry's writings (Peters, "Wendell Berry's Vindication of the Flesh").

61. Berry, *Jayber Crow*, 160.

62. Ibid.

and the courting couples sat thigh to thigh, full of yearning and joy, and the old people thought of the beauty of their children. And when church was over they would go home to Heavenly dinners of fried chicken, it might be, and creamed new potatoes and creamed new peas and hot biscuits and butter and cherry pie and sweet milk and buttermilk.[63]

The problematic dichotomy, evident in the lives of the church-goers, between the sacred and ordinary becomes strikingly clear to the town barber, but not the young clergy. They bathe in the goodness of their God's creation, yet intellectually reject it as so. Berry's point here is overtly sacramental, especially in his Eucharistic employment of cherry pie and milk in the last line above.[64] Jayber reminisces about his "best duty" as janitor, which was to ring the bell on Sunday mornings. Berry's emphasis on sensual spirituality comes out in Jayber's explanation of the bell-ringing as voicing "the best sermon of the day."[65] He explains he "would feel the weight of the bell . . . and then it struck 'Dong!' . . . the sound of the bell boomed out in all directions over the countryside . . . I so delighted in that interval of pure sound."[66] The sensuality of this experience emerges clearly from the text.

Ultimately, Jayber remains convinced that the people believed in a religion that 'scorned the beauty and goodness of the world,' though their words spoke otherwise. They believed in the world's limited goodness, but tolerated the quasi-Gnostic preaching. Jayber declares, "What they came together for was to acknowledge, just by coming, their losses and failures and sorrows, their need for comfort, their faith always needing to be greater, their wish (in spite of all the words and acts to the contrary) to love one another and to forgive and be forgiven, their need for one another's help and company and divine gifts, their hope (and experience) of love surpassing death, their gratitude."[67] Jayber concludes that the foundation of their ecclesial gatherings rests in communal solidarity, an undying commitment to each other apart from theological similarities and differences.[68] Jayber catches a glimpse of this sacramental *sobornost* after falling asleep in the back pew of the church and waking (or perhaps remaining in a dream state,

---

63. Ibid., 161 (italics his).

64. A similar scene takes place in the well-known film "The Seventh Seal," in which Jof, Mia and the Knight enjoy a communal meal of wild strawberries and milk, which might suggest that the director, Ingmar Bergman, is pointing to the natural goodness of the world and its potential to render God present thusly.

65. Berry, *Jayber Crow*, 164.

66. Ibid., 163–64.

67. Ibid., 163.

68. Zosima also articulates this spirituality of *sobornost* (solidarity).

for reports Jayber that he "couldn't tell which") to see what Barkley Thompson, drawing on Josiah Royce, refers to as "God's eternal perspective,"[69] an eschatological vision of all in time, yet beyond time. In his wake/sleep state, Jayber recalls,

> I saw all the people gathered who had ever been there . . . I saw them as I had seen them on the Sunday before. I saw them in all the times past and to come, all somehow there in their own time and in all time and in no time: the cheerfully working and singing women, the men quiet or reluctant, the dying, the little children tucked into the pews beside their elders, the young married couples full of visions, the old men with their dreams, the parents proud of their children, the grandparents with tears in their eyes, the pairs of young lovers attentive only to each other on the edge of the world, the grieving widows and widowers, the mothers and fathers of children newly dead, the proud, the humble, the attentive, the distracted—I saw them all . . . They were just there . . . I seemed to love them all with the love that was mine merely because it included me.[70]

Second, there is the well-known 'sacramental occasion,' similar to that of Jayber's vision eternal presence above, of Andy Catlett's 'hilltop experience' in the novel *Remembering*, an experience Thompson recognizes as eschatological and transformative.[71] It is an experience that resonates with the overall context of Berry's pansacramental spirituality, and comes strikingly close to Zosima's river epiphany. Like Jayber, having awakened from a forest slumber on a log above town on a hill, Andy,

> looks and sees the town and the fields around it . . as he never saw or dreamed them, the signs everywhere upon them of the care of a longer love than any who have lived there have ever imagined. The houses are clean and white, the great trees stand among them and spread over them. The fields lie around the town, divided by rows of such trees as stand in the town and in the woods, each field more beautiful than the rest. Over town and fields the one great song sings, and is answered everywhere; every leaf and flower and grass blade sings. And in the fields

---

69. Thompson, "Eschatological Moments in the Theology of Josiah Royce and the Novels of Wendell Berry," 44. Thompson's article eloquently examines this passage and others similar to it in Berry's fiction as they pertain to eschatological glimpses of eternity.

70. Berry, *Jayber Crow*, 164–65.

71. Thompson, "Eschatological Moments in the Theology of Josiah Royce and the Novels of Wendell Berry," 44–45.

and town, walking, standing, or sitting under trees, resting and talking together in the peace of a Sabbath profound and bright, are people of such beauty that he weeps to see them. He sees that these are the membership of one another and of the place and of the song or light in which they live and move . . . He sees that they are dead and they are alive. He sees that he lives in eternity as he lives in time.[72]

Pansacramentalism is evident here in Andy's eschatological vision in addition to the themes of solidarity, the fulfillment of creation, and the collapse of the sacred/ordinary. Recall Zosima's river experience where he recognizes the divine mystery of the world's beauty, that "each blade of grass" witness to the divine mystery and ceaselessly enacts it.[73] In Andy's experience, Thompson recognizes its transformative call, for Andy is confronted with "the imperative to decide whether or not to live in light of the eschatological vision."[74] In other words, Andy is invited to a new way of seeing.

Finally, it may be that the seeds for this new way of seeing were planted in Andy as a young boy in the novel *A Place on Earth*. An episode takes place in which Aunt Fanny, who is "older than anybody knows," invites the young Andy on a 'ramble.'

> Aunt Fanny walks [in the forest], studying the ground . . . She seems to see everything . . . Watching her, Andy is again aware that hers is a kind of life different from any other that he knows. He is made happy by her pleased easy taking of the good things that the world provides without effort, that nobody else wants, that most do not even see. Aunt Fanny's basket, as it slowly fills with the clutter of her discoveries, comes to have for him the excitement of a chest of treasure found in a cave. That these things have grown out of the ground into their secret places apart from anybody's intention, and that she takes them familiarly and freely without attempting to take them all, that they are the harvest of a ramble and not a search or a labor, all this bespeaks a peaceableness between her and the world.[75]

Not only is Berry's agrarianism evident here in Aunt Fanny, but its relation to seeing the land in a new way ('new' here runs contrary to the young preachers vision of a damned creation) is revealed as well. It may be that

---

72. Berry, *Remembering*, 124.

73. Dostoevsky, *The Brothers Karamazov*, 295.

74. Thompson, "Eschatological Moments in the Theology of Josiah Royce and the Novels of Wendell Berry, 45.

75. Berry, *A Place on Earth*, 254.

coming to see the world sacramentally takes work and comes with practice; that is, one must learn it, such as the young boy Andy does, and as Zosima learns from Markel, and the 'mysterious visitor' learns from Zosima. It is a striving to gain the 'knack for the Here.' This phrase is coined by Burly Coulter, in *A Place on Earth*, in his letter to his nephew Nathan. Nathan's brother, Tom, had just died a soldier on the battlefield. In his letter, Burly recounts the recent episode in which Brother Piston visited Jayber's barbershop, the center of local gossip, to fulfill his pastoral duties of speaking a few last words over Tom's death. Burley resents the preacher's attempt, "What claim did he have to it? . . . Preacher, who are you to speak of Tom to me, who knew him, and knew the very smell of him?" Burly identifies a "difference between people" which,

> has got to be taken notice of. There's the preacher who has what I reckon you would call a knack for the Hereafter. He's not much mixed with this world. As far as he's concerned there is no difference, or not much between Tom Coulter and Virgil Feltner. Their names fit into the riddle he thinks he knows the answer to. I wouldn't try to say he ain't right. I do say that some people's knack is for the Here. Anyhow, that's the talent I'm stuck with.[76]

Berry's suggestion here is that both Aunt Fanny and Burly Coulter have this 'knack for the Here,' while the young clergymen seem to miss it at the expense of their 'knack for the Hereafter.' In acquiring the 'new way of seeing,' evident in Berry's literary agents, these sharp distinctions are softened and perhaps altogether dissolved.

Anti-dualism, kenotic *theōsis*, and the sacramental vision evident in writings of Dostoevsky and Berry exhibit a spirituality connected to the sensual as mediated through sacramental categories. One implication for such a spirituality is that it results in a way 'of apprehending the whole of reality'—a new 'way of seeing.' The strength of employing sacramental language, which can successfully mediate between God and world (and between God as such and experience of God) allows for the retention of an immanent God that dwells in the world, yet is not reduced to the world as such. The medium of literature, especially in the gifted prose of Dostoevsky and Berry, remains helpful in articulating this spirituality in ways that strict philosophy and theology might not otherwise be able to do. For this reason, as Peter Kreeft reminds us, "Story is more powerful than philosophy in convincing us . . . No philosopher was able to convince me that 'we are

---

76. Ibid., 104.

each responsible for all.' But Dostoevsky did: he *showed* it in *The Brothers Karamazov*."[77]

---

77. Kreeft, *An Ocean Full of Angels*, dust-jacket, inside (italics his).

PART 3

"Finding All Things in the Divine"

11

A Philosophy of Sacramental Mediation[1]

THIS BOOK, SO FAR, has argued for the retention of sacramental language and categories in the mediation between the fields of theology and the study of spirituality. By proposing a robust criteriology of symbol, this chapter ventures deeper into the relationship between the two fields as mediated through a philosophy of symbolic sacramentality. The burden of the chapter is to bring part one (chapters one through six) and part two (chapters seven through ten) into a reconciliatory dialogue concerning the operation and functionality of sacramentality as mediator between theology and the study of spirituality. First, I apply Hegel's method of sublation to theology, spirituality and sacramentality, and offer two examples to demonstrate this. Second, I discus the philosophic function of sacraments as symbols with an emphasis on how symbols relate to signs, how symbols concretize, and how symbols invite participation. This definition of symbol is then applied to the concept of sacrament and followed up with a brief consideration of Thomist analogical language as applied to sacramental (re)presentations. Finally, I discuss the turn to relationality in philosophical theology and how it relates to a pansacramental proposal which implies the abolishing of false dichotomies.

---

1. Variations of sections of this chapter were presented in Gustafson, "Sacramentality as a Philosophical Model of Mediation and Reconciliation."

Applying Hegel's Method to Theology, Spirituality, and Sacramentality

Hegel claims that his well-known method of dialectic "alike engenders and dissolves" categories,[2] while "the thinking activity is, in general, the apprehension and bringing together of the Manifold into unity."[3] Thus, the process of dialectical thinking arises out of pure thought and seeks to sublate (*aufheben*) and overcome the mere externalities (to which the "Manifold" belongs) of the world via reconciliation. In this way, identity is mediated through difference, and external fractures are negated, transcended, and affirmed. The method consists of three successive moments; "the *first moment* is, as always, the *concept*. The *second moment* is the *determinateness of the concept*, the concept in its determinate forms . . . in the *third place* the concept . . . comes forth to itself out of its determinateness, out of its finitude, as it reestablishes itself out of its own finitude, its own confinement."[4] These three moments constitute the three steps of his method of dialectic, and Hegel applies these to the concept of God.

The first step commences in the examination of an initial category, the concept as such, resulting in the recognition that it yields a second category that is both different from and contrary to the initial category. Likewise, the examination of this new category results in the recognition that it too yields the initial category. One is left with two opposing categories that yield each other. In this way, the Manifold of the world is realized—that is, a world that appears differentiated in its mere externality is recognized. When applied to the concept of God, Hegel proposes this first step as the beginning of the philosophical treatment which is the concept of the universal as such as such. The Christian tradition recognizes this in the Father, the first part of the Trinity. In the Father, the concept of God is understood in and for itself as one, abstract, conceptual, inexpressible, and inconceivable beyond all concepts. The idea is universal and resides in the realm of pure thought alone.[5]

The second step surfaces in the process of the first two categories differentiating and determining themselves from one another, which gives rise to a third category understood as *determinate negation* since it negates the second step (the determinate category) and unites it with the first category.

---

2. Hegel, *Philosophy of Right*, par. 31.

3. Hegel, "Philosophical Propadeutics," 99.

4. Hegel, *Lectures on the Philosophy of Religion*, 100–102 (italics his).

5. One may immediately think of Kant here and his philosophical project of pure reason that sought to distinguish between the noumenon and phenomenon. Hegel's method of *aufheben* showcased here demonstrates an attempt to abolish this dichotomy.

The determinate concept both self-determines and manifests itself in the concrete particular. This second step considers religion in its determinate and finite aspect. It is a move in which the pure concept of God (first category) exists determinately (second category).[6] The concept develops and comes forth concretely in the world exposing the Manifold. It is the realization of the pure concept of God entering concrete existence and becoming explicit and particular. Hegel claims that the Christian tradition recognizes this concretization in the Son, the second part of the Trinity. In Jesus Christ, the infinite becomes a finite being demonstrating elements of change and variety. This second step gives rise to the third category, which unites the first two.

The third step employs the third category as a means to sublate the first two categories. In so doing, the first two categories are no longer opposed and contradictory, but united. Further, this third category now successfully replaces the initial first category. This dialectical process of unification then bounds onward and upward like a tightening spiral all the while removing contradictions. In the third part of the Trinity, the Holy Spirit, God has overcome the finite limitations of the Son and has become absolute. In order for this process to have culminated, it was necessary for the pure concept to have first been alienated from itself; that is, the Spirit (in the first step) must have been alienated from itself in order to find itself. For the Christian tradition, this third moment results in the outpouring of the Spirit (the Holy Spirit) in the community (*ekklesia*), for it is in the community that the Spirit remains truly present and "at-hand." This is the moment in which true reconciliation is achieved. In Hegel's history of the philosophy of religion, this third moment is one in which the pure concept (first category) reestablishes itself and returns out of its determinateness. He ultimately deems this the consummate religion, which he considers the most fully developed form of religion. For him this form of religion is Christianity, the absolute religion.[7]

---

6. Concerning the particular manifestation of God's determinateness, Hegel has written extensively in an engaging and imaginative fashion. See his *Lectures on the Philosophy of Religion*.

7. However, prior to manifesting itself in the consummate religion of Christianity, the divine Spirit must endure a process in which it seeks its own essential structure. In one of the most imaginative and creative "philosophical theology of religious pluralism" (although Hegel does not use this phrase) that I am aware of, Hegel's history of the philosophy of religion evaluates and ranks the religions in the context of identifying the process of the Spirit coming to know itself through the method of sublation in the world's great religions traditions.

Like the sun that passes from east to west, the Spirit passes through the determinate religions beginning first with the "nature religions" in Asia towards the absolute and

Hegel's method or "logic" is to be applied to all categories in an effort to know what both Hegel and Raimundo Panikkar might refer to as "the Whole." The philosopher seeks the truth and for Hegel "*Das Wahre ist das Ganze*"[8] ("the true is the Whole"). Knowing the whole is more than knowing the sum of its parts, since the whole *is* more than the sum of its parts. One must strive to investigate the parts, or at the very least to know something about the parts, in order to know the totality.[9] Knowing the whole as differentiated from itself, in its parts, yields the true, which for Hegel exists only as totality.

Hegel's textbook example of this dialectical method dwells on the first category of Being. The first step commences with the recognition that the category Being contains its opposite, Nothing, thus demonstrating two contrary categories: Being and Nothing. "Being is the simple empty immediateness which has its opposite in *pure Naught*."[10] Pure being alone entails its indeterminateness and emptiness, thus nothing can be intuited in it, which yields Nothingness. The second moment brings forth the recognition of

---

consummate religion of Christianity. In the religions of nature (e.g., shamanism, Chinese Confucianism, Taoism, Buddhism, and Hinduism), the Spirit develops by moving through the stages of manifestation from, for instance, the Chinese religion in which the Spirit communicates through the emperor alone, to Hinduism which exhibits a pluralistic explosion of particular spiritual manifestations.

Second are the religions of transition, which include Persian religion (the religion of light) and the Egyptian religion. They demonstrate the Spirit's transition from universality to subjectivity and particularity. In these traditions the Spirit develops further in knowing and distinguishing itself from the Hindu pluralistic context. For instance, the Persian tradition distinguishes Spirit as light, which is in stark contrast to darkness (or the absence of light), while the Egyptian tradition overcomes this light/dark dualism by positing Spirit "represented in a human fashion" (Hegel, *Lectures on the Philosophy of Religion*, 317). "In a human fashion" here is not to say an immediate human being, but rather it "still lacks clarity and transparency on the part of the natural or external features of the configuration" (Hegel, *Lectures on the Philosophy of Religion*, 326). Think, for example, of the great sphinx representing subjectivity in human fashion emerging out of the cat shaped rock.

Third are the religions of the spiritual which illustrate the elevation of the spiritual above the natural. These religions include the religion of the Greeks (the religion of beauty), the religion of the Jews (religion of sublimity), and the religion of the Romans (religion of expediency and purpose). These religions represent the Spirit particularized in more concrete ways: beauty, sublimity, and expediency. However, it is only in the Christian tradition, the consummate religion, that the Spirit has entered into itself and has itself as the purpose. After the Spirit has run its full course of self-manifesting and determining, it completes itself in the absolute singularity Jesus, after which it returns to itself.

8. Hegel, *Phenomenology of Spirit*, p. 11, par. 20.
9. Panikkar, *The Rhythm of Being*, 28.
10. Hegel, "Philosophical Propadeutics," 104.

a third category, Becoming, which unites the first two self-contradictory categories. In so doing, this third category sublates the first two by preserving their identity while transcending their contrariness. For, "what is simply in a state of becoming *in a sense* is or *has being* and also *in a sense* is not or *is nothing*."[11] This new category of Becoming then serves as the commencement point for the ensuing round of dialectic, and so on spiraling upward negating contradictions while simultaneously preserving and transcending them.[12]

Hegel's method can be applied to the concerns of this book when theology is taken to be that which proffers the universal absolute and spirituality (and the study of spirituality) is understood as that which proffers the particular, relative, and determinate. In Hegel's philosophy of the Christian religion, each person (relation) of the Trinity represents a moment in the dialectical process. Each person of the Trinity operates with a specific and defining relation to the world, which corresponds to its assigned moment in the dialectical process. The Father represents the pure abstract idea of God as such, undifferentiated. The Son represents the occurrence of God's concrete and determinate manifestation of God's self in time and space; that is, the Son represents the negation of pure abstraction in its concrete manifestation. The Holy Spirit, then, brings about the third moment by sublating the distinction between Father and Son, the first two moments. The Spirit transcends the finite, yet still remains dependent on the finite for meaning (e.g., dwelling in the *ekklesia* or community of believers in time and space). The Hegelian method of dialectical sublation is thus played out here in the Christian tradition. God finds and knows God's self, by going out from God's self and differentiating God's self from God's self via negation. In this process, God comes to know God's self (God becomes self-conscious) in the Spirit. Further, the negation of God's self leads to the transcendence of God's determinate differentiation, yet simultaneously preserves the uniqueness of each determinate manifestation. This is the intent of the method.

The method can be applied to the category of theology, understood as that which strives for and declares universal claims about the nature of God. Theology's abstractness and universality (category A) negated yields the particularities of the study of spirituality (category B), which is understood as that which strives for and reports particular and relative claims of lived religious experience (of God and/or the divine) in determinate time and space.[13] Thus, the abstractness and universality of theology negated yields

11. Forster, "Hegel's Dialectical Method," 133 (italics his).
12. Ibid.
13. Theology negated yields spirituality in the sense that universality negated

the particularities of spirituality. This gives rise to a new category (category C) of mediation, which I will deem *sacramentality* and is to be understood broadly in the manner that this book has sought to claim. It is this new category that unites the first two; thus, a sacramental sublation of theology and the study of spirituality surfaces. Sacramentality functions as the sublating mediator in the whole process. It negates theology's abstractness (absolute universal claims about the nature of God) and transcends the particularities of the study of spirituality (the mere particularity and determinateness of lived religious experience) all the while preserving the validity and uniqueness of each field. To be clear, in the first moment theology as such is not negated but rather it is the pure abstractness and universality of theology that is negated. Likewise, it is not the study of spirituality as such that is transcended. Rather it is the particularities of the study of spirituality that are negated.

A concept's negation of itself illuminates it; that is, in negating itself a concept comes to know itself. Understood thusly, spirituality might be deemed theology that comes to know itself via sacramentality (that is, via self-consciousness). In a similar manner to the relationships found in the Trinity, the reconciliation of theology's abstractness and universality with the study of spirituality's particularities via sacramentality demonstrate God's coming to know God's self in God's finite manifestations in both time and space; hence, sacramentality emerges from this process of sublation in a similar manner to the Spirit emerging from the sublation of the first two persons of the Trinity. The following two examples serve as attempts to apply this method to sacramentality.

Example One: "Finding God in All Things"

The Ignatian principle of "finding God in all things," as espoused in chapter seven, lends itself to the application of Hegelian sublation. The method of sublation includes three moments: negation, transcendence of the negation, and the preservation at a higher level of that which was negated. In his articulation of the Ignatian principle, Karl Rahner has suggested that one must first love all things prior to finding God in all things. In arguing thusly, he proceeds in a manner reminiscent of Hegelian sublation by suggesting that the path towards "loving all things" begins with its negation, which he deems a life of *indiferencia*. In opposition to loving all things, one is called to be indifferent towards all things. To love all things in the world (category A), one must *fuga saeculi*, "flee from the world" (category B). One detaches

---

yields particularity, and absoluteness negated yields relativity.

from the world (*fuga saeculi*) in order to ultimately attach to the world and find God in the world (in all things). In negating A (loving all things in the world) via B (fleeing from the world), one emerges with category C (finding God in all things) via sublation. This third category, in this particular case, constitutes a return to the world with a cosmic vision of God as infinitely knowable in the world. In the process of sublation, the concept of loving God in all things is negated, the determinate *fuga saeculi* is preserved at a higher level, and the distinction between them is simultaneously united and transcended in the finding of God in all things. In short, to love and find God in all things, first one must negate the concept by detaching from the world. Without this first step of negation, the world offers the dangerous temptation to love it as such, thus flirting with pantheism. Second is the transcendence of the negation which yields the love of God apart from the world. Third, in God (at the higher level) one discovers their true relationship to the world and preserves the love of all things. The world is then restored to its proper place without its dominating claim and threat of pantheism. Thus, the method of sublation as negation, transcendence, preservation is demonstrated in the Ignatian principle.

Example Two: Bede Griffiths

An instance of sublation can be drawn from the spiritual mysticism of Bede Griffiths,[14] the twentieth century British Benedictine monk, who spent the majority of his life in southern India seeking "a life as close to that of a traditional Hindu *sannyasi*[15] or monk as it is possible for a Christian monk to live."[16] Unity remains a goal for both Hegel's method of dialectic and Griffiths' spirituality. For Griffiths, a Christocentric approach to mysticism allows for a person's union with the divine. This union

> has to take place in the center of our own being, in the darkness of the interior where alone we can encounter God who is hidden in the depths of the soul. We have to pass beyond all the images

---

14. Much of the content here on Bede Griffiths was also published and expanded upon in much greater detail in Gustafson, "Substance Beyond Illusion."

15. In Bede's own words, "A sannyasi is one who renounces the world to seek for God, but his renunciation goes far beyond what is ordinarily understood by the 'world.' A sannyasi is one who renounces not only the world in the biblical sense of the world of sin, the world which today is so clearly set on the path of destruction. A sannyasi renounces the whole world of 'signs,' of appearances" (Griffiths, *Bede Griffiths*, 97).

16. Moffitt, "A Christian Approach to Hindu Beliefs," 60 (italics mine).

of the sense, beyond all the concepts of the mind, beyond ourselves, if we are really to find God.[17]

Negation is the first step. The spiritual journey of sensory negation described above requires a mediator. For Griffiths, who maintains that people "have lost the thread in the maze,"[18] the mediator of Christ is required to make possible the illumination of this hidden depth of the soul. He coined this process "The Golden String [which] is Christ . . . The sacrifice of Christ is the central event of human history; it is the event which alone gives meaning to life."[19] Among other things, this experience of spiritual union, for Griffiths, is a harmonic reconciliation of the feminine and masculine. It is an occasion of recapturing that cosmic unity between self and God, and humans and world. Similar to *sublation*, in this spiritual union, Griffiths writes,

> we are recovering that unity beyond duality. Humanity had to go through dualism, to learn the difference between right and wrong, good and evil, truth and error. It is necessary to go through that stage of separating and dividing, but then you have to transcend it.[20]

Through his Christian yoga, which functions as apophatic mediation, Griffiths endorses a return to the understanding of the world in a sacramental unity with the divine. He writes, "when you stop the mind, you discover the unifying principle behind everything."[21] For Griffiths, a mediator is required to move from dualism (determinateness) to unity (consummation), which for him is a form of sacramental yoga. It grounds his cosmological vision of "The whole universe [as] a sacrament, which mirrors the divine reality . . . Every hill and tree and river is holy, and the simplest human acts of eating and drinking, still more of birth and marriage, have all retained their sacred character."[22]

Griffiths' spirituality consists of his Christian yoga, understood as the holistic union of all the aspects of personhood. It is a striving towards knowing the totality of the *anthros*, which commences with negation and duality. He writes that "the steps by which we approach union are also yoga. The union is primarily union with God, but it involves the uniting

17. Ibid., 119.
18. Ibid.
19. ibid.
20. Griffiths, *Essential Writings*, 121.
21. Ibid., 122.
22. Ibid., 31–36.

or integrating of all aspects of our being."²³ Griffiths draws on traditional Hindu yoga, such as classical *Patañjali* yoga, which strives to separate the masculine principle of "pure consciousness" (*Purusha*) from the feminine principle of "nature" (*Prakriti*), which when entwined, induce suffering and despair. The goal of *Patañjali* yoga is to free the person from this suffering and despair "so that consciousness becomes free from every movement of nature and enjoys the bliss of pure contemplation, untouched by any taint of mortality."²⁴

In this scheme, Christ functions as a Hegelian reconciler by providing the way to preserve cosmic unity within divine and beyond duality. Griffiths' Christ-centered yoga proceeds with the conceptual negation of the cosmos resulting in a duality between self and world. On the cross, Christ negated the cosmos by dying and passing into the depths of absolute no-thing-ness, only to return and preserve his relationship to and in the cosmos. Christ's self-sacrifice, for Griffiths, is the way, the path, the Golden String, towards unity beyond duality. In a similar manner, Griffiths' Christian yoga calls the practitioner to put to death the conceptual self and pass into the depths of conceptual absolute no-thing-ness. In so doing, he negates his unity to the cosmos, transcends it, and preserves it. Unity is preserved beyond duality via Christocentric reconciliation.

The two examples above and the preceding explication of Hegelian *aufheben* have served to demonstrate the intuition behind this book, which proposes that one of the primary functions of sacramentality is that of a sublating mediator.²⁵ Hegel understood his method as the sole approach to all science, which begins in the self-explicating concept and proceeds through self-determination after which it returns to itself united. With the concept of self, the method commences in the concept of I as such (e.g., I am myself as such). If the I is to be real, then it must be related to the world; thus, the second step examines the I's relations to the world distinct from others (e.g., I am not you as such, I am a father related to my children, I am a son related to my parents, I am a husband related to my wife, I am a teacher related to my students, I am a student related to my teachers, and so on). The I cannot be the same I related to all things in the same way at all times, but rather distinctions must be made and reconciled if the I is to go on living as a real concept. I cannot be a father and a son to all persons (or just one person for that matter) at the same time. This is a contradiction. With these

23. Ibid., 85.
24. Ibid., 86.
25. I am not making the claim that Hegel's method of dialectical sublation is the only way to understand sacramental mediation, rather it serves as one possible way to illuminate the philosophical functionality of sacramentality to mediate.

distinctions of the I exposed, one returns to the concept of I in its totality with these distinctions sublated (negated, transcended, and preserved). With the contradictions removed (e.g., I am the same I related to all things in the same way at same time), the totality of the I is then preserved at a higher level as a real concept related to the world, and can thus continuing to live as a concept.

A similar process emerges, as proffered above, when one examines the process of dialectic applied to theology, the study of spirituality, and the sacramental mediation between the two. In reconciling the study of God as such (theology) with the study of lived experience of God in the world (the study of spirituality), sarcamentality *can* be placed in this Hegelian role of sublator. Hegel's method, however, need not be the end all and be all of approaches to sacramentality as mediator. It offers one possible approach among several. For instance, in the final section of this chapter I present an alternative approach to the whole posed by Raimundo Panikkar.

The Philosophic Functionality of Sacraments as Symbols

In the first part of this book, I made the claim that sacraments, as symbols, particularize the universal and conversely universalize the particular, thus demonstrating their inherent mediatory functionality. More precisely, sacramentality particularizes theology and universalizes spiritual experience. To probe this central insight it is necessary to offer here a "criteriology of symbol"[26] and to distinguish sign from symbol in order to demonstrate the philosophical function of sacramentality.

Drawing on Paul Ricoeur and Sandra Schneiders, this section, the bulk of this chapter, puts forth a definition of symbol followed by its application to sacramentality. First, all symbols are signs, but not all signs are symbols. Second, symbols concretize that which they symbolize. Third and finally, symbols invite transformative participation. The following treats each of these three in turn.

All Symbols Are Signs, but Not All Signs Are Symbols

Paul Ricoeur writes, "that symbols are signs is certain . . . but not every sign is a symbol."[27] This is to say that all symbols signify, but not all signs symbol-

---

26. A phrase borrowed from Paul Ricoeur.
27. Ricoeur, *The Symbolism of Evil*, 14–15.

ize. To signify is to point to something real beyond oneself. To symbolize is to point to something real both beyond and within itself. While signification has a single intentionality (pointing from itself to something beyond itself), symbolism has a "double intentionality"[28] (pointing from itself to something both beyond itself and within itself). For instance, a sign, such as a red stop sign, signifies to the traffic goers the command to bring one's vehicle to a stop. There is nothing intrinsic to the stop sign as such that communicates the reality of stopping one's vehicle. The color red and octagonal shape are arbitrary qualities assigned to the command of stopping one's vehicle. The same function could be achieved with equal success with a green circle should a given society employ it.

Signs are not grounded in reality, but rather point to a reality beyond them, whereas symbols are grounded in reality and (re)present it as such. The stop sign does not cause the reality of stopping vehicles, but rather suggests it. Stopping vehicles is left to human agency. The stop sign employs sensible qualities (colors, shapes, language) to point beyond itself to the reality of traffic coming to a stop, but the stop sign as such does not cause or present that reality on its own. Symbols on the other hand, as signs, employ sensible qualities in order to point to a reality beyond them, but also point inwardly by making present the reality they symbolize.[29]

For instance, in most families there are many strong traditions. Some die out, while others are born, and old ones reborn. Imagine a family that maintained the tradition of cooking and eating garlic mushroom oyster soup with their Christmas meal. The recipe is a traditional recipe passed down from Grandma's family and introduced to the grandchildren by Grandma herself. The recipe calls for mushrooms and oysters, and year after year the recipe is prepared in the same manner so everyone can expect that same garlic, mushroom, oyster taste. Time goes by and the family expands as grandchildren and great grandchildren are born into the family. They are introduced to the tradition of mushroom oyster soup. Many of the younger children grumble about the oysters in their soup, as children are wont to do. For these picky eaters, their parents suggest they simply negotiate their spoon around the oysters and not eat them, but the oysters must remain. Time goes by, new children are born and grandparents pass away. Grandma is no longer around to demand the retention of the mushroom oyster soup tradition, yet the soup continues to be made as always. One of the youngsters suggests not making the soup or removing the oysters and mushrooms from

28. Ibid., 15.

29. "The symbol presents its meaning transparently in an entirely different way than by translation . . . it evokes its meaning . . . It presents its meaning in opaque transparency of an enigma and not by translation" (Ricoeur, *Symbolism of Evil*, 16).

the recipe, since many in the family seem to discard them. This suggestion falls on the deaf ears of his elders who kindly remind him that this is how Grandma did it and this how they shall continue to do it. They explain to the child that even though Grandma is no longer "here," her memory lives on. They commemorate her in a variety of ways. One way is by keeping alive her soup recipe as a symbol of her. "Yes, but Grandma is not here anymore, it's only a symbol!" the child impatiently reminds his elder.

Only a symbol? Yes, it is "only" a symbol, but a symbol is a rather powerful thing indeed, and that which remains rooted in, and plunges the subject into, reality. The ritualistic reenactment of replicating and partaking in Grandma's mushroom oyster soup every Christmas symbolizes—that is, it makes present or (re)presents—Grandma via sensible reality. As a symbol it points both beyond itself to something greater—Grandma—while simultaneously drawing the participant into itself as the concrete representation of Grandma. It demands that one participate in—that is, eat—the soup. Another soup will not do in this context.[30] An oyster-less and mushroom-less soup will not represent Grandma here as well. Symbols cannot be merely exchanged with one another or rearranged with the same effect. The color red and the octagonal shape might be easily interchanged with the color green and circular shape to signify the same reality of stopping traffic; however, with Grandma, tomato or chicken or butternut squash soup will not do on Christmas. Those soups do not (re)present Grandma.

The soup symbolizes Grandma and, as such, sensibly mediates her non-sensible presence to her kin partaking of it. In the process, there is a double movement of 1) the literal signification of the soup and 2) the symbolic representation of Grandma. Yet, this double move is essentially one for the participant.[31] The literal soup facilitates the partaker in the experience of Grandma, and thus holds the potential for a spiritual experience. Going forward, as the philosophical function of the symbol is fleshed out below, keep in mind Grandma and her mushroom oyster soup, for this philosophical

---

30. However, one might imagine a scenario where the soup might be rethought out of necessity (e.g., mushrooms and oysters are either no longer available nor considered responsible to eat) or innovation (e.g., current culture has evolved in a manner wherein the mushrooms and oysters of the soup no longer convey the presence of Grandma in an effective manner and new qualities may need to be employed to achieve a similar effect in the new cultural context).

31. Paul Ricoeur writes, "for the one who participates in the symbolic signification there are really not two significations, one literal and the other symbolic, but rather a single movement, which transfers him from one level to the other and which assimilates him to the second signification by means of, or through, the literal one" (Ricoeur, *Interpretation Theory*, 55).

definition of symbol is employed to yield the theological definition of sacrament as a religious symbol of God and of ultimate significance.

Symbols Concretize

Symbols make real, in a sensible concrete manner, that which they symbolize.[32] In the process, they mediate the double movement of pointing both beyond and within by bringing together opposed aspects: particular and universal, subjective and objective, and experience and reflection. More precisely, *a) symbols particularize the universal* (and universalize the particular); *b) symbols subjectify the objective* (and objectify the subjective); and *c) symbols render inner reflection experiential.*

a) Symbols Particularize the Universal:[33] Symbols make particular the universal (e.g., idea, concept, person) in context (both time and place) via concrete (re)presentation. In this way, the symbol renders present (in its own unique way) that which transcends the symbol, but could not otherwise be represented by an arbitrarily alternative symbol or sign. In other words, the symbol facilitates concrete representation. For instance, an architect designs a house and the general contractor and subcontractors build the house.[34] The house functions as a concrete symbol of the builders (architect and contractors) and, as such, (re)presents them (in its own unique way) in time and place. The house as symbol facilitates the (re)presentation of the builder(s). Despite the literal absence of the architect in the house, one may enter the house and declare "the architect is present in this house." This is not a misguided statement about the literal location of the architect, but rather a claim that this particular house makes present, in a concrete manner (the sensible reality of the house), the presence of the architect herself, who is universally present to all who know her. One may not go to the next

---

32. Sandra Schneiders recognizes this as the first element in her definition of symbol (Schneiders, "Symbolism and the Sacramental Principle in the Fourth Gospel," 222–35).

33. Sandra Schneiders recognizes, as the second element in her definition of symbol, that "unlike the sign which merely points to or stands for an absent reality which is totally other than itself, the symbol *renders present* the Transcendent because and insofar as it participates in what it re-presents. The symbol is an epiphany of present reality, not an indication of an absent one" (Schneiders, "Symbolism and the Sacramental Principle in the Fourth Gospel," 224 (italics hers).

34. This analogy of the builder related to her building (i.e., artist related to her artwork) is expanded on in the final chapter (chapter 13) in the context of panentheistic pansacramentality.

house over and state the same thing about the same architect. The particular house matters.

The same is true with artists and their respective art. The symbol blurs the line between the symbol itself and that which is symbolized, as well as the line between art and artist, creation and creator. For instance, a painting particularizes the painter, but also renders present in a particular manner the universal idea embedded in the context of the painting (e.g., the art of Rembrandt discussed below). A poem particularizes not only the poet, but also the universal idea, feeling, truth, or sentiment the poet is seeking to communicate. For this reason, the conceptual content of a symbol remains almost infinitely expressible, or inexhaustible. Ricoeur writes, "We readily concede that a symbol cannot be exhaustively treated by conceptual language, that there is more in a symbol than in any of its conceptual equivalents."[35] In other words, if the artist is present in her art, there may be no point at which we cease speaking conceptually about the art as it expresses and represents her. The conversation may continue on without exhaustion; however, given the content of the artwork as symbol, the point at which speaking conceptually about it may differ. A poem (or any symbol or piece of art) stands on its own;[36] that is, it cannot be summarized, which is to say it cannot be reduced to a mere summary of conceptual terms. The painter paints a painting, the poet writes a poem, and the builder builds a building, because what they want to communicate can only be done so through their artwork. A summary of Shakespeare's "Sonnet 18" cannot be written, a photo of the Mona Lisa cannot be taken, a video of the Taj Mahal cannot be filmed, without lessening them. It is one thing to view a photograph of the Grand Tetons, but it is entirely something else to experience them in person. Symbols point inwardly to, and stand for, themselves.[37] They make particular that which is universally accessible to all. We quote poems and lines of literature for a reason—because they are effective in concretizing the universal; they make present and particular, in a strikingly real manner, that which universally resonates with persons. If they are effective in doing so, they stand the test of time and never fade away or become irrelevant. These are what David Tracy refers to as "classics." They are transcendent, remain stable, never go out of style, impose their meaning on all eras, take on lives of their own, and take over the recipient (thus, they are not dominated by the reader, viewer, participant, etc.). These classics are

---

35. Ricoeur, *Interpretation Theory*, 57.

36. By this I am not referring to the autonomy of a text (popular in postmodern, but rather the idea that art cannot be reduced to, or replaced by, a summary of concepts.

37. Himes, "Theology Lecture."

symbols in the richest sense, and "because they plunge their roots into the durable constellations of life, feeling, and the universe, and because they have such an incredible stability, [they] lead us to think that a symbol never dies, it is only transformed."[38]

b) Symbols Subjectify the Objective:[39] Symbols facilitate the subject relating to that which is symbolized via objectification in time, space, and corporeality. On one hand, they objectify (make objective) the subject (be it that which is symbolized, the transcendent, etc.); while on the other hand they subjectify (present in a subjective manner) the object.[40] To demonstrate, I turn here to Kierkegaard (under the pseudonym Johannes Climacus) and his description of the moment of passion in *Concluding Unscientific Postscript to the Philosophical Fragments*. The Kierkegaardian moment of passion, "the infinite passion of inwardness,"[41] assists in making intelligible this function of the symbol of subjectifying the object and objectifying the subject. To be sure, it is not clear whether Kierkegaard understood the moment of passion as symbolic. In fact, he most likely did not. Rather, the claim here is that his language about the moment of passion illuminates the philosophical function of the symbol. The experience of the moment of infinite passion of inwardness can function symbolically either on its own, or be symbolized through our person.

In this text, Climacus' philosophical anthropology proffers persons as "becomers." Persons are subjects that exist in time and are thus dynamic movers in, and subject to, both space and time. The subject is engaged in the ongoing process of striving, reaching, climbing, becoming and self-realization. Persons are finite subjects constantly seeking to realize themselves in the achievement of union with the object of the infinite, hence they commence on the project of uniting subject with object. In this union of subject and object, the moment of passion flickers forth. When the truth becomes

---

38. Ricoeur, *Interpretation Theory: Discourse and the Surplus of Meaning*, 64.

39. Sandra Schneiders recognizes, as the third element in her definition of symbol, that the symbol "reveals by involving the person in a *subject-to-subject relationship* with the Transcendent" (Schneiders, "Symbolism and the Sacramental Principle in the Fourth Gospel," 224, italics hers). Similarly, Panikkar recognizes that "symbolic knowledge overcomes the subject-object epistemological split. The symbol is neither merely objective nor purely subjective" (Panikkar, *Rhythm of Being*, 281).

40. In a similar manner, Panikkar proposes that one discovers the 'Rhythm of Being' in *advaitic* experience, which is the "experience [of the] subjective difference of an objective identity . . . In rhythm we find the (re)conciliation between an objective physical process and a subjective human feeling" (Panikkar, *The Rhythm of Being*, 48).

41. Søren Kierkegaard, *Concluding Unscientific Postscript to the Philosophical Fragments*, 200.

subjective for the knower, in the moment of passion, the subject is united with the object.

Climacus proposes two modes of knowing and knowledge, objective knowledge (the *what*) and subjective knowledge (the *how*), the latter of which is deemed higher and that which yields the subjective path to truth, hence the well-known Kierkegaardian epistemological claim that "subjectivity is truth."[42] For instance, Climacus distinguishes between knowing God and knowing *about* God, the former of which employs the subjective mode and the latter the objective. The subjective is preferred to the objective since it allows the subject to relate to God as a subject and not an object; while the objective way only yields knowledge about God apart from relating to God; that is, it approaches God as an object.

Knowing God subjectively is a certain kind of relationship to truth. It is not just relationship as such, but rather it is a relation that involves passionate commitment, risk, and trust. In such a relationship to God, held fast in a moment of passion, the knowing person is subjectively related to the truth. For Climacus, subjective truth is "*an objective uncertainty, held fast through the appropriation with the most passionate inwardness,* [this] *is the truth*, the highest truth there is for an *existing* person."[43] A key distinction between objective and subjective truth rests on the person's relation[44] to the truth. A person's relationship to objective truth is secure, indifferent, uncommitted, and dispassionate. However, a person's relationship to subjective truth is risky, interested, committed, and passionate. "The way of objective reflection . . . leads to abstract thinking, to mathematics, to historical knowledge of various kinds, and always leads away from the subjective individual."[45] For instance, the propositions that two and two are four and the earth is spherical are known in an indifferent detached objective manner. To know what love is, on the other hand, one must be approach it in an attached, devoted and committed fashion. For the existing person, knowing God subjectively takes precedence over the objective grasp of God, which

---

42. Ibid., 203.

43. Ibid., (italics his).

44. Here Kierkegaard's emphasis on relationality surfaces. For instance, recall Kierkegaard's well-known opening anthropological declaration in *The Sickness Unto Death*, "But what is the self? The self is a relation that relates itself to itself or is the relation's relating itself to itself in the relation; the self is not the relation but is the relation's relating itself to itself. A human being is a synthesis of the infinite and the finite, of the temporal and the eternal, of freedom and necessity, in short, a synthesis" (Kierkegaard, *The Sickness Unto Death*, 13).

45. Kierkegaard, *Concluding Unscientific Postscript*, 193.

Climacus suggests belongs to the realm of accidental knowledge and holds little bearing on *how* one exists.

The experience of relating to God subjectively—the subject knowing (relating to) God as subject—constitutes the moment of passion, and illustrates the symbolic function of subjectifying that which can be known objectively. However, Climacus' point is that there is more truth in the subjective knowledge of God, which rests in the moment of infinite passion. That momentary experience of knowing God subjectively in infinite passion functions symbolically in that it subjectively approaches that which can be approached objectively. Approaching God objectively "enters upon all approximating deliberation intended to bring forth God objectively, which is not achieved in all eternity, because God is a subject and hence only for subjectivity in inwardness."[46] Whereas the subjective approach to God in the moment of subjective passionate inwardness, the person "at that very moment he has God, not by virtue of any objective deliberation but by virtue of the infinite passion of inwardness."[47]

What has Climacus' thought here have to do with sacramental functionality? The moment of passion is the highest point the subject can achieve in approaching what might otherwise be sought objectively. This explanation of the experience of the passionate commitment as a mode of subjective knowing describes well the moment of symbolic and sacramental experience. In the experience of the sacred, the person remains in time and space. She does escape her context and subjectivity. The objective truth is grasped out of a subjective disposition, which the existing person can never escape from.

Since one cannot transcend subjectivity, objective truth[48] is known through subjective commitment, or passionate experience of decisive significance. For Climacus, the existing person achieves the nearest glimpse of the Absolute when he is in relation to the Absolute via subjectivity. However, in such a relation, the existing person knows God without necessarily knowing *about* God, thus God remains God; God remains absolute mystery.

Objective truth is known and realized in and through subjective experience. The symbol functions as that point of contact between the subjective knower, in his or her experience of symbol, and objective reality as such. Further, according to Climacus, a passionate commitment is required. The *what* (objective truth) is neither nullified nor negated in the face of subjective experience, but remains important since it is the object which is

---

46. Ibid., 199–200.
47. Ibid., 200.
48. The absolute eternal truth, the reality of the absolute, divine, God, etc.

sought. Yet, it can only be realized through the *how* (subjective experience). It must be appropriated to, and experienced in, existence via subjectivity and subjective reflection.[49] The *what* is attained via the *how*; therefore *how* one seeks remains preliminary to *what* she understands.

The moment of passion, which functions as an experience of symbolic-like sacramentality, takes places in existence for the becoming person. "At that very moment he has God, not by virtue of any objective deliberation but by virtue of the infinite passion of inwardness."[50] The symbol mediates the subjective experience of objectivity at its highest point of truth. It is an experiential moment of the real; it is an experience of the truth realized and the objective truth manifested in a subjective manner. The "moment of passion" is the precipice upon which objective truth and subjective experience teeter. As symbolic and sacramental experience, the moment of passion ignites and catalyzes the vehicle that launches subjectivity into objective truth.

The moment of passion is ultimately one of commitment (faithful disposition), in which the knower transcends his finitude (his subjectively) *momentarily* and holds fast to that 'objective uncertainty' that is God. Without recognizing subjectivity, a person seeks the Absolute objectively. Apart from his subjectivity, this approach ends in error. It is what Climacus terms "sin" and what Paul Tillich cautions as the pursuit of idolatrous "demonic" symbols.[51] In the moment of passion, the person experiences the objective truth mediated through subjectivity. This experience is facilitated, in part, by religious symbols and sacramentality. The moment of passion, understood as symbolic sacramental experience, prods the existing person to realize her reflection on that experience.

c) Symbols Render Inner-Reflection Experiential: Symbols mediate between the experiential and the reflective. They *experientialize* (make concrete and sensible) inner reflection; they make inner reflection experiential in the manner that symbols *a) particularize the universal, b) subjectify the objective* and further, as I argue below, as sacramental symbols spiritualize the theological. Symbols bring out the reflective in a concrete and sensible way. This functional aspect of the symbol is demonstrated in the well-known transformative narrative of Henri Nouwen's experience of, and reflection on, Rembrandt's great painting "The Return of the Prodigal Son." Nouwen narrates the experience,

---

49. Evans, *Kierkegaard's "Fragments" and "Postscript,"* 130.
50. Kierkegaard, *Concluding Unscientific Postscript*, 200.
51. See chapter four on Paul Tillich's Theology of the "Demonic."

A PHILOSOPHY OF SACRAMENTAL MEDIATION 225

Fig. 11.1: **Close-up from Rembrandt's** *Return of the Prodigal Son*

My eyes fell on a larger poster pinned on her door. I saw a man in a great red cloak tenderly touching the shoulders of a disheveled boy kneeling before him. I could not take my eyes away. I felt drawn by the intimacy between the two figures, the warm red of the man's cloak, the golden yellow of the boy's tunic, and the mysterious light engulfing them both. But, most of all, it was the hands—the old man's hands—as they touched the boy's shoulders that reached me in a place where I had never been reached before . . . My heart leapt when I saw it. After my long self-exposing journey, the tender embrace of father and son expressed everything I desired at that moment. I was, indeed, the son exhausted from long travels; I wanted to be embraced; I was looking for a home where I could feel safe. The son-come-home was all I was and all that I wanted to be. For so long I had been going from place to place: confronting, beseeching, admonishing, and consoling. Now I desired to only rest safely in a place where I could feel a sense of belonging, a place where I could feel at home.[52]

Upon seeing the painting for the first time, Nouwen began to question his vocation. He reports that it "set in motion a long spiritual adventure that brought me to a new understanding of my vocation and offered me new strength to live it."[53] It pointed both beyond itself to the parable attributed to Jesus, but also made present the reality of his deep loneliness, homelessness, and vocational confusion. At the time he was considering trading his comfortable position at Harvard University for a challenging pastoral position at a L'Arche community in Toronto. He found himself a wandering pilgrim on an adventure for meaning and a sense of home. He writes, "At the heart of this adventure is the seventeenth-century painting and its artist, a first-century parable and its author, and a twentieth-century person in search of life's meaning."[54] Nouwen's reflection on the painting not only reveals his heart's deepest longings, but prods him to act on, and experience, those longings. It pushes him to concretize those longings.

He reports, "The Dutch master not only brought me into touch with the deepest longings of my heart,[55] but also led me to discover those longings could be fulfilled in the community where I first met him."[56] After two years of reflection, Nouwen decided to make L'Arche his permanent home. "The yearning for a lasting home, brought to consciousness by Rembrandt's painting, grew deeper and stronger, somehow making the painter himself into a faithful companion and guide . . . From the moment of my departure, I knew that my decision to join L'Arche on a permanent basis and my visit to the Soviet Union [to see the painting] were closely linked. The link—I was sure—was Rembrandt's *Prodigal Son*."[57]

The function of artwork in the case of Nouwen's encounter with Rembrandt's painting serves as a powerful demonstration of symbolic concretization and evocation of reconciling reflection with experience. Rembrandt's work symbolically served as the mediatory platform for rendering Nouwen's

52. Nouwen, *The Return of the Prodigal Son*, 4–5.
53. Ibid., 3.
54. Ibid.
55. "Having first viewed the painting while visiting a community of mentally handicapped people allowed me to make a connection that is deeply rooted in the mystery of our salvation. It is the connection between the blessing given by God and the blessing given by the poor. In L'Arche I came to see that these blessings are truly one" (Nouwen, *The Return of the Prodigal Son*, 135).
56. Nouwen, *The Return of the Prodigal Son*, 135.
57. Ibid., 5–6.

reflection experiential. In so doing, it provoked action and invited the individual to participate in self-transformation.

Symbols Invite Transformative Participation

Symbols draw the participant in while offering transformation. They demand participation and interpretation in order to function properly and effectively. A symbol, as Ricoeur says, "only works when its structure is interpreted,"[58] and as Panikkar states, "is only such for those who recognize it as a symbol."[59] One of the major criterions that make a symbol a symbol is the interpreter. One must participate in that which is symbolized in order for the symbol to be effectively symbolic.

Further, the symbol places a transformative demand on the participant. For instance, Nouwen was captivated by the striking truth (the Kierkegaardian type of "truth [that] is subjectivity) presented in the painting. It demanded a subjective concrete commitment on his behalf. The painting, in the life of Nouwen, effected that which it symbolized and thus prodded Nouwen to participate in that reality. In this way, symbols are causal or efficacious, but not coercive.[60] Symbols respect the freedom of their interpreters in allowing persons to ignore their beckoning. However, they continually beckon without exhaustion. Further, in order for symbols to be effective, the participant must participate and not stand idly by. Nouwen must participate in the painting in order to grasp its symbolic reality. A poem must be entered into and lived in order to be grasped. It cannot be read passively in an apathetic manner. It functions properly only when one "gets it." A symbol must be recognized for what it is in order to take root, and take its participant to the root of its reality.

Additionally, one can return again and again to the symbol without wearing it out. Symbols "cannot be exhaustively treated by conceptual language . . . there is more in a symbol than in any of its conceptual equivalents."[61] Symbols cannot be exhausted, for they continually push their symbolic reality outwards and manifest that which they symbolize ever new again and again. For instance, as stated above, a poem stands on its own without a secondary commentary. In fact, a poem is created by a poet for

58. Ricoeur, *Interpretation Theory*, 62–63.
59. Panikkar, *The Rhythm of Being*, 281.
60. This element of sacramental causality is a traditional tenet of classical sacramental theology introduced by Lombard and endorsed by Aquinas, among many others.
61. Ricoeur, *Interpretation Theory*, 57.

the very reason that she knows of no other equally adequate way. The poem is the best way to communicate the message. A commentary or summary of that poem in standard colloquial prose will not do. The poem cannot be reduced nor shortened without turning it into something less.[62] Similarly, a photo of Rembrandt's painting will not do, nor will a summary of the painting. Nouwen was affected by the painting itself.

Symbols continually manifest that which they symbolize regardless of whether or not there is an interpreter there to participate in its symbolic representation. Michael Himes often points to Gerard Manley Hopkins' well-known poem, "Hurrahing in Harvest," in which Hopkins recognizes the steadfastness of reality regardless of the presence or absence of an interpreter. The poem celebrates the end of summer and the dawning of autumn's "barbarous" beauty with its wild whipping winds and majestically stalwart and "azurous hung hills." The poet recognizes the autumn's stark beauty and laments, "These things, these things were here and but the beholder / Wanting."[63] In other words, these things are always there, unchanged, but often (and tragically) unnoticed. But what did change was Hopkins, as one being drawn into the sacred symbolism of nature (the sacramental manifestation of the sacred). Hopkins's eyes become opened like the blind man in the Chapter nine of the Gospel of John.

In the fourth and final element of her definition of symbol, Sandra Schneiders explains that "the involvement of a person with the Transcendent rendered present in the symbol is necessarily a *transformative experience*."[64] Since the symbol transcends itself by pointing both within and beyond, the interpreter becomes involved with the transcendent and is transformed. Thus, the interpreter is necessarily transformed by the experience despite the symbolic reality remaining continually manifested. For instance, Hopkins transforms in his realization of the beauty of autumn which was always there; and Nouwen transforms his life after encountering Rembrandt's art.

The philosophical function of symbols held to here maintains symbols as both outwardly pointing signs, but also inwardly pointing manifestations of their symbolic reality. Symbols concretize and, in so doing, they particularize the universal, subjectify the objective and render inner reflection experiential. Finally, symbols invite transformative participation while encouraging commitment. With this understanding of symbol, the next

---

62. Himes, "Theology Lecture."

63. Himes deems this line "the single most beautiful statement in English of the Catholic sacramental principle" (Himes, "'Finding God in All Things,'" 100).

64. Schneiders, "Symbolism and the Sacramental Principle in the Fourth Gospel," 225 (italics hers).

section applies it to sacramentality by asking what it means to say sacraments are symbols.

Sacraments as Symbols

With the three-point definition of the symbol established above, I shall now apply it to sacrament and define sacrament as a "symbol of God"—that is, sacraments are religious symbols of ultimate significance. A sacrament is that which expresses God and makes God present in the way a symbol represents that which it symbolizes, and as such functions as mediator. With the above description of symbol in mind, it can be stated that a sacrament, as a symbol, is *a) not merely a sign, b) it concretizes*, and *c) is participatory*.

a) A sacrament is not merely as sign. As a symbol of God, sacraments functions as both sign and symbol. It points both outwardly and inwardly. It points beyond itself to God, but also draws one into itself by making God present in time and space. This claim has been made multiple times throughout this book, and demonstrates, in part, the classical theistic claim regarding God's immanence and transcendence; that is, God's immanence and transcendence can be maintained within this pansacramental framework by claiming that God is made present by the sacrament, yet still transcends it. Sacraments are symbols and not merely signs because God is intrinsic to the symbol itself. There is nothing arbitrary about the symbol. A sacrament cannot be replaced with another equally effective sign. The sacrament, as symbol, employs sensible realities to (re)present a non-sensible reality and, in the process, makes God a sensible reality. Chapter three, in tracing the foundations and development of sacramentality, sought to clarify this, for this idea of (re)presenting the non-sensible in a sensible manner has remained a traditional tenet for most Christian sacramental theologies.

b) Sacraments concretize God. As symbols, sacraments mediate and reconcile theological reflection with spiritual experience (among many other aspects). Moreover, sacramentality, as a mode of reconciliation and a making-present of God, functions to mediate between theology and the study of spirituality. It provides a way to relate God's immanence in spiritual experience with God's transcendence in theological study. For instance, the Lakota claim to of spiritual experience occurring in the ceremonies of pipe smoking and "the making of relatives." Likewise, the Christian claim of encountering God in the experience of partaking of the bread and wine of Holy Communion, the Muslim in the reading of the Holy Qur'an, and the Jew in the gathering of fellow believers at synagogue. The corporeal elements of these rituals concretize the divine, which can be understood as fully present in these rituals, yet also beyond. In other words, the divine is represented wholly, but are not the whole of the divine. The sacrament particularizes the universality of God, which is to say God universally pervades the corporeal cosmos and is experienced in and through particular manifestations.[65] These manifestations are spiritually experienced by particular individuals at particular places and at particular times. They are then studied, under the heading of the contemporary study of spirituality, as particular instances of lived religious experience.[66]

The category of sarcamentality, and its implied philosophical function, beckons the retention of the interdependence of the two fields: theology and spirituality. One without the other reduces the authority and authenticity of both. In the manner that a symbol particularizes the universal and subjectifies the objective, a sacrament "spiritualizes"[67] the theological and "theologizes"[68] the spiritual. It provides a bridge language and a conceptual framework to correlate and situate a particular spiritual experience, and the reflection upon that experience, with universal theological claims predicated on criteria other than that particular experience. Likewise, sacramentality as symbolism offers a means to correlate universal theological claims with particular spiritual experience and the study of particular spiritual experiences of others. In this manner, non-sensible theological

---

65. This claim can indeed be accused of being an imperial Christian appropriation of non-Christian rituals and is thus open to the charge that it dominates other traditions by imposing Christian categories (e.g., sacramentality) on non-Christian traditions. That being said, this book remains operative from within the Christian perspective and constitutes an effort to embrace a Christian pluralist approach to religions.

66. Particular spiritual experience takes place in the concrete world. In a pansacramental worldview—that is, a worldview in which all things hold the potential to function as sacramental symbols—spiritual experience will always be rooted in sacramental symbolism. Every particular lived religious experience in the world will entail the presence of potential sacramental mediators (which can and may include all things). In short, all spiritual experience entails sacramental symbols. An argument could be made that spiritual experience as such is symbolic, since it takes places in the concrete world. However, one must decide if it is necessary to distinguish between experience of the world and the world itself. Sacramental experience is experience of God in and through the concrete particularity of the world, and if one were to identify the sacrament in this experience, it would be the world (or something in the world), and not the experience of the world as such. However, I remain very open to the possibility that spiritual experience as such might be understood to be sacramental and symbolic.

67. "Spiritualize" here refers to making something religiously experiential and concrete. It does not refer to the contemporary meaning of "elevation to spiritual nature." This latter meaning rests on the assumption that matter and spirit exist and function independently. This book does not make that assumption.

68. "Theologize" here refers to the process whereby a concept or experience is subjected to theological reflection.

claims and concepts can be identified in sensible concrete lived religious and spiritual experience. This neither absolutizes the particular spiritual experience of the individual to the level of universal human experience nor reduces God to a mere instance of particular experience. In so doing, both God's transcendence is preserved as that which cannot be reduced to a particular concretization and God's immanence is preserved as that which is represented in particular lived religious experiences. Both complement, and require the relation to, the other, and are held fast in sacramental symbolism. The sacramental mediation envisioned here is robust enough to allow for the conceptual abolishment of these dichotomies (e.g., universal/particular, objective/subjective, theological/spiritual, God's transcendence/immanence). Thus, to the question, "Where is God within this scheme?"[69] I concur with Panikkar whose answer is, "unambiguous: inside and outside; the Divine is immanent and transcendent. Many mystics will say god wanders between us, inside and outside, goes in and out, appears and disappears, strays, dwells."[70] Furthermore, the question presumes to reduce God to spatial categories, which confuses the issue. In a Thomist sense, God's immanence follows from God's transcendence; that is, since God is transcendent God can be imminent in things.[71]

c) *Sacraments are participatory.* A sacrament, as symbol, calls attention to itself and draws the person into its depths. What is required is someone to notice it as a symbol. Thus a sacrament might be simultaneously efficacious for some and dormant for others. Regardless, the sacrament expresses itself continuously regardless of the whether or not one participates in it. For instance, Panikkar's vision, which he terms "the Rhythm of Being," calls for the involvement of both Cosmos and Deity, "but Man also plays a crucial role,"—that is, "we have this mysterious power to effectively participate in the free destiny of Being."[72] The role of the individual might constitute the subjective aspect of sacramentality, while the objective aspect remains regardless of participation.[73]

For instance, the Eucharist and the Grand Tetons continually function as sacraments regardless of the disposition of the participant. An individual may be "going through the motions" in his partaking of the bread

---

69. This question, of course, assumes God's dwelling to be 'somewhere,' which is problematic in that it threatens to reduce God to spatial categories and construct unnecessary dichotomies. The collapsing of these dichotomies are explored below.

70. Panikkar, *The Rhythm of Being*, 181.

71. See the sections on Aquinas in chapters five and twelve.

72. Panikkar, *The Rhythm of Being*, 106.

73. The Roman Catholic tradition analogously distinguishes between *ex opere operato* and *ex opere operantis*.

and wine and simply not recognize the symbolic efficacy of the sacrament. Likewise, an individual may be in the presence of the Grand Tetons without any recognition of the mountains bodying forth their sacramental symbolic representation of the divine.[74] In other words, through sacraments, God is always representing God's self, but these sacraments are only effective when one notices them as such. The sacrament invites, and requires, participation in order for the representation of God to be noticed, and thus be engaging and transformative. In this way, sacraments, as symbols of God, effect transformation of the participant. Among other transformations, a sacrament attunes the participant to the sacramental reality of the religious symbol and cosmos. Participatory attunement is what Panikkar refers to as sharing

> in that rhythm [which] is our destiny and our responsibility. For this we need that purity of heart which will allow us to be attentive to the real rhythms of Being, detectable, first, in the revelation that comes to us from the others, the joys as much as the sufferings of humanity and Nature. It is a dance that is as much ethical as it is metaphysical and cosmic.[75]

It is what Thomas Merton (among others) refers to as participating in "the cosmic dance."[76]

Attunement to viewing the cosmos in this sacramental way is the coming to accept, what many Catholic theologians have come to term the *sacramental principle*, which can be understood to mean "that what is always and everywhere the case must be noticed, accepted, and celebrated somewhere sometime. What is always and everywhere true must be brought to our attention and be embraced (or rejected) in some concrete experience at some particular time and place."[77] For instance, at a particular place and time, Nouwen embraced the truth he recognized in the concrete work of Rembrandt's, and this indeed founded one of the most transformative experiences in his life. Hopkins poem cited above ("Hurrahing in Harvest") demonstrated his sudden recognition of what has always been, but not for him. The acceptance of the sacramental principle entails being open

---

74. Michael Himes often speaks of waiting in the dentist's waiting room and fixating on the shrill of the drill in the next room. All the while, music is playing in the waiting room, but you pay no attention to it, until someone leans over and asks you the name of the tune playing. It is then that you realize music is playing. "For the first time, the music goes on *for you*. The music was always there, but it needed to be pointed out before it was there for you. It was present without effect" (Himes, *Doing the Truth in Love*, 107, italics his).

75. Panikkar, *The Rhythm of Being*, 106.

76. Merton, *New Seeds of Contemplation*, 296.

77. Himes, "'Finding God in All Things,'" 91.

to a pansacramental orientation, which is an approach that embraces the possibility of all things sacramentally symbolizing and (re)presenting God. This orientation is what I refer to as a pansacramental cosmology,[78] and will be explored further in the final chapters.

An Insight on Analogy from Aquinas

Aquinas' doctrine of analogy offers insight to this philosophy of sacramental mediation in so far as it assists with determining the various degrees to which sacraments (re)present God. Simply stated, Aquinas states the doctrine of analogy in the *Summa* as follows, "it must be said that names are said of God and creatures in an analogous sense, that is, according to proportion."[79] A name applied to God is proportionate to God's being. Thus, if God is said to be good then God's goodness is proportionate to God's being. Therefore, God is said to be infinitely good and goodness is one with God's essence, since God's being is infinite and one with God's essence. Likewise, if humans are said to be good then their goodness is proportionate to their being, which is finite, imperfect, and "composed of essence plus existence."[80] Therefore a human's goodness is finite, imperfect, and distinct from her essence. In this way, Aquinas famously safeguards against reducing God to the limits of human language and avoids the pitfall of univocally or equivocally naming God.

Applying this doctrine of analogical language to the character of sacramentality envisions an appropriate approach for determining the different degrees of sacramental functionality. Within a Thomist framework, the understanding of the sacramentality of all things must always bear in mind the dictum that sacraments represent God to various degrees. For instance, Aquinas taught that Christ is the first (primary) sacrament. For Aquinas, "Christ was not just a revelation or a sign of God. He was God. He was quite literally divine."[81] The Church and its sacraments then provide a sacramental path for people to participate in God's life, but their function ought to

---

78. I am using the term "cosmos" here in the manner that Panikkar uses the term kosmos. I employ cosmology, and Panikkar employs Kosmology, "in the sense of the subjective genitive: the *logos*, the word of the kosmos that Man should try to hear and to understand by attuning himself to the music of this world, to the mysteries of the kosmos" (Panikkar, *Rhythm of Being*, 369). I do not intend the currently popular definition of the term which refers to knowledge resulting from scientific reasoning applied to the physical data of cosmos.

79. Thomas Aquinas, *Summa Theologica*, I, 13, 5.

80. Kreeft, *A Summa of the Summa*, 127 n99.

81. Davies, *The Thought of Thomas Aquinas*, 352.

be understood analogically. In this manner, the representation of God is not reduced to the sacramental elements as such. Aquinas posited degrees of sacramentality beginning with Christ and followed by the Church which administers the seven sacraments.

In this book's approach to a pansacramental vision of the cosmos, in which all things function as potential sacramental mediators of God's presence, the doctrine of analogy ensures a certain level of humility. In labeling a sacrament a sacrament, one armed with the doctrine of analogy might recognize a similarity in difference among sacramental (re)presentations of God, as well as with God as such. The sacramental (re)presentations are analogically related to each other and to God as such, which is to say they represent God proportionally. In sacraments, God is represented in different but related ways. For instance, the bread and wine may sacramentally reveal God in a different but related way than Mother Theresa of Calcutta sacramentally reveals God; further, these sacramental representations of God remain different but related to God as such. In this manner, using univocal and equivocal language is avoided. When the statements "bread (re)presents God," "Mother Theresa (re)presents God," and "Jesus (re)presents God," are posited, the use of the phrase "(re)presents God" is not used in exactly the same sense (univocally) nor does it refer to three unconnected and different realties (equivocally). All three cases have in mind the same God, but represented in different degrees (analogically) by the various sacraments. By employing analogical language, philosophy of pansacramentality can more easily navigate and recognize the nuances of the varying degrees to which the infinite number of sacraments (re)present God.

Relationality and Abolishing False Dichotomies

In order to articulate an adequate pansacramental cosmology, which assists in demonstrating the mediatory function of sacramentality, it is constructive to recognize that sacramentality holds the potential to dissolve boundaries and collapse dichotomies.[82] Denying dualisms and collapsing dichotomies, for instance between spirit and matter, facilitates an approach to the Whole [of reality] in the spirit of Panikkar's *Advaitic*[83] orientation. Arweck and Keenan recognize this when they write, "discarding this limiting dualism

---

82. Sacraments do this, but not completely. For instance, in the Eucharist the bread and wine remain symbols. God is not reduced to those symbols, but remains irreducibly other. The same applies to the infinite number of symbols potentially functioning in a pansacramental world.

83. "not-two" or non-dual.

allows the pursuit of an integrated or holistic intellectual approach which might trace along those fuzzy, yet critical margins where body-spirit and mind-matter fuse, mix and mingle,"[84] and F. LeRon Shults observes that "escape from such bifurcating tendencies will be good news for a wider public interested in engaging with and accounting for the real insights of both religion and science."[85] There is a yearning in the West among many to move beyond simplistic dualisms towards more holistic and relational approaches.

This sacramental approach to the Whole has been discussed above from a Hegelian dialectical approach, however here a complementary approach is offered: Panikkar's *Advaitic* approach to the Whole. This approach "focuses not on the two things (the Whole and the part, in our case) to be related. This is the classical dialectical approach [of Hegel]. The *Advaitic* intuition intuits the relationship itself."[86] This approach provides a complementary Eastern intuitive approach to our Western dialectical approach. Panikkar trumpets a much-needed caution against placing total confidence, lock, stock, and barrel, into the scientific pursuit of objective truth. James Fredericks notices that "Panikkar called into question the Enlightenment's legacy of scientific objectivism, Christian theology's attachment to Greek notions of substance, and any attempt to divide the sacred from the secular."[87] In his *Advaitic* approach, Panikkar does not intend to embark on a system-building project which imposes a master narrative on all others; although, as a matter of formal logic, one might successfully accuse him of doing so.[88] Rather, he envisions his approach as an attitude, an orienta-

---

84. Arweck and Keenan, "Material Varieties of Religious Expression," 8. F. LeRon Shults cites this passage in "Religious Symbolism at the Limits of Human Engagement."

85. Shults, "Religious Symbolism at the Limits of Human Engagement," 307. In this text, Shults credits Charles Sanders Peirce with shattering these dichotomies in modern philosophy by providing "a new set of categories for promoting transversal dialogue among those interested in the dynamics of religious symbolic engagement in the world" (308).

86. Panikkar, *Rhythm of Being*, 30.

87. Fredericks, "At the Limits," 7–8.

88. Panikkar has insisted that pluralism in theory or as a system is impossible since it will inherently strive to subordinate all other systems to its own, however at the level of myth (orientation, existential attitude) pluralism remains possible as a "cosmic confidence in the ultimate harmony of opposites" and rhythm of being, which is ontologically plural as such. Anselm Min raises the issue that Panikkar, having stated the impossibility of theoretical pluralism, goes on to "theorize by providing anthropological, theological, and ultimately ontological grounds for transcending theory," and thus "it remains valid to ask whether Panikkar . . . has not also explained and subordinated [the irreducibly different realities of other religions] to his own theory and included them all as variants of his own belief." Min tentatively concludes that Panikkar is to

tion, a way of seeing, which yields an ontological religious pluralism.[89] In this way, each religion is not to be understood as either formally true or false, but rather as one language among many, for "language is the human way of being in the world, and the plurality of language shows plainly that there is more than one way to be human."[90] The *Advaitic* approach denies system building and ignores the Hegelian temptation to focus on the two things (e.g., the Whole and the part), and instead dwells on the relationship between the two. Panikkar explains,

> An isolated Isabel does not exist, nor can I know Isabel if I take cognizance of Isabel alone. I have to know also what José Ortega y Gasset called her "circumstance," her world around (*Umwelt* says the German). Then I need to relate both, and this is dialectical thinking—the movements from A to B, Hegel would say. The *advaitic* intuition proceeds differently. It does not look first at Isabel and then her environment, trying afterward to relate the two. The advaitic intuition sees primordially the relationship that "makes" the "two," sees the polarity that makes the poles. It can discover that the poles are neither one nor two. Only by negating the duality (of the poles) without fusing them into one can the relationship appear as constitutive of the poles, which are such only insofar as they are conceptually different and yet existentially or really inseparable.[91]

When applied to theology and spirituality, the *Advaitic* approach does not first look at theology and then at the study of spirituality, trying afterward

---

be understood as an inclusivist, theoretically, and a pluralist, mythically. Gerald James Larson, in "Contra Pluralism," accuses Panikkar of simultaneously trying to assert that different religions are neither objectively true nor false and yet holds that it is true that truth itself is pluralistic, thus falling victim to the law of non-contradiction. Min deems this critique "quite valid as a matter of formal logic, but it also fails to appreciate Panikkar's deeper point: the vocation of the intellect is to recognize something as higher than itself" (Min, "Loving Without Understanding,"71–2, n). In short, Panikkar falls prey to formal logic, and one must accept this, leave formal logic and intellect behind and scandalized, and move beyond it.

89. Anselm Min has proposed six types of religious pluralism represented by its corresponding advocates: 1) "phenomenalist" (John Hick and Paul Knitter); 2) "universalist" (Leonard Swidler, Wildfred Cantwell Smith, Niniam Smart, Keith Ward, and David Krieger); 3) "ethical or soteriological pluralism" (Rosemary Ruether, Marjorie Suchocki, Tom Driver, and Paul Knitter; 4) "confessionalist" (Hans Küng, John Cobb, Jürgen Moltmann, John Milbank, and Mark Heim); 5) "dialectical" (Anselm Min); and 6) "ontological" (Panikkar). (Min, "Loving Without Understanding;" Min, *The Solidarity of Others in a Divided World*, 173–97; and Min, *Paths to the Triune God*, 53).

90. Panikkar, *Rhythm of Being*, 24.

91. Ibid., 30–31 (sic).

to relate the two; rather it strives to intuit the relationship that makes them appear separate and polar.

In the spirit of this approach, here I carry forth one of the key implications stemming from both a pansacramental reality and the turn to the inherent ontological relationality of the Whole. Several contemporary thinkers have advocated for the 'turn to relationality,' or more accurately a (re)turn to relationality in both philosophy and theology. Tracing this (re)turn illuminates what was identified in this book's opening chapters concerning the bifurcation of spirituality from theology stemming, in large part, from the separation of spirit from matter.[92] In the historical scope of Western philosophy, this separation is seen most clearly in the privileging of substance over relation.[93] Shults deems the journey away from and (re)turn to relationality is uniquely a Western one, hence, "for many non-Western Christians, the claim that relationality is central for theological anthropology is nothing new."[94] Furthermore, I concur with Shults' inclination that that "the philosophical turn to relationality per se is not hostile to Christianity theology,"[95] and I will add that nor should it be hostile to Christian spirituality; rather it is one that could be intensely pursued and brought back in to vogue with the utmost rigor. Drawing on Shults, it is worthwhile to briefly sketch here the history (from Plato to Martin Buber) of this turn from, and return to, relationality.

Plato's proposal of a metaphysical dualism that distinguished between material (temporal and changing) and immaterial (unchanging eternal Forms) realms, followed by Aristotle's developed theory of predication, which distinguished substance from accident, serves as one of the foundational moves in the ontological prominence of substance (over relationality) in the Western tradition. Aristotle's metaphysical categories, in particular the sharp distinction between substance and accident, the former of which can exist independently and is thus more real, led to the casting off of accidents as non-essential to the reality of a thing (its *quiddity*). These categories and distinctions, of course, enjoy theological appropriation in the Middle

---

92. Keith Ward, in his chapter "Materialism and its Discontents," argues that the majority of both the classical and contemporary philosophers of the European tradition "have expounded a basically spiritual view of reality." These thinkers include Plato, Aristotle, Anselm, Aquinas, Descartes, Leibniz, Spinoza, Locke, Berkeley, Kant, and Hegel. Similarly, influential thinkers such as Hume, Schopenhauer, and Nietzsche denied that ultimate reality is merely physical (Ward, *God and the Philosophers*, 130–47).

93. For an eloquent sketch of the historical contours of the turn to relationality in Western philosophy, see Shults, *Reforming Theological Anthropology*, 11–36. I am indebted to Shults' sketch, for the following several paragraphs draw from it.

94. Shults, *Reforming Theological Anthropology*, 35.

95. Ibid.

Ages, carried forth, in large part, by Aquinas. In the seventeenth century, Descartes continues the endorsement of dualism while Spinoza heads in the other direction proffering monism.[96] The proliferation of natural philosophy and the scientific method during the age of the Enlightenment sought to separate the so-called "subjective" aspects of what one perceives from the "objective" aspects, which pushed dualism into the realm of empiricist categories.

Kant's Copernican Revolution stood philosophy on its head in its insistence that objective reality and its meaning conforms to the subjective mind, not vice-versa. In this way, the distinction between the phenomenal (things as they appear to the human subject) and the noumenal (things as they are in themselves) is upheld, but only turned on its head. However, Kant contributes to the turn to relationality by subordinating the categories of substance and accident to relation while retaining permanent terminology for substance. Hegel, as evident in the application of his method to theology and the study of spirituality at the outset of this chapter, marks a turning point in the Western move towards relationality, as demonstrated in this chapter as well.[97]

Twentieth century philosophy has trumpeted both the "turn to the other" and now what Shults refers to as the "turn to relationality." Key thinkers include Heidegger, Sartre, Levinas, and Whitehead. Of these, Whitehead is the most outspoken in his criticism of Aristotelian distinctions and categories, most notably substance. Instead, Whitehead proposes "occasions" which are understood to be in relationship to all things by extension.[98] Philosophical and theological anthropology can be profoundly influenced by this turn to relationality. The human person is understood primarily as

---

96. Keith Ward has entertained the possibility that Descartes was not a dualist, but rather a dual-aspect monist in his chapter, "Why Does Everybody Hate Cartesian Dualism?" in *God and the Philosophers.*

97. Shults credits Hegel with three crucial contributions to the turn to relationality. First, Hegel called into question the separation of substance and accident and, with Kant, places the two under the category of "relation." Second, in lifting up the essentiality of "process" in both reflection and being, Hegel ignites the "turn to the subject" in his insistence that substance be replaced by subjectivity. "Process" or "becoming" contributes to what it means to be, and vice-versa. Shults here also recognizes that Hegel's "phenomenology" was "an attempt to overcome the Kantian dualism between" noumenal and phenomena. Third, Hegel offers a substantial contribution to reconciling the infinite and the finite. He sought to understand the relation between the two and, in so doing, relegates the concept of relation to the aspect of quality over and above the aspect of quantity. Kierkegaard, of course, reacts to much of Hegel's thought, but Shults points out that concerning the category of relation, Kierkegaard, like Hegel, insists on its importance (Shults, *Reforming Theological Anthropology,* 22–25).

98. This proposal is not without its own critique. See Neville, *Creativity and God.*

"embedded in relationship,"⁹⁹ and not as an individual substance. This is evident in two important ways (among others) in the Christian and Jewish traditions. I refer here to the Chalcedonian "Definition of Faith" from 451 c.e. and Martin Buber, the twentieth-century Jewish philosopher.

The Chalcedonian definition of the hypostatic union can serve as a functional model for understanding the collapsing of dichotomies set within an anthropological context. It has set the traditional standard for the Christian faithful in understanding the union of divinity and humanity in the person Jesus Christ. In the union, Jesus' perfect and full divinity remains simultaneously (consubstantially) with his perfect and full humanity. Though the two natures remain unconfused and their distinction neither negates nor diminishes their union, their union remains real in the one person Jesus Christ. The human and divine natures are preserved in their union. In other words, real distinction does not mean separation. Humanity and divinity are not the same, but are related to each other in an unconfused manner. Personhood, as exemplified by Jesus, bears the real possibility and *telos* of this hypostatic *theōsis*; that is, human persons hold the potential to unite with the divine in a Jesus-like-manner (though not in the same perfect way without sin) and (re)present God sacramentally in the world. The hypostatic union could serve as a like-model for understanding the collapsing of dichotomies set within the context of anthropology.

In a similar manner, Martin Buber's insistence on the constitutiveness of the relation between the "I and thou" models this turn to relationality. Buber credits the Hasidic movement, in its "soaring up of a genuine vision of unity and a passionate demand of wholeness,"¹⁰⁰ with providing a clear vision of the inherent relationality between God and world. In such a vision, "the image of God that has become greater demands a more dynamic, labile boundary between God and the world,"¹⁰¹ and as such, the so-called dichotomy between the sacred and non-sacred is exposed as illusory. In his essay "Symbolic and Sacramental Existence," Buber makes the case for pansacramental personhood based on the blurring of the sacred non-sacred divide. He argues that "the real existence of the human person can itself be symbolic, itself be a sacrament."¹⁰² In this sense, the *nabis* (the biblical prophets) of the Hebrew tradition function sacramentally in mediating between God and person, for their task enabled "the spoken dialogue between deity and

---

99. Shults, *Reforming Theological Anthropology*, 31.
100. Buber, *The Origin and Meaning of Hasidism*, 172.
101. Ibid.
102. Ibid., 152.

humanity to fulfill itself."[103] The whole person contains the potential to become the prophetic mouth of God; he or she, "with his whole being and life, is speaker of the hidden voice, that 'hovering silence' (1 Kings 19:12), that blows through him."[104] The biblical tradition, according to Buber, maintains that to symbolize God is to embody God; it is to bodily represent God, thus the prophet does not simply act out as a sign of God, but rather he or she lives it via bodily symbolic representation. The sacrament, for Buber, mediates between the Absolute God and the concrete world. "The covenant of the Absolute with the concrete takes place in the sacrament,"[105] and this takes place especially in human existence.

The monotheistic tradition, declares Panikkar, requires "a loving relationship with God," without which it becomes "a dangerous ideology."[106] Persons "need access to the divine. This means that this access has to be, if fully human, a truly personal relationship. God needs an iconic face if it is to be a God for us . . . The monotheistic God is a living and loving divine icon."[107] This sacramental relationship takes place in the covenant between God and person, but also between persons. Buber writes,

> That the divine and the human join with each other without merging with each other, a lived beyond-transcendence-and-immanence, is the foremost significance of sacrament. But even when it is only two human beings who consecrate themselves to each other sacramentally—in marriage, in brotherhood—that other covenant, the convent between the Absolute and the concrete, is secretly consummated.[108]

Buber claims an inherent pansacramental tendency in primordial human nature, which is to say, "'Primitive' man is a naïve pansacramentalist,"[109] for which all things function sacramentally.

> Everything, to [primitive man], is full of sacramental substance, all, each thing and each function, is ever ready to flash up as a sacrament for him. He knows no selection of objects and activities, only the methods and the favorable hours. "It" is everywhere, one must only be able to catch it. For this there are, to be sure, rules and rhythms, but even these one only acquires

---

103. Ibid., 155.
104. Ibid., 157.
105. Ibid., 165.
106. Panikkar, *The Rhythm of Being*, 124.
107. Ibid.
108. Buber, "*The Origin and Meaning of Hasidism*," 166.
109. Ibid., 167.

when one risks oneself therein, and he who is already capable of knowing must expose himself ever anew to the dangerously seizing and claiming contact.[110]

This most ancient of wisdom entails that "primitive man" (to use Buber's language) did not have the crisis of finding the holy or sacramental, but rather was challenged, and thus thrown into crisis, by the "discovery of the fundamentally not-holy, the a-sacramental."[111] This discovery of the fundamentally not-holy, according to Buber, throws humanity into the crisis of no longer being able to find, and rest in, "a holy relationship to the world," since to give into and accept such an all-embracing holy relationship to the world would be to surrender to the reductionist heresy of pantheism.

Buber claims that this threat is combated, for one, by Hasidism, a "great religious movement . . . that has projected a new pansacramentalism," and has attempted "to rescue the sacramental life of man from the corruption of the facile and the familiar."[112] She who lives sacramentally is not mandated to determine the sacred from the non-sacred. The person of sacramental existence "can undertake no selection, no separation; for it is not for him to determine what has to meet him and what not. The not-holy, in fact, does not exist; there exists only the not yet hallowed."[113] Though Buber dwells primarily on the sacramental existence of personhood, he makes clear the position that, according to Hasidism, all worldly things desire hallowedness by way of sacramentality, and further, all things desire "to come to God through us."[114]

The Hasidic pansacramental vision of unity and demand for wholeness suggests that one of the primary functions of sacraments as mediators is that of collapsing the sacred/non-sacred dichotomy. Sacraments also overcome time; that is, they overcome the past/present divide by bridging the two through memory or commemoration. For instance, when the Jewish faithful participate in the Passover feast they "make memorial" (Hebrew –zkr). The Christian believers do something similar when they celebrate the sacrament of the Eucharist as instituted by the words of Jesus who told his followers to "do this *in memory* of me."[115] These celebrations, as memorials, function as real immediate encounters with the original redemptive events themselves, which are, in this case, the initial Passover feast in Egypt

110. Ibid.
111. Ibid.
112. Ibid., 170.
113. Ibid., 171.
114. Ibid., 181.
115. Luke 22:19

and the Last Supper in first-century Palestine. Each generation experiences anew the same determinative events of the past by reinterpreting them in light of their own experience in responding to their God who meets them in history. In this way, the past-present divide is shattered, and the feast becomes sacramental in that it makes present the original redemptive event of the first Passover. The original historical event that takes place at a fixed point in chronological time reverberates through time. When the Jewish and Christian believers *make memorial*, they sacramentalize the celebration and thus participate in this reverberation in the present. To be sure, there is no time travel back to the original event involved, but rather those making memorial remain in the present and resonate with the original event's reverberation. This memorial is very sacramental in that the reverberation is experienced in present time and space. The original event's reverberation is manifested in and through corporeal things and constitutes lived religious experience (spirituality).

The spiritual experience of resonating with an event in the past, via memory, need not be reserved for the celebrations of religious traditions alone, but rather can potentially surface in all things. This is especially the case if what Hasidism and pansacramentalism maintain is true concerning all things functioning as bridges to God, who remains equally in the past as well as the present. For instance, a very spiritual experience for me (and perhaps for many others) occurs in the autumn every year when I encounter the crisp dry air and the smell of fresh cut lawn of a nearby football or soccer field. In a Kierkegaardian "moment of passion," I am figuratively transported back to my youth when I played soccer and football in the autumn. This spiritual experience is facilitated by the corporeal autumn air, fresh cut grass, and nearby cries of children playing in the park. Most recently, I experienced this momentary flash of sacramentality as I walked past a neighborhood park and heard the faint cries of youths playing football, coaches shouting, referees' whistles blowing, and the smell of fresh-cut grass wafting. Though I remained in the present, I sacramentally connected with the past and time was collapsed altogether. The not-yet hallowed was hallowed in that instant. There was no neat separation between past and present, childhood and adulthood. I was embedded in an all-embracing relationship with the world and, as such, experienced the world in its pansacramental reality. In this way, the sacramental functions as that which collapses time within the context of the divine.

This chapter will not come to a close with a final example taken from Augustine's classic *Confessions*. In book nine, he recalls his very spiritual experience at Ostia, a scene in which he and Monica become so wrapped up in their sacramental conversation with each other that they transcended themselves, time, and, for a moment, simply exist outside of time. They experience being beyond time. Augustine recalls,

> Our minds were lifted up by an ardent affection towards eternal being itself. Step by step we climbed beyond all corporeal objects and the heaven itself, where sun, moon, and stars shed light on the earth. We ascended even further by internal reflection and dialogue and wonder at your works, and we entered into our own minds. We moved up beyond them so as to attain to the region of inexhaustible abundance where you feed Israel eternally with truth for good. There life is wisdom by which all creatures come into being, both things which were and which will be. But wisdom itself is not brought into being but is as it was and always will be. Furthermore, in this wisdom there is no past and future, but only being, since it is eternal. For to exist in the past or in the future is no property of the eternal and while we talked and panted after it, we touch it in some small degree by a moment of total concentration of the heart.[116]

Augustine's journey to rest till he rests in God catches momentary respite in this experience. In a flash of Kierkegaardian passion, they achieve a small degree of rest in their hearts; it occurred through sacramental conversation and relationship. In book ten, Augustine dwells on the concept of time and memory. He confesses, "Great is the power of memory, an awe-inspiring mystery my God, a power of profound and infinite multiplicity. And this is mind, this is I myself."[117] He notices that memory functions, in part, as that which allows him to be. It allows him to recognize the almost frightening limit of the present and transcend into the past. Thus, via memory, he discovers that he is not locked in time nor in the present, but rather memories can serve as primary experiences of spiritual transcendence, and even these he can transcend. He declares, "So great is the power of memory, so great is the force of life in a human being whose life is mortal. What then ought I to do, my God? You are my true life. I will transcend even this my power which is called memory."[118] All of his experiences had made him who he was when he wrote this. Since God was equally present to all moments of his life, in reflecting on who he was, Augustine had to employ his memory and expose (and confess) his past experiences. Memory allows one to re-member their dis-membered self. It functions to bridge one's present self with their past self and to resonate with the recognition of God's presence during all life

---

116. Augustine, *Confessions*, 171.
117. Ibid., 194.
118. Ibid.

experiences. In this way, it allows one to know their whole self; hence it is a re-membering of a dis-membered self.

A pansacramental proposal, such as the one presented in this book, advocates for the collapsing of dichotomies and bifurcations on many levels: time, space, and God/world, to name a few. In the spirit of the Hebrew *nabi*, it strives to maintain both the immanence and transcendence of the divine through the category of sacramentality and allow for an all-embracing holy relationship to the whole. Reminiscent of both Hegel's method of dialectical sublation and Panikkar's *Adviatic* approach to the whole, the sacrament, as both sign and symbol, mediates between the particular and universal, the subjective and objective, and renders inner reflection experiential all the while inviting transformative participation.

This pansacramental proposal will inevitably lead to the confrontation of philosophical questions pertaining to God's immanence and transcendence. In particular, my pansacramental proposal echoes traces of a type of sacramental panentheism; thus, it is appropriate to address its relationship to various Christian panentheisms, both classical and contemporary. In the next chapter, by entering into a dialogue with the various proponents of panentheism, while engaging its promises and problems (especially the reality of suffering), I shall both identify and distinguish my proposal from others.

12

Panentheism

A CENTRAL CONCERN OF this book is to reserve space for sacramentality in the mediation between theology and the study of spirituality. I have proposed a worldview that is deeply sacramental in that all things, in their particularity, serve as potential sacramental symbols of the universal divine nature. This is what I refer to as pansacramentality. Drawing on Buber's term pansacramental as employed in understanding the relationship between personhood and genuine conversation, I continue to suggest the benefit of understanding the world as pansacramental. I contend that a pansacramental worldview, such as the one I have suggested, inevitably requires engaging current scholarship in contemporary formulations of panentheism. This chapter is an attempt to do so. A burden of this book has been to show how the world can be understood pansacramentally. Both classical and contemporary panentheistic proposals attempt to also show how the divine is in all things, how all things reveal the divine, and how all things have their existence in the divine. In the final chapter, which draws on panentheism in this chapter and suffering in the next chapter, I offer a model, which I term "panentheistic pansacramentality," to understand the God-World relationship that is conducive to a pansacramental cosmology.

The philosophy of sacramentality presented in the previous chapter, the endorsement of Buber's pansacramental category, and the resulting worldview of all things holding the potential to sacramentally present God in and through worldly material, can facilitate a form of panentheism. There is no simple and shared meaning of panentheism that exist, but rather there is a diversity of panentheisms. Therefore, the aim here is to offer a foundational definition of panentheism (for this book) followed by a brief overview of some of the dominant versions of panentheism that are conducive for pansacramentality.[1]

Prior to reviewing some of the major versions of classical and contemporary panentheism, it may be helpful to relate the scope of this book to panentheism. Sacraments functions as religious symbols of ultimate significance. That which is of genuine ultimate significance constitutes that which is most real in one's life. Hence, in a Tillichian way, an ultimate concern can be made manifest via religious symbols of ultimate significance, whether they are genuine or not. These religious symbols of ultimate significance serve sacramentally as presentations of the ultimate reality of God. In this way they bring together the visible and the invisible by making visible the invisible; that is, they bring together spiritual reality and the material world, which I have suggested are coextensive with one another. Hence the spiritual-material dichotomy is dissolved, shattered, or absorbed. Keith Ward, in his chapter "Materialism and its Discontents," argues that the majority of both the classical and contemporary philosophers of the Western European tradition "have expounded a basically spiritual view of reality."[2] These thinkers include Plato, Aristotle, Anselm, Aquinas, Descartes, Leibniz, Spinoza, Locke, Berkeley, Kant, and Hegel. Similarly, thinkers such as Hume, Schopenhauer, and Nietzsche denied that ultimate reality is merely physical. Ward concludes, "The consensus of the Western philosophical tradition is that there is a supreme and transcendent spiritual reality, though it can be conceived in a number of different ways."[3]

If this inclination about the spiritual value of reality is correct, it prompts a discussion about how this might be understood and the resulting implications. In the previous chapters I gave a pansacramental explanation of how the material world might be conceived as coextensive with spiritual reality, and thus understood as ultimately spiritual. Others, in the discussion under the rubric of panentheism, have similarly sought to explain this. This is most pointed in proposals about how to understand the immanence of God in the world. The recognition of God's immanence in the world, as a means towards understanding the God-World relationship, has, perhaps more than any other factor, ignited the contemporary panentheistic

---

1. I am indebted to a couple of key texts in contemporary panentheism scholarship: Clayton and Peacocke, eds., *In Whom We Live and Move and Have Our Being*; and Cooper, *Panentheism, the Other God of the Philosophers*.

2. Ward, *God and the Philosophers*, 130.

3. Ibid., 147.

discussion in Christianity; it is what Phillip Clayton refers to as "the panentheistic turn" in twentieth century theology.[4]

The origin of the term "panentheism" is commonly credited to Karl Krause, who coined *Allingottlehre* in 1829. The first known English usage was in 1899 by William Ralph Inge's *Christian Mysticism*,[5] though the idea itself, it has been argued, is not new in the least.[6] Quite simply, the term literally translates to positing all-in-God and expounds a view that all things are in God and God is in all things, yet God is not exhausted by the world as a whole.[7] Though God is in the world and the world is in God, God remains more than, and thus transcends, the world as such. It is often praised for providing a promising alternative to both pantheism (all-is-God, which thus identities all things with God as such) and that which might be termed acosmic classical theism, which radically separates God and world. Panentheism, so goes the argument, steers a middle course between these two poles and retains a balanced view of God's immanence and transcendence. Thus the nature of the God-World relationship remains central to the panentheistic discussion. One's approach to this question will entail a number of far reaching theo-philosophical implications about God, world, and human nature among others.

4. Clayton, "The Panentheistic Turn in Christian Theology."

5. Inge, *Christian Mysticism*, 121; cf. Brierley, "Naming a Quiet Revolution."

6. Thinkers that have either openly professed panentheism or who have been identified as implicit panentheists, to varying degrees, include: Plato, Plotinus, Proclus, Pseudo-Dionysius, John Scotus Eriugena, Ramanuja, Mechtild of Magdeburg, Meister Eckhart, Julian of Norwich, Nicholas of Cusa, Martin Luther, Giordano Bruno, Jakob Böhme, Spinoza, Jonathan Edwards, Fichte, Schleiermacher, Hegel, Samuel Taylor Coleridge, Schelling, Karl Krause, Baur, Gustav Fechner, Ralph Waldo Emerson, Isaak Dorner, Jules Lequier, Charles Renouvier, Hermann Lotze, John and Edward Caird, Thomas Hill Green, Charles Sanders Peirce, Otto Pfleiderer, William James, James Ward, Andrew Seth Pringle-Pattison, Samuel Alexander, Henri Bergson, William Ralph Inge, Alfred North Whitehead, James Bethune-Baker, Ernst Troeltsch, Sergei Bulgakov, William Hocking, Nicholay Berdyaev, Karl Heim, Martin Buber, Albert Schweitzer, Teilhard de Chardin, William Temple, Rudolf Bultmann, Paul Tillich, Sarvepalli Radhakrishnan, Heidegger, Charles Hartshorne, Hans-Georg Gadamer, Paul Weiss, Karl Rahner, Norman Pittenger, Dietrich Bonehoeffer, Piet Schoonenberg, Alan Watts, Masao Abe, Charles Birch, John Macquarrie, John A.T. Robinson, Hugh Montefiore, Andrew Louth, Ian Barbour, Arthur Peacocke, Juan Luis Segundo, John cob, Jürgen Moltmann, Helen Oppenheimer, Joseph Bracken, Pannenberg, Hans Küng, Gustavo Gutiérrez, Schubert Ogden, Peter Hodgson, Peter Berger, John Polkinghorne, Sallie McFague, Donald Gelpi, Kallistos Ware, Rosemary Radford Ruether, James Cone, Leonardo Boff, Keith Ward, David Ray Griffin, Matthew Fox, Claude Stewart, Marcus Borg, Paul Davies, Paul Fiddes, Miriam Starhawk, Jim Garrison, Muhammed Iqbal, Christopher Knight, Daniel Dombrowski, Anna Case-Winters, and Phillip Clayton (cf. Cooper, *Panentheism*; Brierley, "Naming a Quiet Revolution").

7. Gregersen, "Three Varieties of Panentheism," 19.

In chapter 5, panentheism was defined in a general sense. There are several good works that discuss the variations of panentheism and that provide useful typologies.[8] Here I offer a basic definition and lay out some of the basic distinctions that separate one panentheism from the others. The *Oxford Dictionary of the Christian Church* defines the term as "the belief that the Being of God includes and penetrates the whole universe, so that every part of it exists in Him, but (as against pantheism) that His Being is more than, and is not exhausted by, the universe."[9] This definition provides the lowest common denominator (or highest common factor) of all panentheisms; that is, it states what is common to all without introducing that which separates one from the other. However, most, if not all, modern and contemporary panentheisms go beyond the mere Oxford definition. The panentheistic turn of the last century in Christian theology is due, in large part, to the desire to balance God's immanence with God's transcendence, the latter of which is often accused of being over-emphasized by classical Christian theism. Thus panentheism exhibits the appeal of functioning as a *via media* between two positions; one that advocates for God's transcendence (classical theism), and one, for God's radical immanence (pantheism). One may adopt panentheism for several reasons and the panentheism they adopt may be highly qualified, ranging from classical and contemporary attempts alike. Since, at its most basic level, panentheism advocates for God being *in* all things and all things remaining *in* God, the crucial word here (and the most often qualified) in both formulas is rightly "in." How are all things *in* God and how is God *in* all things? This question, more than any other, often separates one panentheism from the next.

This section is not meant to systematically treat or propose a certain variety of panentheism, but rather serves to draw some lines of similarity and difference between the pansacramental vision of this project and some of the popular models, themes, and implications of classical and contemporary panentheism scholarship.[10] The final chapter proposes a form of

---

8. cf. Gregersen, "Three Varieties of Panentheism," Ward, "The World as the Body of God," Clayton, "Panentheism Today," and Cooper, *Panentheism*.

9. "panentheism, "*The Oxford Dictionary of the Christian Church.*"

10. Niels Gregersen proposes the following are three varieties of panentheism. I have listed a representative for each one in parentheses: 1) soteriological (Polkinghorne), 2) expressivist (Hegel), and 3) dipolar (Whitehead) (Gregersen, "Three Varieties of Panentheism"). Phillip Clayton proposes the following thirteen varieties with their respective representative: 1) Participatory (A. Louth), 2) "Divine Energies" (K. Ware), 3) Ecclesial (A. Nesteruk), 4) Eschatological/Soteriological (Polkinghorne), 5) Sapiential (C. Deane-Drummond), 6) Emergentist (A. Peacocke & P. Clayton), 7) Sacramental (A. Peacocke, C. Knight), 8) Trinitarian (D. Edwards), 9) Pan-sacramental naturalistic (C. Knight), 10) Process/dipolar (D. Griffin & J. Bracken), 11) "Body of

panentheistic pansacramentalism that engages key issues and distinctions within contemporary panentheism scholarship.

At the very least, this chapter necessarily attempts to draw some broad lines between classical and contemporary panentheism as employed in this chapter and current theological scholarship. It has become clear that the definition of the term panentheism has been stretched to include a diverse variety of types. Here, for the sake of simplicity, I suggest two types, classical and contemporary, both within which (especially the latter) one can make several more qualifications and types. Classical panentheism here simply refers to affirming the Oxford Dictionary definition of panentheism given above as well as the traditional orthodox tenets of Christianity, both East and West. On the other hand, contemporary panentheism has come to entail a rejection of many of these classical tenets, and instead entertains the claims that God is mutable, God suffers, God is affected by creatures, God is dependent on the world, and the world is part of God's nature to name a few. However, due to the sheer diversity of contemporary panentheism, it is impossible and inappropriate to make generalized claims about it. Thus it is important to take each panentheist in his or her own right when evaluating. This is what this chapter endeavors.

Prior to proposing a model of panentheistic pansacramentality in the final chapter, this chapter presents several foundational thinkers in so far as they explicate both classical and contemporary panentheism that have contributed to, and have helped to clarif, my own theological position. These thinkers are Thomas Aquinas, Friedrich Schelling, Karl Rahner, Arthur Peacocke, John Polkinghorne, and Matthew Fox, in addition to the *theōtic* tradition of Gregory Palamas and Eastern Orthodox Christianity. Aquinas, Rahner, and Eastern Orthodox Christianity (represented by Palamas) serve as representatives of classical panentheisms, while Schelling and Peacock fall within the vast spectrum of modern or contemporary panentheisms. Polkinghorne remains a provisional contemporary panentheist and Fox is

God" (Ramanuja), 12) Neopanentheism (H. Morowitz), and 13) Pansyntheism (R. Page) (Clayton, "Panentheism Today," 250). Michael Brierley recognizes eight common themes which he believes serve as a preliminary test to determine whether or not one might be described as a panentheist. They are: 1) The Cosmos as God's Body, 2) Language of "In and Through," 3)The Cosmos as Sacrament, 4) Language of Inextricable Intertwining, 5) God's Dependence on the Cosmos, 6)The Intrinsic, Positive Value of the Cosmos, 7) Passibility, and 8) Degree Christology (Brierley, "Naming a Quiet Revolution," 5- 12). John W. Cooper discerns five key distinctions amongst the varieties of panentheisms. I have listed Cooper's suggested representative for some of the categories in parentheses. They are 1) explicit (Harthshorne) and implicit (Hegel), 2) personal (Teilhard) and nonpersonal (Tillich), 3) part-whole and relational, 4) voluntary and natural, and 5) classical divine determinist (Schleiermacher) and modern cooperative (Schelling) (Cooper, *Panentheism*, 26–30).

more difficult to pin down in his progressive spiritual explicit panentheism. Here the goal is not to argue for one over the other (classical vs. contemporary), but rather to affirm the basic inclination behind panentheism as such: to show the nature of the pansacramentality of all things. Drawing on these thinkers, the final chapter will then offer a new panentheistic pansacramental proposal which may be able to serve, at some level, both camps, classical and contemporary.

Thomas Aquinas (1225–1274)[11]

Though it is certainly anachronistic to label Aquinas a panentheist, he can be deemed a classical panentheist if the Oxford dictionary definition is employed in the strict sense. This is not to say that Aquinas qualifies as a panentheist in the contemporary sense. However, he can represent a classical ontological panentheism since God is in all things ontologically as the ground of their being. For Aquinas, God causes and sustains all things in the cosmos. "Every being in any way existing is from God."[12]

For Aquinas, all that exists within the cosmos can be distinguished by employing the language of essence and existence. In all finite created things, the essence remains distinct from its existence. God, as the principal cause and creator of the cosmos, is beyond such distinction and comprehensibility. God's essence is identical with God's existence. The reason for this is that for Aquinas, to create is to create anew, to make something from nothing (*ex nihilo*), and only God can create. Only God can give being since God is being as such. Aquinas writes, "We must consider not only the emanation of a particular being from a particular agent, but also the emanation of all being from the universal cause which is God; and this emanation we designate by the name of creation."[13]

As indicated in chapter five, an effect of creation is existence itself, "which accordingly should be the proper effect of the first and most universal cause, which is God."[14] This is supported by what Etienne Gilson refers to as the "Great Syllogism,"

1. "God is very being (*esse*) by His own essence,"

---

11. A more comprehensive overview of Aquinas' classical panentheism can be found in chapter 5.
12. Thomas Aquinas, *Summa Theologica*, I, 44, 1.
13. Ibid., I, 45, 1.
14. Ibid., *Summa Theologica*, I, 45, 5.

2. "being (*esse*) is innermost in each thing and most fundamentally inherent in all things since it is formal in respect of everything found in a thing."
3. "Hence, it must be that God is in all things, and innermostly."[15][/NL]

God sacramentally expresses God's self (*esse*) in the world via creaturely representation or imaging. This further highlights the mutual entanglement of God's transcendence and immanence in a Thoimist classical framework. Contemporary panentheists sometimes complain that classical Christian orthodoxy has traditionally overemphasized God's transcendence at the expense of God's immanence, and thus propose panentheism as a means to balance the two more equally. However, Thomists point out that the very nature of this accusation confuses the relationship between God's transcendence and immanence; it treats them as two distinct things and possibly mutually exclusive, hence the proposed possibility of an imbalance. According to Aquinas, they cannot be separated nor in an imbalance; since God is being as such, God is both totally transcendent and totally immanent to all things. God's immanence and transcendence are not two things. God is immanent in all things since God is totally transcendent. God cannot be one without the other. Each entails the other.[16] God is fully immanent in God's presence in the world, but remains fully transcendent in God's nature.

A classical conception of panentheism retains this Thomist understanding of the relationship between God's transcendence and immanence as well as the classical attributes ascribed to God such as immutability, simplicity, omnipotence, omniscience, self-sufficiency, and omnipresence to name the major ones. In Aquinas, who remains *the* representative of classical Western orthodoxy *par excellence*, these tenets are retained within an implicit panentheistic framework.

Friedrich Schelling (1775–1854)

Friedrich Schelling, greatly influenced by Plato, Meister Eckhart, Nicholas of Cusa, Jakob Böhme and Baruch Spinoza, defended what he referred to as "pantheism,"[17] which John Cooper reasonably deems, "modern (dy-

15. Ibid., *Summa Theologica*, I, 8, 1.

16. In his *Summa of the Summa*, Peter Kreeft interprets Aquinas on this as follows: "Nothing is more inner, present, and intimate to every being than God. God activates every being from within, so to speak. N. b.: God can be thus supremely present and immanent only because He is supremely transcendent" (Kreeft, *Summa of the Summa*, 101–2).

17. Schelling, *Schelling: Of Human Freedom*; 10.

namic, cooperative) panentheism."[18] Both Schelling and Hegel represent a transition from classical panentheism to contemporary panentheism.[19] The main difference between the two lies in the approach to God's (im)mutability. The classical approach affirms the "unmoved mover" God while the modernist-contemporary approach proffers a more dynamic and cooperative God. German idealism, ignited by Schelling and developed by Hegel, proposed a God that develops and rises to consciousness in and through the world. For these reasons, Cooper anoints Schelling and Hegel as the "godfathers of modern panentheism"[20]

Schelling preserved human freedom and posited a personal God (which may distinguish him from those panentheists who posit a non-personal God). These two positions should not scandalize the classical Christian theist in the least, for both free will and a personal God remain well within their theological comfort zone. However, in order to preserve human moral freedom and autonomy, Schelling departs from classical Christianity and places humans in God, concluding that as parts of God, humans too have freedom like God.[21] Since God is free and humans participate in God, humans are free as well. For Schelling, it follows that God is dynamic since within God there are free autonomous subjects that are yet to be determined and thus God develops dynamically in and through human history. This entails a codependence of God and humans on one another since "we are collaborators of the whole and have ourselves invented the particular roles we play."[22] In this way, God provides the *telos* of human history while persons remain free to determine the minutiae of their movement towards that *telos*.

This might be likened to a kayaker (human agent) paddling down a whitewater river (God) flowing from summit to sea. The source and destination are predetermined and put into incessant motion by the moving water;

---

18. Cooper, 95; Cooper recognizes that "a number of scholars regard Schelling as a panentheist," including Charles Harthshorne, William Reese, Steve Wilkins, Alan Padgett, and Philip Clayton (Cooper, 105).

19. Cooper refers to contemporary panentheism as modern panentheism. I employ the two terms interchangeably.

20. Cooper, 90; While Cooper ranks Schelling ahead of Hegel when it comes to contributing more to modern panentheism, the authors of *In Whom We Live and Move and Have Our Being*, as Roger Olson has pointed out, "treat Hegel as the early paradigmatic modern panentheist (rather than Schelling)" (Olson, "A Postconservative Evangelical Response to Panentheisms Old and New").

21. "Every individual intelligence can be regarded as a constitutive part of God or of the moral world-order. Every rational being can say to himself: I too am entrusted with the execution of the law, and the practice of righteousness within my sphere of influence" (Schelling, *System of Transcendental Idealism*, 206).

22. Schelling, *System of Transcendental Idealism*, 210.

however, the details of the journey are left to the paddler. He may shoot rapids, portage around falls, rest in eddies, and/or allow the flowing water to move him without rudder. The river and he cooperate and "codetermine the course of their mutual self-actualization." I suspect that if you ask enough whitewater paddlers about this experience, you're likely to receive quasi-spiritual answers about "dancing" and being "at one" with the river in the movement towards its end. This analogy can be very easily translated into many gravity-assisted activities such as downhill skiing and surfing.[23]

Schelling posits a panentheism in which humans are located in God as part of his philosophical system of the Absolute that identifies God and world. To preserve human freedom and avoid determinism in this scheme, he posits a free and personal God from which creatures haven fallen (which Schelling refers to as a defect, or sin). Borrowing from Böhme, Schelling extends this creaturely fall to all of creation resulting in a cosmic fall from God. He then distances himself from the pantheism of Spinoza by positing a personal God in distinction from Spinoza's "abstract conception of . . . eternal Substance itself."[24] By positing a fallen cosmos and a personal God, Schelling can be understood as a panentheist in his view of the Absolute as containing the cosmos yet not exhausted by it. As persons receive their freedom from their location in a free God, God is thus able to self-actualize in world-history via human action. This raises one of Michael Brierley's key themes of panentheism: the question of God's (in)dependence of, or on, the cosmos.[25] For Schelling, it appears that God is indeed dependent on the world in order to be God, but this dependency is on free persons who resemble God.[26]

In and through God's participation with cosmos, God's passibility remains; that is, God experiences suffering since the cosmos experiences suffering. Like persons, "God is a life, not a mere being. All life has a destiny and is subject to suffering and development. God freely submitted himself to this too."[27] Like Aquinas, Schelling maintains that God's essence remains eternal and immutable, but unlike Aquinas, for Schelling, God's existence is dynamic which entails becoming, growing, changing and suffering. He writes, "The one being really divides itself into two beings in its two functions, that in the one it is *only* the basis of existence, in the other only essence (and therefore only ideal); moreover . . . only God as spirit is the

23. cf. Kreeft, *I Surf, Therefore I Am*.
24. Schelling, *Of Human Freedom*, 22.
25. Brierley, "Naming a Quiet Revolution," 9–10.
26. Schelling, *Of Human Freedom*, 19.
27. Ibid., 84.

absolute identity of both principles, but only because and insofar as both are *subjected* to his personality."[28]

God, like human persons, develops and comes to know God's personhood in and through this existential becoming and suffering in the world. This is how God is involved in human history. The anthropomorphizing of God and God's suffering in Schelling has earned him the rank of being one of the earliest, if not the first, thinkers to articulate a version of contemporary panentheism. For Schelling, "all history remains incomprehensible without the concept of a humanly suffering of God."[29] Note here that God suffers in a human way. This addresses an important question to be asked when discussing the mode of God's suffering. God suffers in God's own existence, yet remains eternal and immutable in God's own essence. Hence there is a distinction between God's essence and existence. For God, like human persons, "participating in everything blind, dark, and evil, the suffering of God's nature is necessary in order to elevate God to the highest consciousness."[30]

In addition to preserving human freedom, Schelling exhibits remnants of the romantic spirit in his high place for art and aesthetic intuition. In this way, art functions sacramentally in its revelation of the Absolute; in fact, it is only through art that the absolute is revealed. Schelling relies on this aesthetical intuition as the epistemological foundation for the whole of philosophy. He declares, "The whole of philosophy starts, and must start, from a principle which, as absolute principle, is also at the same time the absolutely identical. An absolutely simple and identical cannot be grasped or communicated through description, not through concepts at all. It can only be intuited. Such an intuition is the organ of all philosophy."[31] This intuition is the intuition of the aesthetic.

Unlike Hegel, Schelling preserves the infinite knowability of God in his skepticism of whether philosophy can fathom the mystery of God.[32] Cooper provides an eloquent and succinct summary of Schelling's panentheistic vision,

> His "God or Freedom" is different than Spinoza's "God or nature." Even his early philosophy of absolute identity strongly distinguishes God and creatures, grants both freedom, and locates humanity "in God." His panentheism gains clarity with

---

28. Ibid., 90 (italics and parenthesis his).
29. Ibid., *Of Human Freedom*, 84.
30. Schelling, *The Ages of the World*, 101; also quoted by Cooper, 103–4.
31. Ibid., 229.
32. Cooper, 105.

his Böhmian theology of divine and human personhood. But his existence is a progressive self-actualization of his essence in and through the action of free creatures, their suffering, and eventual triumph.[33]

Schelling ignites the fire under Hegel, who takes several of these themes and develops them, while denying others. Schelling's importance for this chapter lies in his move towards articulating, in a more explicit manner, contemporary panentheism, his preservation of human freedom, and solidarity of God with the world in suffering, and his preservation of God's transcendence.

Karl Rahner (1904-84)

Among all thinkers presented in this book thus far, Karl Rahner has had the most significant and far reaching influence on the pansacramental vision offered here. His Ignatian roots ground his thoroughly sacramental view of finding God in all things. Though he does not use the term panentheism, he might be considered an implicit classical panentheist or an "anonymous panentheist," and certainly an incarnational pansacramentalist.[34] John Cooper has labeled Rahner's panentheism "cosmic-incarnational panentheism."[35] However, just because Rahner is an incarnationalist and pansacramentalist does not necessarily mean that he is a contemporary panentheist, thus I label Rahner an implicit classical panentheistic pansacramentalist. Rahner still maintains the classical attributes of God (e.g., God is other than the world and God suffers in that otherness, but not anthropomorphically).

An appealing aspect of Rahner's theological project, for the aspiring Christian panentheist, lies in his incarnational view of the cosmos.[36] The source and summit of this view rests in his "Christology [from] within an evolutionary view of the world."[37] The world, especially the person, evolves through transcendence towards God, and towards ultimate unification of all things in God. In this scheme, the material world functions as a vehicle for the spirit; that is, in the person matter and spirit are united, and in this way move the cosmos towards fulfillment. In the Incarnation, this ultimate fulfillment "has already begun [in] what we call the 'hypostatic union,' . . .

33. Cooper, 105.
34. Cf. Edwards, "A Relational and Evolving Universe."
35. Cooper, 225.
36. A detailed excursus of Rahner's view is not necessary here since chapter 5 was devoted to sketching his pansacramentalism.
37. Rahner, *Foundations of Christian Faith,* 178.

[which] appears as the necessary and permanent beginning of the divinization of the world as a whole."[38] All creatures, especially the human person, and all of creation are invited to follow suit and participate in the transcendence of the world and in the life God. In this pursuit, humans and nature share the common goal of transforming the material world into spirit. In other words, the whole of creation is invited to realize and actualize itself in transcending its matter in a movement towards spirit and, in this way, sacramentally express and present God.

Rahner's implicit classical panentheism, although it clearly stresses God's immanence in the world, holds firm to God's transcendence—in a manner reminiscent of Aquinas. God becomes incarnate in the world so that matter might realize its spiritual nature. God "cannot simply be God himself as acting in the world, but must be a part of the cosmos, a moment within history, and indeed at its climax."[39] Matter remains distinct from the Logos, yet also expresses the Logos. For Rahner, "there is no problem in understanding what is called creation as a partial moment in the process in which God becomes world."[40] Both God's act of creation and the process of God becoming world are not to be understood as two distinct acts, but rather "two phases of *one* process of God's self-giving and self-expression."[41] What has been decisively accomplished in Christ (Logos and human matter have become one) continues in the cosmos and its fulfillment in God.

Rahner's God remains immutable despite the ability to become. His case for this rests on a dialectical understanding of God's immutability and his claim that the Logos incarnates a human person, which has the ability to become. In other words, the immutable incarnates the mutable and is thus able to mutate itself—however the immutability of God remains. "He who is not subject to change in himself can *himself* be subject to change *in something else*."[42] This is a crucial distinction to be noted when distinguishing between classical and contemporary panentheisms. Rahner's insistence on God's immutability is thoroughly classical and clearly distinguishes him from contemporary panentheism. God's attribute of immutability must be dialectically balanced alongside God's attribute of willingness to incarnate in the same manner one dialectically balances the mystery of the unity of God in the Trinity.[43] One attribute ought not negate or trump the other, but

---

38. Ibid., 181.
39. Ibid., 195.
40. Ibid., 197.
41. Ibid. (italics his).
42. Ibid., 220 (italics his).
43. "The assertion of God's immutability is a dialectical assertion in the same sense

rather must be dialectally placed alongside one another and affirmed in their apparent contradiction. In the manner unity is expressed in the Trinity, "so too do we learn through the doctrine of the Incarnation that God's immutability, without thereby being eliminated, is by no means simply the only thing that characterizes God, but that in and in spite of his immutability he can truly become something: he himself, he in time."[44] Thus Rahner holds firm to the classical Christian claim that God is immutable.

God's divine will remains free, for God's willingness to incarnate things does not entail God's dependence on it, but rather it demonstrates "the height of his perfection."[45] God expresses God's self in and through the material world not because God needs to do so in order to be God, but rather because that is what God is and does in God's perfection. Rahner's vision here is held together by defining God, with scripture, as self-giving and self-emptying free love (*agape*).[46] "The kenosis and genesis of God himself," God's self-emptying and incarnation in the world, establishes "the other as his own reality by dispossessing *himself*, by giving *himself* away," and in this sense God is in God's self as *agape*.[47]

In short, Rahner maintains a pansacramentally imbued cosmos which is invited to transcend itself towards and in God. Though God remains mysteriously other and "infinitely knowable," Rahner holds fast to his Ignatian foundation of promoting the principle of finding God in all things which, for him, entails all things finding themselves in God. Hence, Rahner is understood here to be an implicit panentheist who relies on the evolutionary cosmic potential of all things to sacramentally facilitate God's self-communication in space and time in order that the world might be unified in God.

Arthur Peacock (1924-2006)

Arthur Peacocke stresses, more than other contemporary thinkers, Michael Brierley's third main panentheistic theme: the understanding of "the cosmos

---

as is the assertion of the unity of God in and in spite of the Trinity, that is, both of these assertions remain in fact really correct only if we immediately add the other two assertions, namely, about the Trinity and about the Incarnation respectively" (Rahner, *Foundations*, 221).

44. Rahner, *Foundations*, 221.

45. Ibid., 222.

46. "God goes out of himself, he himself, he as the self-giving fullness. Because he can do this, because this is his free and primary possibility, for this reason he is defined in scripture as love" (ibid.).

47. Ibid. (italics his).

as sacrament."[48] Peacocke emphasizes the sacramental through a naturalistic approach to panentheism[49] and credits William Temple for speaking of the "sacramental universe."[50] Consequently, he builds on this theme to become one of the first thinkers to explicitly promote a naturalistic sacramental panentheism. Peacocke does so, in large part, due to his background in science. He boasts an impressive resume in scientific research spending the first twenty-five years of his career teaching and researching physical biochemistry with an emphasis on DNA structure and macromolecules.[51] He devoted the latter thirty years of his career examining the relationship between science and religion, and held several prestigious academic positions and memberships in the U.K.[52] Given Peacocke's impressive career, it is not surprising that his approach to panentheism was naturalistic.

Peacocke understands the cosmos as having evolved over billions of years from potency to act into a complex emergent system of systems, including animals, humans, and everything else. He writes, "The original fluctuating quantum field, quark soup or whatever, has in twelve or so billion years become a Mozart, a Shakespeare, and Buddha, a Jesus of Nazareth—and

48. Brierley, "Naming a Quiet Revolution," 8.

49. Christopher C. Knight puts forth a similar case for what he terms "pansacramental naturalism" in his *Wrestling with the Divine*. In fact, he recommends renaming Peacocke's panentheism to either "sacramental panentheism or pansacramentalism," two labels I do not use synonymously. Knight follows Peacocke and credits Eastern Orthodox conceptions of the cosmos as well as Alexander Schmemann's claim of "The World as Sacrament" (Knight, *Wrestling with the Divine*, 18). His pansacramental naturalism, like Vladimir Lossky's Eastern Orthodox tradition, "knows nothing of 'pure nature' to which grace is added as a supernatural gift... [there is] no natural or normal state, since grace is implied in the act of creation itself... The world, created in order that it might be deified, is dynamic, tending always towards its final end," and thus nature as such is inherently engraced or incessantly actualized (Lossky, *The Mystical Theology of the Eastern Church*, 249; quoted by Knight, 18–19).

50. Peacocke references Temple, *Nature, Man, and God,* chapter 19, in Peacocke "Articulating God's Presence in and to the World Unveiled by the Sciences," 154.

51. "Dr. Peacocke was involved in founding the Science and Religion Forum in the United Kingdom, the corresponding European society (ESSSAT), and the Society of Ordained Scientists, a new dispersed religious order. He was made a member of the Order of the British Empire by Queen Elizabeth II in 1993" (Clayton and Peacocke, *In Whom We Live and Move and Have Our Being,* 270).

52. Peacocke, "scientist-theologian and Anglican Canon, . . . was Warden Emeritus at the Society of Ordained Scientists and Council Member of the European Society for the Study of Science and Theology, and he demonstrated the viability and the necessity of regarding theology and science as interacting approaches to reality during more than forty years of scientific and theological scholarship. In so doing, he produced creative, insightful, and thought-provoking resources for the reinterpretation and reconstruction of theological models of God and the God-world relationship compatible with evolutionary science" (Schaab, *The Creative Suffering of the Triune God,* 34–35).

you and me!"⁵³ For Peacocke, the evolutionary process of nature sacramentally reveals or (re)presents the real presence of God. This "real presence" might be understood in a way reminiscent of Luther's understanding of the real presence; that is, one that remains skeptical of Aristotelian substance metaphysics and transubstantiation, yet nonetheless affirms the real presence. God employs the natural "process as an instrument of God's purposes and as a symbol of the divine nature, that is, as the means of conveying insight into these purposes [and] in the Christian tradition, this is precisely what its sacraments do."⁵⁴ Peacocke here is alluding to the efficacy of the sacramental as that which effects what it symbolizes. In *God and the New Biology*, Peacocke builds his pansacramentalism on the understanding of the incarnation as the complete realization of the God who is present in the world. In turn, nature as symbolic of God makes God present in an "obscure and partial" way. Just as "a new value [is] assigned by God himself in Christ" to Jesus, so too in Eucharist a new value is assigned to its material aspects. However, "that to which a new value was imputed was not only these particular elements of bread and wine used in *this* way, but the whole created material world."⁵⁵ Since the cosmos is imbued with, and constituted by, nature as such, God's real presence is represented in all ways through the natural process and thus, the cosmos functions pansacramentally.

For Peacocke, God is immanent in the natural process of the cosmos, yet God remains other; that is, "God is the immanent creator creating through the processes of the natural order. The processes are not themselves God, but the *action* of God as creator. God gives existence in divinely created time to a process that itself brings for the new—thereby God is creat*ing*."⁵⁶ God is immanent in the processes, but God as such transcends the processes. Peacocke affirms a panentheism similar to that of Jürgen Moltmann which employs, "the 'in' (the *en* of 'pantheism') to express the idea of the world, including humanity, as enveloped by God without losing its true distinctiveness as a way of intensifying the traditional believe in God's immanence in the world."⁵⁷ Thus, all is in God including all that is not God. In this way Peacocke avoids committing to the position that identifies the world with God, which he believes flirts too closely with pantheism. However, even though God is not a person for Peacocke—rather, God is "suprapersonal

53. Peacocke, "Articulating God's Presence in and to the World Unveiled by the Sciences," 153–54.

54. Ibid., 154.

55. Peacocke, *God and the New Biology*, 117–118.

56. Peacocke, "Articulating God's Presence in and to the World Unveiled by the Sciences," 144 (italics his).

57. Ibid., 146 (italics his).

or transpersonal" since there are aspects of God's nature which "cannot be subsumed under the categories applicable to human persons"[58]—suffering remains within and present to God. Peacocke explains,

> Creating is costly *to God*. Now, when the natural world, with all its suffering, is panentheistically conceived of as "in God," it follows that the evils of pain, suffering, and death in the world are internal to God's own self: God must have experience of the natural. The intimate and actual experience of God must also include all those events that constitute the evil intentions of human beings and their implementation—that is, the moral evil of human society.[59]

One value, among many, that Peacocke retains in the panentheistic conversation is his insistence on the role and functionality of the sacramental as an adequate mode of God's presence in the world. His approach, in addition to that of Christopher C. Knight, to sacramental panentheism rests on the process of nature as symbol, whereas the approach I advocate for in this project rests on the philosophical function of sacramentality and its mediatory role between theology and the study of spirituality as well as between God and world.

John Polkinghorne (1930–)

John Polkinghorne is an English physicist, theologian, and Anglican priest who, like Peacocke, brings together the fields of religion and science. Although Polkinghorne himself rejects the term panentheism,[60] he proffers what others[61] have labeled a provisional eschatological, soteriological, or eschatological sacramental panentheism. The appeal of his approach lies

---

58. Ibid., 151

59. Ibid. (italics his).

60. In *Science and Providence*, Polkinghorne writes that the "the problem [of panentheism] then lies in the danger that such a view compromises the world's freedom to be itself, which God has given to his creation, and also the otherness that he remains for himself." Further, "all panentheistic theories are going to threaten the mutually free relation of God and his creation" (Polkinghorne, *Science and Providence*, 20, 28). In *The Faith of a Physicist*, he writes, "While I am sympathetic to what panentheism sets out to achieve by way of balance between divine transcendence and divine immanence, I cannot myself see that it succeeds in doing so in an acceptable way" (Polkinghorne, *The Faith of a Physicist*, 64f). In *Science and Creation*, he writes "Panentheism's defect is its denial of the true otherness of the world from God, which is part of our experience" (Polkinghorne, *Science and Creation*, 66).

61. cf. Clayton, "Panentheism Today," 250; Cooper, 315–17.

in his conservation of the classical eschatological "not yet" while providing space for God's sacramental reign as partially realized in the "now." Thus God is sacramentally in the world "now," but God's fullness in the world remains "not yet," but is to come at the eschaton. John Cooper deems this a "provisional" panentheism,[62] since Polkinghorne qualifies it when he writes, "I do not accept panentheism (the idea that the creation is in God, though God exceeds creation) as a theological reality for the present world, but I do believe in it as the form of eschatological destiny for the world to come."[63]

In this manner, Polkinghorne separates himself from a hard or strong form of panentheism that affirms God's presence in the world presently, and instead he advocates for a soft or weak form of panentheism by affirming the goal of panentheism (all things existing in God) at the eschaton. The benefit of such an approach leaves room for the claim that the here and now represents God incompletely; that is, revelation is blurred or veiled. God may be present in momentary sacramental glimpses similar to a Kierkegaardian moment of passion, but the fullness of God being in the world, and all things being in God, remains incomplete until the end of time. Polkinghorne strives to balance what he deems an overemphasis of God's transcendence in classical theism with God's immanence in the world without overemphasizing it, as he believes panentheism does.

Polkinghorne makes a move similar to that of the Eastern Orthodox in making the Palamite distinction between God's essence and energies, positing that it is God's energies which are operative and immanent in the world now, while God's essence remains transcendent. For Polkinghorne this distinction surfaces in the dipolarity of the God: God is both infinite and finite in Christ, God is both immanent and transcendent, eternal and temporal, etc. An example of this dipolarity plays out in the temporal world, in which God's worldly knowledge remains limited to the present; that is, "God does not yet know all that will eventually become knowable . . . [But like] William James' picture of the Grandmaster of cosmic chess, who will win the game whatever moves the creaturely opponent may make,"[64] God's intended *telos* will ultimately be realized. Think here of the scenes from the 1993 Bill Murray film *Groundhog Day*, in which Murray's character, who lives the same February 2nd day over and over again, attempts to save a homeless beggar from his destiny to pass away on that particular day. Each reoccurring day Murray tries to buck fatalism in his attempts to save the homeless beggar in new ways (e.g., bringing him to a hospital, feeding him

---

62. Cooper, 315.
63. Polkinghorne, *The God of Hope and the End of the World*, 114–15.
64. Polkinghorne, *Science and the Trinity*, 108. Cited by Cooper as well.

a warm meal). His efforts are futile, for fate prevails and the beggar passes away regardless of Murray's free acts to save him. The Grandmaster of cosmic chess wins regardless of Murray's freedom. In the end, the temporal knowledge of God does not reduce God's power to push the world towards its destiny and fulfillment.

Sacraments function, for Polkinghorne, in a fairly traditional and orthodox way in that they make God present. He employs the terminology of "real presence" in describing sacramental functionality and is clear that it should "by no means [be] confined to the Catholic and Orthodox traditions alone; it is to be found for example in Luther and Calvin,"[65] albeit with qualification. Polkinghorne conceives of the real presence not in terms of some magical manipulation of natural elements, nor as a merely symbolic remembrance that conjures up thoughts of the tradition. Rather, he takes it seriously and is probably the closest to Catholic, Lutheran, and Orthodox understanding of the real presence. However, he parts with the classical tradition in an explicit rejection of substance metaphysics.

> The medieval doctrine of transubstantiation was a brilliant attempt to deal with this problem in terms of the substance which was held to underlie the accidents of material composition, so that the former became in the sacrament the body and blood of Christ, while the latter remained unchanged. Unfortunately, that metaphysical scheme of substance and accident no longer seems persuasive.[66]

The action of God in this sacramental scheme relies not on the concept of substance, but rather on the claim that God is present in "the gathered community of believers."[67] God is immanent and sacramentally present through the work of the Spirit which dwells in the openness of the community. Moreover, Polkinghorne upholds the First Anglican—Roman Catholic International Commission on the "Eucharistic Doctrine" which denies any material change in the bread and wine becoming the body and blood of Christ. He affirms the commission's statement that *becoming*, "does not imply that Christ becomes present in the eucharist in the same manner that he was present in his earthly life. It does not imply that this *becoming* follows the physical laws of this world."[68] Polkinghorne accepts this understanding of sacramental functionality as consistent with the provisional eschatological panentheism he strives to articulate. Citing Colossians 3:11, he writes,

65. Polkinghorne, *Science and Providence*, 105.
66. Ibid.
67. Ibid., 106.
68. *First Anglican/Roman Catholic International Commission, Eucharistic Doctrine.*

"Our present sacramental experience can be seen as a foretaste and earnest of that ultimate consummation in which 'Christ is all and in all.'"[69]

According to Polkinghorne, the fullness of God is not present in the here and now, thus the world neither exists nor participates fully in God currently, but the destiny of the cosmos is *theōtic* in that the cosmos is divinized and participates in God fully at the eschaton. This dipolar aspect of God distinguishes between God's absence from the world and God's sacramental presence in the world, both now and not yet. With respect for Polkinghorne's right to not self-identify as a panentheist, I do not regard him as a strict panentheist, but rather as a potential (or provisional) panentheist; that is, he is one who rejects panentheism for the present world but remains hopeful for the panentheistic fulfillment at the eschaton. Regardless, his emphasis on the sacramental nature of reality in the here and now resonates well with the pansacramental vision I have strived to set forth in this book. It allows for the function of sacramental mediators in the present and offers glimpses and representations of God. I have included Polkinghorne's vision here as an example of a provisional panentheism that can accommodate my understanding of sacramental mediation.

Gregory Palamas and Theōsis in Eastern Orthodox Christianity

Having already offered Aquinas as a Western representative of classical panentheism, I now turn to Gregory Palamas as an Eastern representative of classical panentheism. Pope John Paul II famously stated in *Ut Unim Sint* that "the Church must breathe with her two lungs," both East and West. Bishop Kallistos Ware argues that "Regrettably, from the seventeenth century onward, among all too many Christian thinkers—chiefly Western but sometimes also Eastern Orthodox—the delicate equilibrium between transcendence and immanence has been impaired and God's otherness has been overemphasized at the expense of his immanence."[70] Panentheism offers a promising path for bringing the two lungs here back together to breathe synergistically between East and West while emphasizing both God's transcendence and immanence. The Eastern Orthodox tradition, with their emphasis on *kenosis* and *theōsis*, makes a good case for the assertion that the Abrahamic traditions can understood to be inherently panentheist without violating the classical attributions of the Godhead. Ware asserts that God is both "immanent as well as transcendent: all things have been created 'in

---

69. Polkinghorne, *Science and Providence*, 107.
70. Ware, "God Immanent yet Transcendent," 159.

him . . . through him and for him . . . and in him all things hold together' (Col. 1:15–17)."[71] Thus, "God is *pantokrator*, a term which means not only 'almighty,' 'all-powerful,' but 'he who holds all things in unity.'"[72] In this manner, Christianity (as well as Judaism and Islam) can be deemed "fundamentally 'panentheist,'" and does not require the reevaluation of the adequacy of God's attributes as defined by classical theism. The Eastern approach to this classical panentheism rests on both the Palamite distinction between God's essence and God's energies, as well as the emphasis on *kenosis* and *theōsis*.

For the Eastern Orthodox tradition, a case for panentheism can be made from within the confines of classical theism via Gregory Palamas and his essence-energies distinction. Simply put, God's essence remains transcendent while God's energies—"which are nothing less than God himself in action"—render God "inexhaustibly immanent, maintaining all things in being, animating them, making each of them a sacrament of his dynamic presence."[73] As ancient as Philo of Alexandria and developed systematically by Palamas in the late Middle Ages, the essence-energies distinction in God has remained prominent in Eastern Orthodoxy. The world is imbued with and rests in God's energies; that is, God's energies descend from God to world while God's essence remains inaccessibly transcendent. This kenotic self-emptying of God, via God's energies imbued in the world, places God in all things and all things in God. The cosmos becomes divinized through *theōsis*. Just as individuals can be mystically united to God's energies in deification while remaining a distinct personal subject,[74] the cosmos can be mystically united to God's energies and deified while retaining its otherness from God as well. In this way, "Palamas [is able] to avoid monistic pantheism."[75] In order to maintain the classical claim of God's simplicity (which the essence-energies distinction allegedly violates), Eastern Orthodoxy denies any "synthesis or compositeness in the Godhead," but rather affirms that God remains "one, single, living, and active God [who] is present wholly and entirely."[76] God's *ousia* is totally simple; the hypostasis contains a Trinitarian "threefold diversity of the divine persons," in a unified whole; and the *energia* of God are God's self wholly and entirely. Ware summons

---

71. Ibid., 158.
72. Ibid.
73. Ibid., 160.
74. Ibid., 164.
75. Ibid.
76. Ibid., 165.

the declaration of the Council of Constantinople in 1351, "When speaking of God, we distinguish while uniting and we unite while distinguishing."[77]

Palamas is an implicit panentheist since he never employed the word, but espoused a theology that claims the mutual indwelling of God in all things and all things in God, with qualification. Ware has argued that Palamas can placed alongside Polkinghorne as a soteriological panentheist.[78] Palamas affirms the "now and not yet-ness" of Polkinghorne's eschatological vision. God is present ontologically via God's energies in creation "now," however due to the fallen state of the world, the complete subsistence of all things in God is "not yet," but is to come. "In that sense it can indeed be said on Palamite principles that the existence of the world 'in God' is not merely a static datum by a dynamic gift of grace, a gift to be revealed to an ever increasing extent through the voluntary cooperation of humankind."[79]

With classical Christian theism, Palamas denies evil as having any substantive existence. He also denies God's dependence on the world in order for the doctrine of energies to stand. Evil remains a perversion of the essentially good created nature of things as ordered by God and thus functions as "an adjective, not a noun."[80] God is independent of the world but the world remains dependent on God. God freely chose to create the world, but could have refrained from doing so without diminishing God's self. However, in creating the world, God expresses God's self as love, and this love is made manifest through God's divine energies.

Palamas has provided the Eastern Orthodox tradition with a version of classical Christian panentheism which serves as the counterpart to Aquinas' panentheism in the West. Without denying classical tenants, the Eastern orthodox tradition has employed the themes of God's kenosis and the world's *theōsis* in articulating a version of intelligible panentheism. Drawing on this foundation, various contemporary thinkers such as Kallistos Ware, Alexei Nesteruk, Andrew Louth, and Nicolai Berdyaev have all proposed several versions of Eastern Orthodox panentheism. One central thread, among others, remains the *theōtic* tradition. This divinization/deification aspect of spiritual experience provides generous opportunities for experiencing God in the world via the divine energies as sacraments of God's dynamic presence in the world.

---

77. Synodical Tome of 1351, §29: ed. I. N. Karmiris, *Ta Dogmata kai Symvolika Mnimeia tis Orthodoxou Katholikis Ekklisias*, 2nd ed., vol. 1 (Athens, Greece: Apostoliki Diakonia, 1960), 391; quoted in Ware, "God Immanent yet Transcendent," 165 n25.

78. Ware, "God Immanent yet Transcendent," 166–67.

79. Ibid., 167.

80. Ibid.

Matthew Fox (1940–)

Matthew Fox has a well-known and controversial history with the Catholic Church from serving as a Dominican priest in good standing for twenty-five years to being censored in 1989 and dismissed from the Dominican Order in 1995, after which he became an Episcopal priest. He remains a popular writer and thinker on progressive Christian spirituality. As an explicit panentheist,[81] Fox's contribution to the panentheistic conversation is largely spiritual and mystical; that is, his approach is less theologically constructive and more spiritually constructive. He grounds his spirituality (practical lived religious experience of God) in his understanding of traditional Christianity resting on Western thinkers such as Hildegaard of Bingen, Francis of Assisi, Aquinas, Meister Eckhart, Dante, Julian of Norwich, and Nicholas of Cusa (many of whom Fox deems panentheists).[82]

His "creation spirituality" is founded on the biblical concept of the creator God who creates, sustains, and continually dwells in all things created. He deems the honoring of God's creativity in the world,

> the number-one survival issue of our time: the sustainability achieved when creativity is honored and practiced not for its own sake but for justice and compassion's sake. *This* is the way of the Holy Spirit, who *is* the Spirit of Creativity and compassion. And who *was present* hovering over the waters at the beginning of creation and *is present* still at the continuance of creation (Aboriginals call this the "Dream-time") and who *is present* in the mind of the artist at work- which is each of us.[83]

The scriptural foundation for Fox's panentheistic creation spirituality relies on concept of the "Cosmic Christ." Though Fox clearly borrows here from Pierre Teilhard de Chardin, he reaches back to scripture to ground his Christology in that of early Christian communities who "applied the Wisdom motif to Jesus or, better, to the Christ in Jesus."[84] For Fox, Christ is the life and connectivity of all creation in a panentheistic way. Fox argues that the Sophia tradition, as applied to the Christ in Jesus, espouses a theology of co-creatorship. The early Christians were influenced by the Sophia tradition developed in Judaism and cast her qualities onto the Christ figure

---

81. Fox writes, "Theism (the idea that God is 'out there' or above and beyond the universe) is false. All things are in God and God is in all things (panentheism)" (Fox, *A New Reformation*, sixth thesis in chapter 5; quoted in Cooper, 297).

82. Cooper, 298.

83. Fox, *Creativity*, 11 (italics his).

84. Ibid., 112.

which transformed Jesus "from teacher to personification of Wisdom, to a Wisdom that was like God."[85] Following Marcus Borg, Fox cites the Wisdom of Solomon, a scriptural text that Borg argues contains the most developed exposition of Sophia.[86] Chapter seven of the Wisdom of Solomon claims that "all good things" come with Lady Sophia, for she "leads them" as "their mother."[87] She is "the fashioner of all things,"[88] and "because of her pureness she pervades and penetrates all things. For she is a breath of the power of God, and a pure emanation of the glory of the Almighty."[89] Though Sophia "is but one, she can do all things, and while remaining in herself, she renews all things."[90] The implication here is the understanding of Sophia as a co-creator with God, "thus she becomes our co-worker when we give birth; the work of creation gets carried on as co-creation between ourselves and Sophia, ourselves and Spirit."[91] Relying on Jesus Seminar fellows, Marcus Borg and John Dominic Crossan, Fox links Jesus to Sophia while pointing out that the early sources of the historical Jesus imply that he understood himself as Sophia.[92] Fox agrees with Borg that Sophia Christology constitutes the earliest attempt on behalf of Christians to understand Jesus as the Christ. It both undergirds and bridges Fox's cosmic Christology, thus for Fox, "creativity and cosmology are central to the earliest development of Christology."[93]

Fox's spirituality demonstrates the implications of this scripturally based cosmic-creative panentheism. It reveals a masterful breadth of far-reaching applications, from understanding Christ as operative in the cosmos to promoting social and ecological justice in the world. To a great degree, Fox demands a reorientation of the Christian consciousness: an

---

85. Ibid., *Creativity*, 113. The Wisdom of Solomon claims that in Sophia there exists "a spirit that is intelligent, holy, unique, manifold, subtle, mobile, clear, unpolluted, distinct, invulnerable, loving the good, keen, irresistible, beneficent, humane, steadfast, sure, free from anxiety, all-powerful, overseeing all, and penetrating through all spirits that are intelligent, pure, and altogether subtle" (Wisdom of Solomon 7:22–23).

86. Borg, *Meeting Jesus Again for the First Time*, 101.

87. Wisdom of Solomon 7:11–12.

88. Wisdom of Solomon 7:22.

89. Wisdom of Solomon 7:24–25.

90. Wisdom of Solomon 7:27.

91. Fox, *Creativity*, 113.

92. Ibid.

93. Ibid., 116. Fox writes, "*To say that Sophia is central to the earliest Christian message and to the work of the historical Jesus is to say that creativity is central to the earliest Christian message and to the work of the historical Jesus*" (Fox, *Creativity*, 116, italics his).

"aesthetic revolution"[94] and an "embracing [of] the Cosmic Christ [which] will demand a paradigm shift, and . . . will empower us for that shift."[95] This multi-faceted paradigm shift remains deeply grounded in a panentheistic cosmology. Matthew Fox remains important for this brief survey of contemporary panentheists because he provides a spiritual approach to a panentheistic cosmos, and although Fox does little by way of theology, his spirituality refreshingly provides the much needed practical implications that stem from such a view.

∞

These seven thinkers exhibit panentheistic proposals (both implicit and explicit) with various qualifications. The field of panentheism, of course, is vast and growing ever more diverse. This makes it necessary to distinguish one panentheism from another and pay attention to their nuances and qualifications. The seven thinkers I have outlined above by no means represent the vastness of panentheism, but rather demonstrate, in their own way, aspects of panentheism I find appealing and noteworthy for this book.

Aquinas maintains a view that can be understood as a classical western version of panentheism. Schelling, an implicit panentheist, preserves human free will and the personality of God. Rahner, an implicit or "anonymous" panentheist, provides one of the most developed and profound systematic treatments of a Christian pansacramental vision while promoting an incarnational approach. Peacocke, an explicit panentheist, draws on his scientific resume and offers a naturalistic approach the cosmos as sacrament. Polkinghorne rejects the label panentheist and offers a provisional panentheism that emphasizes the soteriological and eschatological dimensions of the conversation. Palamas and Eastern Orthodoxy offer an implicit panentheism that promotes balancing God's transcendence with God's immanence via the Palamite distinction between God's essence, which remains beyond

---

94. Fox, *Creativity*, 11.

95. Fox, *The Coming of the Cosmic Christ,* 134. Here Fox includes a table illustrating his call for a shift from X to Y:

from X	to Y
Anthropocentrism	a living cosmology
Newton	Einstein
parts-mentality	wholeness
Rationalism	mysticism
obedience as a prime moral virtue	creativity as a prime moral virtue
personal salvation	communal healing, i.e., compassion as salvation
theism (God outside us)	panentheism (God in us and us in God)

the world, and God's divine energies, which imbue and dwell in the world. Finally, Matthew Fox's creation spirituality provides the scripturally based antecedents of panentheism as it pertains to ones lived religions experience in the world.

In the next chapter I explore the challenge of accounting for suffering in a panentheistic and pansacramental vision, and in the final chapter, drawing on these thinkers above I offer a model for the God-world relationship in what I label panentheistic pansacramentality. The goal of this brief summary was just that: a summary of some of the various panentheisms without dwelling on the finer points or criticisms. These models shall serve as the backdrop for the working model I sketch in the final chapter.

13

Suffering in God and World[1]

HAVING TRACED SOME OF the prevailing contours of panentheism, both classical and contemporary, in the previous chapter, this chapter confronts the reality (and so-called "problem") of suffering in a pansacramental proposal such as the one suggested in this book. In the next and final chapter, which draws on the previous and present chapters on panentheism and suffering respectively, I offer a model, which I term "panentheistic pansacramentality," to understand the God-World relationship that is conducive to a pansacramental cosmology.

A perennial challenge to any monotheistic vision, especially one flirting with panentheism, is the burden of dealing with the existence of suffering (and evil). If God is in all things and all things are in God, and all things sacramentally express God, then the existence of suffering and evil demands to be confronted, reckoned with, and explained. One intention of this chapter is to raise the following question as an entry into wrestling with a God that is sacramentally manifested and mediated in and through all things, including suffering: 'if the sacrament is that which represents the divine in time and space, or is that which invites the participant into commemoration of God's acts in history, and all things serve as potential sacramental mediators, then are suffering and evil in God, and God in them, as well?' The short, though qualified, answer here might be yes, and although I do not intend to solve the classic problem of evil here, I offer a few promising approaches to the existence of suffering from within a pansacramental or qualified

---

1. Variations of sections from this chapter were presented in the paper Gustafson, "The Awe-Filledness of Awfulness: Experiencing God in Suffering."

provisional panentheistic vision. The claim that God is sacramentally revealed in suffering can scandalize, to a certain degree, classical Christianity. However, any serious pansacramental or panentheistic proposal ought to be willing to take on questions regarding the possibility of the sacramental authenticity of suffering. This is to entertain the affirmation of the claim and the experience of suffering can potentially (re)present the divine in a sacramental fashion. To assist in the development and articulation of such a view, this chapter explores the approaches of classical Thomism, Martin Buber's sacrament of suffering, Abraham Heschel's and Jürgen Moltmann's theology of divine pathos, and Polkinghorne's realized eschatological panentheism. First, I turn to classical Thomism and second, under the rubric of "divine pathos" I draw on Buber, Heschel, and Moltmann, and finally I turn to Polkinghorne's realized eschatology.

Classical Thomism

The problem of suffering from within classical Christian theism is addressed by Aquinas' response to objection four in the first article of question eight in the *Summa Theologica*. The objection is raised to counter his claim that God is in all things. It takes issue with the existence of "demons"[2] as beings. God supposedly is not in demons, yet demons still have being. Thus, according to objection four, it cannot be possible that God is in all things. In other words, all things are in God, yet demons exist, and therefore demons must exist in God as well. If this is a case, then it appears to be a contradiction and therefore problematic. To put it another way, all things are in the divine, yet evil exists, and therefore evil must exist in the divine as well. This is essentially the argument levied against panentheism.

For Aquinas (and Augustine) evil is "pure negation within a substance. It is not an essence, nor a reality."[3] It is neither a being nor from God, "neither a being nor a good,"[4] and thus its presence cannot be made sense of. It is a privation of the good that should be. It is blindness in an eye, cancer in a body, and so on. "In the case of evil, we have the opposite of good. We have what ought to be there but is not—a kind of non-being which only

---

2. For the sake of this chapter's proposal, I simply understand Aquinas' use of the term "demon" here to serve as a figurative stand-in for "evil," regardless of whether or not Aquinas himself (or anyone else for that matter) accepts or denies the ontological status of demons as beings.

3. Gilson, *The Christian Philosophy of St. Thomas Aquinas*, 156.

4. Thomas Aquinas, *Summa Theologica* I, 48, 1.

exists because something is failing in some respect."[5] How is the existence of evil to be reconciled with all things being in God? Aquinas answers with a reference to demons, which, he says, receive their nature from God but are deformed by sin, which is not from God. This is because sin is the denial of God. "Therefore," concludes Aquinas, "it is not to be absolutely conceded that God is in the demons, except with the addition, inasmuch as they are beings. But in things not deformed of their nature, we must say absolutely that God is."[6] In other words, God is in demons in so far as they have being, but their sinful deformity negates that Godliness. In this sense, evil is to be understood as a fallen or failed state of being. However, an appropriate conclusion here might be that since angels can fall into the level of the demonic and become void of their goodness (and Godliness), then humans can fall (and indeed have fallen) as well. This raises the need for a criterion or set of criteria on which the things might be gauged and deemed either demonic or sacramental. A measure similar to Tillich's "Protestant Principle"[7] would provide assistance in gauging the authenticity of an experiences' sacramental or demonic genuineness. Furthermore, evil in the classical sense, as non-being and negation of God, limits the revelation of God in the world. If suffering and evil are understood as what should not be in place of the good, then where suffering and evil occur God is absent. This limits the sacramental and revelatory capacity of the world in that particular instance.[8] However, this does not mean that wherever there is suffering God is not to be found. After all, suffering is a part of the world and a part of the human condition. The human body grows old, weak, and eventually passes. There is suffering involved on many levels in this process, but this is what should be. The task then is to find God in that experience of suffering.

5. Davies, *The Thought of Thomas Aquinas*, 91.
6. Thomas Aquinas, *Summa Theologica* I, 8, 1.
7. See chapter 4.
8. In his essay, "The Dialectic of God's Presence and Absence in the World," Anselm K. Min asks the question, "How do finitude, evil, and sin qualify our perception of God's presence in the world?" He analyzes "the epistemological condition, the nature and conditions of the human perception of God's presence" via three conditions: "[1] finitude and its incapacity to reveal God in her own essence including the finitude of the human knowledge of God, [2] the tendency to non-being and evil on the part of finite creation, and [3] the sinfulness of human existence in all its modalities" (110). Drawing on ontological, epistemological, and phenomenological conditions, his overarching argument seeks to make the case "that we can never experience God as pure positivity but only in a dialectic of presence and absence: we can only experience God as present as the absent one, absent as the present one, or, more accurately, as a constant and simultaneous dialectic of presence and absence, of unveiling and veiling" (111), (Min, "The Dialectic of God's Presence and Absence in the World," 109–128).

Within this classical Thomist view, God retains the classical attributes of simplicity, immutability, self-sufficiency, omnipotence, omniscience, impassiblity, and pure actuality to name the major ones. Many of these classical attributes have come under the gun in the context of contemporary panentheism. Various Christian and Jewish thinkers are becoming increasingly uncomfortable with one or more of these and have deemed them unhelpful and unbiblical ideas that have seeped in from classical Greek metaphysics. "Dissatisfaction with traditional answers [to the problem of evil[9] are] part of the reason most panentheists prefer a more limited view of God's power,"[10] thus denying God's omnipotence. In so doing, explanations for the existence of evil and suffering emerge that posit a God that suffers and changes with the world. However, for some of these contemporary proposals of God's suffering, more explanation and clarification is needed regarding precisely the nature of God's suffering and how it is related to, similar to, and/or different from human suffering.

In his 1986 article, "The Suffering of God," Ronald Goetz's recognized that,

> The age-old dogma that God is impassible and immutable, incapable of suffering, is for many no longer tenable. The ancient theopaschite heresy that God suffers has, in fact, become the new orthodoxy. A list of modern theopaschite thinkers would include Barth, Erdyaev, Bonhoeffer, Brunner, Cobb, Cone and liberation theologians generally, Küng, Moltmann, Reinhold

---

9. The traditional view of the Western tradition for both Protestants and Roman Catholics rests on Augustine and Aquinas, which maintains a good world created by a good God, but also a world that has fallen into evil disarray through free rejection on behalf of God's creatures (both angels and humans). Thus God allows humans to remain free to reject God. This gets God off the hook for being responsible for the existence of evil. "This disobedience [on behalf of humans and angels], although known and permitted by God from eternity, is freely chosen and not causally determined by the nature or circumstances of creatures. The mystery in this account is why creatures created good would choose to sin, not they are free to do so" (Cooper, *Panentheism, the Other God of the Philosophers*, 335). This is remains a problematic and weak argument for many. Panikkar writes, "That in order to create us free God was bound to allow our free will to go against his Will and choose evil is a very weak argument—besides the fact that it put on our shoulders the burden of the entire evil of the world does not explain either how a just and omnipotent God allows that we have to suffer from bad *karma* of our ancestors. The suffering of the innocent may be explained by *karma*, but not by an omnipotent and good God. The argument of freedom is weak on three mutually related accounts." The three are 1) God's freedom is eroded, 2) human freedom in this argument is weak and whimsical freedom, and 3) the assumption that God has free will to create or not create crudely anthropomorphizes God (Panikkar, *The Rhythm of Being*, 144, 144–45).

10. Cooper, *Panentheism, the Other God of the Philosophers*, 335.

Niebuhr, Pannenberg, Ruether, and feminist theologians generally, Temple, Teilhard and Unamuno.[11]

While several others could be added to this list, the point here is to recognize the growing appreciation for the claim of God's passiblity and potential to suffer. Building on the work of Peacocke and operating out of a panentheistic framework, Gloria Schaab has added the most recent contribution to this growing list of approaches to a suffering God. In particular, her approach is "informed by the understandings of evolutionary cosmology and biology."[12] In her work, she briefly recognizes and critiques four contemporary approaches to divine passibility, but ultimately deems them inadequate for various reasons. These four ways are "the biblical theology of Jürgen Moltmann, the liberation theology of Jon Sobrino, the process theology of Daniel Day Williams, and the feminist-ecological theology of Sallie McFague."[13] Without denying or ignoring Schaab's critique, I suggest that aspects of Moltmann's approach and, to a greater extent, Abraham Joshua Heschel's work on the divine pathos provides a promising way to intelligibly approach the suffering of God in the world from within a panentheistic and pansacramental framework.

Divine Pathos

Abraham Joshua Heschel writes that God "does not simply command and expect obedience; He is also moved and affected by what happens in the world, and reacts accordingly."[14] This refers to the pathos of God; that is, God's susceptibility to being moved and affected by emotion. This is a departure from the classical Aristo-Thomist claim of God as the "Unmoved Mover," but rather, as Fritz Rothchild has described it, posits God as "the Most Moved Mover."[15] These labels (unmoved mover and most moved mover) can be helpful only to a certain extent, however fall short in getting at the heart of the matter of whether and how God moves others and is moved by others. For instance, the classical conception of God as the Unmoved Mover still allows for the suffering of God, but not in the way humans suffer. Cyril of Alexandria writes, "we say that [Christ] suffered and rose again; not as if God the Word suffered in his own nature stripes, or the

11. Goetz, "The Suffering of God," 385.
12. Schaab, *Creative Suffering of the Triune God*, 5.
13. Ibid., 7.
14. Heschel, *The Prophets*, 288.
15. Rothschild, "Varieties of Heschelian Thought," 89.

piercing of the nails, or any other wounds, for the Divine nature is incapable of suffering, inasmuch as it is incorporeal, but since that which had become his own body suffered in this way, he is also said to suffer for us; for he who is in himself incapable of suffering was in a suffering body."[16] In this classical conception of divine suffering elicited by Cyril's passage above, it is clear that the nature of God is immune to suffering. Suffering is something that happens to the body, and since God does not have a body, then God does not suffer in the same manner as humans. However, in the Christian tradition, God takes on the condition of the human via Jesus Christ and thus suffers, yet remains impassible by nature.

John C. Merkle[17] reminds us that, "while Heschel's philosophical argument for the pathos of God challenges the tradition of classical metaphysical theology, as Rothchild rightly claims, it is not meant to challenge traditional Jewish understanding."[18] However, some Christian theologians have affirmed this understanding of God and argued for its use within Christian theology as well, especially in the affirmation of a God that suffers. For instance, Jürgen Moltmann recognizes that "before the 'suffering of God' had become a theme of Christian theology in the present, Jewish theology had already been discussing the theme. Christian theology cannot but learn from this new Jewish exegesis of the history of God in the Old Testament and in the present suffering of the Jewish people."[19]

In the spirit this assertion by Moltmann's, here I suggest that it is appropriate to apply Heschel's theology of divine pathos to the God of Christianity within a pansacramental framework, for it assists in bringing meaning to the reality of suffering in the world and in God in a sacramental fashion. In this brief section, I turn to two prominent Jewish philosophers, Martin Buber and Abraham Joshua Heschel, as guides for the Christian adoption of the theology of divine pathos. Buber offers insight into the Hasidic approach to pansacramental unity in the world and wrestling with the contradiction of the existence of evil, while Heschel provides an explicit treatment of God's pathos. Jürgen Moltmann then serves here as a prominent Christian representative who appropriated "the *pathetic theology* of later Jewish philosophy of religion" in order to overcome the Christological difficulties caused by the early church's adoption of "the *apathetic theology* of Greek

---

16. Cyril of Alexandria, Second epistle to Nestorius.

17. John C. Merkle has written the classic text on Heschel's philosophical theology. For a substantive treatment on Heschel's theology of divine pathos, see Merkle, *The Genesis of Faith,* and *Approaching God.*

18. Merkle, *Approaching God,* 4.

19. Moltmann, *The Crucified God,* 267.

antiquity" and a "God incapable of suffering."[20] However, although I respect Moltmann's right to assert that for Christians "we can only talk about God's suffering in trinitarian terms,"[21] with Merkle, I do not agree that a trinitarian framework is necessary to articulate a suffering Godhead as many Jewish thinkers have clearly demonstrated.[22]

Martin Buber

If the cosmos is imbued with God pansacramentally and possibly panentheistically, and all things maintain the potential to reveal and express God, it is then to be taken with the utmost seriousness that "all things" truly includes "all things," which entails that suffering too might function sacramentally. Martin Buber refers to this as the primal question; that is, how to reconcile the contradiction of intensified despair in the world with the being of God. In order to be grasped on a significant level of being, Buber suggests an approach that considers "Hasidic pansacramentalism" in relationship to the approach of the Kabbala.[23] Their respective approaches to this contradiction of experiencing suffering in a world reveals God. Here Hasidism both builds on and "breaks with the basic principles of the Kabbala."[24] While the Kabbala is esoteric and withholds its ultimate meaning from the uninitiated and the unenlightened (i.e., to those without gnosis), Hasidism demands "the mystery is valid for all or none," especially "the simple man [since] he has a united soul; [for] where unity of the soul is, there will God's unity dwell."[25] For Buber, the "Sacramental covenant means the life of the unity with the unity,"[26] and for him, the Hasidic movement is to be understood as "the soaring up of a genuine vision of unity and a passionate demand

---

20. Ibid.

21. Moltmann, *The Trinity and the Kingdom,* 25; also cited in by Merkle, "God's Love, Suffering, and Power," 10, n40.

22. Merkle writes, "without the help of our doctrine of the Trinity, Heschel, [Hans] Jonas, and [Melissa] Raphael, as well as countless other Jews, express compassion not only for creatures who suffer but also for the Creator whom they believe shares in that suffering. And without our Christian doctrine of the Incarnation, Jews have come to believe in God's suffering in the midst of the flesh and blood suffering of God's creatures" (Merkle, "God's Love, Suffering, and Power," 10); see also Merkle, "God's Love, Suffering, and Power," 10 n40.

23. Buber, "Symbolic and Sacramental Existence," 173.

24. Ibid.

25. Ibid., 174.

26. Ibid.

for wholeness."²⁷ The Kabbala shares this vision of unity as a goal, however pursues it through an anti-dualistic gnosis and, in so doing, encounters the primal question regarding the contradiction of suffering and despair in the world. Scripture gives rise to this question, but does not answer it. Buber writes,

> The Biblical experience of unity—one decisive power, a superior partner of man—met the experience of contradiction that announced itself out of painful depths by pointing to the hiddenness of the mystery: the determination of what appears as contradiction or absurdity is an insurmountable barrier for knowledge (Job), but dimly perceivable in the lived mystery of suffering (deuteron-Isaiah); just here arises the strongest expression of sacramental existence in which the suffering itself becomes a sacrament (Isaiah 53).²⁸

The experience of the contradiction reveals its hidden mysteriousness which lies beyond explanation or gnosis. Gnosis, in this case an attempt to see through the contradiction by employing various reasoned theodicies and removing oneself from it, remains the way of the Kabbala. Hasidism, on the other hand, accepts suffering as sacramental and prescribes a faithful endurance of the contradiction thereby redeeming the contradiction itself.²⁹ This attitude reveals the humble piety of Hasidism,³⁰ which distinguishes it from the systematic rigor of the Kabbala which proceeds via "principles of a certitude that almost never stops short, almost never shudders, almost never prostates itself. In contrast, it is precisely in stopping short, in letting itself be disconcerted, in deep knowledge of the importance of all 'information,' of the incongruence of all possessed truth, in the 'holy insecurity,' that Hasidic piety has its true life."³¹

Experience of the contradiction is the reality of this world and to remove oneself from it, or to give in to the inclination to "get behind" the problem, would be both contrary to Hasidism and to forsake the mission.³² Instead, Buber calls one to dwell and rest in the contradiction, to concern oneself with "this lower world, the world of corporeality, [and] to let the hidden life of God shine forth."³³ He proclaims, "The absurd is given to me

27. Ibid., 172.
28. Ibid., 175–76.
29. Ibid., 178.
30. *Hasidut* is often translated to "piety."
31. Buber, "Symbolic and Sacramental Existence," 179.
32. Ibid.
33. Ibid., 181.

that I may endure and sustain it with my life; this, the enduring and sustaining of the absurd, is the meaning which I can experience."[34] In this sense, Buber calls for a rather Kierkegaardian fideist approach to the problem, one that seeks to draw on the strength of the absurd without striving to solve it.[35]

In Buber's pansacramental vision of unity, the problem of suffering is not to be reconciled nor ignored, but rather to be recognized, sustained, and dwelt in. Suffering is part of the absurd reality of the world which must be endured as a sacrament that reveals the hiddenness of God.

Abraham Joshua Heschel

In his monumental work *The Prophets,* Heschel provides his most substantial treatment of the theology of divine pathos. For him, it is the "central category in prophetic theology."[36] The core insight of the theology of divine pathos is that, "God does not reveal himself in an abstract absoluteness, but in a personal and intimate relation to the world. He does not simply command and expect obedience; He is also moved and affected by what happens in the world, and reacts accordingly. Events and human actions arouse in Him joy or sorrow, pleasure or wrath."[37] Thus, the classical notion of Aristotle's concept of the Unmoved Mover as applied to God is rejected in favor of what Rothchild calls the Bible's "Most Moved Mover."[38] God is affected by human suffering and historical events in the world, for "pathos is concern unto suffering, and God's concern is full of pathos."[39] Heschel goes to lengths to distinguish between the God of the Bible from the God of Greek philosophical thought, the former being more dynamic, changing, loving, and in solidarity with the world, while the latter remains "conscious of Himself, but oblivious of the world."[40]

---

34. Ibid., 179.

35. Recall here Kierkegaard's *Fear and Trembling,* under the pseudonym Johannes de Silentio, which depicts Abraham as a Knight of Faith who retained his son Isaac on the strength of the absurd.

36. Heschel, *The Prophets,* 286.

37. Ibid., 288.

38. Rothschild, "Varieties of Heschelian Thought," 89.

39. Merkle, *Approaches to God,* 44.

40. Heschel, *The Prophets,* 289; In rejecting the static idea of divinity, Heschel accuses two strands of thought for its influence, "The static idea of divinity is the outcome of two strands of thought: the ontological notion of stability and the psychological view of emotions as disturbances of the soul" (Heschel, *The Prophets,* 335). For a clarifying exegesis of Heschel on this point see Merkle, *The Genesis of Faith,* 131–35 and Merkle, *Approaching God,* 44–48. Merkle draws parallels between Heschel and Whitehead

God exists in an intimate relation to the world and God's pathos "is not an attribute, but a response... It is rather a reaction to human history, an attitude called forth by man's conduct; a response, not a cause."[41] This response is primarily one of solidarity with the world in its suffering. It is a recognition of, and a being moved by, the suffering that is part of the world's condition and reality. In this sense, the problem of evil and suffering is not only a problem for humans, but also for God, who dwells in solidarity with the world. "The predicament of man is a predicament of God Who has a stake in the human situation. Sin, guilt, suffering, cannot be separated from the divine situation... It is a frustration to God."[42] Human work and failure affect the life of God "insofar as it is directed to man."[43] Heschel's vision of God is one in which the human person acts and reacts as "a consort, a partner, a factor in the life of God."[44]

Though Heschel endorses a relational, dynamic, and self-moving God that remains involved in the world and is affected by the world, he does not deny the immutability of God's essence. He does not think "of God's nature or essence as changeable but that God's mode of being in relation to the world may change."[45] God's essence remains immutable, but not unrelated to the world. This holds profound anthropological implications.

> It is man's being relevant to God. To the biblical mind the denial of man's relevance to God is as inconceivable as the denial of God's relevance to man. This principle leads to the base affirmation of God's participation in human history, to the certainty that the events in the world concern Him and arouse His reaction. It finds its deepest expression in the fact that God can actually suffer.[46]

---

when he writes, "Heschel would surely concur with one of the most famous comments by Alfred North Whitehead, the patriarch of modern process philosophy, 'God is the great companion—the fellow-sufferer who understands,'" (Whitehead, *Process and Reality*, 532) and "although [Heschel] never addresses the question of affinity between Whitehead's process philosophy and his own biblical philosophy, it seems clear that, whatever differences there may be between the two, Heschel would be able to endorse one of Whitehead's central tenants: 'God is not to be treated as an exception to all metaphysical principles" but as "their chief exemplification'" (Whitehead, *Process and Reality*, 521), (Merkle, *Approaches to God*, 44–45).

41. Heschel, *The Prophets*, 290.
42. Ibid., 291.
43. Ibid., 292.
44. Ibid.
45. Merkle, *Approaches to God*, 45.
46. Heschel, *The Prophets*, 333–34.

Heschel has proposed a biblical vision in which God remains emotionally attached, shows compassion for, and is affected by, world events and history. According to this view God suffers, which far from threatening God's perfection, is an expression of it. She who remains unaffected by emotion is not the more perfect person, as the Stoics may have advocated, but for the biblical mindset, to strive for perfection is to be moved and motivated by passion and emotion. "The ideal state of the Stoic sage is apathy, the ideal state of the prophet is sympathy"[47] (i.e., pathos). Here Heschel relies on psychiatry, which as Edmond Cherbonnier points out, has demonstrated that "the healthy personality is open and vulnerable, willing to take risks and able to bear the hurt. This describes the biblical God *par excellence*."[48] Authentic personhood entails the capacity for compassion and ability to love. Love opens itself up to rejection and suffering. "If you love, you will suffer. The only way to protect yourself against suffering is to protect yourself against love—and that is the greatest suffering of all, loneliness."[49] Thus, both the perfect God and the perfect person loves, and subsequently suffers (albeit perhaps in different ways and to different extents).[50]

Heschel is keenly aware that his theology of divine pathos is open to the charge of anthropomorphism, and in *The Prophets* he devotes a chapter to defending his view against it. He writes, "A major motive for the rejection of the idea of pathos has been the fear of anthropomorphism, by which we mean the endowment of God with human attributes."[51] Heschel, in my view, successfully and constructively defends himself against this charge, suggesting that the Hebrew prophets "had to use anthropomorphic language in order to convey [God's] nonanthropomorphic Being."[52] They recognized that "*All expressions of God are attempts to set forth God's aliveness. One must not forget that all our utterances about Him are woefully*

---

47. Ibid., 332.

48. Cherbonnier, "Heschel as a Religious Thinker," 33; quoted in Merkle, *Approaches to God*, 46.

49. Kreeft, *Three Philosophies of Life*, 113.

50. "Clearly, Heschel believes that the idea of divine pathos is both religiously important and philosophically credible, superior to the idea of an impersonal, disengaged deity. A god unaffected by human concerns and cries, unmoved by the plight of creatures, would be religiously irrelevant to us. And such a god would be both ontologically and psychologically inferior to us, since we human beings are able to respond to the concerns and cries of each other, and also to the plight of other creatures. What in this regard we human beings may do humanly, the God of biblical revelation does divinely, supremely" (Merkle, *Approaches to God*, 47).

51. Heschel, *The Prophets*, 345.

52. Ibid., 354.

inadequate."[53] It is the nature of prophetic language to combine "otherness and likeness, uniqueness and comparability, in speaking about God,"[54] thus often the error of mistaking divine pathos as anthropomorphism arises when this otherness and uniqueness is not understood in its total structure, but is rather taken in isolation apart from its context.[55] Heschel makes the ever crucial distinction between anthropomorphic *conceptions* and anthropomorphic *expressions*, and maintains that "the use of the latter does not necessarily prove belief in the former."[56] In other words, to speak of God in human terms does not necessarily entail conceiving of God as human as such. To illustrate, Heschel recalls Michelangelo's depiction of the Creator in human form and reminds the reader that Michelangelo "can hardly be accused of believing that God possesses the shape of man."[57] All the more, Hescehl suggests, when speaking of God as full of pathos, the prophets of Israel were not depicting God as human. Instead, he sees the attribution of pathos—like virtues such as love—to human beings as form of "theomorphism. It is not a matter of casting imperfect human traits onto God but of casting perfect divine traits imperfectly onto humans." For instance, when God is deemed absolutely selfless and loving,

> absolute selflessness and mysteriously undeserved love are more akin to the divine than to the human. And if these are characteristics of human nature, then man is endowed with attributes of the divine.
>
> God's unconditional concern for justice is not an anthropomorphism. Rather, man's concern for justice is a theomorphism . . . The language of the prophets employed to describe that supreme concern was an anthropomorphism to end all anthropomorphism.[58]

In short, Heschel assertively defends the idea of divine pathos against any charge of anthropomorphism and instead stresses the prophets' use of metaphorical theomorphic language. For "to speak about God as if He were a person does not necessarily mean to personify Him, to stamp Him in the image of a person . . . The idea of the divine pathos is not a personification of God but an exemplification of divine reality . . . It does not represent a

---

53. Ibid., 355 (italics his).
54. Ibid., 347.
55. Ibid.
56. Ibid., 348.
57. Ibid.
58. Ibid., 349; also quoted in Merkle, *The Genesis of Faith*, 99.

substance, but an act or a relationship."⁵⁹ In this perspective, God's nature is both relation and immutable, for as Heschel states: "The divine pathos which the prophets tried to express in many ways was not a name for His essence but rather for the modes of His reaction to Israel's conduct which would change if Israel modified its ways."⁶⁰

Heschel was not an explicit panentheist;⁶¹ nor did he explicitly advocate for the pansacramentalism that Buber did. However, he did go further than most thinkers in his development of the concept of divine pathos and its theological, philosophical, and anthropological implication. Moltmann situates Heschel's biblical philosophy of divine pathos within a Christian Trinitarian context in order to expound a suffering God in Christian theology.

Jürgen Moltmann

At the outset of *The Crucified God*, Moltmann draws heavily on, and quotes, "Schelling's words: 'Every being can be revealed only in its opposite. Love only in hatred, unity only in conflict.'"⁶² He then applies this to the being of God and surmises that God is reveled in God's opposite, the absence of God. Moltmann's theology, like Heschel's, is rooted deeply in the biblical tradition, and in particular, the kenotic engagement of the trinitarian God in Christ on the cross. In fact, Moltmann contends that "we can only talk about God's suffering in trinitarian terms."⁶³ As noted above, although I do not share this

---

59. Heschel, *The Prophets*, 350–51.

60. Heschel, *Man Is Not Alone*, 245.

61. Scholars of Heschel differ on whether or not he can be appropriately deemed a panentheist. Fritz Rothchild and Maurice Friedman have advocated that Heschel's view tends towards panentheism, while John Merkle concludes that well-known statements by Heschel, such as God is "being in and beyond all things" "should not be read in a panentheistic sense because, for Heschel, while God's being is within all beings, it is not in them as a part of them, and all beings are not parts of God's being" (Merkle, "Heschel's Monotheism Vis-à-vis Pantheism and Panentheism"). If one were to ascribe panentheism to Heschel (as is the case with many others), it should be done in a careful and qualified way so as to distinguish his variety of implicit panentheism from other contemporary panentheisms (e.g., process theology) that might advocate for the world as God's body in more than a metaphorical sense. Heschel's panentheism, if one were to make the case, would be more similar to a classical or provisional Polkinghornian panentheism.

62. Moltmann, *The Crucified God*, 27 (quoting Schelling, *Über das Wesen der menschlichen Freiheit*, 89). I am indebted to John Cooper's chapter on Moltmann in *Panentheism, the Other God of the Philosophers*, 237–58.

63. Moltmann, *The Trinity and the Kingdom*, 25; also cited in by Merkle, "God's Love, Suffering, and Power," 10, n40.

contention with Moltmann I do respect his attempt to make this claim from within Christian tinitarian framework, especially for Reformed Christians. However, I resonate more with Merkle's commentary and suggestion on this that "it is good for Christians, even those who reject the classical view of God's impassibility, to realize that others, without our doctrines of the Incarnation and the Trinity, affirm the suffering of God, suffering born of love."[64] Though Moltmann's approach is not without critique,[65] it remains fruitful to provide a brief overview here of Moltmann's approach, for it helps to broaden the appeal of a suffering God within a panentheistic framework for Christians who might not otherwise be open to such a construct.

Moltmann suggests that God, on the cross, self-empties (*kenosis*), goes away from God (God abandons God), and enters into the depths of God's opposite, which lies in the human condition of suffering. The Markan suffering Jesus provides Moltmann's point of departure. The author of the gospel of Mark, unlike the other gospel writers, depicts a confused Jesus in despair on the cross who famously cries out in agony, "*Eloi, Eloi, lema sabachthani?*" which means "My God, my God, why have you forsaken me?"[66] On the cross, according to Moltmann, there was "a deep division in God himself, in sofar as God abandoned God and contradicted himself, and at the same time a unity in God, in so far as God was at one with God and corresponded to himself."[67] Schelling's philosophy of 'revelation in the opposite' is clearly evident here.

Influenced by Heschel and the Kabalistic rabbinic theology of God's self-humiliation and *Shekinah*,[68] Moltmann recognizes a dipolar concept of God. On one hand, "God is free in himself" while, on the other hand,

64. Merkle, "God's Love, Suffering, and Power," 10.

65. Merkle asks, "How could Moltmann have missed the point that Heschel did not speak of God's suffering in trinitarian terms? Adding to the irony, right after his claim that speaking of God's suffering can only be done in trinitarian terms, Moltmann adds: 'In monotheism it is impossible.' It is one thing for Moltmann to idiosyncratically contrast trinitarian doctrine and monotheism (playing right into the hands of monotheists who suspect that the Christian doctrine of the Trinity indicates an attenuation of monotheism); it is another and more inexplicable thing for him to do this on the same page where he cites one of Judaism's great defenders of monotheism as a source of inspiration for his own theology of divine suffering!" (Merkle, "God's Love, Suffering, and Power," 10 n40).

66. Mark 15:34

67. Moltmann, *The Crucified God*, 244.

68. "The Term *Shekinah* is derived from the Hebrew *shakan*, meaning "presence" or 'act of dwelling.' In the early rabbinic sources, the *Shekinah* 'connotes the personification and hypostatization of God's presences in the world,' of God's immanence and immediacy in a specific place on the earth (Urbach, *The Sages, Their Concepts and Beliefs*, 40)." (Schaab, *The Creative Suffering of the Triune God*, 18).

God remains "interested in his covenant relationship and affected by human history."[69] God is thus present in two opposite ways: in God's self (what Moltmann refers to as "in heaven"[70]) and in God's *Shekinah*. God enters into and dwells in the world. "He enters not only into the situation of the limited creature, but even into the situation of the guilty and suffering creature . . . God goes with Israel into the Babylonian exile. In his 'indwelling' in the people he suffers with the people, goes with them into prison, feels sorrow with the martyrs."[71] Thus, the God of Moltmann is the God of Heschel in so far as they both recognize a God who suffers, and is in solidarity, with the human condition. However, the God of Moltmann is clearly not the God of Hescehl in so far as the former affirms the necessity of a trinitarian concept of God while the latter obviously does not. For Moltmannm God's suffering restores the union between God and God's people. This is the fundamental thrust of the *theologia crucis*—the theology of the cross—and the most "shattering expression" of this, he suggests, is Elie Wiesel's witness account in *Night* of being imprisoned at Auschwitz.

> The SS hanged two Jewish men and a youth in front of the whole camp. The men died quickly, but the death throes of the youth lasted for half an hour. 'Where is God? Where is he?' someone asked behind me. As the youth still hung in torment in the noose after a long time, I heard the man call again, 'Where is God now?' And I heard a voice in myself answer: 'Where is he? He is here. He is hanging there on the gallows.'[72]

The story recounted here by Wiesel demonstrates the implication of both a pansacramental vision and a God that suffers. The utter and disturbing human suffering in this story reveals God and is thus sacramental. With Wiesel, Moltmann contends that, "any other answer would be blasphemy. There cannot be any other Christian answer to the question of this torment. To speak here of a God who could not suffer would make God a demon."[73]

Recall that for Heschel, divine pathos is expressed in God's relationship to Israel, and since Israel routinely falls into disobedience, God is injured (and therefore suffers) in that relationship (despite God's nature remaining immutable). However, for Moltmann, suffering is naturally a part of the created order, which is eventually conquered at the eschaton. God's suffering is most fundamentally expressed in Christ's death on the cross in a display of

---

69. Moltmann, *The Crucified God*, 272.
70. Ibid., 273.
71. Ibid.
72. Wiesel, *Night*, 75; quoted by Moltmann, *The Crucified God*, 274.
73. Moltmann, *The Crucified God*, 274.

the suffering love intrinsic to the trinitarian divine life of God. The event on the cross is for Moltmann the window into how God suffers and is necessarily Trinitarian. His insistence on Christian trinitarianism distinguishes his theology of divine pathos from that of Heschel. While for Heschel the suffering of God is in God's love being forsaken by Israel, for Moltmann the suffering of God is in God's forsaking God. It is exhibited on the cross where

> the Son suffers in his love being forsaken by the Father as he dies. The Father suffers in his love the grief of the death of the Son ... The doctrine of two natures must understand the event of the cross statically as a reciprocal relationship between two qualitatively different natures, the divine nature which is incapable of suffering and the human nature which is capable of suffering.[74]

Instead, Moltmann proposes to interpret "the event on the cross in Trinitarian terms as an event concerned with a relationship between persons in which these persons constitute themselves in their relationship with each other. In so doing we have not just seen one person of the Trinity suffer in the event of the cross, as though the Trinity were already present in itself, in the divine nature,"[75] but rather it demonstrates the Trinity as such being actualized on the cross. In this manner, Trinitarian thought and the event on the cross are mutually interdependent on each for their respective meaningfulness. "The content of the doctrine of the Trinity is the real cross of Christ himself. The form of the crucified Christ is the Trinity."[76]

Regardless of whether one stands more with Moltmann's trinitarian account or Heschel's monotheistic account, it is indeed clear that for them, and Wiesel, God is not indifferent and removed from the depths of human suffering, but rather is so concerned and moved by pathos that God is to be understood as a God who suffers with, and dwells in, the human predicament, in all its beauty and disturbing torment. A pansacramental proposal such as the one this book advocates for must necessarily reckon with the reality of suffering in the world. Suffering must be taken seriously as potentially sacramental in its capacity to mediate and (re)present God in the world. Heschel and Moltmann's insistence on the pathos of God and God's suffering in solidarity with the world provides a way to begin to bring meaning to the human experience of suffering within a Jewish-Christian context.

---

74. Ibid., 245.
75. Ibid.
76. Ibid., 246.

However, their view of course has its critics.[77] Gloria Schaab remains unsatisfied pointing out that, "Moltmann clearly stressed the Father's deliberate subjection and abandonment of the Son on the cross, an emphasis that raises concerns from a pastoral standpoint and that opens [his] proposal to the critique . . . that the cross was an event of divine child abuse in which the Father sacrificed the Son according to the divine will." This charge does not apply to Heschel's non-trinitarian account, however. Further, Schaab raises the concern that, "Moltmann risks the conclusion that the very God who suffers is the God who willed it so."[78] These are pointed critiques which demand some response from those who affirm Moltmann's proposal. For some, restricting divine agency might be one response, which is to say that God unwillingly suffers with God's creation, but does so because that is what love entails. Perhaps this would be like a parent enduring the suffering of her child. The parent takes on the suffering of her child and lives in solidarity. However, this still does not necessarily satisfy the charge that Moltmann proposes a God that, by divine will, subjects his son to deliberate abandonment, abuse, and suffering.

The purpose of this section is not to fully endorse Heschel and/or Moltmann, lock, stock, and barrel, but rather raise their theology of divine pathos and a suffering God as an entry into wrestling with a God that is sacramentally manifested and mediated in and through all things, including suffering. However, critiques such as Schaab's above remain appropriate and beckon a response. The final chapter offers a proposal that aims to address some of these concerns. To be sure, the claim that God is sacramentally revealed in suffering can be scandalous. However, any serious pansacramental or panentheistic proposal ought to, at the very least, be willing to wrestle with the possibility of the sacramental authenticity of suffering. Though Moltmann is an explicit panentheist and Heschel is not, in rejecting various tenets of classical theism, both provide a promising way to approach suffering from within their own respective biblical traditions. The final chapter sounds echoes of their thought in its proposed model of panentheistic pansacramentality.

Realized Eschatology and Soteriological Panentheism

An alternative way to deal with the existence of suffering in the world within a pansacramental vision is to endorse a realized eschatology that affirms what

---

77. Most recently, Paul Gravilyuk has defended the impassible God though an examination of early church writers (Gravilyuk, *The Suffering of the Impassible God*).

78. Schaab, *The Creative Suffering of the Triune God*, 20.

might be referred to as soteriological panentheism. The main contemporary proponent of this is John Polkinghorne, mentioned in the previous chapter. This view rejects strict panentheism as a reality for the current world, but affirms it as a cosmological *telos*. The present world as it is experienced and known sacramentally reveals God in an incomplete manner; that is, the sacramental mediation of God in the world as experienced in one's spirituality through lived religious experience must be approached with the caution that it mediates divine in a less than complete manner. God is in all things and all things are in God, provisionally and incompletely, which implies the necessary caution not to mistake these incomplete manifestations of God for God as such. This view allows one to affirm God's qualified immanence in the world, yet also maintain God's radical otherness and transcendence. More importantly perhaps, realized eschatological pansacramentalism provides hope for a better world to come. One on hand, God is realized in all things sacramentally, yet on the other hand there is more to come. What you see is not what you get, but rather what you see is what you get with the hope for a more complete future. God's life is sacramentally shared now and is to be realized fully in the future. In this vein, Polkinghorne deems panentheism "true as an eschatological fulfillment, not a present reality."[79]

The philosophic function of sacramentality and sacramental language provides a promising way to talk about and make intelligible the mediation between God and world without reducing one to the other (pantheism) or separating them in such a radical manner that one has nothing to do with the other. It provides a meaningful way to approach one of the main questions of panentheism, that of the relation between God and world. The problem of suffering in a pansacramental vision can be dealt with in a number of ways. This chapter outline two promising ways: 1) recognizing the pathos of the biblical God and 2) recognizing a provisional pansacramental panentheism. Drawing on relevant sacramental and panentheistic scholarship, the final chapter offers the beginning of a sacramental model for approaching the God-world relationship in so far as it raises implications for the relationship between theology, spirituality, and the study of spirituality. Further, it broadens the focus to consider implications for a theology of religious pluralism and interreligious encounter.

---

79. John Polkinghorne, *Faith of a Physicist*, 168.

14

Towards a Pansacramental Theology of Religious Pluralism and Doing Theology Interreligiously

THIS FINAL CHAPTER DEMONSTRATES an attempt to place the view proposed thus far, a pansacramental view of the world in which all things are in God sacramentally and thus can serve as mediators of the divine, in the context of doing theology interreligiously. In so doing, first I propose "panentheistic pansacramentalism" as a new model for understanding the God-world relationship. This view relies on the metaphors of the relation of the artist to her art and the mother to her child. Second, I apply this model to the context of interreligious encounter by sketching a preliminary attempt at a "pansacramental theology of religious pluralism." Third, I propose the method of doing theology interreligiously, offer an example based on the content of this book, and then place it within the context of the interdisciplinary field of interreligious studies. Finally, I conclude with some very brief comments on potential avenues for theological exploration going forward.

Panentheistic Pansacramentalism[1]

F. LeRon Shults has proclaimed that one of the current pressing critical tasks for the contemporary Christian theologian is "to present a Christian

---

1. Content from this this section was presented in Gustafson, "Pansacramentality as a New Model for the God-World Relationship in Panentheism."

understanding of the relation between God and the world that overcomes the problems of dualism (or deism) without collapsing into the opposite problems associated with monism (or pantheism), that is, without conflating the concepts of Spirit and matter."[2] The pansacramental proposal laid out in this book, in which all things function as potential revelations of the ultimate, has sought just this.[3] Positing the divine and world together in an intimate and interdependent fashion while respecting and preserving their mutual irreducible difference, pansacramentalism and the philosophic function of sacraments as religious symbols not only avoid Shults' concern for monism, but also offer the constructive promise for the doing of theology in the context of religious pluralism and interreligious encounter; a context that is emerging as increasingly important and prevalent in the twenty-first century. In this book, I have not sought to advocate for, or construct, an explicit coherent panentheistic model from within which a philosophy of pansacramentality functions intelligibly, but rather I have instead sought to raise the category of pansacramentality in so far as it relates to similar issues and concerns that panentheism has dealt with. In this book, I operate on the working premise of "pansacramental panentheism." This is to say that I work on the assumption that panentheism is an adequate and accommodating model for the philosophy of sacramental mediation proposed in this book, until demonstrated otherwise. Although I share a certain kinship with Christopher Knight's pansacramental naturalism, Peacocke's naturalistic sacramental panentheism, and Polkinghorne's eschatological sacramental panentheisms, I do not fully identify wholly with any of them. There is great merit in the proposals of all three of these thinkers, but here in this section I sketch my own view on the heading "panentheistic pansacramentalism."

At present, I prefer "panentheistic pansacramentalism" over "pansacramental panentheism," since it emphasizes pansacramentality and avoids imposing any restrictions on panentheism as such. However, I remain open to the use and possible prominence of the latter term, should it be sufficiently demonstrated (which is most likely the case in certain contexts and under certain circumstances). The following beginning sketch of my panentheistic pansacramental proposal is an attempt to understand the God-world relationship while highlighting the role of sacramentality.

The God-world relationship is often conceptualized in panentheism through the understanding of the world as God's body, thus God and world are understood to be related in an analogous manner to mind and body.

---

2. Shults, "Current Trends in Pneumatology."

3. In similar fashion, Keith Ward has proposed an "iconic vision" (Ward, *Concepts of God*, 3).

Many panentheists find this attractive, while others remain cautious.[4] Without rejecting this metaphor of divine embodiment straight away, I offer here an alternative metaphor to supplement, complement, and/or replace it. This metaphor likens the God-world relationship to the artist-art relationship (broadly conceived) and, more to the point, to the mother-child relationship.

The relationship of God to the world can be likened to that of the artist to her art.[5] For instance, a builder designs a house and builds it. He stands in distinction to his house, but remains "in" it in a symbolic way. He remains both immanent and transcendent in relation to the house. He is more than the house, transcends the house, and is thus not reduced to the house, yet he also dwells in the house artistically, that is, symbolically. The house is a product of his intellect and thus expresses his mind concretely. The house represents him, but he is not exhausted by the house. He can also design and build other houses, as well as do other things. This analogy, like all analogies, breaks down at a certain point. For instance, although the builder can design and build a house, he cannot create the materials used to build the house. In this way the builder is limited by, and dependent on, the materials and their capabilities. Further, this means that the builder is not completely present in the house since he did not create the materials. So in a very important sense, the house remains external to him. However, God is completely present in the creator-creation model since God created (and sustains) the materials of the creation.

When others enter the house, they not only experience the house as such, but they experience the builder as well. They get to know the builder, for the house symbolically (re)presents the builder. It bears the marks of the builder. The artist and his art mutually dwell in one another; they mutually indwell. The builder is symbolically "in" all his houses through design, material, function, and feel, while all of the houses are "in" the builder, who is the source of their origination and actualization. I come from a long line

---

4. Michael W. Brierley identifies advocates as Philip Clayton, David Ray Griffin, Jay McDaniel, and Sallie McFague. He identifies those who remain cautious as John Macquarrie and David Pailin. And he identifies Arthur Peacock as one who outright rejects this model (Brierley, "Naming a Quiet Revolution, fn 136–138). One of the most lucid and far-reaching writings on the metaphor of the world as God's body has been written by Keith Ward, "The World as the Body of God: A Panentheistic Metaphor," in which he traces its roots to twelfth-century Indian philosopher, Ramanuja. Ward contrasts Ramanuja's proposal with that of Hegel, Whitehead, and Christian panentheism (Ward, "The World as the Body of God," 62–72).

5. This model focuses on the relationship between the artist and her art, but broadly conceived so as to include the relationship of creator to creation and even, as discussed later in the chapter, the parent-child relationship.

of homebuilders: my grandfather, my father, and now my eldest brother. They have built hundreds of painstakingly artistic homes. In experiencing these homes you come to experience and know them as builders as they learned, grew, and evolved through the decades. These houses make present my homebuilding kin. I have had many experiences in one of their homes where a visitor says "your father is in this house," in an effort to articulate the house bearing the mark of the builder. It is like many other artist's relationship to her art: a poet to his poetry, a painter to her paintings, a musician to her music, and a photographer to his photos, etc.

Reflecting on the parent-child metaphor, recall hearing the phrases, "you have your mother in you; you are your father; I see you in your mother." Not to be understood literally, these figurative exclamations nonetheless point to something the speaker believes to be true about whom they say it. Further, any parent knows that these comments are not only a one-way street. That is, it is not always about simply seeing the parent in the child, but also about seeing the child in the parent. Mothers know that not only was their child literally inside them at one time, but also the child remains in both her and father. This latter sense is obviously meant metaphorically to indicate the ability of the child to impress upon her spirit upon her parents. Far from being threatened, intimated, or subordinated in this process, the parent (at least in my experience) feels proud and blessed. This two-way street is like Heschel's God of pathos which both affects and is affected by persons and the world. The mother-child metaphor is, to my knowledge at present, the most apt for maintaining either a panentheistic or pansacramental understanding of God-world-person relationship that preserves immanence and transcendence throughout. Further, it concretizes the pathos, possibility, dynamism, and relationality of God and world (the latter of which includes persons).

This model posits the artist in her creation, yet preserves her transcendence and otherness. This proposal need not be understood as a strict panentheistic model, but rather can be understood as a pansacramental model with panentheistic overtones. It advocates for both all things existing in God and God existing in all things; however, it proposes that the crucial "en" (in) of "pan-en-theism" be understood pansacramentally. This in answer to the question about panentheism of how do all things exist "in" God, the answer here is that they exist "in" God sacramentally. Panentheism states that all things are in God and God is in all things, just as all fish are in the sea and the sea is in all fish. Here I propose the pansacramentally qualified version of this formula and offer the following analogy: all houses are in the builder and the builder is in all the houses (yet the builder is not reduced to his houses). Likewise, regarding the parent-child metaphor: the parent is in the child and the child in the parent, yet both remain other to one another (one is not reduced to the other).

The artist-art relationship as a pansacramental and panentheistic metaphor might then be employed as a beginning to the conversation concerning the various crucial questions within any pansacramental or panentheistic vision. These include the question of God's independence and self-sufficiency, the problem of suffering and God's passibility, immutability, and the question of divine and human freedom to name a few. For instance, likening the God-world relation to artist-art, the question of freedom for God and humans might be approached as follows. When an artist produces art (such as builder does a house), the work is now "out there" and in a certain sense, autonomously on its own, though still a part of the artist. Others are free to interpret and treat it how they wish, which is beyond the control of the artist. The art is like the child of the artist and once set free it is opened to the reality of suffering. If the art suffers, so too does the artist. When a child suffers, the parent does as well in a similar, but not identical, manner. The parent and artist suffer in solidarity with their child and art respectively. Thus, the "in" of "in all things" here might be understood as "in solidarity with;" that is, God exists in solidarity with all things, just as an artist or parent is in solidarity with their respective art and child. The implication of this depicts a God that Heschel depicted above, a God of pathos, which challenges the tenets of classical theism. Since the art and artist mutually indwell, they both hold the potential to affect one another.

This pansacramental art-artist metaphor for the God-world relationship, in which all things hold the potential to sacramentally (re)present God in the world in the manner that art (re)presents its creator, is an endorsement here for a soft panentheism. By soft I simply intend to avoid strict panentheism which might reduce God to the totality all things (which few panentheists, in my experience, do). Rather, the sacramental qualification placed on this form of panentheism, which implies pansacramentalism since it includes "all things," serves to preserve the otherness and transcendence of God without negating God's radical immanence in all things.

The intention here is not to construct and propose a fully coherent and "new and improved" model of panentheism, but rather the intention is to raise the function and category of pansacramentality in so far as it might prove promising for clarifying the God-world relationship. The grand scope of this book is interested in what implications this might raise for the mediation between theology and spirituality, as well as the study of spirituality. It has been argued that theology (knowing God), spirituality (experiencing God), and the study of spirituality (examining one's lived religious experience of God) can be facilitated through (pan)sacramental mediation.

This panentheistic pansacramental model, with its proposed artist-art and parent-child metaphors, further assists in demonstrating the function of sacramental mediation.

For instance, in this metaphor, knowing God (theology) is likened to knowing the builder, while experiencing God (spirituality), and the study of that experience (study of spirituality) is likened to experiencing the builder and studying one's experience of the builder. In order for one to know the builder, he must know the houses, and in order to know[6] the houses one must experience the houses. The houses themselves function symbolically as the mediator between builder and non-builder. To truly know an artist as an artist, one needs to experience the art of the artist, which functions symbolically. Likewise to truly know a mother as a mother, one must meet, experience, and know her child(ren). Thus art as such functions as a sacramental mediator between God and God's world, and this is experienced precisely in and through God's world. In the examination of the this experience (the study of spirituality), the employment of this panentheistic pansacramental metaphor assists in maintaining both God's radical immanence and irreducible otherness, as well as retaining the legitimacy of grounding the quest for knowledge of God (theology) in the experience as such.

These metaphors help to facilitate the taking seriously the sacramental experience of divine's real presence in all things. As such, theology is required to take lived religious experience seriously and thus depend on the study of spirituality. Likewise, if the study of spirituality, as the examination of lived religious experience in the world, takes seriously the pansacramental function of the cosmos as mediator of the divine, it is required to take seriously the attempt of correlating the individual and particular spiritual experiences in pursuit of coherent theological knowledge. In short, just as lover of Shakespeare immerses himself into Shakespeare's work in order to get to know the artist himself, the lover of God must immerse herself into God's work (God's art, creation, cosmos, all things) in order to get to know God as such.

Towards a Pansacramental Theology of Religious Pluralism

The philosophy of pansacramental mediation proposed in this book contains a foundation from which to propose a preliminary attempt at a pansacramental theology of religious pluralism. For decades, the *en vogue*

---

6. To know here refers to subjective knowledge (not objective knowledge) as distinguished by Johannes Climacus (Kierkegaard), which was examined in chapter 11.

Christian approach to other religions, under the title "theology of religions," was often reduced to the single issue of discerning the possibility and mode of salvation for non-Christians. Generally, all approaches fell under one of three types, exclusivism, inclusivism, and pluralism famously posed in 1983 by Alan Race in his book *Christians and Religious Pluralism*. Theology of religious pluralism used under this soteriocentric typology can refer to a number of constructs, but all seek to respond to the question of salvation. Although not a fruitless nor uninteresting pursuit, the salvation question is one I move beyond here. Going beyond "theology of religions" (often limited to Race's three-fold typology) to the broader "theology of religious pluralism," I resonate with Jacques Dupuis who makes this distinction. For him, this "new perspective is no longer limited to the problem of 'salvation' for members of the other religious traditions or even to the role of those traditions in the salvation of their members. It searches more deeply, in the light of Christian faith, for the meaning of God's design for humankind of the plurality of living faiths and religious traditions with which we are surrounded."[7] With Dupuis I intend here to broaden the conversation under the rubric theology of religious pluralism, and with Diana Eck, I employ the term pluralism not simply to refer to the mere acceptance of religious diversity, but also to refer to the "energetic engagement with [that] diversity."[8] In this section, I have in mind Dupuis' understanding of theology of religious pluralism in proposing a pansacramental theology of religious pluralism. In the next section, I have more in mind Eck's understanding of pluralism as I draw on interreligious encounter as it can take place within the context of comparative theology.

In *Paths to the Triune God*, Anselm Min proposes a soteriocentric "sacramental theology of religions" based on a Thomist trinitarian theology of salvation. In particular, his is "a pluralist theology of religions which considers each religion a sacrament in the same way that contemporary Catholic theology considers the church the 'basic' sacrament out of which the particular sacraments flow."[9] Contemporary Roman Catholic theology proclaims that the church is the "basic" sacrament which stems from Christ, the primordial sacrament. As such, the church serves as the foundation from which all other sacraments flow and function. In an analogous theology of religions in which the church serves as the basic sacrament of salvation and from which all others flow, each religion functions salvifically

---

7. Dupuis, *Toward a Christian Theology of Religious Pluralism*, 10; also quoted in Kärkkäinen, *An Introduction to the Theology of Religions*, 206.

8. Eck, "What Is Pluralism?"

9. Min, *Paths to the Triune God*, 77.

and authentically only in so far as it flows from, and relates to, the Christian church. Going further, each non-Christian religion as such functions as the basic sacrament for its constituents. In other words, "Non-Christian religions . . . can be regarded as basic sacraments for non-Christians."[10] Min's proposal might be understood as a pansacramental theology of religions, albeit inclusive and not necessarily pluralist. It is pansacramental since it rests on the sacramental principle which states, "the material, the sensible, the visible can serve as signs of the spiritual, the intellectual, and the invisible. The whole universe as such can serve as a sign or sacrament of God's presence and activity."[11] Presumably this includes other religions.

In contemporary theology of religions, this theory cannot be properly deemed a pluralist position and is, at best, what Min admits "could be called 'pluralistic inclusivism.'"[12] Min however strives beyond inclusivism towards a position of genuine pluralism in which each religion is understood as an "irreducibly different totality."[13] In so doing, Min avoids a "common essence" or common *telos* theory, however he is not inclined to affirm this mutual incommensurability as something permanent.[14] In other words, he remains open to a future-oriented convergence theory, in which all religions *may* ultimately converge in so far as their essence and *telos* are concerned. Ultimately, Min reconciles the desire for a genuine theology of religious pluralism with Aquinas via the notion of "light" drawn from "the light of faith and grace."[15] Light of faith illuminates that towards which it is directed, which includes all things as potential material objects of faith, "but only insofar as faith considers them . . . in relation to God [*in ordine ad Deum*] and on account of the divine truth [*propter divinam veritatem*]."[16] The light of faith, Min claims, provides a believing community with a mode of seeing "things differently," which contrasts with seeing things from the position of lacking faith. "In short, the light of faith, when shared, produces a church, a believing community with its own internal criteria and horizon, distinguishing it from all other communities who do not share that light."[17] Each community functions under the light of faith as an authentic expression of the quest for religion. Thus, the criterion becomes whether a

10. Ibid., 105.
11. Ibid., 104.
12. Ibid.
13. Ibid.
14. Ibid.
15. Ibid., 106
16. Ibid. (italics mind)
17. Ibid., 107

community has the light of faith or not, wherein lack of faith is not a unique form of faith on its own, but rather is simply unbelief and a product of sin, according to Min.[18] Although one goal of this section is to engage and affirm Min's proposal, I do not advocate that such a pansacramental Christian theology of religious pluralism is only possible by relying on the Thomist criterion of "light of faith" to gauge the authenticity of one's faith. There may be other criterions or sets of criteria that allows one to navigate the waters of religious authenticity[19]. Further, a purpose of this section is to also begin to both build on and complement Min's proposal.

One addition I propose is turning to the "theomorphic principle" for guidance in dealing with the question of whether something is sacramental and to what extent. Although there may be a number of legitimate criterions or set of criteria for determining the sacramental strength of a person, thing, or action, and in addition to Min's "light of faith," I propose looking again to Abrahams Joshua Heschel's theology on theomorphism as a criterion for determining sacramental robustness. In defending his theology of divine pathos against the charge of anthropomorphism, Heschel turns the criticism on its head and argues for theomorphism.

> The idea of the divine pathos combining absolute selflessness with supreme concern for the poor and the exploited can hardly be regarded as the attribution of human characteristics. Where is the man who is endowed with such characteristics? Nowhere in the Bible is man characterized as merciful, gracious, slow to anger, abundant in love and truth, keeping love to the thousandth generation . . . if these are characteristics of human nature, then man is endowed with attributes of the divine.[20]

In other words, a person concerned with and working for justice in the world exhibits theomorphic traits. Thus where one exhibits theomorphic (God-formed) qualities in the world, the more God-like, and sacramentally representative, they are of God. Without a doubt, Mother Teresa of Calcutta exhibited to a much greater degree than I the combination of "absolute selflessness with supreme concern for the poor and the exploited,"[21] and thus is sacramental to a much greater degree than I (at least, for much more of her life than I of my life). In short, she is more sacramentally robust than I. The criterion for determining the sacramental robustness of a person then is a theomorphic principle which states that wherever God-like traits are

---

18. Ibid.
19. Cornille, ed., *Criteria of Discernment in Interreligious Dialogue*.
20. Heschel, *The Prophets*, 348–49.
21. Ibid.

exhibited in a human person, the more sacramental that person is. Hence, there can be degrees of sacramentality exhibited by persons. The question then becomes one of determining what the God-like traits are apart from the usual suspects found in both the Hebrew Bible and the New Testament such as compassion, justice, virtue, mercy, love, honesty, courage, wisdom, discernment, and so on. Further, criteria is also needed for determine the sacramental robustness of experiences, not just human actions.

Min claims to have properly demonstrated a theology of religious pluralism supported by Aquinas, "who expressed the confidence that for pagans God would provide the necessary means of salvation provided they followed the lead and light of natural reason in their moral praxis."[22] All persons are endowed with this "light of natural reason" mediated through different cultural, linguistic, and religious contexts.[23] As such, "there is no common light of faith for all religions."[24] Min confesses that this may be provisional, for there is no reason to reject the idea, especially in an increasingly globalized and shrinking world, that cultural and linguistic barriers cannot be overcome. It remains within the realm of possibility that religious convergence and respect (that is, respecting the authenticity and validity of divine revelation in religions other than one's own) can be achieved. "Ultimately, to abandon humanity to all their stark differences is not only to ignore the growing interdependence of the world and the growing convergence of human needs and concerns but also to despair reconciliation and solidarity."[25]

Avoiding this despair remains the hope of a genuine pansacramental theology of religious pluralism, a position which advocates for the revelatory authenticity of each religious tradition set within its own context. The criterion for authenticity may very well be Min's campaign for Aquinas' "light of faith," or simply an honest devotion to striving for the divine. In a pansacramental proposal, each religious tradition, as well as its particular symbols, texts, rituals, and customs, can function as sacramental symbols. The qualification of potentiality here remains, for all things hold the *potential*

---

22. Min, *Paths to the Triune God*, 108

23. Wilfred Cantwell Smith proposed a view that resonates in some sense with Min's proposal in that Cantwell Smith famously distinguished between universal "faith" (that which all persons are capable of due to it being a part of human nature) and particular "beliefs," which are mediated through different contexts, cultures, practices, theologies, languages, and so forth. Cantwell Smith's view tends towards a theology of religious pluralism founded on the principle that faith is a universal aspect of human nature and as such serves as one way humanity is united in via common religious quest.

24. Min, *Paths to the Triune God*, 108.

25. Ibid., 109

to function sacramentally, but this is not to say that all things *actually* function sacramentally at all times. Where there is "light of faith," or genuine striving for the divine, the potential for sacramental mediation is actualized in and through a particular context. These contexts remain irreducibly different. Thus, the Lakota ritual of "having a sweat" (to put it colloquially) is not to be reduced to simply an acceptable, yet confused, version of the communal solidarity expressed through the rituals of the Christian church (e.g., communion). Rather, "having a sweat" might be understood as a genuine sacrament (or symbol of religious significance) in its own right to be placed alongside all other sacraments, whether they are "the seven Sacraments" of the Catholic and Orthodox churches, or the infinite number of informal sacramental experiences that occur in all other traditions. "Having a sweat" might be a unique sacrament reserved for those communities that practice it and thus provides insight for to learn from for those communities that do not practice it. This moves beyond a Rahnerian Christocentric or ecclesiocentric theology of religious "inclusivism" towards a genuine pansacramental theology of religious pluralism. This is an elevation of Rahner's sacramental theology of "symbolic reality," to radically include all things as genuine revelations of the divine.

A note here about the language of sacrament. The term sacrament, although perhaps appropriate for the Christian to employ from within her own context, may be discarded for the phrase "symbol of religious significance" since the latter phrase (as explained in chapter 11) aims to articulate what is understood by the term sacrament here. However, the term sacrament often connotes the Christian tradition in particular or exclusively, for better or for worse. In the spirit of a theology of religious pluralism, it ought to remain up to the adherents, leaders, thinkers, and practitioners of the various traditions to propose their own linguistic terms and philosophical categories for understanding the relation between and among their tradition and others.

This pansacramental theology of religious pluralism aims to get beyond the salvation question and, as Dupuis has proposed above, get to "search more deeply" for God's design between and among the divine-world-person relationship in the context of religious plurality. This entails moving beyond the sole obsession of whether and how persons achieve salvation (not to mention the problematic presumption of a shared definition of "salvation"), but also takes seriously the mode, content, and context of the rich plurality of religious experience claimed by the traditions throughout history. As such, this model naturally lends itself to the constructive task of doing theology interreligiously.

Doing Theology Interreligiously and Interreligious Studies

Doing theology interreligiously does not need to be understood in a manner which requires one to leave behind their particular religious or theological orientation, but it does require the commitment to doing theology in the context of other religious traditions and their theological and philosophical claims. First, drawing on Wilfred Cantwell Smith, Keith Ward, and Francis X. Clooney, this section elaborates further on the theological method of doing theology interreligiously and provides an example that draws on several themes and ideas introduced in this book. Second, it nudges the conversation into the interdisciplinary field of interreligious studies by asking what doing theology interreligiously might practically offer the emerging field of interreligious studies.

Doing Theology Interreligiously

Wilfred Cantwell Smith's proposed the doing of "world theology" in his well-known book by the same title.[26] He suggested that a new era has arrived, which calls for the recognition that all people share a common religious story based on one universal faith expressed through many different particular beliefs.[27] This common religious story emerges, in part, in the doing of "world theology," which involves people of faith reinterpreting their beliefs in light of this common experience of faith. Perhaps more provocative still, Cantwell Smith advocates for no longer categorizing theologies under religious designators such as Christian theology, Islamic theology, Hindu theology, and so on. Rather, going forward there only ought to be "world theology," which is to draw on all of the theologies (of the world's religious traditions) in an effort to express the universal faith through the various particular beliefs of the religions.[28] This process entails persons of faith modifying their own beliefs in a manner that will adequately square with those from other religious traditions. The result, then, is a belief system developed by people from around the world who are consciously aware of the one history of faith that undergirds all separate religions.

For Cantwell Smith this new era upon us is one in which we can no longer stay isolated in our own theological systems and do theology without

---

26. Smith, *Towards a World Theology*.

27. I am indebted to James Fredericks' examination of Cantwell Smith's theology in Fredericks, *Faith among Faiths*, 79–89.

28. Ibid., 84.

taking into account other religious traditions. To demonstrate, he recalls key developments in the history of the Christian tradition which required reinterpretation and revision of theological beliefs, language, and philosophical categories. For instance, just as the discovery of Greek philosophy in the Middle Ages or scientific discoveries about the physical world in the modern era forced a rethinking of religion, so too now does the reality of religiously plurality force just such a constructive rethinking as well.[29] In other words, going forward all theology is to be done interreligiously; that is, it is to be done in light of the data offered by all religious traditions and not just one's home tradition alone. If a theology refrains from this, so goes the argument, it will not be taken seriously and simply die just as today one cannot do theology or philosophy, and be taken seriously without recognizing the claims of modern science or the influence of Greek philosophy (especially on Christian and Islamic theologies). For Cantwell Smith, and this is an important point this section stresses, theology can no longer be done without reference to other religions and their claims. Any theology that fails to do this will simply pass into irrelevancy as it falls on deaf ears of an educated public that lives, and moves, and breaths in a religiously plural world. Therefore, in the spirit of Cantwell Smith's "world theology," below I offer a pansacramental view of the divine-world-person relationship that engages tenets of various traditions and introduced throughout this book. However, unlike Cantwell Smith I do not suggest that one need to refrain from doing Christian theology, Islamic theology, Hindu theology, and so on. It is entirely appropriate for one to remain within one's home tradition and do theology from primarily that context but with a keen eye to the wisdom, claims, and insights made by the world's religions.

Keith Ward is a modern pioneer in contemporary field of comparative theology in the context of philosophical theology.[30] He produced an impressive five volume series[31] that sought to rethink, in light of the world's religions, major Christian themes (e.g., revelation, creation, human nature, community, and human fulfillment). Ward describes these as his attempt

---

29. Smith, "The Christian in a Religiously Plural World," 47–48.

30. Here I do not want to suggest that Ward was among the first to engage in the task of doing theology interreligiously, but rather his project represents one of the more robust examples in the modern era of one that strives to investigate key philosophical theological concepts within the world's religions in a fashion that makes an enduring impact on how he, as a committed Christian theist, understands God's disclosure in Jesus. Francis X. Clooney rightly recognizes that "interreligious and comparative learning has always been an inescapable dimension in the life of every religious community. [And] early Christianity . . . was no exception" (Clooney, *Comparative Theology*, 24).

31. Ward, *Religion and Revelation, Religion and Creation, Religion and Human Nature, Religion and Community,* and *Religion and Human Fulfilment.*

to develop a Christian systematic theology that is "radically influenced by a global religious perspective" as well as "to show how the world's major religious traditions can interact positively and fruitfully in the modern world."[32] His five volume project beautifully demonstrates his attitude that "once an understanding of faith as acceptance of exclusively correct propositions is given up, one can no longer simply say that the Christian faith has the only truth, and that all others are wrong. If faith is a response to a disclosure of the divine in this community, then why should there not be different disclosures of the divine in other communities?"[33] With Cantwell Smith and Ward, I agree that the future of theology is indeed one that will require the theologian, in order to be taken seriously, to certainly be aware of and well versed in religions other than her own, but to also engage them. After all,

> The great religious traditions are histories of developing reflection on the primal disclosures that constitute a tradition. In their meeting, the opportunity exists for conversations in which each tradition is modified by its greater empathy for the insights embodied in other traditions. It is in this way that diversity, and the freedom it requires, can be helpful to the discovery of the partiality in one's own views, and thus of a more expansive truth.[34]

Francis X. Clooney is "in substantial agreement with Ward," but suggests a "further step" is needed so that one's "faith itself is deeply infused with the spirit and influence of comparative work;" a "Ward-plus."[35] Clooney's approach is text-centric and proceeds by reading religious texts, "preferably scriptural and theological texts that have endured over centuries and millennia, back and forth across religious borders."[36] His approach exemplifies a modern comparative theological approach through texts in which one reads the religious texts of another tradition alongside the texts of her home tradition with the aim being able to see each in light of the other with new eyes. Fresh questions and insights are often generated in the process which encourages the theologians to rethink, revise, and revisit beliefs, convictions, concepts, and worldviews. The idea is that the scholar, though crossing over into another tradition (in this case, the texts of another tradition), returns to her own tradition with "fresh theological insights."[37]

32. Ward, "Books."
33. Ward, "The Importance of Liberal Theology," 51.
34. Ward, "Liberal Theology and the God of Love," 198.
35. Clooney, *Comparative Theology*, 45
36. Ibid, 58.
37. Ibid, 10.

In her 2006 presidential address to the American Academy of Religion, Diana Eck, stressed the challenge of pluralism (energetic engagement with religious diversity) for the academy, the public sphere, and for theology:

> Understanding and interpreting religious diversity is not only an academic and civic challenge, it is a theological challenge, a question of faith—age old, and yet insistent and new in our time. A theological argument utilizes the language, the symbols, and the authoritative sources of one's own religious tradition. It is plainly evaluative and interpretive. It speaks from the tradition to the tradition.[38]

A Christian pansacramental theology of religious pluralism and the doing of theology interreligiously speaks from the Christian tradition to the Christian tradition in its promotion of constructively seeking out and recognizing shared symbols. This is not just an advance towards synthesizing and syncretizing sacraments, symbols, texts, and concepts, although that may be part of it, but more importantly it entails recognizing and appreciating the theological thrust behind non-Christian sacraments, symbols, texts, and concepts, and learning from them (which does not necessarily entail incorporation and acceptance within one's own tradition).[39] In this manner, I work in the spirit of Cantwell Smith, Ward, and Clooney, in an energetic engagement with religious diverse concepts of the divine, world, and person as I put the panentheistic pansacramental proposal in conversation with the world's traditions.

---

38. Diana L. Eck, "Prospects for Pluralism," 767.

39. A starting point in the quest for shared symbols and theology can be found in comparative spirituality. Comparative theologian Catherine Cornille has rightly pointed out that it is "no coincidence that the individuals who appear most often as examples of multiple religious belonging belong to the spiritual branches of the traditions and that the intermonastic dialogue has offered much of the food for thought on this question" ("Introduction," 5). This should be of no surprise if spirituality functions as the most common bridge between faith traditions. Here Cornille is speaking of those who have embraced two traditions simultaneously, however this need not be the aim of comparative spirituality. Rather, spirituality can serve as an entry point into theological reflection. In other words, comparative spirituality naturally lends itself and leads to comparative theology. As this book argued, sacraments and religious symbols function as a natural bridge language. Spirituality, via shared symbols and sacraments, is only a beginning, a promising path, towards which recognition, reconciliation, respect, and acceptance (and at times convergence, synthesis, and syncretism where appropriate) of faith traditions other than one's own can begin. Certainly this is not the only way to achieve this goal. Other promising paths are available. Perhaps, the most common of these is through shared ethics, service, and concern for social justice. Sharing symbols, revelatory worldviews, and spiritual practices, can also promote interfaith learning, cooperation, and service within and among faith traditions.

As an example, in what follows I offer an instance of doing theology interreligiously by focusing on the construction of an interreligious approach to a changing planet.[40] The aim here is to provide an example of bringing the main thrust of this book into a project of doing theology interreligiously and then ask what it might offer the broader, more interdisciplinary, audience of interreligiously studies. It commences with Michael Murphy's rather intuitive premise that "if we view ourselves as one with the cosmos in our beginnings and our essential aims, we will be less inclined to war and world-weariness than we are if we see the world as fundamentally hostile or illusory ... [panentheism] may well provide a conceptual gathering place for the global village."[41] The idea, quite simply, is that if the relations between and among the divine, world, and human persons are envisioned as intimate, in this case panentheistically, then persons (which are parts of the cosmos) will supposedly be more hesitant to act not only against the best interest of the earth (that is, we will theoretically avoid harming the earth), but also will avoid harming one another since this construction understands persons as part of the cosmos as well.

With this premise in mind, I turn to four traditions (represented by four various figures) in an effort to construct an interreligious approach to the divine-world-person relationship and offer a panentheistic and pansacramental approach to a changing planet. The four traditions are the Lakota view (represented by Nicholas Black Elk from chapter 9), the Hindu *Advaita* view (represented by Anantanand Rambachan), the Jewish view of God's pathos (represented by Abraham Joshua Heschel from chapter 13), and the Christian pansacramental view (represented by myself). In addition to offering insight that facilitates an overall pansacramental view of the cosmos, and without contradicting a Christian view, this proposal may have implications for those working outside strict philosophical theology and under the general interdisciplinary field of interreligious studies.

Nicholas Black Elk, recall, espoused a Lakota view of the sacredness of all things. Informed by both his Lakota spiritual tradition and the Ignatian tradition, he presented the view that all things "are the works of the Great Spirit[42] ... [who] is within all things[43] [and] also above all these things and

---

40. Based on the content that follows, I presented the paper Gustafson, "Interreligious Panentheistic Approaches to a Changing Planet in Comparative Theology and Interfaith Studies."

41. Murphy, "The Emergence of Evolutionary Panentheism," 180–181.

42. See chapter 9.

43. E.g., "the trees, the grasses, the rivers, the mountains, and all the four-legged animals, and the winged peoples" (Black Elk, xx).

peoples."[44] An element of panentheism is clear in his view: the divine is within all things (immanence), but also above or beyond all things (transcendence). Hence, Black Elk's Lakota earth-view provides a non-Christian approach to understanding the relation between God and world that need not contradict nor compete with a Christian perspective. Notice too, that Black Elk's view need not be understood panentheistically since there is no claim of all things being in the divine, but rather the claim is that the divine is within and beyond all things.

Anantanand Rambachan self-identifies as a "committed insider"[45] of the Hindu *Advaita* tradition and describes *Advaita* as that which, "characterizes the relationship between the infinite (*brahman*), the world (*jagat*), and the human being (*jiva*) as not-two (*Advaita*) while affirming the ultimate ontological non-difference among all three. *Brahman* is the ultimate self of the world and the human being."[46] The panentheistic overtones are immediately evident, for *Advaita* understands the relationship between God and world as not-two (nondual) in such a manner that the world partakes of the nature of the divine (Brahman) yet does not fully express it. In other words, the world is in Brahman and Brahman is in the world, but Brahman remains more than the world, for Brahman is limitless. Not only does Rambachan clearly articulate the fundamental claims of an *Advaita* worldview, but he also, perhaps more importantly, eloquently argues that the "Advaita teaching about the fundamental ontological unity of *brahman*, world, and human beings is understood as promoting a reverence and value for nature that is conducive to sound environmental ethics."[47]

Rambachan's *Advaita* view is especially important since it has been commonplace to lay blame on the Western dualistic worldview as a significant culprit in the devaluation of nature and the alienation of the world from humans and God. The result is a view which understands the world as a transient piece of trash radically separated from the divine and humans that ought to be ultimately relegated to the rubbish heap at the end times or completely recreated anew. It takes no large imagination to employ this view to justify an attitude that has little to no concern for, or care of, the world and its ills. In short, if nature is desacralized, then it is easier to justify exploiting it. Traditionally, the *Advaita* view itself has not been immune to these critiques either. Rambachan and others have pointed out that *Advaita* has often been understood in a manner than devalues nature as well since it

---

44. Ibid.
45. Rambachan, *A Hindu Theology of Liberation*, 9.
46. Ibid, 131.
47. Ibid, 132.

promotes indifference to the world; that is, the world has been understood as an illusion, a dream, and so forth. "The predominant Advaita concern has been to explain the world away and to inculcate attitudes of world renunciation and detachment."[48] Various Christian traditions, of course, can be accused of this apathetic stance towards the world as well. Rambachan's work is important, especially for the Hindu *Advaita* tradition but also for non Hindus as well because he turns this apathetic interpretation on its head and argues that, to the contrary, "because *brahman* has ultimate value, the non-dual relationship enriches the value of the world."[49] Put differently, "if the world can be seen positively as the outcome of the intentional creativity of *brahman*, expressing and sharing *brahman's* nature, it does not have to be rejected, negated, or argued away."[50]

Abraham Heschel, recall, promoted a God that "does not simply command and expect obedience [but] is also moved and affected by what happens in the world, and reacts accordingly."[51] This is a God of pathos, a God that is susceptible to being moved and affected by emotion. The core insight gleaned from Heschel's theology of divine pathos might be that God reveals God's self "in a personal and intimate relation to the world . . . [And] is also moved and affected by what happens in the world, and reacts accordingly."[52] An implication is that God is affected by human suffering and historical events in the world, which includes the ills of the natural and human world on a changing planet. A God of pathos that is also understood as in the world, with the view of the world being in God, mutually aligns with the interests of God, persons, and the world. If one suffers, all suffer. Since God exists in an intimate relation to the world, and God's pathos "is not an attribute, but a response . . . a reaction to human history, an attitude called forth by man's conduct; a response, not a cause,"[53] then God's response to the suffering world (which includes human suffering) can be understood as primarily one of being in solidarity[54] with the world. Therefore, in responding to the ills of changing world, the human relation to God can be

---

48. Ibid, 136.
49. Ibid, 139.
50. Ibid., 7–8.
51. Heschel, *The Prophets*, 288.
52. Ibid., 288.
53. Ibid., 290.
54. Here I am in agreement with Enrique Dussel and Oddbjørn Leirvik on a general understanding of the term solidarity to mean "'suffering with' the other" (Leirvik, *Interreligious Studies*, 101).

understood as one in which humans act and react as "a consort, a partner, a factor in the life of God."[55]

In conversation with Black Elk (the Lakota sacredness of all things), Rambachan (Hindu *Advaita*), and Heschel (Judaism's divine pathos), and in an effort to demonstrate the doing of theology interreligiously, I turn again to my proposal of panentheistic pansacramentalism detailed above. With Black Elk, it supports the understanding that all things serve to represent and express the divine in a real way by mediating God in the world. Rambachan's *Advaita* view emphasizes that in this construction of the God-world relationship, "*brahman* remains limitless and non-dual after the emergence of the world. Without any diminution or loss, therefore, *brahman* brings forth the world out of itself as an act of self-multiplication."[56] It takes little imagination to recognize the kinship between Rambachan's *Advaitic* view described above and the metaphor proposed at the outset of this chapter of God giving birth to the world in a manner a mother does a child. Heschel provides one of the most eloquent and thorough going proposals for how to understand God as capable of suffering and pathos. If the pansacramental worldview is to be taken seriously, along with Black Elk and *Advaitic* cosmology, then the understanding of all things serving as potential mediators of divine must indeed include suffering. Further, if a panentheistic proposal is to be held (in one manner or another), the possibility of God's suffering in some fashion must be entertained and articulated. In short, doing theology interreligiously here renders an open and relational constructive Christian theology which maintains the following: with Nicholas Black Elk, all things are sacred; with Rambachan's *Advaita* tradition, the divine-world relationship inherently calls for recognition of the intimate nondual relation between god, world, and persons while paying sufficient attention to, and care for, the world; and with Heschel, God suffers in solidarity with the world. All of this is especially the case if it can be affirmed that the world is somehow in God (in some manner) and God is in the world (in some manner). All things, then can function as sacraments in their making God present, including (or perhaps especially) suffering. Therefore, God is present in the suffering of the world and human persons and, for the Christian, God suffers in the world as a human person in Jesus as well.

This brief example of doing theology interreligiously retains the spirit of the thinkers mentioned above, especially Keith Ward's conviction that when religious traditions converse, "the opportunity exists for conversations in which each tradition is modified by its greater empathy for the insights

---

55. Heschel, *The Prophets*, 292.
56. Rambachan, *A Hindu Theology of Liberation*, 138.

embodied in other traditions."[57] Perhaps it is the case that the Lakota, Jewish, and Hindu traditions have been able to discover and clearly articulate various aspects of a theological view of reality more than the Christian tradition has, and it does the Christian tradition well to listen to those views in an attempt to square them with its own.

Interreligious Studies

Given the explanation above about the spirit of doing theology interreligiously in addition to the demonstrative example that places this book's panentheistic pansacramentalism in conversation with Black Elk, Rambachan, and Heschel, this penultimate section of the final chapter very briefly serves the purpose of pushing the conversation beyond the confines of theology by asking what interdisciplinary implications might be generated from such a project under the general academic field of interreligious studies. The field of interreligious and interfaith studies[58] has emerged relatively recently in the academy, with several graduate and seminar programs, and a small but growing number of undergraduate programs in Europe and North America. In fact, the Association of Theological Schools has implemented the standard that Master of Divinity programs ought to now "engage students with the global character of the church as well as ministry in the multifaith and multicultural context of contemporary society. This should include attention to the wide diversity of religious traditions."[59] There are several academic journals[60] and institutes devoted to the field as well. A

---

57. Heschel, *The Prophets*, 198.

58. Beginning with their inaugural session in Baltimore in 2013, the "Interreligious and Interfaith Studies Group" met at the annual meeting of the American Academy in Baltimore, MD. This Group creates a space for critical interdisciplinary engagement with interfaith and interreligious studies, which examines the many modes of response to the reality of religious pluralism (theological, philosophical, historical, scriptural, ethical, praxological, and institutional). The group strives to "expand and enrich the modalities of interreligious and interfaith discourse in a diverse set of academic disciplines that have grappled with religious pluralism; give voice to what has already been happening for years at the cutting-edge of institutional and pedagogical innovation and at the intersection of the academy and civic engagement in many disciplines; [and] encourage the rigorous analysis necessary to establish the contours of this emerging field. Similarly, we will encourage critical analysis of both national and international interfaith organizational models and other praxis-oriented responses to religious pluralism" (American Academy of Religion, "Interreligious and Interfaith Studies Group").

59. Association of Theological Schools, "Commission Accrediting Degree Program Standards Handbook," 3 (sec. A.2.3.2).

60. E.g., *Journal of Inter-Religious Dialogue, Studies in Interreligious Dialogue, Interreligious Insight: A Journal of Dialogue and Engagement*, and *Journal of Ecumenical*

rising consensus among scholars seems to be that the field, not unlike religious studies, is inherently interdisciplinary.[61] Much more can be said about this emerging field, and much more will be said, to be sure, in the coming years as it continues to define itself and find a home within the research and teaching of academia. It is sufficient here to comment on four key elements (among others) of the field in so far as they relate to the example above of doing theology interreligiously. Interreligious studies is a) self-implicating, b) descriptive, c) prescriptive, and d) experiential.[62]

As self-implicating, interreligious studies involves the examination of religious encounters that one is already a part of. It implicates the researcher by placing him or her in concrete situations were religious identities and concepts intersect and call for sensitivity and action. Therefore, interreligious studies goes beyond descriptive approaches by embracing prescriptive and experiential approaches as well. The descriptive element is indispensable "because it records and documents the dialogue process for the present and future generations."[63] Further, the field needs "the critical outside perspective of religious studies in order not to be controlled by the dialogue of the insiders who are well aware of their role as agents but perhaps not always able to see themselves from a critical distance."[64] Interreligious Studies is also prescriptive in the questions it generates, such as "can interreligious dialogue play a role in resolving religious conflicts and healing past injustices?"[65] Can it play a role in responding to the current sufferings of the world and in the world? The experiential component becomes important in order to respond to the ills, conflicts, and injustices in the world. This

---

Studies.

61. Still in its infancy, this field is still undergoing the process of self-definition. However, there are several good resources out there for distinguishing this field in relation to religious studies and theology while situating it within the greater context of academic discipline such as Dunbar, "The Place of Interreligious Dialogue in the Academic Study of Religion"; Gustafson, "Interreligious and Interfaith Studies in Relation to Religious Studies and Theological Studies"; Leirvik, *Interreligious Studies*; Patel, "Toward a Field of Interfaith Studies."

62. These four elements are drawn from my article Gustafson, "Interreligious and Interfaith Studies in Relation to Religious Studies and Theological Studies."

63. Dunbar, "The Place of Interreligious Dialogue in the Academic Study of Religion," 462; (cited by Leirvik, "Interreligious Studies: a Relational Approach to the Study of Religion, 16).

64. Leirvik, "Interreligious Studies: a Relational Approach to the Study of Religion," 17. Leirvik draws on Cheetham, "The University and Interfaith Education."

65. Dunbar, 462; (cited by Leirvik, "Interreligious Studies: a Relational Approach to the Study of Religion," 16.

entails immersing into the situations themselves in order to collect data, experience, and to realize one's subjective agency therein.

The brief example above of doing theology interreligiously proposed a view of God and world that entails, with Black Elk, that all things are sacred, with Rambachan's *Advaita* tradition, that the God-world relationship inherently calls for attention to, and care of, world; with Heschel, that God suffers in solidarity with the world; and with a panentheistic pansacramental view, that all things (including suffering) serve as potential representations of the divine in the world. What might this mean for the non-theologian (or the theologian working beyond the confines of theology, for that matter)? There is the obvious implication, articulated already by Rambachan, of the mandate to tend to and care for a changing planet. Doing so, fosters the mutually aligned interests of God, world, and persons by promoting the healing of a suffering planet and suffering persons. This ethic can be facilitated well by either a panentheistic or pansacramental view that posits the world as part of or in God in some manner (even if God is understood to be "more than" or transcendent of the world). The hope here is that this construct can provide a non-threatening alternative narrative of the presupposition (the quote from Murphy above[66]) for those to embrace the tending to the planet since a changing planet entails a changing God. More accurately, a changing and suffering God (a God of pathos) entails a changing and suffering planet; and tending to one entails tending to the other. This is not to lose sight of an appropriate emphasis on the healing of human suffering. The conversation on environmental justice issues can sometimes radically separate humans from the world and relegate human suffering to a separate and distinct phenomenon apart from the planet's suffering. The view offered here wraps them together in a mutually interdependent manner. Clearly, the mandate for environmental stewardship cannot neglect the care of the human condition and basic needs of communities on the planet. Rather, this view situates human persons within, or perhaps at the center of, environmental stewardship since what is good for the world is good for humans in the long term.

This brief worldview proposed on the heels of doing theology interreligiously above necessarily requires the knowledge, wisdom, and practice of non-theological disciplines. Religious studies may provide the religious resources to generate a constructive theological proposal for understanding the divine-world-person relationship as panentheistic and/or

---

66. "If we view ourselves as one with the cosmos in our beginnings and our essential aims, we will be less inclined to war and world-weariness than we are if we see the world as fundamentally hostile or illusory . . . [panentheism] may well provide a conceptual gathering place for the global village" (Murphy, "The Emergence of Evolutionary Panentheism," 180–81).

pansacramental, but other disciplines must be involved in order to properly and intelligently implement the mutual care of world, God, and person. Concerning issues stemming from the reality of a changing planet, (e.g., land, communities, climates, cultures), the immense complexity is readily apparent. In order to understand intricate relations, tensions, and histories between and among traditions, cultures, nations, value-systems, ecologies, geopolitical relations, economic dynamics, and so forth, the necessity of the many academic research disciplines remains essential. However, the approaches to understanding the various dynamics (interreligious or otherwise) that might exist on a changing planet can be shaped in particular manners with an adopted pansacramental worldview (articulated any number of ways). In other words, with the view that God, world, and person are interdependent and share, between and among them, mutually aligned interests, clarity might be brought to how we ought to practically act as involved agents in our approach to one, two, or all three.

Going Forward

Though this book traverses significant philosophical and theological terrain, there remains more territory for further exploration. Perhaps most interesting is the seemingly infinite number of possible case studies on the philosophical function of pansacramental spirituality in the world. Part II included three such cases with in chapter 8 on Thomas Merton and the sacramental function of place, chapter 9 on Nichols Black Elk's Lakota-Catholic spirituality, and chapter 10 on the sacramental spirituality in the literature of Dostoevsky and Wendell Berry. It is in these cases of applied pansacramental philosophy that some of the most interesting and concrete work surfaces. Further, as hinted at in the chapter 9 on Black Elk, they can often provide fertile soil from which constructive interreligious learning can spring. The focus of this book, and these particular case studies, centered on the role of the philosophic functionality of pansacramental mediation, however this, of course, need not be the central thrust behind such examinations of spiritual experience in the world.

More work can be done at the level of theory with an examination of the further implications that pansacramentalism yields. For instance, this book has already provided some degree of measure for establishing a criterion and mode of discerning genuine sacramental symbols as authentic representations of the divine in the world. However, this perhaps could be expanded to include a set of systematically organized, yet intentionally flexible and non-rigid, criteria. Based on the philosophy of pansacramental mediation proposed in chapter 11, this final chapter has offered several constructive proposals for engaging religious pluralism. These include a vision of panentheistic pansacramentalism (drawing on the metaphors of the artist-art and mother-child relationships) as a model for the God-world relationship, the beginning of a pansacramental theology of religious pluralism, and an example of doing theology interreligiously. These are only a beginning and each is deserving of a text devoted to itself alone.

In proposing a panentheistic pansacramentalism, pansacramental theology of religious pluralism, a method of doing theology interreligiously, and especially in entertaining the theology of divine pathos (e.g., Heschel and Moltmann), classical orthodox Christian claims concerning the attributes of God can come under fire. It may be that such proposals need not negate these classical claims. There may be a manner in which a theology of pansacramental mediation might accommodate the affirmation of these various classical divine attributes, however the challenge of the problem of suffering and theodicy remain. These challenges do not entirely disappear regardless of one's affirmation or denial of classical divine attributes. In any case, there is a constructive lesson in this: the continual reminder of the fragility of life and the need to humbly reduce the human quest to the alleged[67] Socratic creed "ἓν οἶδα ὅτι οὐδὲν οἶδα" ("I know that I do not know)." With such a guiding creed, perhaps as true philosophers we can rest in the blessed ignorance of "wonder" (αῦμα).[68]

Resting in wonder can open the horizon to finding that "medicine in the water" that Danny spoke of in the opening chapter, whether it be literally, metaphorically, sacramentally or a combination thereof. Wonder opens the horizon to finding the divine in all things and, as this book has suggested, finding all things in the divine. In this way, I am in wholehearted agreement with David Brown who writes, "one way to recover enchantment and so a holistic view of how God relates to human experience in its totality is through a reinvigorated sense of the sacramental."[69] Through a philosophy of pansacramental functionality, one can both engage the theology of his own tradition and share symbols, spiritual experience, and theological concepts with other faith traditions. When we strive to engage our own theol-

---

67. It is disputed whether this claim can be rightly attributed to Socrates since it does not appear in Plato's Socrates.

68. Plato, *Theaeteus*, 155d.

69. Brown, *God and Enchantment of Place*, 5.

ogy (or lack therof), as well as the theology of another, through particular lived religious experience (spirituality). The process, as advocated for in this book, can occur through symbols, narratives, and experiences, both our own and shared. The situating of particular lived religious experience within the context of universal theological claims, from a Christian perspective, can proceed via sacramental and religious symbols, especially if all things (including other religions, suffering, etc.) can function as authentic religious symbols). This is to say that one can appreciate and find the symbolic significance of the "the medicine in the water" as taught by the spirituality of her Ojibwa neighbor, and seek to correlate it with the theology of her own tradition. This carries out the task of pansacramental spirituality and the doing theology interreligiously *par excellence*.

By retaining sacramental and symbolic language and categories, with an eye to their philosophical functionality and openness to the pansacramental vision, this book has suggested a vision of the relationship between theology, spirituality, and the study of spirituality. To be sure, there remains plenty of work to be done to further integrate these horizons and constructively apply them to particular lived religious experience. Far from daunting and overwhelming, this prospect can be enlivening, liberating, and exciting. This is the ongoing task I charge others and myself with going forward.

Bibliography

Albert, Samantha. "I'll Have That to Stay Please—Swedish Coffee Culture." Visit Sweden. Accessed January 3, 2014. http://www.visitsweden.com/sweden/Featured/Sweden-Beyond/Food/Ill-Have-That-To-Stay-Please—Swedish-Coffee-Culture.
Alexander, Jon. "What Do Recent Writers Mean by Spirituality?" *Spirituality Today* 32 (1980) 247–56.
Allen, Diogenes. "The Restoration of Sacramentality in a Post-Modern World." *Reformed Liturgy and Music* 19.2 (1985) 85–88.
American Academy of Religion. "Interreligious and Interfaith Studies Group." https://papers.aarweb.org/content/interreligious-and-interfaith-studies-group.
[Anonymous] Monk of the Eastern Church. "The Essentials of Orthodox Spirituality." In *Exploring Christian Spirituality: An Ecumenical Reader*, edited by Kenneth J. Collins, 108–21. Grand Rapids: Baker, 2000.
Archambault, Marie Therese. *A Retreat with Black Elk: Living in the Sacred Hoop*. Cincinnati: St. Anthony Messenger, 1998.
Arnold, Philip P. "Black Elk and Book Culture." *Journal of the American Academy of Religion* 67 (1999) 85–111.
Arweck, Elisabeth, and William J. F. Keenan. "Introduction: Material Varieties of Religious Expression." *Materializing Religion: Expression, Performance and Ritual*, edited by Elisabeth Arweck and William J.F. Keenan, 1–20 Aldershot, UK: Ashgate, 2006.
Ashley, J. Matthew. "The Turn to Spirituality? The Relationship between Theology and Spirituality." *Christian Spirituality Bulletin* 3.2 (1995) 13–18.
Association of Theological Schools. "Commission Accrediting Degree Program Standards Handbook." In *Association of Theological Schools, The Commission on Accrediting*, approved June, 2012; posted January 21, 2015. http://www.ats.edu/uploads/accrediting/documents/degree-program-standards.pdf.
Augustine. *Confessions*. Translated by Henry Chadwick. Oxford: Oxford University Press, 2008.
———. *De Civitate Dei*.
———. *On Christian Teaching*. Translated by R. P. H. Green. Oxford: Oxford University Press, 2008.
Barron, Robert E. *And Now I See—: A Theology of Transformation*. New York: Crossroad, 1998.
Bechte, Regina. "Theological Trends: Convergences in Theology and Spirituality." *The Way* 25 (1985) 305–14.

Berling, Judith A. "Christian Spirituality: Intrinsically Interdisciplinary." In *Exploring Christian Spirituality: Essays in Honor of Sandra M. Schneiders*, edited by Bruce H. Lescher and Elizabeth Liebert, 35–52. New York: Paulist, 2006.

Berry, Wendell. *Jayber Crow*. Berkeley: Counter Point, 2000.

———. *A Place on Earth*. Washington, DC: Counterpoint, 1999.

———. *Remembering*. San Francisco: North Point, 1988.

Black Elk. "Foreword." In *The Sacred Pipe: Black Elk's Account of the Seven Rites of the Oglala Sioux*. Edited by Joseph Epes Brown. Norman: University of Oklahoma Press, 1953, 1989.

———. "Gift of the Sacred Pipe." In *The Sacred Pipe: Black Elk's Account of the Seven Rites of the Oglala Sioux*, edited by Joseph Epes. Brown. Norman: University of Oklahoma Press, 1989.

Black Elk, and John Gneisenau Neihardt. *Black Elk Speaks: Being the Life Story of a Holy Man of the Oglala Sioux*. Illustrated by Standing Bear. Lincoln: University of Nebraska Press, 2000.

Boeve, Lieven. "Theology in a Postmodern Context and the Hermeneutical Project of Louis-Marie Chauvet." In *Sacraments: Revelation of the Humanity of God: Engaging the Fundamental Theology of Louis-Marie Chauvet*, edited by Philippe Bordeyne and Bruce Morrill. Collegeville, MN: Liturgical, 2008.

Boeve, Lieven, and Lambert Leijssen, eds. *Sacramental Presence in a Postmodern Context*. Bibliotheca Ephemeridum theologicarum Lovaniensium 160. Leuven: Leuven University Press, 2001.

Borg, Marcus J. *Meeting Jesus Again for the First Time: The Historical Jesus & the Heart of Contemporary Faith*. San Francisco: HarperSanFrancisco, 1994.

Borg, Marcus J., and N. T. Wright. *The Meaning of Jesus: Two Visions*. San Francisco: HarperSanFrancisco, 2007.

Boyarin, Daniel. *A Radical Jew: Paul and the Politics of Identity*. Berkeley: University of California, 1994.

Breton, Jean Claude. "Retrouver les Assises Anthropologiques de la Vie Spirituelle." *Sciences Religieuses* 17 (1988) 97–105.

Brierley, Michael W. "Naming a Quiet Revolution: The Panentheistic Turn in Modern Theology." In *In Whom We Live and Move and Have Our Being: Panentheistic Reflections on God's Presence in a Scientific World*, edited by Philip Clayton and Arthur Peacocke, 1–15. Grand Rapids: Eerdmans, 2004.

Brown, David. *God and Enchantment of Place: Reclaiming Human Experience*. Oxford: Oxford University Press, 2006.

Brown, Joseph Epes. "Letter to Father Gall." November 12. Scourmont Abbey, Belgium, 1947.

Buber, Martin. *Between Man and Man*. Translated by Ronald Gregor Smith. New York: Macmillan, 1948.

———. "Symbolic and Sacramental Existence." In *The Origin and Meaning of Hasidism*. Translated by Maurice Friedman. New York: Harper & Row, 1966.

Chauvet, Louis Marie. *The Sacraments: The Word of God at the Mercy of the Body*. Collegeville, MN: Liturgical, 2001.

———. *Symbol and Sacrament: A Sacramental Reinterpretation of Christian Existence*. Translated by Patrick Madigan and M. Beaumont. Collegeville, MN: Liturgical, 1995.

Cheetham, David. "The University and Interfaith Education." *Studies in Interreligious Dialogue.* 15.1 (2005) 16–35.

Chenu, Marie-Dominique. *Nature, Man, and Society in the Twelfth Century: Essays on the New Theological Perspectives in the Latin West.* Chicago: University of Chicago Press, 1968.

———. *Toward Understanding Saint Thomas.* Chicago: University of Chicago Press, 1963.

Cherbonnier, Edmond La B. "Heschel as a Religious Thinker." *Conservative Judaism* 23 (1968) 25–39.

Cherkasova, Evgenia V. "The Ambiguity of Suffering: Dostoevsky and the Russian Orthodox Tradition." In *Mother Tongue Theologies: Poets, Novelists, Non-Western Christianity,* edited by Darren J. Middleton, 3–15. Eugene, OR: Pickwick Publications, 2009.

Childs, Brevard S. *Memory and Tradition in Israel.* Studies in Biblical Theology 1/37. London: SCM, 1962.

Clayton, Philip. "Panentheism Today: A Constructive Systematic Evaluation." In *In Whom We Live and Move and Have Our Being: Panentheistic Reflections on God's Presence in a Scientific World,* edited by Philip Clayton and Arthur Peacocke, 249–64. Grand Rapids: Eerdmans, 2004.

———. "The Panentheistic Turn in Christian Theology." *Dialog* 38 (1999) 289–93.

Clayton, Philip, and Arthur Peacocke, eds. *In Whom We Live and Move and Have Our Being: Panentheistic Reflections on God's Presence in a Scientific World.* Grand Rapids: Eerdmans, 2004.

Clifford, Anne M. "Re-membering the Spiritual Core of Theology: A Response." *Christian Spirituality Bulletin* 3.2 (1995) 6–21.

Clooney, Francis X. *Comparative Theology: Deep Learning across Religious Borders.* Malden, MA: Wiley-Blackwell, 2010.

Connolly, Julian W. "Dostoevskij's Guide to Spiritual Epiphany." *Studies in East European Thought* 59 (2007) 39–54

Cooper, John W. *Panentheism, the Other God of the Philosophers: From Plato to the Present.* Grand Rapids: Baker Academic, 2006.

Cornille, Catherine. "Conditions for Inter-Religious Dialogue." In *The Wiley-Blackwell Companion to Inter-Religious Dialogue,* edited by Catherine Cornille, 20–33. Hoboken, NJ: Wiley-Blackwell, 2013.

———. ed. *Criteria of Discernment in Interreligious Dialogue.* Eugene, OR: Cascade Books, 2009.

———. *The Im-Possibility of Interreligious Dialogue.* New York: Crossroad, 2008.

———. "Introduction." In *Many Mansions?: Multiple Religious Belonging and Christian Identity,* edited by Catherine Cornille, 1–6. 2002. Reprinted, Eugene, OR: Wipf & Stock, 2010.

———. ed. *Many Mansions?: Multiple Religious Belonging and Christian Identity.* 2002. Reprinted, Eugene, OR: Wipf & Stock, 2010.

Costello, Damian. *Black Elk: Colonialism and Lakota Catholicism.* Faith and Culture Series. Maryknoll, NY: Orbis, 2005.

Cross, Frank Leslie, and Elizabeth Anne. Livingstone, eds. *The Oxford Dictionary of the Christian Church.* London: Oxford University Press, 1984.

Crowley, Paul. "The Crisis of Transcendence and the Task of Theology." In *Finding God in All Things: Essays in Honor of Michael J. Buckley*, edited by Michael J. Himes and Stephen J. Pope, 197-214. New York: Crossroad, 1996.

Culp, John. "Panentheism." In *Stanford Encyclopedia of Philosophy*. May 19, 2009. http://plato.stanford.edu/entries/panentheism/.

Cunningham, David S. "'The Brothers Karamazov' as Trinitarian Theology." In *Dostoevsky and the Christian Tradition*, edited by G. Pattinson and D. O. Thompson, 134-55. Cambridge Studies in Christian Literature. Cambridge: Cambridge University Press, 2001.

Cunningham, Lawrence S. *Thomas Merton and the Monastic Vision*. Grand Rapids: Eerdmans, 1999.

Cyril of Alexandria. *Second Epistle to Nestorius*.

Davies, Brian. *The Thought of Thomas Aquinas*. Oxford: Clarendon, 1992.

DeMallie, Raymond J., ed. *The Sixth Grandfather: Black Elk's Teachings Given to John G. Neihardt*. Lincoln: University of Nebraska Press, 1984.

Dostoyevsky, Fyodor. *The Brothers Karamazov*. Translated by Richard Pevear and Larissa Volokhonsky. New York: Farrar, Straus & Giroux, 1990.

———. "Letter to editor Nikolai Lyubimov." August 1879.

Dunbar, David Scott. "The Place of Interreligious Dialogue in the Academic Study of Religion." *Journal of Ecumenical Studies* 35 (1998) 455-70.

Dupuis, Jacques. "Christianity and Religions: Complementarity and Convergence." In *Many Mansions? Multiple Religious Belonging and Christian Identity*, edited by Catherine Cornille, 61-75. 2002. Reprinted, Eugene, OR: Wipf & Stock, 2010.

———. *Toward a Christian Theology of Religious Pluralism*. Maryknoll, NY: Orbis, 1997.

Dwyer, John C. "The Implications of Tillich's Theology of the Cross for Catholic Theology." In *Paul Tillich: A New Catholic Assessment*, edited by Raymond F. Bulman and Frederick J. Parrella. Collegeville, MN: Liturgical, 1994.

Eck, Diana L. "Prospects for Pluralism: Voice and Vision in the Study of Religion." *Journal of the American Academy of Religion* 75 (2007) 743-76.

———. "What Is Pluralism?" The Pluralism Project at Harvard University. http://www.pluralism.org/pluralism/what_is_pluralism.

Edwards, Denis. "A Relational and Evolving Universe: Unfolding within the Dynamism of the Divine Communion." In *In Whom We Live and Move and Have Our Being: Panentheistic Reflections on God's Presence in a Scientific World*, edited by Philip Clayton and Arthur Peacocke, 199-210. Grand Rapids: Eerdmans, 2004.

Egan, Keith J. "The Divorce of Spirituality from Theology." In *Theological Education in the Catholic Tradition: Contemporary Challenges*, edited by Patrick W. Carey and Earl C. Muller, 296-307. New York: Crossroad, 1997.

Eliade, Mircea. *No Souvenirs: Journal, 1957-1969*. New York: Harper & Row, 1977.

———. *The Sacred and the Profane: The Nature of Religion*. Translated by Willard R. Trask. San Diego: Harcourt Brace Jovanovich, 1987.

Endean, Philip. "Introduction." In *Karl Rahner: Spiritual Writings*, edited by Philip Endean. Modern Spiritual Masters Series. Maryknoll, NY: Orbis, 2004.

Evans, Charles Stephen. *Kierkegaard's "Fragments" and "Postscript": The Religious Philosophy of Johannes Climacus*. Atlantic Highlands, NJ: Humanities, 1983.

Feldmeier, Peter. "Comparing the Non-Objectifying Aim of Zen to Christian Apophatic Mysticism." Paper presented at the Upper Midwest Regional Meeting of the American Academy of Religion, Luther Seminary, St. Paul, MN, April 1, 2011.

First Anglican/Roman Catholic International Commission, Eucharistic Doctrine—Elucidation. [Information Service 49 (1982/II-III), Pp. 79–82; The Final Report (London: CTS/SPCK, 1982), Pp. 17–25]. doi:http://www.vatican.va/roman_curia/pontifical_councils/chrstuni/angl-comm-docs/rc_pc_chrstuni_doc_1979_eucharistic-elucidation_en.html.

Fletcher, Frank. "Towards a Contemporary Australian Retrieval of Sacral Imagination and Sacramentality." *Pacifica* 13 (February 2000) 1–10.

Flood, Gavin. *Beyond Phenomenology: Rethinking the Study of Religion*. London: Cassell, 1999.

Forster, Michael. "Hegel's Dialectical Method." In *The Cambridge Companion to Hegel*, edited by Frederick C. Beiser. Cambridge: Cambridge University Press, 1993.

Fox, Matthew. *The Coming of the Cosmic Christ: The Healing of Mother Earth and the Birth of a Global Renaissance*. San Francisco: HarperSanFrancisco, 1988.

———. *Creativity: Where the Divine and the Human Meet*. New York: Putnam, 2002.

———. *A New Reformation: Creation Spirituality and the Transformation of Christianity*. Rochester, VT: Inner Traditions, 2006.

———. *Sheer Joy: Conversations with Thomas Aquinas on Creation Spirituality*. New York: Putnam, 2003.

Fredericks, James. "At the Limits: Raimundo Panikkar's Long Theological Journey." *Commonweal*, November 19, 2010.

———. *Faith among Faiths: Christian Theology and Non-Christian Religions*. New York: Paulist, 1999.

García-Rivera, Alejandro. "Interfaith Aesthetics: Where Theology and Spirituality Meet." In *Exploring Christian Spirituality: Essays in Honor of Sandra M. Schneiders*, edited by Bruce H. Lescher and Elizabeth Liebert, 178–95. New York: Paulist, 2006.

Gavrilyuk, Paul L. *The Suffering of the Impassible God: The Dialectics of Patristic Thought*. The Oxford Early Christian Studies. Oxford: Oxford University Press, 2004.

Gilkey, Langdon. *Gilkey on Tillich*. New York: Crossroad, 1990.

Gilson, Etienne. *The Christian Philosophy of St. Thomas Aquinas*. Compiled by Ignatius Theodore Eschmann. Translated by Laurence K. Shook. Notre Dame, IN: University of Notre Dame Press, 1994.

Goetz, Ronald. "The Suffering of God: The Rise of a New Orthodoxy." *The Christian Century* 103.13 (1986) 385–89.

Gregersen, Niels Henrik. "Three Varieties of Panentheism." In *In Whom We Live and Move and Have Our Being: Panentheistic Reflections on God's Presence in a Scientific World*, edited by Philip Clayton and Arthur Peacocke, 19–35. Grand Rapids: Eerdmans, 2004.

Griffiths, Bede. *Bede Griffiths: Essential Writings*. Edited by Thomas Matus. Maryknoll, NY: Orbis, 2004.

Gustafson, Hans. "The Awe-Filledness of Awfulness: Experiencing God in Suffering " Plenary paper presented at *Wondrous Fear and Holy Awe*: A Meeting of the Society for the Study of Christian Spirituality, University of Notre Dame, South Bend, IN, July 2, 2013.

———."Collapsing the Sacred and the Profane: Pan-Sacramental and Panentheistic Possibilities in Aquinas and Their Implications for Spirituality." *The Heythrop Journal* 52 (2011). doi:10.1111/j.1468-2265.2011.00684.x.

———. "Descandalizing Multiple Religious Identity with Help from Nicholas Black Elk and His Spirituality: An Exercise in Interreligious Learning." *Journal of Ecumenical Studies* 51.1 (2016).

———. "Encountering the Painful Past in the Present: A 'Cloudy Spirituality' of Remembering the US-Dakota War of 1862." *StateofFormation.com*. Oct. 1, 2012.

———. "Interreligious and Interfaith Studies in Relation to Religious Studies and Theological Studies." *StateofFormation.com*. January 6, 2015.

———. "Interreligious Panentheistic Approaches to a Changing Planet in Comparative Theology and Interfaith Studies." Paper presented at the annual convention of the College Theology Society, University of Portland, Portland, OR, May 28–31, 2015.

———. "Luther and Loyola in Context: Spirituality, Saintliness and Divine Communication." Paper presented at the Upper Midwest Regional Meeting of the American Academy of Religion, Luther Seminary, St. Paul, MN, April 13–14, 2007.

———. "Multiple Religious Belonging and Interfaith Panentheistic Spirituality in the Liberal Theology of Nicholas Black Elk." Paper presented at the annual meeting of the American Academy of Religion, Chicago, Illinois, Nov. 17–20, 2012.

———. "Pansacramentality as a New Model for the God-World Relationship in Panentheism." Paper presented at the Upper Midwest Regional Meeting of the American Academy of Religion, Luther Seminary, St. Paul, Minnesota, April 6, 2013.

———. "Place and Selfhood in the Later Years." Paper presented at the 12th General Meeting and Conference of the International Thomas Merton Society, Loyola University, Chicago, IL, June 9–12, 2011.

———. "Place, Spiritual Anthropology, and Sacramentality in Merton's Later Years." In *The Merton Annual: Studies in Culture, Spirituality, and Social Concerns, Volume 25*, edited by David Belcastro and Joseph Raab, 74–90. Louisville: Fons Vitae, 2013.

———. "Revisiting the Multiple Religious Belonging of Nicholas Black Elk in the Context of the Catholic Sacramental Imagination." Paper presented at the annual meeting of the American Academy of Religion, Baltimore, MD, Nov. 23–26, 2013.

———. "Sacramental Caution and Finding God in All things: Sacramentality and Spirituality in Luther and Loyola." Paper presented at the 59th annual meeting of the Renaissance Society of America, San Diego, CA, April 5, 2013.

———. "Sacramentality as a Philosophical Model of Mediation and Reconciliation: with an Emphasis on Christian Theology and Spirituality." Paper presented at annual Moberg Conference on Sociological Perspectives on Reconciliation, Bethel University, St. Paul, MN, February 22–23, 2013.

———. "Sacramental Mediation between Theology and Spirituality." In *Spirituality in the 21st Century: Explorations*, edited by John L. Hochmeier and William S. Schmidt, 63–82. Oxford: Inter-Disciplinary Press, 2013.

———. "Sacramental Mediation between Theology and Spirituality." In S*pirituality: Theory, Praxis and Pedagogy*, edited by Martin Fowler, John D. Martin III, and John L. Hochmeier, 341–48. Oxford: Inter-Disciplinary Press, 2012.

———. "Sacramental Mediation between Theology & the Contemporary Study of Spirituality." Paper presented at the First Global Conference on Spirituality in

the 21st Century: At the Interface of Theory, Praxis and Pedagogy, Prague, Czech Republic, March 20–22, 2011.
———. "Sacramental Spirituality in *The Brothers Karamazov* and Wendell Berry's Port William Characters." *Literature and Theology* 27 (2013) 345–63.
———. "Substance beyond Illusion: The Spirituality of Bede Griffiths." *The Way* 47.3 (2008) 31–48.
———. "What a Christians might learn about Sacramentality from the Spirituality of Nicholas Black Elk?" Paper presented at the annual convention of the Catholic Theological Society of America, St. Louis, MO, June 7–10, 2012.
Hartshorne, Charles. *The Divine Relativity: A Social Conception of God*. New Haven: Yale University Press, 1948.
Hegel, Georg Wilhelm Friedrich. *Lectures on the Philosophy of Religion*, edited by Peter C. Hodgson. Translated by R. F. Brown, P. C. Hodgson, J. M. Stewart, and H. S. Harris. Berkeley: University of California Press, 1984.
———. *Phenomenology of Spirit*. Translated by Arnold Vincent. Miller. Oxford: Oxford University Press, 1977.
———. "Philosophical Propadeutics." In *Hegel Selections*, edited by J. Loewenberg, translated by W. T. Harris. New York: Scribner, 1929.
———. *The Philosophy of Right*. Oxford: Oxford University Press, 1976.
Heschel, Abraham Joshua. *Man Is Not Alone: A Philosophy of Religion*. New York: Farrar, Straus & Young, 1951.
———. *The Prophets*. New York: Perennial Classics, 2001.
Himes, Michael J. *Doing the Truth in Love: Conversations about God, Relationships, and Service*. New York: Paulist, 1995.
———. "'Finding God in All Things': A Sacramental Worldview and Its Effects." In *As Leaven in the World: Catholic Perspectives on Faith, Vocation, and the Intellectual Life*, edited by Thomas M. Landy. Franklin, WI: Sheed & Ward, 2001.
———. "The Last Lecture Series." Public lecture given at Boston College, Chestnut Hill, MA, November 18, 2008 [online Video Retrieved Nov. 5th, 2010, http://frontrow.bc.edu/program/himes2/.
———. "Theology Lecture." Lecture given at Boston College, Chestnut Hill, MA, January 14, 2002.
Hoffman, Bengt. "Lutheran Spirituality." In *Exploring Christian Spirituality: An Ecumenical Reader*, edited by Kenneth J. Collins. Grand Rapids Mich.: Baker, 2001.
Holler, Clyde. "Black Elk's Relationship to Christianity." *American Indian Quarterly* 8 (1984) 37–49.
———. "Lakota Religion and Tragedy: The Theology of Black Elk Speaks." *Journal of the American Academy of Religion* 52 (1984) 19–45.
Hoppál, Bulcsú Kál. "Karl Rahner's Notion of Vorgriff." *Verbum* 6 (2004) 451–59.
Hugh, of St. Victor. *On the Sacraments of the Christian Faith*. 1951.
Hugh, of St. Victor, and Brother Charles Henry Buttimer. *Hugonis De Sancto Victore Didascalicion De Studio Legendi: A Critical Text*. Washington, DC: Catholic University of America Press, 1939.
Ignatius of Loyola. *Ignatius of Loyola: The Spiritual Exercises and Selected Works*. Edited by George E. Ganss. Classics of Western Spirituality. New York: Paulist, 1991.
Inge, William Ralph. *Christian Mysticism*. London: Methuen, 1948.
Isidore of Seville. *Etymologies*.

Jeanrond, Werner. "Belonging or Identity? Christian Faith in a Multi-Religious World." In *Many Mansions?: Multiple Religious Belonging and Christian Identity*, edited by Catherine Cornille, 106–20. 2002. Reprinted, Eugene, OR: Wipf & Stock, 2010.

John, of Damascus, Saint. *On the Divine Images: Three Apologies against Those Who Attack the Divine Images*. Translated by David Anderson. Crestwood, NY: St. Vladimir's Seminary Press, 1994.

Jones, Alan. "Spirituality and Theology." *Review for Religious* 32.2 (1980) 161–76.

Kärkkäinen, Veli-Matti. *An Introduction to the Theology of Religions: Biblical, Historical, and Contemporary Perspectives*. Downers Grove, IL: InterVarsity, 2003.

Kelly, Anne F. "To 'Reconstitute the World' the Sacramental Imagination and a Spirituality of Embodiment." In *Candles Are Still Burning: Directions in Sacrament and Spirituality*, edited by Mary Grey, Andree Heaton, and Danny Sullivan, 13–21. Collegeville, MN: Liturgical, 1995.

Kelly, Geffrey B. *Karl Rahner: Theologian of the Graced Search for Meaning*. Making of Modern Theology. Minneapolis: Fortress, 1992.

Kidwell, Clara Sue, Homer Noley, and George E. "Tink" Tinker. *A Native American Theology*. Maryknoll, NY: Orbis, 2001.

Kierkegaard, Søren. *Concluding Unscientific Postscript to the Philosophical Fragments*. Translated by Howard V. Hong and Edna H. Hong. Vol. 1. Kierkegaard's Writings 12. Princeton: Princeton University Press, 1992.

———. *The Sickness unto Death: A Christian Psychological Exposition for Upbuilding and Awakening*. Translated by Howard V. Hong and Edna H. Hong. Kierkegaard's Writings 19. Princeton: Princeton University Press, 1980.

King, Peter. "Peter Abelard." In *Stanford Encyclopedia of Philosophy*. August 4, 2004. http://plato.stanford.edu/entries/abelard/.

Klibansky, Raymond. *The Continuity of the Platonic Tradition: During the Middle Ages*. London: Warburg Institute, 1939.

Knight, Christopher C. *Wrestling with the Divine: Religion, Science, and Revelation*. Minneapolis: Fortress, 2001.

Knight, Mark. *An Introduction to Religion and Literature*. London: Continuum, 2009.

Knitter, Paul F. *Introducing Theologies of Religions*. Maryknoll, NY: Orbis, 2002.

Kreeft, Peter. "Aquinas and the Angels." Talk given, ChristiFideles, April 1999.

———. *I Surf, Therefore I Am: A Philosophy of Surfing*. South Bend, IN: St. Augustine's Press, 2008.

———. *An Ocean Full of Angels*. South Bend, IN: St. Augustine's Press, 2011.

———. *A Summa of the Summa: The Essential Philosophical Passages of St. Thomas Aquinas' Summa Theologica*. San Francisco: Ignatius, 1990.

———. *Three Philosophies of Life: Ecclesiastes—Life as Vanity, Job—Life as Suffering, Song of Songs—Life as Love*. San Francisco: Ignatius, 1989.

Lane, Belden C. "Writing in Spirituality as a Self-Implicating Act: Reflections on Authorial Disclosure and the Hiddenness of the Self." In *Exploring Christian Spirituality: Essays in Honor of Sandra M. Schneiders*, edited by Bruce H. Lescher and Elizabeth Liebert, 53–69. New York: Paulist, 2006.

Larson, Gerald James. "Contra Pluralism." In *The Intercultural Challenge of Raimon Panikkar*, edited by Joseph Prabhu. Maryknoll, NY: Orbis, 1996.

Leclercq, Jean. Introduction to *The Spirituality of Western Christendom*. Edited by E. Rozanne Elder. Cistercian Studies 30. Kalamazoo, MI: Cistercian, 1976.

———. "Spiritualitas." *Studi Medievali* 3 (1962) 279–96.

———. *The Love of Learning and the Desire for God: A Study of Monastic Culture.* Translated by Catharine Misrahi. New York: Fordham University Press, 1961.
Leirvik, Oddbjørn. "Interreligious Studies: A Relational Approach to the Study of Religion." *Journal of Inter-Religious Dialogue* 13 (2014).
———. *Interreligious Studies: A Relational Approach to Religious Activism and the Study of Religion.* London: Bloomsbury, 2014.
Léon-Dufour, Xavier. *Le Partage Du Pain Eucharistique Selon Le Nouveau Testament.* Paris: Seuil, 1982.
Lindbeck. George. A. *The Nature of Doctrine: Religion and Theology in a Postliberal Age.* Philadelphia: Westminster, 1984.
Lindberg, Carter. *The European Reformations.* Oxford: Blackwell, 1996.
Loades, Ann. "Sacramentality and Christian Spirituality." In *The Blackwell Companion to Christian Spirituality*, edited by Arthur G. Holder, 254–68. Oxford: Blackwell, 2005.
Lombard, Peter. *The Sentences.*
Lossky, Vladimir. *The Mystical Theology of the Eastern Church.* Cambridge: Cambridge University Press, 1996.
———. *Orthodox Theology: An Introduction.* Translated by Ianand Ihita Kesarcodi-Watson. Crestwood, NY: St. Vladimir's Seminary Press, 1978.
Louth, Andrew. *Discerning the Mystery.* Oxford: Clarendon, 1983.
Luther, Martin. "The Babylonian Captivity of the Church." In *Martin Luther's Basic Theological Writings*, edited by Timothy F. Lull and William R. Russell, 210–38. Minneapolis: Fortress, 2005.
———. "A Brief Instruction on What to Look for and Expect in the Gospels (1521)." In *Martin Luther's Basic Theological Writings*, edited by Timothy F. Lull and William R. Russell, 93–97. Minneapolis: Fortress, 2005.
———. "Lectures on Genesis 6–14." In *Luther's Works 2.* St. Louis: Concordia, 1970.
———. "Letter to Hans Luther, Wartburg, Nov. 21, 1521." In *Martin Luther's Basic Theological Writings*, edited by Timothy F. Lull and William R. Russell, 3–5. Minneapolis: Fortress, 2005.
———. *Luther's Works.* Vol. 37, 54, 57.
Lévi-Strauss, Claude. *Anthropologie Structurale.* Paris: Plon, 1958.
Martinez, David. "Review of Damien Costello, Black Elk: Colonialism and Lakota Catholicism." *Journal of the American Academy of Religion* 74 (2006) 1014–17.
Martos, Joseph. *Doors to the Sacred: A Historical Introduction to Sacraments in the Catholic Church.* Rev. ed. Liguori, MO: Liguori/Triumph, 2001.
McCluskley, Sally. "Black Elk Speaks: And so Does John Neihardt." *Western American Literature* 6 (1972) 231–42.
McGinn, Bernard. *The Growth of Mysticism.* New York: Crossroad, 1994.
———. "The Letter and the Spirit: Spirituality as an Academic Discipline." In *Minding the Spirit: The Study of Christian Spirituality*, edited by Elizabeth A. Dreyer and Mark S. Burrows, 25–41. Baltimore: Johns Hopkins University Press, 2005.
Merkle, John C. *Approaching God: The Way of Abraham Joshua Heschel.* Collegeville, MN: Liturgical, 2009.
———. "God's Love, Suffering, and Power." Paper presentation at a *Pursuit of Wisdom* gathering. Collegeville, MN: College of Saint Benedict/Saint John's University Oct. 24, 2014.

———. "Heschel's Monotheism vis-à-vis Pantheism and Panentheism." *Studies in Christian-Jewish Relations* 2.2 (2007) 26–33.
———. *The Genesis of Faith: The Depth Theology of Abraham Joshua Heschel.* New York: Macmillan, 1985.
Merton: A Film Biography. Directed by Paul Wilkes and Audrey Glenn. New York: First Run Features, The Merton Project 2004, 1984. DVD.
Merton, Thomas. *The Asian Journal of Thomas Merton.* New York: New Directions, 1973.
———. *Conjectures of a Guilty Bystander.* New York: Doubleday, 1966.
———. *The New Man.* New York: Farrar, Straus, & Cudahy, 1961.
———. *New Seeds of Contemplation.* Norfolk, CT: New Directions, 1972.
———. *The Other Side of the Mountain: The End of the Journey.* Edited by Patrick Hart. Vol. Seven 1967–1968. The Journals of Thomas Merton. San Francisco: HarperSanFrancisco, 1998.
Miller, Vincent J. "An Abyss at the Heart of Mediation: Louis-Marie Chauvet's Fundamental Theology of Sacramentality." *Horizons* 24 (1997) 230–47.
Min, Anselm Kyongsuk. "The Dialectic of God's Presence and Absence in the World." In *The Presence and Absence of God: Claremont Studies in the Philosophy of Religion, Conference 2008,* edited by Ingolf U. Dalferth, 109–28. Tübingen: Mohr Siebeck, 2009.
———. "Loving Without Understanding: Raimon Panikkar's Ontological Pluralism." *International Journal for Philosophy of Religion* 68.1–3 (2010).
———. *Paths to the Triune God: An Encounter between Aquinas and Recent Theologies.* Notre Dame, IN: University of Notre Dame Press, 2005.
———. *The Solidarity of Others in a Divided World: A Postmodern Theology after Postmodernism.* New York: T. & T. Clark, 2004.
Moffitt, John. "A Christian Approach to Hindu Beliefs." *Theological Studies* 27 (1966) 58–78.
Moltmann, Jürgen. *The Crucified God: The Cross of Christ as the Foundation and Criticism of Christian Theology.* Minneapolis: Fortress, 1993.
———. *The Trinity and the Kingdom: the Doctrine of God.* Minneapolis: Fortress, 1993.
Moore, Rebecca. "The Primacy of Faith in Hugh of St. Victor's Sacramental Theology." Paper presented at the 35th International Congress of Medieval Studies Kalamazoo, MI, May 6, 2000.
Morrill, Bruce T. "Building on Chauvet's Work: An Overview." In *Sacraments: Revelation of the Humanity of God: Engaging the Fundamental Theology of Louis-Marie Chauvet,* edited by Philippe Bordeyne and Bruce Morrill, xv–xxiv. Collegeville, MN: Liturgical, 2008.
Mounier, Emmanuel. *The Character of Man.* New York: Harper, 1956.
Mowinckel, Sigmund. *Psalmenstudien.* Amsterdam: Schippers, 1966.
Murphy, Michael. "The Emergence of Evolutionary Panentheism." In *Panentheism Across the World's Traditions,* edited by Loriliai Biernacki and Philip Clayton, 177–99. New York: Oxford University Press, 2013.
Neville, Robert C. *Creativity and God: A Challenge to Process Theology.* Albany: State University of New York Press, 1995.
New York Times (New York, NY). "The Messiah Craze Spreading." November 26, 1890.

Neihdardt, John G. *Black Elk Speaks: Being the Life Story of a Holy Man of the Oglala Sioux as told to John G. Neihardt (Flaming Rainbow)*, illustrated by Standing Bear. Lincoln: University of Nebraska Press, 2000.

Nouwen, Henri J. M. *The Return of the Prodigal Son: A Story of Homecoming*. New York: Doubleday, 1994.

O'Connor, June. "Sensuality, Spirituality, Sacramentality." *Union Seminary Quarterly Review* 40 (1985) 59–70.

Olson, Roger. "A Postconservative Evangelical Response to Panentheisms Old and New." Paper presented at the Upper Midwest Regional Meeting of the American Academy of Religion, Luther Seminary, St. Paul, MN, March 31, 2012.

Osborne, Kenan B. *Sacramental Theology: A General Introduction*. New York: Paulist Press, 1988.

———. "Tillich's Understanding of Symbols and Roman Catholic Sacramental Theology." In *Paul Tillich: A New Catholic Assessment*, edited by Raymond F. Bulman and Frederick J. Parrella. Collegeville, MN: Liturgical, 1994.

Peelman, Achiel. "Native American Spirituality and Christianity" In *The Wiley-Blackwell Companion to Inter-Religious Dialogue*, edited by. Catherine Cornille, 346–359. Hoboken, NJ: Wiley-Blackwell, 2013.

"Panentheism." In *The Oxford Dictionary of the Christian Church*, edited by F. L. Cross and E. A. Livingstone. *Oxford Reference Online*. Oxford University Press.

Panikkar, Raimundo. *The Intrareligious Dialogue*. New York, NY: Paulist, 1999.

———. *The Rhythm of Being: The Gifford Lectures*. Maryknoll, NY: Orbis, 2010.

Patel, Eboo. "Toward a Field of Interfaith Studies." *Liberal Education* 99.4 (Fall 2013).

Peacocke, Arthur. "Articulating God's Presence in and to the World Unveiled by the Sciences." In *In Whom We Live and Move and Have Our Being: Panentheistic Reflections on God's Presence in a Scientific World*, edited by Philip Clayton and Arthur Peacocke, 137–54. Grand Rapids: Eerdmans, 2004.

———. *God and the New Biology*. San Francisco: Harper & Row, 1987.

Peters, Jason. "Wendell Berry's Vindication of the Flesh." *Christianity and Literature* 56 (2007) 317–32.

Phan, Peter C. "Multiple Religious Belonging: Opportunities and Challenges for Theology and Church." *Theological Studies* 64 (2003) 495–519.

Plato. *Theaeteus. The Collected Dialogues of Plato, including the Letters*. Edited by Edith Hamilton and Huntington Cairns. Bollingen Series LXXI. Princeton: Princeton University Press, 1961

Polkinghorne, John. C. *The Faith of a Physicist: Reflections of a Bottom-up Thinker*. Princeton: Princeton University Press, 1994.

———. *The God of Hope and the End of the World*. New Haven: Yale University Press, 2002.

———. *Science and Creation: The Search for Understanding*. Philadelphia: Templeton Foundation Press, 2006.

———. *Science and Providence: God's Interaction with the World*. Philadelphia: Templeton Foundation Press, 2005.

———. *Science and the Trinity: The Christian Encounter with Reality*. New Haven: Yale University Press, 2004.

Pourrat, Pierre. *Christian Spirituality*. 4 vols. Translated by W. H. Mitchell and S. P. Jacques. Westminster, UK: Newman, 1953–55.

Prabhu, Joseph. *The Intercultural Challenge of Raimon Panikkar*. Maryknoll, NY: Orbis, 1996.
Principe, Walter. "Toward Defining Spirituality." *Sciences Religieuses* 12 (1983) 127–41.
"Prologue." In *The Story of Christian Spirituality: Two Thousand Years, from East to West*, edited by Gordon Mursell, 9–10. Minneapolis: Fortress, 2001.
Rahner, Karl. *The Church and the Sacraments*. Translated by W. J. O'Hara. New York: Herder & Herder, 1963.
———. "The Concept of Mystery in Catholic Theology." In *A Rahner Reader*, edited by Gerald A. McCool, 108–20. New York: Seabury, 1975.
———. *Foundations of Christian Faith: An Introduction to the Idea of Christianity*. New York: Crossroad, 1982.
———. *Kirche und Sakramente*. Freiburg: Herder, 1960.
———. *The Mystical Way in Everyday Life: Sermons, Prayers, and Essays*. Translated and edited by Annemarie S. Kidder. Maryknoll, NY: Orbis, 2010.
———. "The Mysticism of Loving All Things in the World according to Ignatius." In *The Mystical Way in Everyday Life: Sermons, Prayers, and Essays*, edited by Annemarie S. Kidder. Maryknoll, NY: Orbis, 2010.
———. *The Practice of Faith: A Handbook of Contemporary Spirituality*. New York: Crossroad, 1983.
———. "The Theology of Mysticism." In *The Practice of Faith: A Handbook of Contemporary Spirituality*, 70–77. New York: Crossroad, 1983.
———. "The Theology of the Symbol." In *Theological Investigations*, translated by Kevin Smyth. Vol. IV, *More Recent Writings*. Baltimore: Helicon, 1966.
———. "What Is a Sacrament?" In *Theological Investigations*. Translated by David Bourke. Vol. XIV, *Theology, Anthropology, Christology*. New York: Seabury, 1976.
Rambachan, Anantanand. *A Hindu Theology of Liberation: Not-Two Is Not One*. SUNY Series in Religious Studies. Albany: SUNY Press, 2015.
Renard, John. "Comparative Theology: Definition and Method." *Religious Studies and Theology* 17 (1998) 3–18.
Richter, Friedrich. *Martin Luther and Ignatius Loyola, Spokesmen for Two Worlds of Belief*. Westminster, MD: Newman, 1960.
Ricoeur, Paul. *Interpretation Theory: Discourse and the Surplus of Meaning*. Fort Worth: Texas Christian University Press, 1976.
———. *The Symbolism of Evil*. Translated by Emerson Buchanan. Boston: Beacon, 1967.
Rothschild, Fritz A. "Varieties of Heschelian Thought." In *Abraham Joshua Heschel: Exploring His Life and Thought*, edited by John C. Merkle. New York: Macmillan, 1985.
Sandoz, Mari. *Old Jules: A Bison Book*. Lincoln: University of Nebraska Press, 1985.
Sayers, Dorothy L. *Further Papers on Dante*. London: Methuen, 1957.
Schaab, Gloria L. *The Creative Suffering of the Triune God: An Evolutionary Theology*. New York: Oxford University Press, 2007.
Schelling, Friedrich. *The Ages of the World: (fragment) from the Handwritten Remains, Third Version (c. 1815)*. Translated by Jason M. Wirth. SUNY Series in Contemporary Continental Philosophy. Albany: SUNY Press, 2000.
———. *Of Human Freedom: A Translation of F.W.J. Schelling's Philosophische Untersuchungen über das Wesen der Menschlichen Freiheit und die Damit Zusammen-*

hängenden Gegenstände, with a Critical Introduction and Notes. Translated by James Gutmann. Chicago: Open Court, 1936.

———. *System of Transcendental Idealism*. Translated by Peter Heath. Charlottesville: University Press of Virginia, 1978.

———. *Über das Wesen der menschlichen Freiheit*. Stuttgart: Reclam, 1809.

Schneiders, Sandra M. "Approaches to the Study of Christian Spirituality." In *The Blackwell Companion to Christian Spirituality*, edited by Arthur G. Holder, 15-34. Malden, MA: Blackwell, 2005.

———. "The Discipline of Christian Spirituality and Catholic Theology." In *Exploring Christian Spirituality: Essays in Honor of Sandra M. Schneiders*, edited by Bruce H. Lescher and Elizabeth Liebert, 196–212. New York: Paulist, 2006.

———. "Religion vs. Spirituality: A Contemporary Conundrum." *Spiritus: A Journal of Christian Spirituality* 3 (2003) 163–85.

———. "Spirituality in the Academy." *Theological Studies* 50 (1989) 676–97.

———. "Spirituality in the Academy." In *Exploring Christian Spirituality: An Ecumenical Reader*, edited by Kenneth J. Collins, 249–69. Grand Rapids: Baker, 2000.

———. "Symbolism and the Sacramental Principle in the Fourth Gospel." In *Segni E Sacramenti Nel Vangelo Di Giovann*, edited by Puis-Ramon Tragan, 221–35. Rome: Anselmiana, 1977.

———. "Theology and Spirituality: Strangers, Rivals, or Partners?" *Horizons* 13 (1986) 253–74.

The Seventh Seal. Directed by Ingmar Bergman. Stockhold, Sweden: Svensk Filmindustri, 1957. DVD.

Sheldrake, Philip. *A Brief History of Spirituality*. Malden, MA: Blackwell, 2007.

———. "Human Identity and the Particularity of Place." *Spiritus: A Journal of Christian Spirituality* 1 (2001) 43–64.

———. "Some Continuing Questions: The Relationship between Spirituality and Theology." *Christian Spirituality Bulletin* 2.1 (1994) 15–17.

———. *Spirituality and History: Questions of Interpretation and Method*. 2nd ed. Maryknoll, NY: Orbis, 1998.

———. "Spirituality and Its Critical Methodology." In *Exploring Christian Spirituality: Essays in Honor of Sandra M. Schneiders*, edited by Bruce H. Lescher and Elizabeth Liebert, 15–34. New York: Paulist, 2006.

———. *Spirituality and Theology: Christian Living and the Doctrine of God*. Maryknoll, NY: Orbis, 1998.

Shults, F. LeRon. "Current Trends in Pneumatology." Paper presented at the Nordic Systematic Theology Conference: "Spirit and Spirituality," Denmark, Copenhagen, January 4–7, 2007.

———. *Reforming Theological Anthropology: After the Philosophical Turn to Relationality*. Grand Rapids: Eerdmans, 2003.

———. "Religious Symbolism at the Limits of Human Engagement." *Theology and Science* 8 (2010) 303–18.

———. "Spirit and Spirituality: Philosophical Trends in Late Modern Pneumatology." *Pneuma* 30 (2008) 271–87.

Smith, Wilfred Cantwell. "The Christian in a Religiously Plural World." In *Christianity and Other Religions: Selected Readings*, revised and edited by John Hick and Brian Hebblethwaite, 44–58. Oxford: Oneworld, 2001.

———. *Towards a World Theology: Faith and the Comparative History of Religion.* Library of Philosophy and Religion. Houndmills, UK: Macmillan, 1989.
Southern, R. W. *The Making of the Middle Ages.* New Haven: Yale University Press, 1953.
Steinmetz, D. C. "Luther and Loyola." *Interpretation* 47 (1993) 5–14.
Steinmetz, Paul B. *Pipe, Bible and Peyote among the Oglala Lakota: A Study in Religious Identity.* Stockholm Studies in Comparative Religion 19. Stockholm: Almqvist & Wiksell, 1980.
Steltenkamp, Michael F. *Black Elk: Holy Man of the Oglala.* Norman: University of Oklahoma Press, 1993.
———. *Nicholas Black Elk: Medicine Man, Missionary, Mystic.* Norman: University of Oklahoma Press, 2009.
Stolzman, William. *The Pipe and Christ.* Chamberlain, SD: Tipi, 1995.
Stover, Dale. "Eurocentrism and Native Americans." *Cross Currents* (1997) 390–97.
Sugirtharajah, R. S. *The Bible and the Third World: Precolonial, Colonial and Postcolonial Encounters.* Cambridge: Cambridge University Press, 2001.
Temple, William. *Nature, Man and God.* London: Macmillan, 1934.
Thatamanil, John. "We Are All Multiple: Identity and Conversion after 'Religion.'" Paper presented at the annual American Academy of Religion, Baltimore, MD, November 25, 2013.
Thomas, Aquinas, Saint. *Summa Contra Gentiles.*
———. *Summa Theologica.*
Thompson, Barkley. "Eschatological Moments in the Theology of Josiah Royce and the Novels of Wendell Berry." *Journal of Pastoral Theology* 15 (Spring 2005) 39–47.
Thurston, Bonnie. "'I Spoke Most of Prayer:' Thomas Merton on the West Coast (September 11–October 15, 1968)." *The Merton Seasonal* 35.3 (2010) 10–19.
Tickle, Phyllis. *Re-discovering the Sacred: Spirituality in America.* New York: Crossroad, 1995.
Tillich, Paul. *The Essential Tillich: An Anthology of the Writings of Paul Tillich.* Edited by F. Forrester Church. 1987. Reprinted, Chicago: University of Chicago Press, 1999.
———. "The Permanent Significance of the Catholic Church for Protestants." *Dialog* 1 (spring 1962).
———. "Religious Symbols and Our Knowledge of God." *Christian Scholar* (September 1955) 180–97. Reprinted in *The Essential Tillich*, 44–56.
———. *Systematic Theology.* Vol. 2, *Existence and the Christ.* Chicago: University of Chicago Press, 1975.
———. *Systematic Theology.* Vol. 3, *Life and the Spirit, History and the Kingdom of God.* Chicago: University of Chicago Press, 1976.
Tinker, George E. "Tink." *American Indian Liberation: A Theology of Sovereignty.* Maryknoll, NY: Orbis, 2008.
Urbach, Efraim Elimelech. *The Sages, Their Concepts and Beliefs.* Translated by Israel Abrahams. Cambridge: Harvard University Press, 1987.
Van Deusen, Nancy. "The Harp and the Soul: The Image of the Harp and Trecento Reception of Plato's Phaedo." In *The Harp and the Soul: Essays in Medieval Music*, edited by Nancy Van Deusen, 384–416. Studies in the History and Interpretation of Music 3. Lewiston, NY: Mellen, 1989.
Van Engen, John H., ed. *Devotio Moderna: Basic Writings.* New York: Paulist, 1988.

Van Rossum, Joost. "Deification in Palamas and Aquinas." *St. Vladimir's Theological Quarterly* 47.3-4 (2003) 365-82.
Vandenbroucke, Francois. "Le Divorce entre Théologie et Mystique: Ses Origines." *Nouvelle Revue Théologique* 72 (1950) 372-89.
Vogel, Dwight W., and Linda J. Vogel. "Sacramental Living: A Distinctive Spirituality." *Liturgical Ministry* 9 (2000) 219-24.
Vorgrimler, Herbert. *Sacramental Theology*. Translated by Linda Maloney. Collegeville, MN: Liturgical, 1992.
Ward, Keith. "Books." Keith Ward's Personal Website. http://www.keithward.org.uk/books-all/.
———. *Concepts of God: Images of the Divine in Five Religious Traditions*. Oxford: Oneworld, 1998.
———. *God and the Philosophers*. Minneapolis: Fortress, 2009.
———."The Importance of Liberal Theology." In *The Future of Liberal Theology*, edited by Mark D. Chapman. Aldershot, UK: Ashgate. 2002.
———. "Liberal Theology and the God of Love." In *The God of Love and Human Dignity: Essays in Honour of George M. Newlands*, edited by Paul Middleton, 191–202. London: T. & T. Clark. 2007.
———. *Religion and Community*. Oxford: Clarendon, 2000.
———. *Religion and Creation*. New York: Oxford University Press, 1996.
———. *Religion and Human Fulfilment*. London: SCM, 2008
———. *Religion and Human Nature*. New York: Oxford University Press, 1998
———. *Religion and Revelation: A Theology of Revelation in the World's Religions*. New York: Oxford University Press, 1994.
———."The World as the Body of God: A Panentheistic Metaphor." In *In Whom We Live and Move and Have Our Being: Panentheistic Reflections on God's Presence in a Scientific World*, edited by Philip Clayton and Arthur Peacocke, 62-72. Grand Rapids: Eerdmans, 2004.
Ware, Kallistos. "God Immanent Yet Transcendent: The Divine Energies according to Saint Gregory Palamas." In *In Whom We Live and Move and Have Our Being: Panentheistic Reflections on God's Presence in a Scientific World*, edited by Philip Clayton and Arthur Peacocke, 157-68. Grand Rapids: Eerdmans, 2004.
———. *The Orthodox Church*. London: Penguin, 1993.
Whitehead, Alfred North. *Process and Reality: An Essay in Cosmology*. New York: Macmillan Company, 1929.
Wiesel, Elie. *Night*. New York: Avon, 1969.
Williams, Rowan. *Dostoevsky: Language, Faith, and Fiction*. Waco, TX: Baylor University Press, 2011.
Wirzba, Norman. "The Dark Night of the Soil: An Agrarian Approach to Mystical Life. " In *Wendell Berry and Religion: Heaven's Earthly Life*, edited by Joel James. Shuman and L. Roger Owens, 148-69. Lexington: University Press of Kentucky, 2009.
Ziolkowski, Margaret. "Dostoevsky and the Kenotic Tradition." In *Dostoevsky and the Christian Tradition*, edited by George Pattinson and Diane Oenning Thompson, 31-40. Cambridge: Cambridge University Press, 2001.

Name Index

Abe, Masao, 247
Abelard, Peter, 27–28, 320
Albert, Samantha, 164
Alexander, Samuel, 247
Anne, Elizabeth, 315
Aquinas, Thomas, xiii, xv, 10, 27, 29–30, 45, 58, 65–68, 80–89, 106–12, 119, 130, 134, 233–34, 237–38, 249–51, 253, 271–73, 297, 316–17, 326–27
Archambault, Marie Therese, 158–60, 165, 168–69, 171, 313
Aristotle, xiv, 25–27, 30, 73–74, 112, 177, 191, 237, 246
Arnold, Philip P., 157, 171, 313
Arweck, Elisabeth, 234–35, 313
Ashley, Matthew, 45, 313
Augustine, xiii, 7, 45, 47, 58–64, 66, 86, 137, 152, 242–43, 271, 273, 313
Aumann, Jordan, 39

Balthasar, Hans Urs von, 39
Barbour, Ian, 247
Barron, Robert, 134
Barth, Karl, 273
Baur, Gustav Fechner, 247
Bechte, Regina, 31, 313
Bede Griffiths, 172, 213, 317, 319
Beiser, Frederick C., 317
Belcastro, David, 318
Berdyaev, Nicolai, 247, 265
Berger, Peter, 247
Bergman, Ingmar, 199, 325
Bergson, Henri, 247

Berling, Judith A., 21, 314
Bernard of Clairvaux, 27–28
Berry, Wendell, 124, 183–85, 197–202, 310, 314, 326–27
Biernacki, Loriliai, 322
Birch, Charles, 247
Black Elk, Nicholas, xiv, 124, 153–55, 157–82, 303–4, 306–7, 309–10, 313–15, 318–19, 321, 326
Boeve, Lieven 21, 113, 116, 314
Boff, Leonardo, 247
Böhme, Jakob, 247, 251, 253
Bonhoeffer, Dietrich, 273
Bordeyne, Philippe, 314, 322
Borg, Marcus, 172, 247, 267, 314
Boyarin, Daniel, 18, 314
Boyer, Louis, 38
Bracken, Joseph, 247–48
Breton, Jean Claude, 38–39, 314
Brierley, Michael W., 247, 249, 253, 257–58, 290, 314
Brown, David, 20, 311
Brown, Joseph Epes, 175, 314
Brunner, Emil, 273
Buber, Martin, 135, 167, 237, 239–41, 247, 271, 275–77, 282, 314
Buchanan, Emerson, 324
Buckley, Michael J., 316
Bulgakov, Sergei, 247
Bulman, Raymond F., 316, 323
Bultmann, Rudolf, 247
Buttimer, Charles Henry, 27

Caird, Edward, 247
Calvin, Jean, 262

NAME INDEX

Caravaggio, Michelangelo Merisi da, 134
Carey, Patrick W., 316
Case-Winters, Anna, 247
Chauvet, Louis-Marie, xiv, 17, 19, 22, 53, 68, 111–20, 314, 322
Cheetham, David, 308, 315
Chenu, Marie-Dominique, 29, 315
Cherbonnier, Edmond, 280, 315
Cherkasova, Evgenia, 189
Childs, Brevard 315
Clayton, Philip, 246–49, 252, 258, 260, 290, 314–17, 322–23, 327
Clifford, Anne, 6–7, 31, 315
Clinton, President Bill, 56
Clooney, Francis. X., 299–302, 315
Cobb, John B., 178, 236, 273
Collins, Kenneth J., 313, 319, 325
Cone, James, 247
Connolly, Julian W., 193
Cooper, John W., 246–49, 251–52, 254–55, 260–61, 266, 273, 282, 315
Cornille, Catherine, 156, 168, 173–74, 176, 296, 302, 315–16, 320, 323
Costello, Damien, 155, 160–64, 166–68, 173, 181–82, 315, 321
Crazy Horse, 155
Crossan, John Dominic, 267
Crowley, Paul, 21, 316
Cunningham, David S., 185, 316
Cunningham, Lawrence, 133, 316
Cusa, Nicholas, 247, 251, 266
Cyril of Alexandria 274–75, 316

Damascus, John, 105, 320
Dante, 27, 32, 266, 324
Davies, Brian, 29, 68, 87, 233, 272, 316
Deere, Phillip, 180
DeMallie, Raymond, 158–59, 162, 164, 166, 171, 316
Descartes, René, 237–38, 246
Dietrich Bonhoeffer, 134, 247
Dombrowski, Daniel, 247
Day, Dorothy, 134

Dostoevsky, Fyodor, 16, 17, 124, 183–86, 188–89, 191–97, 201–3, 310, 315–16, 327
Dreyer, Elizabeth A., 321
Dunbar, David Scott, 308, 316
Dupuis, Jacques, 173, 294, 298, 316
Dussel, Enrique, 305
Dwyer, John C. 78, 316
Dylan, Bob (Robert Zimmerman), 134

Eck, Diana L., 294, 302, 316
Eckhart, Meister, 247, 251, 266
Edwards, Denis, 248, 255, 316
Edwards, Jonathan, 247
Egan, Keith J., 6, 25, 30, 316
Einstein, Albert, 268
Eliade, Mircea 4, 137–38, 163, 316
Elliot, T.S., 33
Emerson, Ralph Waldo, 247
Endean, Philip, xiii, 6, 101, 316
Evans, Charles Stephen, 224, 316

Feldmeier, Peter, 195, 317
Fichte, Johann Gottlieb, 247
Fiddes, Paul, 247
Fletcher, Frank, 20, 317
Flood, Gavin, 40, 70, 317
Forster, Michael, 211, 317
Fox, Matthew, xv, 26, 29, 109, 247, 249, 266,-68, 317,
Francis de Sales, 13, 32
Francis of Assisi, 266
Fredericks, James, 235, 299, 317

Gadamer, Hans-Georg, 247
García-Rivera, Alejandro, 20, 317
Garrison, Jim, 247
Gavrilyuk, Pavel (Paul) L., 286, 317
Gilkey, Langdon, 75, 317
Gilson, Etienne, 85, 107, 250, 271, 317
Glenn, Audrey, 322
Goetz, Ronald, 274, 317
Gregersen, Niels Henrik, 107, 109, 247–48, 317
Griffin, David Ray, 247–48, 290
Griffiths, Bede, 172, 213–15, 317, 319
Groote, Gerard, 31

Gutiérrez, Gustavo, 247
Gutmann, James, 325

Hanson, Bradley, 6, 38
Harnack, Adolf von, 177
Hartshorne, Charles, 107, 247, 249, 252, 319
Hegel, Georg Wilhelm Friedrich, 101, 108, 208–10, 215, 235–38, 246–49, 252, 254–55, 290, 317, 319
Heidegger, Martin, 91, 112–13, 238, 247
Heim, Karl, 247
Heim, S. Mark, 178, 236
Heschel, Abraham Joshua, xv, 271, 274–76, 278–86, 291–92, 296, 303, 305–7, 309, 311, 319, 321–22, 324
Hick, John, 178, 236, 325
Hildegaard of Bingen, 266
Himes, Michael J., 16–17, 40, 42, 90, 100, 103, 105, 220, 228, 232, 316, 319
Hodgson, Peter, 247, 319
Hoffman, Bengt, 71, 319
Holder, Arthur G., 321, 325
Holler, Clyde, 160, 162, 167, 175, 319
Hong, Edna H. and Howard V., 320
Hosmer, Rachel, 39
Hugh of St. Victor, xiii, 27, 58, 63–65, 319, 322
Hume, David 237, 246

Ignatius of Loyola, 32, 38, 70, 72, 124–30, 317–20, 324
Inge, William Ralph, 247, 319
Isidore of Seville, xiii, 58, 62–63, 319

James, Gerald, 320
James, Joel, 327
James, William, 247, 261
Jeanrond, Werner, 176, 320
Jesus, 55–58, 78, 81–82, 94–100, 105–6, 124–25, 134, 184, 186, 188–89, 191–92, 239, 241, 258–59, 266–67
Jones, Alan, 27, 31, 320

Joyce, James, 134
Julian of Norwich, 7, 23, 247, 266

Kant, Immanuel, 113, 208, 237–38, 246
Kärkkäinen, Veli-Matti, 294, 320
Kelly, Anne F., 21, 320
Kelly, Geoffrey, xiii, 101, 320
Kidder, Annemarie S., 324
Kidwell, Clara Sue, 179–80, 320
Kierkegaard, Søren, 221–22, 224, 238, 293, 316, 320
Klibansky, Raymond, 10–11, 320
Knight, Christopher C., 99, 247–48, 258, 260, 289, 320
Knitter, Paul, 77, 178, 236, 320
Krause, Karl, 107, 247
Kreeft, Peter, 29, 83, 89–90, 134, 202–03, 233, 251, 253, 280, 320
Krieger, David, 178, 236
Küng, Hans, 178, 236, 247, 273

Lane, Belden 40, 320
Law, William, 13
Leclercq, Jean, 8, 25–26, 35, 320
Leech, Kenneth, 38
Leibniz, Gottfried Willhelm, 237, 246
Léon-Dufour, Xavier, 47–48, 321
Lequier, Jules, 247
Leirvik, Oddbjørn, 40, 305, 308, 321
Lescher, Bruce H., 314, 317, 320, 325
Levinas, Emmanuel, 238
Lévi-Strauss, Claude, 117–18, 128, 321
Lewinsky, Monica, 56
Liebert, Elizabeth, 314, 317, 320, 325
Lindbeck, George, 42–43, 321
Lindberg, Carter, 71, 321
Loades, Ann, 19–20, 321
Locke, John, 237, 246
Lombard, Peter, xiii, 58, 65–66, 227, 321
Lossky, Vladimir, 188–90, 196, 258, 321
Lotze, Hermann, 247
Louth, Andrew, 6, 25, 27, 30, 33–34, 109, 247–48, 265, 321
Lucy Looks Twice, 158, 160, 162

NAME INDEX

Lull, Timothy F., 321
Luther, Martin, xiii, 69–74, 77, 79, 124–25, 247, 262, 318, 321, 324

Macquarrie, John, 247, 290
Madigan, Patrick, 314
Maloney, Linda, 327
Marrowbone, Ben, 166
Martinez, David, 162–63, 182, 321
Martin III, John D., 318
Martos, Joseph, 54–58, 113–16, 321
Martyr, Justin, 45
McCluskley, Sally, 155, 321
McCool, Gerald A., 324
McDaniel, Jay, 290
McFague, Sallie, 247, 274, 290
McGinn, Bernard, xii, 6, 8, 25–30, 36, 39, 41, 321
Merkle, John C., 275–76, 278–83, 321, 324
Merton, Thomas, xiv, 123, 131–47, 150–52, 232, 310, 318, 322, 326
Michelangelo, 281
Middleton, Paul, 327
Milbank, John, 178, 236
Miller, Vincent J., 116, 319, 322
Milton, John, 134
Min, Anselm Kyongsuk, vii, 18, 29, 82–3, 85–7, 88–9, 108, 178, 235–6, 272, 294–97, 322
Moffitt, John A., 213, 322
Moltmann, Jürgen, 178, 236, 246, 259, 271, 273–76, 282–86, 311, 322
Moore, Rebecca, 64, 322
More, Thomas, 76
Morrill, Bruce, 114–15, 314, 322
Mounier, Emmanuel, 142, 322
Mozart, 258
Murphy, Michael, 303, 309, 322
Murray, Bill, 261–62
Mursell, Gordon, 8, 324

Neihardt, John G., 155, 157–58, 160–63, 171, 181–82, 316, 321, 323
Nesteruk, Alexei V., 109, 248, 265
Neville, Robert C., 238, 322
Newlands, George M., 327

Newton, Isaac, 268
Niebuhr, Reinhold, 273–274
Nietzsche, Friedrich 237, 246
Nouwen, Henri, 224, 226–28, 232, 323

O'Connor, June, 21, 323
Ogden, Schubert, 247
Olson, Roger, 252, 323
Origen, 24, 134
Ortega, José, 236
Osborne, Kenan, 19, 77–78, 323
Owens, Roger, 327

Padgett, Alan, 252
Pailin, David, 290
Palamas, Gregory, xv, 23, 189–91, 249, 263–65, 327
Panikkar, Raimon, xii, 136, 172, 178–79, 210, 216, 221, 227, 231–33, 235–36, 240, 273, 320, 323–24
Pannenberg, Wolfhart, 247, 274
Parrella, Frederick J., 316, 323
Patel, Eboo, 308, 323
Pattinson, George, 316, 327
Peacocke, Arthur, xv, 246–49, 257–60, 268, 274, 290, 314–17, 323, 327
Peelman, Achiel, 154, 323
Peirce, Charles Sanders, 247
Peters, Jason, 198
Phan, Peter C., 156, 323
Plato, 11–13, 237, 246–47, 251, 311, 315, 323
Plotinus, 247
Polkinghorne, John, xv, 247–49, 260–63, 265, 268, 271, 287, 323
Pope John Paul II, 263
Pourrat, Pierre, 14, 323
Prabhu, Joseph, 320, 324
Principe, Walter, 8–10, 13–14, 39, 324
Pringle-Pattison, Andrew Seth, 247
Pseudo-Dionysius, 24, 247

Raab, Joseph, 318
Race, Alan, 294
Rahner, Karl, xiii, xv, 16, 22, 34, 38, 40, 45, 47, 68, 75, 78, 79–81,

87–88, 91–106, 111, 119, 126–30, 212, 247, 249, 255–57, 316, 320
Ramanuja, 247, 249, 290
Rambachan, Anantanand, 303–04, 306–7, 309, 324
Reese, William, 252
Rembrandt, 220, 224, 232
Renouvier, Charles, 38, 247, 314
Rice, Julian, 162
Richter, Friedrich, 70, 72, 125, 324
Ricoeur, Paul, xiv, 216–18, 220–21, 227, 324
Rothchild, Fritz, 274–75, 278, 282, 324
Rowan Williams, 39, 192, 327
Royce, Josiah, 200–201, 326
Ruether, Rosemary Radford, 178, 236, 247, 274
Russell, William R., 321
Ryman, Frank, 144

Sandoz, Mari, 159, 324
Sayers, Dorothy, 32, 324
Schaab, Gloria, 258, 274, 283, 286, 324
Schelling, Friedrich, xv, 247, 249, 251–55, 268, 282, 324
Schleiermacher, Friedrich, 33, 247, 249
Schmemann, Alexander, 258
Schmidt, William S., 318
Schneiders, Sandra M., xii, 6, 8–10, 13–15, 21, 30, 35–45, 216, 219, 221, 228, 314, 317, 320, 325
Schoonenberg, Piet, 247
Schopenhauer, Arthur, 237, 246
Schweitzer, Albert, 247
Scott, David, 316
Segundo, Juan Luis, 247
Semmelroth, Otto, 87
Shakespeare, William 220, 258
Sheldrake, Philip, xii, 4, 6–9, 13, 19, 21, 23–25, 30–32, 34, 36–40, 43, 129, 150, 157, 325
Shook, Laurence K., 317
Shults, F. LeRon, 46, 235, 237–39, 288–89, 325
Smart, Niniam, 178, 236

Smith, Wilfred Cantwell, 178, 236, 297, 299–302, 325
Sobrino, Jon, 274
Socrates, 11–13, 83, 311
Spinoza, Baruch, 237, 246–47, 251, 253–54
Steinmetz, Paul, 161–62, 166
Steltenkamp, Michael F., 158, 160–62, 165–67, 170, 172, 174–75, 326
Stewart, Claude, 247
Stoltzman, William, 162, 326
Stover, Dale, 162, 326
Suchocki, Marjorie, 178, 236
Sugirtharajah, R.S., 181, 326
Swidler, Leonard, 178, 236

Teilhard de Chardin, Pierre, 134, 247, 249, 266, 274
Temple, William, 247
Teresa of Calcutta, 234, 296
Teresa of Avila, 32
Tertullian, 54
Thatamanil, John, 156, 326
Thompson, Barkley, 200–201, 316, 326
Thurston, Bonnie, 143, 326
Tickle, Phyllis, 41, 326
Tillich, Paul, xiii, 40, 69, 75–79, 133, 224, 247, 249, 272, 316–317, 323, 326
Tinker, George E., 154, 161, 179–80, 320, 326
Tracy, David, 220
Troeltsch, Ernst, 247
Turner, Victor, 117

Urbach, Efraim Elimelech, 283, 326

Vandenbroucke, Francois, 30–31, 327
Van Deusen, Nancy, 10–12, 326
Van Rossum, Joost, 190, 327, 190–91, 327
Vauchez, André, And39
Vincent, Arnold, 319
Vivekananda, 14
Vogel, Linda J., 21, 327
Volokhonsky, Larissa, 316

Vorglimer, Herbert, 19, 55–56, 64, 75–76, 81–82, 87, 105, 327

Ward, Keith, 13, 127, 157–158, 172, 175–79, 236–38, 246–47, 248, 289–90, 299–302, 327
Ware, Kallistos, 109, 189, 191, 247, 265, 327
Watts, Alan, 247
Weiss, Paul, 247
Wesley, John, 13

Whitehead, Alfred North, 238, 247–48, 278–79, 290, 327
Wiesel, Elie, 284–85, 327
Wilkes, Paul, 322
Wilkins, Steve, 252
Wirzba, Norman, 197, 327
Wiseman, James, 38
Wovoka, 159–60

Ziolkowski, Margaret, 188–89, 196–97, 327

Subject Index

accidents, 66–68, 73, 82–83, 88, 237–38, 262
advaita, 304–5
anthropology
  spiritual, 131–33, 318
  theological, 91, 94, 123, 132, 237–38
anthropomorphism, 280–81
appropriation, 163, 174, 182, 222
art, xv, 33, 59, 220, 254, 288, 290–93
asceticism, 6, 14, 35, 125
attributes, classical divine, 311
attunement, 11–12, 169, 232
axis mundi, 132, 137–39, 152, 163

beatific vision, 85, 92, 94, 134
beauty, 4, 12, 84, 141, 187, 195, 198–99, 201, 210, 228, 285
Bible, 166, 181, 278, 296, 326
blood, 56–58, 61, 74, 187, 262, 276
brahman, 304–6
bread, 56–58, 114, 231
bread and wine, 56–58, 114, 229, 234, 259, 262
Brothers Karamazov, xiv, 16–17, 124, 183–86, 189, 192–93, 195–97, 201, 203, 316, 319

Catholic, 32, 58, 75, 156, 162–63, 173, 262, 298, 316
Catholicism, 69, 72, 79, 155, 158, 161, 166, 173, 321
Christian Identity, 17, 115, 156, 176, 315–16, 320

Christology, 7, 81, 91, 94–96, 98, 101, 104, 255, 266–67, 324
contemplation, 30–31, 132, 134–37, 139, 232, 322
Cosmic Christ, 266, 268, 317
cosmology, theological, xiii, 135
covenant, 49, 240
creation, 16, 67–68, 82, 84, 86–89, 101, 104–5, 108–10, 128–29, 195–96, 256, 260–61, 265–67, 290–91, 300

deification, 188–92, 194, 196, 264, 327
dialectic, 13, 28, 208, 211, 213, 216, 272, 317, 322
divine
  energies, 248, 265, 269, 327
  Logos, 87–88, 98–99
  nature, 38, 68, 87, 188, 239, 259, 275, 285
divine pathos, xv, 271, 274–75, 281–82, 284, 296, 305
  theology of, 275, 278, 280, 285–86, 296, 311
divinization, 95, 99, 133, 165, 188, 191, 195, 256
doctrine, 7, 38, 43, 46, 70, 73, 82, 185–86, 257, 265, 276, 283, 285, 321–22, 325
dogmatic, 27, 30, 34–35, 37, 39
duality, 214–15, 236

earth, 60, 84, 98, 126, 132, 138–39, 159, 163–65, 169, 186–87, 196, 201–2, 222, 243, 303

Eastern Orthodox Christianity, xv, 249, 263
Eastern Orthodox traditions, 75, 95, 263–65
emptiness, 18, 95, 114, 141, 151, 195, 210
Enlightenment, 25, 31, 33, 43, 238
Eucharist, 54, 61–62, 74, 114–15, 157, 166–67, 182, 231, 234, 241, 259, 262
evil, 13, 76, 78, 133, 214, 216–17, 254, 260, 265, 270–73, 279, 324
existence of, 272–73, 275
experience
lived religious, xiv, 6, 15, 32, 40, 43, 71, 91, 101, 123, 156, 161, 211–12, 287, 293
mystical, 35, 197
subjective, 24, 223–24

faith
religious, 28, 173
understanding of, 175, 301
universal, 299

Ghost Dance, 159–60, 182
gnosis, 276–77
God
knowing, 133, 222–23, 292–93
suffering, 272, 274, 282–83, 286, 309
symbol of, 229, 232
God in all things, 82, 126–30, 165, 196, 213, 248
God-world-person relationship, 291
God-world relationship, xv, 15, 245–47, 258, 269–70, 287–90, 292, 306, 309, 311
gospel, 56–58, 74, 154, 160, 166, 189, 228, 283, 321
grace, 15–16, 62, 64–65, 68, 72, 75, 81, 85–89, 92–94, 96, 98–102, 118–19, 188, 190–91, 258
Greek philosophy, 185, 300

history, redemptive, 52–53, 58
Holy Spirit, 9, 38, 46, 56, 60, 72–73, 196, 209, 211, 266

human condition, 28, 77–78, 88, 152, 191, 272, 283–84, 309
human experience, 37–38, 41–42, 92, 94, 183, 285, 311
humanity, 78, 95, 97–99, 175, 188, 191, 214, 232, 239–41, 254, 259, 297, 314, 322
human nature, 28, 38, 88, 92, 95, 98–99, 104, 191, 240, 247, 281, 285, 296–97, 300, 327
hypostatic union, 87–89, 98–99, 133, 239, 255

idolatry, 61, 69, 75–76, 116, 180
Ignatian Principle, xiv, 101, 123–24, 126, 130, 158, 172, 212–13
Ignatian spirituality, 123–24
immanence, xv, 80, 229, 231, 246, 248, 251, 256, 259, 261, 263, 268, 283, 304
and transcendence, 186, 229, 244, 247, 251, 291
immutability, 109, 251, 256–57, 273, 279, 292
inclusivism, 178, 294–95, 298
Interfaith Studies, 303, 307–8, 318, 323
interreligious
and interfaith studies, 307–8, 318
dialogue, 168, 296, 307–8, 315–16
encounter, xv, 287–89, 294
studies, 40, 299, 307–8, 321

Jesus, historical, 97, 267, 314
justice, 266, 281, 296–97

Kabbala, 276–77
kenosis, 136, 188–89, 194–96, 257, 263–65, 283
Kenotic tradition, 188–89, 196–97, 327
knowledge, 7, 19, 24, 26–27, 29, 33, 35, 38, 76, 101–2, 115, 132, 135–36, 222, 277
subjective, 222–23, 293

Lakota, 50, 156–57, 162–63, 167–68, 170, 173, 179, 182, 303, 307, 321

SUBJECT INDEX

materiality, 10, 88–89, 171
memorial, 47–49, 54–55, 78, 167, 241–42
  making, 47–49, 52, 56, 68, 87, 242
memory, 47–50, 52–53, 56, 58, 147, 218, 241–43, 315
metaphor, xv, 84, 188, 288, 290, 293, 306, 311
metaphysics, symbolic, 81
monotheism, 60, 283
Multiple Religious Belonging, 153, 155–56, 315–16, 318, 320, 323
multiple religious identity (MRI), 153–57, 160, 172–75, 177, 182, 318
mysteria, 54–55, 57
mysticism, 5, 14, 24, 26–27, 29–32, 34–35, 213, 268, 317, 321, 324

otherness, 255, 260, 263–64, 281, 291–92

panentheism, xv, 106–9, 244–53, 258–59, 261, 263–64, 266, 268–71, 273, 282, 287–89, 291–92, 303–4, 315–18, 322–23
  Christian, 106, 108, 290
  classical, 249–50, 252, 263–64
  modern, 252
  soteriological, xv, 286–87
panentheistic
  pansacramentalism, xv, 107, 249, 288–89, 306, 311
  pansacramentality, 178, 219, 245, 249, 270, 286
pansacramentalism, xi, xiv, 135, 172, 201, 242, 255, 258–59, 282, 289, 292, 310
pansacramentality, 15, 21, 80, 88, 124, 130, 137, 172, 179, 183–84, 234, 245–46, 250, 288–89, 292
pansacramental
  mediation, 5, 10, 15, 81, 178, 293, 310–11
  panentheism, 289
  principle, 156, 179–80
  reality, 237, 242

vision, xiv, 124, 163, 184, 195, 197, 234, 248, 255, 263, 269, 284, 286–87
pantheism, 82, 88, 106, 109, 185, 190, 213, 241, 247–48, 251, 253, 259, 282, 287, 289
participation, multiple religious, 155–56
pathos, 275, 278–81, 285, 287, 291–92, 303, 305–6, 309
pluralism, 178, 235, 294, 302, 316
postcolonialism, 181–82
prophets, 240, 274, 278–82, 296, 305–7, 319
Protestant Principle, xiii, 69, 75, 77–79, 272

relationality, xv, 136, 207, 237–39, 291
religions
  philosophy of, 21, 208–10, 319, 322
  study of, xii, 129, 308, 316–17, 321
  theology of, 294, 320
religious pluralism, 178, 209, 236, 289, 294–96, 302, 307, 311, 316
  theology of, 19, 287, 294, 297–98
religious studies, 6, 15, 40, 137, 308–9, 318, 324
revelation, 7, 24, 29–30, 39, 93, 98, 179, 232–33, 254, 261, 300, 314, 320, 322, 327
rituals, 47, 55, 57–58, 67, 73, 113–14, 117, 162–64, 166, 172, 230, 297–98, 313

sacramental
  experience, xiii, 16, 75, 115, 223–24, 230, 293
  mediation, xiv, 17, 19, 21, 45, 183, 215–16, 231, 263, 287, 292–93, 298, 318
  panentheism, 109, 111, 244, 258, 260
  reality, 81, 232
  spirituality, xiv, 19–20, 123–24, 157, 183–86, 189, 310, 319
  theology, xiii–xiv, 19–21, 47, 55–56, 62–67, 76, 78–82, 87, 90–91, 99, 105, 111, 294, 327

sacramental *(continued)*
  vision, 132, 184–85, 202
  worldview, xiv, 68, 79, 91, 123, 164,
    186, 319
sacramentality and spirituality, 19–20,
  318
sacramentum, xiii, 47, 54, 58, 62–64
scholasticism, 10, 21, 23, 25–27,
  29–30, 35, 119
scripture, 7, 24, 26–28, 30, 35, 38, 59,
  61, 65, 71–74, 76, 116, 166, 257,
  266
sensuality, 21, 187, 199, 323
signs, xiv, 57–61, 63–67, 79, 86,
  96, 102–3, 112, 200, 207, 213,
  216–17, 219, 229, 295
sin, 28, 70–72, 74, 78, 125, 127, 192,
  194, 196, 213, 224, 239, 253,
  272–73, 279
solidarity, 18, 48, 178, 193, 198–99,
  201, 236, 255, 278–79, 284–86,
  292, 297, 305–6, 309, 322
spirituality
  Christian, xii, 5, 8, 14–15, 19–21,
    38–39, 41, 237, 314, 317, 321,
    323–25
  comparative, 302
  contemporary study of, 6, 8, 21, 25,
    30, 32, 34–38, 40–41, 91, 120,
    230, 318
  creation, 266, 317
  Lutheran, 71, 319
  pansacramental, 123, 310, 312
  study of, xii, xiv, 5–6, 10, 14–16, 19,
    23, 36, 38, 207, 211–12, 216, 236,
    238, 292–93
substance, 31, 62, 66–67, 73, 82,
  87–88, 116, 118, 235, 237–39,
  262, 271, 282, 319
suffering, xv, 18, 189, 194, 196,
  244–45, 253–55, 260, 269–80,
  282–87, 292, 305–6, 308–9,
  311–12, 320–21
symbolic reality, xiv, 16, 81, 91, 96,
  101, 103–4, 120, 227–28, 298
symbolism, 18, 217, 219, 221, 228,
  230, 325

symbols, xii, xiv–xv, 75–79, 96–97,
  101–6, 113–16, 118, 207, 216–21,
  223–24, 227–29, 231–32, 234,
  298, 302

theism, classical, 247–48, 261, 264,
  286, 292
theology
  biblical, 23, 274, 315
  Catholic, 69, 78–79, 93, 324–25
  comparative, 123, 294, 300–303,
    324
  dogmatic, 37–38
  Hindu, 299–300, 304, 306, 324
  Islamic, 299–300
  monastic, 5, 8, 26–27, 34–35
  moral, 23, 30–31, 34–35, 37
  mystical, 5, 8, 14, 24, 32, 34–35,
    188, 190, 196, 258, 321
  pansacramental, 88, 157, 165, 295
  philosophical, xv, 45, 207, 209, 300
  process, 274, 282, 322
  scholastic, 26, 35, 112–13
  spiritual, 5, 8, 23, 25, 30, 33–35,
    37, 152
  systematic, 7, 16, 35, 45, 78–79, 94,
    301, 326
  world, 299–300, 326
theomorphism, 281, 296
theōsis, xv, 95, 133, 136, 165, 188–89,
  194–96, 263–64
  kenotic, 124, 184–85, 188–89, 194,
    202
transcendence, xv, 39, 92–95, 97–98,
  211–13, 229, 231, 244, 247–48,
  251, 255–56, 261, 263, 287, 291
transubstantiation, 73, 114, 259, 262
Trinity, 24, 27, 96, 99–102, 104, 106,
  177, 208–9, 211–12, 256–57,
  261, 276, 282–83, 285, 322–23

ultimate reality, xi, 54–55, 90, 115,
  174, 178, 237, 246

Wakan Tanka, 50–51, 156, 164–165,
  168–70, 172, 179
water, 3–4, 89, 159, 171, 198, 266, 296

wine, 56–58, 114, 229, 232, 234, 259, 262

wisdom, 26, 51, 84, 157, 174, 241, 243, 267, 297, 300, 309, 321

worship, 20, 60–61, 116

www.ingramcontent.com/pod-product-compliance
Lightning Source LLC
Chambersburg PA
CBHW061424300426
44114CB00014B/1534